1927

1927

A Day-by-Day Chronicle of the Jazz Age's Greatest Year

Thomas S. Hischak

ROWMAN & LITTLEFIELD
Lanham • Boulder • New York • London

Published by Rowman & Littlefield
An imprint of The Rowman & Littlefield Publishing Group, Inc.
4501 Forbes Boulevard, Suite 200, Lanham, Maryland 20706
www.rowman.com

6 Tinworth Street, London, SE11 5AL, United Kingdom

British Library Cataloguing in Publication Information Available

Library of Congress Cataloging-in-Publication Data

Names: Hischak, Thomas S., author.
Title: 1927 : a day-by-day chronicle of the Jazz Age's greatest year / Thomas
   S. Hischak.
Other titles: Nineteen twenty-seven | Day-by-day chronicle of the Jazz Age's
   greatest year
Description: Lanham, MD : Rowman & Littlefield, [2019] | Includes
   bibliographical references and index.
Identifiers: LCCN 2018050158 (print) | LCCN 2018051205 (ebook) | ISBN
   9781538112786 (electronic) | ISBN 9781538112779 (cloth : alk. paper)
Subjects: LCSH: United States—History—1919–1933—Chronology. | United
   States—Social conditions—1918–1932. | Nineteen twenty-seven, A.D.
Classification: LCC E791 (ebook) | LCC E791 .H57 2019 (print) | DDC
   973.91—dc23
LC record available at https://lccn.loc.gov/2018050158

∞™ The paper used in this publication meets the minimum requirements
of American National Standard for Information Sciences—Permanence of
Paper for Printed Library Materials, ANSI/NISO Z39.48-1992.

Printed in the United States of America

For Jamie Duncan,
who loves music and baseball

A ticker-tape parade down Wall Street was the sign of ultimate fame as stockbrokers tossed rolls of ticker tape out the windows like confetti. The parade for Charles Lindbergh on June 13 might serve as the iconic image of 1927 at its most optimistic. *Everett Collection Historical / Alamy Stock Photos*

CONTENTS

PREFACE

Many historians point out that the year 1927 was the high point of the Roaring Twenties. The economy was booming, the Jazz Age was in full swing, social mores were looser than ever, and the nation was celebrating heroes, new dances and music, movie stars, original gadgets and inventions, and a sense of power that Americans felt about themselves. That year saw hundreds of silent films released and movie attendance was at record levels. On Broadway, more plays and musicals opened than in any year before or since. Many of America's greatest novelists, poets, artists, composers, and playwrights were busy producing classic works. In sports, records were broken and several champions in different fields thrilled fans with outstanding feats. It was the year of Charles Lindbergh's famous transatlantic flight; the first talking picture, *The Jazz Singer*; the musical classic *Show Boat*; the discovery of Peking Man; the invention of the jukebox; and the birth of the Academy of Motion Picture Arts and Sciences, Laurel and Hardy, and the music business genre of country music. There were many somber events as well, such as the execution of Sacco and Vanzetti, coal mining strikes and accidents, the Shanghai massacre and civil wars in China as well as in Nicaragua, the ongoing debacle of Prohibition and the power of organized crime, and the Great Mississippi River Flood and other natural disasters. All in all, a diverse and complicated year.

The aim of *1927: A Day-by-Day Chronicle of the Jazz Age's Greatest Year* is to let the reader experience this important year day by day, describing events and accomplishments as they happened. Each day, from January 1 to December 31, 1927, is explored. Major news events, national and international, are described, as well as minor curiosities or news items that would prove to be more important in the future. Activities in music, literature, film, theatre, sports, inventions, politics, business, science, and other areas are included, as are the births and deaths of notable people. Throughout the chronology a series of boxes provide statistics and general information regarding the year 1927.

While no one event can be discussed at great length, the hope is that the reader gets a feel for what it was like to live through this complex and fascinating year. For those looking for more depth and detailed information on these events and people, the bibliography suggests many books that focus on specific topics. In *1927: A Day-by-Day Chronicle of the Jazz Age's Greatest Year*, the reader will take an informative tour through the greatest year of the Roaring Twenties. We point out the sights, describe the highlights, and meet the many famous people. In so doing, we hope to capture one outstanding year during that dizzy time known as the Jazz Age.

ACKNOWLEDGMENTS

I wish to express my thanks to my wife and proofreader, Cathy; my editor, Stephen Ryan; my production editor, Jessica McCleary; and Jamie Duncan and Robert Spitzer for their knowledge and help in making this book as accurate as possible.

PROLOGUE

New Year's Eve, 1926

Prohibition, now in its sixth year, barred the manufacture, sale, and transportation of intoxicating beverages; it did not outlaw the possession or consumption of alcohol. Thus, many people celebrated New Year's Eve with parties serving alcoholic drinks. In fact, the consumption of alcohol was higher during Prohibition (1920 to 1933) than in the years preceding it. For the arrival of 1927, Times Square in Manhattan was filled with people celebrating, even though it was raining and one thousand policemen were on duty to control the crowd. By dawn, eight of the partygoers had died of alcohol poisoning. And so began a year of contradictions. While 1927 has often been depicted as one long party, it was also a year of crisis, disaster, and injustice. Those revelers on New Year's Eve were more concerned with the optimistic side of life. Under the administration of Calvin Coolidge, president of the United States since 1923, business was booming (the gross national product was $93.8 billion), unemployment was low (4.1 percent of the labor force), and spending was high (the consumer price index was 17.4). But these numbers cannot measure the level of optimism most Americans felt as 1927 began. For many, life was good and promised to get better. There was a feeling that anything was possible, particularly in the areas of aviation, science, medicine, communications, and newfangled inventions not yet imagined. At the same time, there was a feeling of frustration and injustice, particularly among minority groups, immigrant laborers, and farmers. And if one looked beyond the borders of the United States, there was much to be concerned about on the international scene. Americans may have been celebrating, but elsewhere there were wars, revolutions, and the rise of Fascism, Communism, and other ideologies that would eventually affect just about every person in the forty-eight states. So as the New Year's parties come to an end, let us start our day-by-day journey through a remarkable year.

JANUARY

SATURDAY, JANUARY 1

For many Americans in 1927, as with today, New Year's Day meant the Tournament of Roses Parade in Pasadena, California, followed by the college football game known as the Rose Bowl, which was the only college football bowl game at the time. Today marked the thirty-seventh annual parade and the eleventh annual football game in the nearby Rose Bowl Stadium. There was extra excitement this year because the competition was between two of the nation's undefeated teams: the Stanford University Indians (with a record of 10-0-0) and the University of Alabama Crimson Tide (9-0-0). Stanford led 7-0 until the final minute of the game, when Alabama blocked a punt, recovered the ball on the fourteen-yard line and scored, stopping a Stanford victory with a 7-7 tie. Additional college bowl games would not be introduced to the American public until the 1930s and beyond.

Also in sports news today, the Brooklyn Robins announced that they were releasing left fielder Zack Wheat, who had been with the team since 1909. "Buck," as he was nicknamed, was picked up by the Philadelphia Athletics, but he played only one season for them. After a year in the minor leagues, Wheat retired. He still holds the Robins/Dodgers' (both in Brooklyn and Los Angeles) franchise records for at bats, hits, doubles, triples, total bases, and hit by pitches.

The United States had occupied the country of Nicaragua since 1912 to keep any other power from taking over the Central American nation and possibly building a Nicaraguan canal. On December 1 of 1926, civil war had broken out between liberal and conservative factions and the Nicaraguan Congress pleaded with President Coolidge for military help. The president hesitated a whole month, then today approved support in the form of four hundred marines, who didn't arrive until three weeks later.

SILENT CAL

Calvin Coolidge was vice president under Warren Harding, and when that scandal-plagued president died in office in August of 1923, Coolidge moved into the White House. He quickly restored confidence in the government, not because of what he did but because he had a talent for doing as little as possible. Business was booming, and Coolidge believed any action by a president might upset the boom. Born in Vermont, the fifty-five-year-old politician led a colorless and quiet life as he moved through Massachusetts politics, serving as state senator and governor. He was little known to the public when he succeeded Harding but was easily elected in his own right in 1924. Except for reading prepared speeches, he said little in public or, legend has it, in private. Stories (mostly apocryphal) about how "silent Cal" went out of his way to avoid conversation have proliferated to this day. His actions as president and as a man were equally reticent. In 1927, it is estimated he spent less than five hours a day working. He was a notorious nap taker and yawned through many an official presidential ceremony. If a crisis arose, he either hesitated to act or turned the matter over to someone else. Coolidge hated living in hot and humid Washington and took many vacations. In 1927, he spent less than nine months in the White House. Yet he was extremely popular with the public, particularly with the middle-class businessman. Coolidge ran the country successfully by leaving everyone and everything alone.

Calvin Coolidge (center in white suit) was not a president who liked to talk to the press (or practically anyone), but he loved to have his picture taken. Here he poses on the White House lawn with visiting Native Americans. *Courtesy of the Library of Congress, LC-DIG-hec-34570*

Two British institutions were born today. The British Broadcasting Corporation (BBC) was created by royal charter as a publicly funded company. Sir John Reith was named the first director-general. The BBC delivered its first news bulletin two days later. The other newcomer on this date was Imperial Chemical Industries, which was formed by the merger of four chemical companies. Imperial Chemical, which went on to make all forms of chemicals, paints, plastics, and polyethylene products before expanding into building motorcycles and even nuclear weapons, was the United Kingdom's largest manufacturer for several decades. It was bought out by the Dutch firm Akzo Nobel in June of 2007.

Massachusetts became the first U.S. state to make it compulsory for car owners to buy liability insurance in order to register their vehicles.

The tomb of Tutankhamen in Egypt's Valley of the Kings, discovered by Howard Carter in 1922, was opened for public viewing today for the first time. All of the treasures had been removed to the Egyptian Museum in Cairo, but the tomb itself attracted many visitors. The site was opened to the public certain days through the end of March. The young King Tut's tomb has been closed at different times over the decades, but today is again open to the public.

Turkey today became the last European country to switch from the Julian Calendar to the Gregorian Calendar which had been established by Pope Gregory XIII in 1582. The change required Turkey to remove thirteen days in order for today to be January 1.

German philosopher Martin Heidegger's groundbreaking philosophical work *Being and Time (Sein und Zeit)* was published today in Germany. Both controversial and influential, the book reopened and redefined the science of ontology (the study of being) that was first introduced by the ancient Greeks. Also published on this date was *God's Trombones*, a book of poems by African American writer James Weldon Johnson. Subtitled *Seven Negro Sermons in Verse*, the collection relates tales from the Bible in African American folklore terms. *God's Trombones* was praised, read, and celebrated by black and white readers in America and Europe. The Harlem Renaissance was going strong in 1927 as African American authors, musicians, singers, artists, composers, and poets such as Johnson were thriving in Upper Manhattan.

Of the handful of Hollywood movies that premiered on New Year's Day, the best of them was the Pola Negri vehicle *Hotel Imperial*. The Paramount melodrama involved romance, suspense, spies, and the Great War, but it all came down to Negri. The Polish-born screen favorite was one of the most sensual stars of the silent era, and she could also act. Negri was at the peak of her powers in 1927, when she made three films. In this movie she played the chambermaid Anna in the small, rural Hotel Imperial behind the Russian lines. She helps hide the Austrian soldier Paul, and the two fall in love. When a Russian general makes the hotel his headquarters, he is distracted by the pretty Anna, while Paul tries to find out the identity of the German spy working for the Russians. *Hotel Imperial* is a surprisingly engaging movie that still holds up today.

The British painter Isabelle de Steiger, who had many other interesting careers, died today at the age of ninety. The Liverpool-born artist had her works shown at the Royal

Academy of Art; then, while illustrating some books on the occult, Steiger became interested in spiritualism and theosophy, writing books on both subjects and becoming a leading figure in several mystic societies in London.

SUNDAY, JANUARY 2

The Cristero War, a bloody struggle in the Mexican central and western states between secular, anti-Catholic factions and those who supported the dominance of the Catholic Church, raged from 1926 to 1929, but the conflict earned a formal declaration of war today. The young rebel René Capistrán Garza, leader of the Mexican Association of Catholic Youth, sent a manifesto "to the nation" declaring themselves "Cristeros," warriors who fought for Christ. This was followed by attacks on villages in the Los Altos region in the Mexican state of Jalisco.

The Horror at Red Hook, a demonic horror story by H. P. Lovecraft, was published in the January issue of *Weird Tales* magazine and has mesmerized readers ever since. Set in the crime-ridden section of Brooklyn known as Red Hook, the reclusive Robert Suydam and his bride are found murdered in the stateroom of the ship that was to take them on their honeymoon. Police detective Thomas Malone investigates and soon finds himself in an underworld filled with occult rituals and human sacrifices.

MONDAY, JANUARY 3

The year 1927 was a pivotal one in China for the rise of Communism. It was also the beginning of a movement to rid the nation of foreigners, particularly the British, who had large concessions in the country. Today anti-British riots broke out in two cities, Hankow and Kiukiang, as throngs of protesters took to the streets. Tensions escalated when a British soldier fired into the crowd at Hankow, killing one protestor and wounding dozens of others. To avoid further trouble, the British relinquished control of the two cities and turned them over to the Chinese government. But Britain was not about to give up its interests in China and began making plans to fortify and hold on to Shanghai.

The new year on Broadway began with two admirable and very different offerings, though neither was a financial hit. The renowned Theatre Guild presented a powerful stage adaptation of Fyodor Dostoyevsky's novel *The Brothers Karamazov* using a French script cowritten by the distinguished director Jacques Copeau and his friend Jean Croué. The Theatre Guild, founded in 1918 to offer classics as well as new American and foreign plays, was at its artistic peak in the late 1920s and this production boasted a superb cast. Dudley Digges was in top form as the drunken and suspicious father, Feodor, who is murdered by his dim-witted bastard son, Smerdiakov (Edward

G. Robinson). The other sons were played by Morris Carnovsky as the religious but disenchanted Alioecha, Alfred Lunt as the volatile Dmitri, and George Gaul as the smitten Ivan. Lynn Fontanne was the seductive whore Agrafena, and Clare Eames was the tragic Katerina. Some critics complained of the extremely condensed version of the novel but applauded the superior cast. Playgoers were not so much interested in Russian tragedy and only the Guild's subscribers kept the play on the boards for seven weeks. The night's other new offering, the romantic musical *The Nightingale*, was more to the audience's taste, but it ran only twelve weeks, not enough for such an expensive production to make money. The nightingale of the title was the popular Swedish songbird Jenny Lind (Eleanor Painter) who bewitched American audiences when P. T. Barnum brought her to America in the middle of the nineteenth century. The plot was a fictional romance between Lind and a promising West Pointer, whom she gives up in order to avoid hurting his promising military career. The songs by Armand Vecsey (music), Guy Bolton, and P. G. Wodehouse (lyrics) were serviceable at best, and the Painter was not the box office draw she once was. The lavish Shubert Brothers' production met with mixed notices and the show closed in the red.

The acclaimed Mexican architect Antonio Rivas Mercado died today at the age of seventy-four in Mexico City, where he had designed or restored many notable buildings and landmarks. He is perhaps best known for his Independence Column in central Mexico City and the Teatro Juárez in Guanajuato.

TUESDAY, JANUARY 4

Broadway had its first major flop of the year with *Ballyhoo*, a melodrama about a carnival bronco rider, Starlight Lil (Minna Gombell), who charms the high-society youth Cameron MacDonald (Eric Dressler) then realizes she's too low-class for him. Both try to make the other jealous with other lovers but are brought together thanks to Lil's highstrung horse Mesquite. *Ballyhoo* mercifully closed in a week. That same night a "musical comedy of New Orleans" titled *Lace Petticoat* opened and only lasted two weeks. It told a torrid tale of the desirable Renita (Vivian Hart), who is kept from her sweetheart by a jealous suitor who falsely claims she is a quadroon (having one-fourth Negro blood). She believes him, and there is much anguish and several forgettable songs before the truth comes out.

WEDNESDAY, JANUARY 5

To protect the American embassy in Managua, the capital city of Nicaragua, in the midst of a civil war, one hundred sixty American marines set sail today on the USS *Galveston*

AMERICAN MILITARY PERSONNEL

In 1927, the number of American military personnel on extended or continuous active duty was 248,943:

U. S. Army	134,829
U.S. Navy	94,916
U.S. Marine Corps	19,198

These numbers do not include reserves on active duty for training. The U.S. Air Force was not established until 1946.

and arrived at the port of Corinto the next day. The Nicaragua Congress was still waiting for the troops Coolidge promised to help bring order to the war-torn nation.

The National Museum of Canada was officially created today from the Museum Branch of the Federal Department of Mines. Today the National consists of four different museums in Ottawa.

THURSDAY, JANUARY 6

It was a busy day for executioner Robert G. Elliott, who was the principal operator of the electric chair in five Northeast states between 1926 and 1939. In the early morning, Elliott put to death three men in Boston for the 1925 murder of a night watchman. He then went to New York City by train, took in a movie matinee with his family, and then traveled to Sing Sing prison in Ossining, New York, where he electrocuted three men for the 1926 murder of a different watchman.

Exotic singer-dancer Josephine Baker recorded Irving Berlin's "Blue Skies" today on the Odeon label. Although the song had been heard briefly on Broadway in 1926, it did not become popular until recorded in 1927 by artists such as Baker, Ben Bernie, Johnny Marvin, Whispering Jack Smith, Jack Olsen, Harry Richman, Vincent Lopez, and others. By the end of the year, Al Jolson would sing it on screen in *The Jazz Singer*.

FRIDAY, JANUARY 7

The first transatlantic telephone call was officially made today at 8:44 a.m., New York time, when Walter S. Gifford of AT&T spoke with Sir G. Evelyn V. Murray of the General Post Office in London, where it was 1:44 p.m. Actually, the two men tested the system the day before, but today the conversation was covered by the press in both cities.

The exotic and tantalizing singer-dancer Josephine Baker came across like some kind of African jungle princess, but in fact she was born in St. Louis, Missouri, and created her Jazz Age persona all by herself. Although she was a sensation in Manhattan in 1927, much of Baker's later career was in Europe, where she encountered less racial prejudice. *Photofest © Photofest*

The Globetrotters, an African American exhibition basketball team founded by Abe Saperstein in Chicago in 1926, played their very first road game today when they traveled forty-eight miles west of Chicago to compete with a local team in Hinckley, Illinois. That first season, the "Savoy Big Five," as they were sometimes known, played 117 games throughout the Midwest, winning 101 of them. In 1928, they changed their

Only 56 percent of American households had a telephone in 1927.

name to the New York Harlem Globetrotters, then the next year simply to the Harlem Globetrotters. The celebrated basketball team is still very active, having played over 26,000 games in more than one hundred countries.

SATURDAY, JANUARY 8

The first of the year's many Hollywood classics, MGM's *The Scarlet Letter*, was given a wide release today after its New York City premiere the previous August. Nathaniel Hawthorne's 1850 novel is about the Puritan Hester Prynne, who gives birth to a child out of wedlock and is shunned by the Massachusetts Colony and forced to wear a red letter *A* as a symbol of her adultery. The tale had already been the subject of five silent films since 1908, most of them lost today. But this version starring Lillian Gish survives and has been restored, so it is possible to see what is today the finest screen adaptation

Filmmakers have always been fascinated by Nathaniel Hawthorne's novel *The Scarlet Letter*. Of the many screen versions of the tale of Puritan hypocrisy, the 1927 adaptation starring Lillian Gish and Lars Hanson remains the finest. *MGM / Photofest © MGM*

of the novel if not one of the finest of all silent films. The screenplay by Frances Marion begins before the novel does, showing the meeting and romance of Hester and the Reverend Dimmesdale (Lars Hanson), Hester's unknown lover. Beautifully directed by Victor Sjöström with even some of Hawthorne's symbolism presented visually, the movie is most remembered for the indelible performance by Gish. Her Hester is no mere waif but a romantic, eager, and even obstinate woman, whose sweetness can quickly turn to anger when her illegitimate daughter, Pearl, is threatened. Swedish actor Hanson is also outstanding as the tormented Dimmesdale, and Henry B. Walthall is sinister and fascinating as the presumed-dead husband, Roger Chillingworth. *The Scarlet Letter* was remade with sound in 1934 and 1995 and there were television versions in 1950 and 1979, but this silent version is still considered the best.

Alban Berg's celebrated string quartet *Lyrische Suite* premiered today in Vienna. Written between 1925 and 1926, the six-movement piece is known for the way Arnold Schoenberg's twelve-tone techniques are used throughout. In 1928, Berg arranged three of the movements for a string orchestra.

The steam-powered riverboat *Kate Adams* was destroyed by a fire today while it was moored on the Mississippi River in Memphis, Tennessee. Built in 1898, the ship was one of the last surviving "side-wheeler" steamboats in the country.

SUNDAY, JANUARY 9

Seventy-eight children between the ages of four and sixteen were killed today in the panic that ensued when a fire broke out during a matinee at the Laurier Palace movie theatre in Montreal. About eight hundred children were in the cinema watching the comedy short *Get 'Em Young* when flames and smoke appeared. Children using three of the theatre's four fire exits got out safely, but those in the balcony were trapped behind a blocked stairwell and some exit doors that only opened inward. Most of the young victims were either crushed or asphyxiated to death. There was already a movement in conservative Montreal to keep children out of cinemas for moral reasons. A few months after the fire, a local law was passed that forbade children under sixteen from entering a movie house. The law stayed on the books for thirty-three years.

MONDAY, JANUARY 10

American financial interests in Nicaragua, Mexico, and China were at stake when civil unrest and rioting broke out in those countries during the past two months. President Coolidge was not overly concerned about political affairs overseas but he was convinced to act because of business reasons. Today, Coolidge informed Congress that fifteen American warships and five thousand U.S. Navy and Marine personnel would be dispatched to Nicaragua and Mexico to protect American interests. On the same day, the U.S. Department of the Navy announced that eight hundred marines would be transported from Guam by the cruiser USS *Huron* to China for the same reason.

A cinema masterpiece, a high point of the Weimar period of filmmaking in Germany, premiered today in Berlin. The movie was Fritz Lang's *Metropolis*, an expressionistic science fiction drama that still thrills. In the year 2026, the citizens of the Utopian city of Metropolis enjoy a life of luxury living in stylish skyscrapers and traveling about in airplanes. What they don't know is that there is another city under them, a dark and oppressive factory in which workers slave away at giant machines to keep Metropolis running smoothly. The system is run by Joh Fredersen, and his son, Freder, discovers this underground world when he follows the beautiful evangelist Maria, who is preaching to the workers below about bringing justice to Metropolis. The plot that follows is action packed with Freder falling in love with Maria and joining the cause, Fredersen having a robot made who looks just like Maria, plans to destroy the main power station for Metropolis, the flooding of the underground city, the mob turning against Fredersen, and the emergence of the Mediator, who will change the way Metropolis is run. As gripping as the story is, it is the visuals in *Metropolis* that are so fascinating. Both the gleaming, sleek upper city and the dark, mechanical underground are portrayed expressionistically and filmed with dramatic shadows, silhouettes, mirrors, and special effects. *Metropolis* was the first feature-length (153 minutes) science fiction movie ever made, and it greatly influenced later movies in the genre. Audiences at the Berlin premiere were dazzled, but the authorities found it politically inflammatory. The film was severely edited, and it was decades before all the cut footage was found and *Metropolis* was fully restored and shown in 2010.

Hollywood's only notable contribution that day was a Walt Disney cartoon short titled *Alice the Golf Bug*. As in the previous "Alice" shorts, the heroine was played by a live-action actress, in this case Margie Gay, but the backgrounds and all the other characters were animated. In *Alice the Golf Bug*, Alice and her cat friends Junius and Pete play a round of golf, which is interrupted by physical comedy gags.

Of the three openings on Broadway that day, the classiest affair was a revival of Henrik Ibsen's *Ghosts* starring the legendary Mrs. Fiske. Some critics carped about

EARLY DISNEY CHARACTERS

Walt Disney offered his first "Alice" cartoon, *Alice's Wonderland*, in 1923. It was so popular he made forty-five other Alice shorts, including sixteen during 1927. Disney began with child actress Virginia Davis playing Alice, but as the years passed, he had to hire other actresses. Eventually Disney moved on to a series of Oswald the Lucky Rabbit cartoons. Mickey Mouse was not introduced until 1928.

Science fiction and German expressionism meet in Fritz Lang's masterpiece *Metropolis*, and both critics and moviegoers didn't know what to make of it. The film remains as audacious, crazy, and mesmerizing today as when it premiered in 1927. *UFA / Photofest © UFA*

the modern-dress production, but playgoers filled the Mansfield Theatre for her three-week stay. The comedy *Tommy* also pleased audiences, running six and a half months. It was a slight but entertaining play about mixing politics and romance in a small town. Coauthor Howard Lindsey would later enjoy a spectacular career on Broadway as a playwright, producer, and actor.

TUESDAY, JANUARY 11

Thirty-six Hollywood celebrities were gathered at the Ambassador Hotel in Los Angeles by MGM producer Louis B. Mayer to discuss the creation of an organization to control labor management and arbitration among the various studios. A secondary purpose of the new group would be to acknowledge cinematic excellence. Mayer suggested the name: International Academy of Motion Picture Arts and Sciences. A subsequent meeting was held on May 6 before the organization was officially founded as the Academy of Motion Picture Arts and Sciences on May 11.

The S.S. *John Tracy*, an American steamer with a cargo of coal and a crew of twenty-seven men on board, encountered a fierce storm today and sank off the coast of Cape Cod. There were no survivors; only the ship's nameplate was recovered ten days later.

There was a building boom on Broadway in 1927 that began with the opening of the Royale Theatre, a midsize playhouse seating just over one thousand patrons and suitable for both plays and musicals. Spanish flavored in design, the Royale boasted two large murals showing Spanish lovers and the color scheme was red, orange, and gold. In 2005 the playhouse was renamed the Bernard B. Jacobs Theatre; Jacobs was for many years the president of the producing Shubert Organization, which owned the theatre. The premiere production in 1927 was the musical *Piggy*, which was based on the popular comedy *The Rich Mr. Hoggenheimer* (1906). Sam Bernard played the low-class but monied "Piggy" Hoggenheimer, the role he introduced two decades earlier, and fussed and fumed when his son prefers to marry a shop girl over the daughter of a British lord. The musical version met with unfavorable notices except for Bernard's performance. Business was so bad, the producers curiously changed the title to *I Told You So*, hoping for better box office. Still the musical struggled and finally closed after ten weeks. Before the year was out, Bernard died at the age of sixty-three, and Broadway lost one of the great stage comics of the turn of the century.

NEW THEATRES ON BROADWAY

During Broadway's busiest year on record, eight new playhouses opened in the Theatre District in 1927:

Alvin Theatre	New Yorker Theatre
Erlanger Theatre	Royale Theatre
Hammerstein Theatre	Theatre Masque
Majestic Theatre	Ziegfeld Theatre

Fortunately, all are still standing and in use except for impresario Florenz Ziegfeld's playhouse. Only the Majestic Theatre retains its original name. Today the Alvin is the Neil Simon Theatre, the Erlanger is the St. James Theatre, the Hammerstein is the Ed Sullivan Theatre, the New Yorker is called Studio 54, the Royale is the Bernard B. Jacobs Theatre, and the Theatre Masque is the John Golden Theatre.

For movie palaces built in 1927, see March 11.

The philosopher Houston Stewart Chamberlain died today at the age of seventy-one, just as some of his anti-Semitic ideas were helping to form the Nazi Party in Germany. Although he was born in Britain, Chamberlain was educated in continental Europe and remained there, where he later wrote the influential philosophical book *The Foundations of the Nineteenth Century*, which argued that the Aryan race was superior and that Jesus Christ was not a Jew. Chamberlain was married to the illegitimate daughter of composer Richard Wagner, and she outlived him by fifteen years.

WEDNESDAY, JANUARY 12

Although the term "Off-Broadway" was not yet commonly used, there was plenty of theatre downtown in Greenwich Village that was an alternative to pricy Broadway shows. A group calling themselves the American Grand Guignol offered a series of one-act plays in the grisly French Grand Guignol tradition. The repertory of horror pieces opened today and entertained audiences for two months.

THURSDAY, JANUARY 13

Tensions between Mexico and the United States over oil interests increased today when Secretary of State Frank B. Kellogg suggested in a public statement that there was Bolshevik influence at work in Mexico.

While gasoline barrels were being unloaded today from the British steamer *Essex Isles* at Tampico, Mexico, there was an explosion and thirty-seven men, mostly Mexican dockworkers, were killed.

FRIDAY, JANUARY 14

Miriam A. Ferguson, the first woman governor of Texas, had only four days left to her term and today decided to halt her office's power of releasing state prisoners. Known popularly as Ma Ferguson, she had over the past two years pardoned or commuted the sentences of a record 3,595 convicted criminals. She was elected governor again in 1933.

SATURDAY, JANUARY 15

The first rugby match to be broadcast by radio in Great Britain was today's Rugby Union International between England and Wales, broadcast from Twickenham with commentary by Teddy Wakelam. England bested Wales 11–9.

The Scopes Trial (*The State of Tennessee v. John Thomas Scopes*), one of the most publicized and controversial cases of the 1920s, took place in 1925, when school teacher John T. Scopes taught the theory of evolution to his students in Dayton, Tennessee, thereby violating the state's Butler Act. The Monkey Trial, as it was dubbed, got national attention as radical lawyer Clarence Darrow defended Scopes and politician William Jennings Bryan prosecuted. After a very colorful trial, Scopes was found guilty and fined $100. The case was appealed and today, in a split decision, the Tennessee Supreme Court upheld the constitutionality of Section 49-1922 of the Tennessee

Code, which prohibited the teaching of evolution, but it reversed the trial's verdict and removed the fine. The law remained on the books in Tennessee until 1967.

Child actor Jackie Coogan, who had become a star in Charles Chaplin's hit *The Kid* in 1921, was thirteen years old in 1927 and was still playing orphaned boys, as in today's movie premiere *Johnny Get Your Hair Cut*. The waif Johnny O'Day is taken off the streets and given a home by the big-hearted racehorse owner Baxter Ryan (Maurice Costello). Johnny does indeed get his hair shorn, but he repays Baxter's kindness by saving the life of Baxter's stepdaughter and riding Baxter's horse to victory in the big race. Coogan was still a box office draw, and the MGM film was a success in its day, but today it is believed to be lost. Between 1922 and 1955, producer Hal Roach presented a series of comedy shorts that went under the names Our Gang, the Little Rascals, or Hal Roach's Rascals. *Bring Home the Turkey*, the first of thirteen such shorts that were released in 1927, premiered today. The mistreated kids at the Happyland Home Orphanage run away and hide out with the poor but kindly African American Uncle Tom (Tom Wilson in blackface). The authorities find the kids but a good-hearted judge orders some reforms at the orphanage, including hiring Tom as the cook. Also beginning on this day was *The Golden Stallion* film serial, put out by Mascot Productions. The ten-part Western offered an honest cowboy, Wynn Kendall (Maurice "Lefty" Flynn), and a greedy villain, Ewart Garth (Jo Bonomo), each looking for a hidden treasure. To find it they must first find the wild horse White Fury, on whose neck a clue to the whereabouts of the gold has been branded. Like most serials, there was a cliffhanger at the end of each episode, and before the treasure is discovered the two men have to shoot it out.

SUNDAY, JANUARY 16

The Wrigley Ocean Marathon, sponsored by chewing gum and sports magnate William Wrigley Jr., ended today when seventeen-year-old Canadian George Young from Toronto became the first person to swim the twenty-two miles between Catalina Island and the California mainland. Competing for the prize of $25,000, 102 competitors dived into the waters at noon the previous day, but Young was the only person to finish the swim, arriving at the Point Vincente Lighthouse at 3:47 a.m. Young, who was thereafter billed as the Catalina Kid, participated in swimming competitions for the next four years.

MONDAY, JANUARY 17

One of the quintessential Roaring Twenties up-tempo songs, "Ain't She Sweet," was recorded for the first time today by bandleader Lou Gold and His Melody Men. Milton Ager composed the Charleston-like music, and Jack Yellen wrote the slaphappy lyric, a list of rhetorical questions about what makes one's sweetheart so sweet. Before

THE JUKE BOX

The year 1927 marked the birth of the coin-operated juke box, which would change the way Americans listened to music in public places. The Automatic Music Instrument Company introduced the machine, in which a coin slot activated a record changer. The idea was soon copied by other companies, such as Wurlitzer, Rockola, and Seeburg. By the end of the year, there were juke boxes in restaurants, bus stations, hotels, stores, and speakeasies. In the South, establishments that served illegal booze and offered juke box music were called "juke joints."

the year was out, "Ain't She Sweet" was recorded by Ben Bernie and His Orchestra, Gene Austin, Johnny Marvin, Annette Hanshaw, and Paul Whiteman's Rhythm Boys, followed by hundreds of other records over the years. The number was also a popular dance song and was played by dance bands and orchestras in all kinds of venues throughout the Depression.

The first automobile bridge over San Francisco Bay, Dumbarton Bridge, opened today for vehicular traffic between the (then) town of Newark and the city of Menlo Park. The drawbridge crossed the southernmost part of the bay and was in use for nearly six decades. The new Dumbarton Bridge opened in 1984 but parts of the original bridge still exist as a fishing pier on the eastern shore of the bay.

Film comedian Harold Lloyd made only one movie in 1927, but it was a comedy classic, Paramount's *The Kid Brother*. The bespectacled weakling Harold is an embarrassment to his gruff father, Sheriff Jim Hickory, and his two brawny elder brothers. Poor Harold is assigned domestic duties in the house and tinkers with clever devices that save manual labor. When the Mammoth Medicine Show comes to Hickoryville and the show wagon burns down, Harold invites Mary (Jobyna Ralston), the daughter of the original owner of the show, to stay in the Hickory house, and they fall in love. Some thugs from the medicine show steal the money that Sheriff Jim was holding for the town to build a new dam, and everyone suspects the sheriff is guilty. He sends his two elder sons to find the culprits, but they are unsuccessful. To everyone's surprise, it is puny Harold who finds the crooks in an abandoned boat and returns the money. Harold clears his father's name, finally gains his respect, and wins the hand of Mary. While *The Kid Brother* is not as well known today as some of Lloyd's other comedy features, it is arguably his best film. Lloyd was at the peak of his popularity in 1927 and *The Kid Brother* was an immediate box office hit.

Juliette Gordon Low, the founder of the Girl Scouts of the USA, died of breast cancer today in her home in Savannah, Georgia. She was fifty-one years old. Low had started the U.S. Girl Guides in 1912, inspired by Sir Robert Baden-Powell's international Scouting Movement. In 1915 the organization changed its name to the Girl Scouts. Low's home in Savannah is today a popular tourist attraction.

TUESDAY, JANUARY 18

The Food, Drug, and Insecticide Administration was established today as part of the U.S. Department of Agriculture. Three years later, the name of the federal organization was changed to the Food and Drug Administration (FDA), a title it retains to this day.

Actor Walter Huston, near the beginning of his celebrated stage and film career, was lauded by the critics for his performance in Kenyon Nicholson's comedy *The Barker*, which opened today on Broadway and pleased playgoers for six months. He played the carnival barker Nifty Miller, who wants his college-educated son Chris (Norman Foster) to become a lawyer. Instead, Chris joins the carnival for the summer and falls in love with the snake charmer Lou (Claudette Colbert), causing plenty of comic grief for Nifty, who decides to quit the tent show business. Chris ends up with both Lou and law school and Nifty rejoins the carnival. In addition to plaudits for Huston, the reviews also pointed out Colbert's sly performance. She appeared in a half dozen other plays in the 1920s before getting a Hollywood contract with Paramount.

WEDNESDAY, JANUARY 19

The massive Council House of India, which opened the day before in New Delhi, held its first legislative session today with a meeting of the Central Legislative Assembly. The House, a circular building with a huge dome covering nearly six acres, is now the Parliament House of India.

The Empress Carlota of Mexico died today in Belgium at the age of eighty-six. The daughter of King Leopold I, King of the Belgians, she married the future emperor Maximilian I of Mexico and the two ruled the troubled nation from 1864 to 1867. Her life was a series of intrigues, affairs, power struggles, and bouts of insanity.

THURSDAY, JANUARY 20

Broadway and silent-film favorite Alice Brady couldn't save the melodrama *Lady Alone*, which struggled to run just over five weeks in New York. She played the headstrong Nina Hopkins, who gives up a rich (and much older) fiancé to have an affair with married man Craig Neilson. When things go wrong, Nina takes an overdose of sleeping pills and dies. The press extolled Brady's performance but little else in the play. She later enjoyed a memorable career as a character actress in talkies before her premature death from cancer in 1939.

FRIDAY, JANUARY 21

Moviegoers got to experience the Fox Movietone sound system for the first time today when a one-reel Movietone film preceded the feature presentation, *What Price Glory?*, in a New York City theatre. The sound system, purchased by the Fox Film Corporation, used a movie projector equipped to play sound-on-film, though visuals and sound were not quite synchronized. The first feature film, released on September 23, to use the Movietone sound system was Fox's *Sunrise*, which had music and sound effects but no dialogue.

Baseball was the subject of the short-lived Broadway play *Damn the Tears*. The talented college athlete Buckland Steele (Ralph Morgan) has a promising future in professional baseball, but when he flubs a much-needed hit in a big game, he quits the sport and tries writing and then the law. His failures continue, however, until he becomes a vagabond roaming the baseball stadiums and is arrested for vagrancy.

SATURDAY, JANUARY 22

A week after the first broadcast of a rugby game in Great Britain, the first broadcast of a soccer football match was made by BBC Radio. The two competing teams were Arsenal and Sheffield United, with Teddy Wakelam again providing the play-by-play of the game at Highbury. The match ended in a tie, each team scoring one point.

While the Baylor University basketball team was traveling on Texas State Highway 2 to a scheduled game against the University of Texas at Austin, the bus they were in was struck at a railroad crossing near Round Rock, Texas. Five members of the team were killed, five other students died, and seven others were seriously injured. Many college basketball games that weekend were canceled out of sympathy for the dead, and legislation was soon passed that required overpasses or underpasses at all places where state highways intersected with railroads.

H. P. Lovecraft finished writing *The Dream Quest of Unknown Kadath* on this date, but the novella was not published until six years after the author's death in 1937. The longest and most encompassing of Lovecraft's *Dream Cycle*, the book is considered by many to be his greatest work. As the title suggests, the story is in the form of a mythic quest. Bostonian Randolph Carter has dreamed of the magical city of Kadath, a sacred place no one has ever seen, and consults with the priests on how to get there. They warn him of the dangers in his quest but Carter sets off and is soon encountering rodent-like zoogs, black galleys rowed by invisible slaves, vicious moon-beasts, helpful ghouls, treacherous slant-eyed men, and other fantastical creatures. When Carter finally reaches Kadath, he is tricked by the Crawling Chaos in disguise and seems doomed to be imprisoned at Azathoth in the center of the universe. But Carter uses what he has learned in his dreams, escapes on the wings of a great bird, and wakes up in his room in Boston, realizing his home is the real Kadath. The novella combines Lovecraft's love of fantasy and horror and utilizes his favorite device, the dream. Since its publication in 1943, the story has inspired everything from comic books to rock music albums.

The Sherlock Holmes story "The Adventure of the Veiled Lodger" by Arthur Conan Doyle first appeared today in *Liberty* magazine. The tale is an unusual one in that Holmes does not solve a crime but merely listens to the confession of an old lady with a disfigured face. She and her lover worked at a circus and plotted to kill her cruel husband by making it look like it was the work of an escaped lion. The husband was killed, but the lion also turned on the wife and clawed her face into a hideous shape. Holmes's only help in the matter is to convince the woman that her life still has value and to not commit suicide. The story was included later in the year in the anthology *The Case-Book of Sherlock Holmes*.

The star power of Ronald Colman and Vilma Bánky helped make the Samuel Goldwyn film *The Night of Love* a box office success and as a costume adventure film it is still entertaining. The romantic but preposterous plot was loosely based on a play by the Spanish Renaissance playwright Calderón. The lecherous Duke de la Garda (Montagu Love) tries to use his aristocratic privilege to seduce a gypsy girl on the night before her wedding, but she kills herself instead. Her fiancé, the gypsy bandit Romani Montero (Colman), swears revenge and when the Duke is to marry the French Princess Marie (Bánky), Montero kidnaps the princess before the wedding and keeps her in his hideout. Of course, Marie falls in love with Montero, so when he is captured by the Duke, she has to save him from being burned at the stake. The production values are lavish and there is some passionate chemistry between Colman and Bánky (they made five movies together) that still sizzles. *The Night of Love* was among Bánky's last movies; her thick Hungarian accent finished her career once talkies came in. John Gilbert, another silent screen favorite who did not have a long career in sound movies, was the star of the day's other film premiere, MGM's *The Show*. Director-producer Tod Browning often used circus and sideshow settings in his films and *The Show* was no exception. For the dashing screen lover Gilbert, however, *The Show* was an exception. He played the barker Cock Robin in a tawdry Budapest sideshow and participated in an act in which Salome (Renée Adorée) danced before Herod and then presents him with the head of Jokanaan on a platter. Robin was the seemingly decapitated head in the act. Salome is lusted after by the Greek (Lionel Barrymore), but she loves Robin and is jealous when he is attracted to the wealthy Lena. The Greek tries to kill Robin by substituting a real sword in the act, but Salome sees through the plot and saves him. *The Show*, rated among Browning's best, is filled with fascinating characters and scenes, and many believe Gilbert gives one of his most disarming performances as Cock Robin. The movie's happy ending is a bit forced, but as directed by horror expert Browning, *The Show* is still fascinating to watch. Unlike Bánky, Gilbert had a fine speaking voice and made some memorable early talkies, but alcohol and depression brought on heart failure and he died in 1936.

SUNDAY, JANUARY 23

Byron Bancroft "Ban" Johnson, president of baseball's American League, had turned a blind eye to the 1919 "Black Sox Scandal" and even publicly criticized the ruling by

Baseball Commissioner Kenesaw Mountain Landis to ban eight players of the Chicago White Sox. Johnson, who had been president of the American League since its founding in 1900, was fired today by vote of the league's eight teams. Although Johnson retained his title, his duties were assumed by Frank J. Navin of the Detroit Tigers.

Tom Mix, Hollywood's favorite cowboy star of the 1920s, made seven westerns in 1927 and probably the best of them was Fox's *The Last Trail*, which was released today. Taken from a Zane Gray novel, the plot centered on a stagecoach race with the winner getting a lucrative contract from the overland company run by Jasper Carrol. Tom Dane (Mix), with the help of his horse, Tony, outwits a murder attempt on his life, finds out who has been robbing Carrol's stagecoaches, and wins the race.

MONDAY, JANUARY 24

Today four hundred American marines arrived in Nicaragua to bring order to the country, which was being torn apart by civil war. It did not take long to see that the situation in the Central American nation was far worse than anticipated. By March there would be two thousand more marines in Nicaragua.

An even larger military force was dispatched today when the United Kingdom sent the Shanghai Defense Force—consisting of twelve thousand men from the British infantry brigades, three thousand naval servicemen, and one thousand marines—to defend the British concession in Shanghai, China.

The pioneering theatre producer, director, and actress Eva Le Gallienne, who had founded the ambitious Civic Repertory Theatre in 1926, offered the 1911 Spanish play *The Cradle Song* for fifty-seven performances on Broadway. It told of an austere nunnery in Spain, under the supervision of Sister Joanna of the Cross (Le Gallienne), which takes in a foundling. She grows up to be the loving Teresa (Josephine Hutchinson), who brings love and warmth to the convent. When Teresa falls in love with a young man and leaves the nunnery to marry, the nuns are a sadder but more human community. Reviewers thought the play sweet yet slight but praised Le Gallienne's production and acting.

TUESDAY, JANUARY 25

The United States and Mexico had been quarreling for some years over oil rights, and at times it looked like the dispute might lead to war. To avoid such an outcome, the U.S. Senate today voted 79–0 to ask President Coolidge to seek arbitration. The president turned the matter over to Secretary of State Frank B. Kellogg, who was not on friendly terms with the Mexican government.

The Remington Typewriter Company and Rand-Kardex Corporation today merged to form Remington Rand, a leading manufacturer of business machines. In

1951 the company would make the UNIVAC, the world's first business computer. A 1955 merger created the company Sperry-Rand, and in 1986 the corporation Unisys was formed.

The controversial Southern Baptist leader and ardent fundamentalist, J. Frank Norris, was acquitted today of a murder charge on the grounds of self-defense. On July 17, 1926, Norris had killed wholesale lumberman Dexter B. Chipps in the Baptist church office in Fort Worth, Texas. Norris had accused the Fort Worth mayor, H. C. Meacham, of misappropriating government money to the Roman Catholic Church. Chipps was a close friend of Meacham's and, during a confrontation between Norris and Chipps, Norris claimed that Chipps threatened his life. The incident and the trial's verdict reflected how powerful Norris was in the South.

The popular comic actor Leon Errol was able to keep the silly musical comedy *Yours Truly* on Broadway for sixteen weeks with his hilarious stunts and drunk scenes, which he had perfected in vaudeville and then on Broadway. The nonsensical plot concerned rich but big-hearted Mary Stillwell, who goes to Chinatown and gets mixed up with petty crooks who are after her inheritance, and the suspicious Shuffling Bill, who turns out to be a detective determined to protect her. The songs were as forgettable as the plot, but Errol in a supporting role was the hit of the evening.

WEDNESDAY, JANUARY 26

A school basketball game in the town of Turner, Idaho, was the site of a freak accident that left seven dead and two dozen others seriously injured. While the game was being played in the recreation room of the Mormon Hall School, there was power failure and acetylene gas leaked from the boiler room. Someone lit a match to see in the dark and the flame triggered a deadly explosion.

Actress Ruth Gordon made a triumphant return to Broadway with her performance as the feisty newlywed Bobby in Maxwell Anderson's comedy *Saturday's Children*, which opened today and entertained playgoers for six months. Bobby snags the man she loves, Rims O'Neal, but their marriage has its rocky moments until she takes a room at a boardinghouse and jealousy drives Rims back into her arms. Gordon had first charmed Broadway audiences in *Seventeen* in 1918, followed by other successes. But the death of her husband Gregory Kelly and her own hospitalization had kept her off the stage since 1925. The press extolled Gordon's comic performance and there were also many compliments for Beula Bondi as the suspicious landlady of the boardinghouse. *Saturday's Children* was filmed twice: in a 1929 silent version with Corinne Griffith as Bobby and in 1940 starring Anne Shirley.

The renowned financier Lyman J. Gage died today at the age of ninety in San Diego. He had served as the secretary of the treasury under Presidents William McKinley and

Theodore Roosevelt and was very influential in passing the Gold Standard Act of 1900. Gage was also active in presenting such famous events as the World's Columbian Exposition in Chicago in 1893 and the Panama-California Exposition in San Diego in 1915.

THURSDAY, JANUARY 27

United Independent Broadcasters, Inc., was incorporated today as a network of sixteen radio stations that were brought together in Chicago by New York talent agent Arthur Judson. The new company was in fragile financial shape from the start, but before the year was out it was rescued and became part of the future Columbia Broadcasting Corporation (CBS).

In 1926, ballplayer Dutch Leonard accused his longtime rivals, outfielders Ty Cobb and Tris Speaker, of having fixed a game between the Detroit Tigers and Cleveland Indians during the 1919 season. The accusation was big news in all the newspapers at the time, and many fans felt that Leonard's charges were retaliatory toward Cobb, who had been Leonard's manager for a time. Baseball commissioner Kenesaw Mountain Landis had conducted an in-depth investigation and today exonerated both Cobb and Speaker of all charges of wrongdoing. Their names cleared, Cobb signed with the Philadelphia Athletics and Speaker with the Washington Senators for the 1927 season.

In the Australian Open Women's Singles Tennis Championship today, held in Melbourne, Esna Boyd beat Sylvia Lance Harper with a final score of 5–7, 6–1, and 6–2. Gerald Patterson defeated John Hawkes 3–6, 6–4, 3–6, 18–16, and 6–3 for the Men's Singles Championship.

William Collins & Sons today published Agatha Christie's mystery *The Big Four*, an unusual Hercule Poirot novel in that it was based on some previously published short stories and it involved international espionage. The plot is episodic and has locations all around the globe rather than the traditional setting of a village or a manor house. The title refers to the four villains—the American soap millionaire Abe Ryland; the Chinese mastermind Le Chang Yen, who is never seen; the French nuclear physicist Madame Olivier; and arch-criminal and assassin Claude Darrell—who are trying to achieve world domination. With the help of assistant Arthur Hastings and Scotland Yard's Inspector Japp, Poirot uncovers their plots and arranges for the destruction of the four villains.

Rising Hollywood star Joan Crawford was the main attraction in the adventure film *Winners of the Wilderness*, which opened today. The forgettable MGM movie was set during the French and Indian War and cast Crawford as René Contrecoeur, the daughter of a French general, who is kidnapped by Chief Pontiac. Colonel Sir Dennis O'Hara (Tim McCoy) is in love with René and rescues her, thereby winning her hand in marriage. The black-and-white film is notable for one scene near the end that is in two-strip Technicolor.

FRIDAY, JANUARY 28

All four countries of the United Kingdom were battered today with gale-force winds that reached 112 mph in some sections. The hurricane-like storm moved north on a line from Land's End in England, to John O'Groats in Scotland, spreading out its path to include Wales and Northern Ireland. Twenty-three people died as a result of the storm.

SATURDAY, JANUARY 29

Moviegoers may have had trouble recognizing Lon Chaney, the "man with a thousand faces," in MGM's *Tell It to the Marines* because in this film the face he used was his own. Playing hardened career officer Sergeant O'Hara of the U.S. Marines, who trains a batch of raw recruits, Chaney insisted on using no makeup at all in order to maintain the documentary look of the movie. One of his most incompetent recruits is Private Skeet Burns (William Haines), and tension between the two men is increased when they both fall in love with the Navy nurse Norma Dale (Eleanor Boardman). The romantic triangle is further complicated when the Marines are sent to Shanghai and Norma and the other nurses are tending the patients of an epidemic in Hanchow. After a raid by Chinese bandits, in which O'Hara is wounded and rescued by a squadron of air support, the threesome survive and return to the States. Skeet and Norma wed and buy a farm, offering O'Hara a partnership in the enterprise. But O'Hara realizes he is married to the Marines and returns to active duty. *Tell It to the Marines* was shot near San Diego with the full cooperation of the U.S. Marine Corps, so it is both realistic and accurate. Chaney so impressed the Marine technical advisor on the film that the actor was later made an honorary marine. His performance is one of his best (Chaney later stated O'Hara was his favorite role) because it is raw and honest and he doesn't hide behind makeup and physical character quirks. The movie had a New York City premiere screening in December 1926, but on this date, it was released to the public and became one of Chaney's biggest hits. Legend has it that the popularity of *Tell It to the Marines* resulted in a sharp rise in enlistment in the Marine Corps. Sadly, before the year was out, many actual marines would be sent to China where they died in that troubled nation's civil war.

As odd as it may seem to modern moviegoers, Hollywood made silent screen versions of popular Broadway operettas and audiences wanted to see them. A case in point is the day's other opening, *The Red Mill* starring Marion Davies. The 1906 Victor Herbert operetta came to the screen in a fanciful production set in Holland and directed by comic Roscoe "Fatty" Arbuckle using the pseudonym William Goodrich. There was no singing, of course, but some of Herbert's music was heard. The screenplay took a secondary character from the stage version, the servant girl Tina, and turned her into the leading role for Davies. The plot is a bit of a mess, with Tina and her pet mouse providing the comedy, and the burgomaster's daughter, Gretchen, and her sweetheart, Captain Jacop Van Goop, as the romantic couple. Gretchen is being forced by her father to marry the elderly governor, so Tina, who is in love with the foreigner Dennis Wheat, helps her escape by exchanging clothes with her, leading to comic mishaps and some confused boyfriends. It is all delightful fun, and Davies carries the movie with her charm and comic skills.

SUNDAY, JANUARY 30

In the Austrian village of Schattendorf today, members of the right-wing veterans' organization Frontkampfer Vereinigung fired on members of the leftist organization Schutzbund, killing one of them, seriously wounding five others, and mortally wounding an eight-year-old boy. The incident would result in a trial in Vienna in July followed by riots and the burning of the Palace of Justice.

Thirty-three-year-old John Ford had already directed nearly forty feature films by 1927 yet had not developed his particular style or been able to film the outdoor subject matter that later made him famous. Such was the case with today's Fox opening, *Upstream*, a comedy-drama set in London's West End. In the theatrical boardinghouse of Hattie Breckinridge Peyton are a variety of performers, including knife-throwing artiste Jack; his pretty assistant, Gertie; and the down-on-his-luck yet still egotistical actor Eric Brashingham. The rivalries and romantic triangles provide dramatic and romantic sparks. *Upstream* is hardly Ford in his stride, yet the movie has its entertainment value. For decades *Upstream* was believed lost, but a copy was found in New Zealand in 2010.

Mabel Normand, considered the greatest screen comedienne of the silent era, was the star of Hal Roach's oddly titled short *Should Men Walk Home?* She plays a bandit who teams up with a gentleman crook (Creighton Hale) as they work their way into a high-society party and try to fleece the guests and break into the owner's safe. A detective at the party is soon onto them, and there is a merry chase throughout the house filled with still-funny gags. Normand was recuperating from drug abuse and a well-publicized scandal when she made the movie, but none of that shows in her sprightly, witty performance.

MONDAY, JANUARY 31

Addressing the Army War College today, Lieutenant Colonel David Sarnoff of the U.S. Signal Corps Reserve explained how the new-fangled invention of television could be used in future warfare by sending images from airplanes of the enemy's movements below. Sarnoff, a pioneer in radio and television and head of the Radio Corporation of America (RCA), was not taken very seriously by the military.

Actress-playwright Mae West, who had stirred up controversy and landed in jail in 1926 with her play *Sex*, went a step further and wrote what is believed to be the first play overtly about homosexuality. It was titled *The Drag* and had its premiere today in Bridgeport, Connecticut. When the production continued on to Bayonne, New Jersey, it was banned by the authorities for indecency. Because of such adverse publicity, West was unable to find a theatre in New York City, so it never opened there. She rewrote *The Drag* in 1928, changing the main gay character into a heterosexual one, and retitling it *The Pleasure Man*. That version opened on Broadway and was still met with charges of indecency.

Of the five productions opening on Broadway this evening, it was the debut of playwright Robert Sherwood that garnered the most attention. His stinging comedy *The Road to Rome* foreshadowed a career of vigorous and thought-provoking playwriting. As the bold conqueror Hannibal (Philip Merivale) and his troops approach the city of Rome, the ineffectual Emperor Fabius Maximus panics, while his wife, Amytis (Jane Cowl), takes matters into her own hands, going to Hannibal and charming him into retreating. The critics praised Cowl's wily performance and credited Sherwood as a playwright to be watched. *The Road to Rome* ran five profitable months. By the end of the year there was a film version that reset the plot during the Trojan War and was titled *The Private Life of Helen of Troy*.

A notable Italian film, *Addio giovinezza!* (*Goodbye Youth!*), premiered in Rome today, the third screen version of a popular Italian play. The Turin student Mario (Walter Slezak) is passionate about the seamstress Dorina but is sidetracked by the seductive Elena. The romantic triangle is dissolved when Mario graduates from school, enters the real world, and says farewell to his youth. Augusto Genina directed the familiar (to Italians) tale, which still felt like a play, but, it pleased audiences enough that another screen version was made in 1940.

The Olympic swimming champion Sybil Bauer died today of cancer in Chicago at the age of twenty-three, cutting short a remarkable athletic career. As a student at Northwestern University, Bauer was on the swim team where she broke world records in swimming events, mostly with the backstroke. She was on the United States swim team for the 1924 Summer Olympics in Paris where she won a gold medal. At the time of her premature death, Bauer was a senior at Northwestern and engaged to newspaper columnist Ed Sullivan, who later went on to have a legendary career in television.

> For households without electricity, a manual washing machine could be purchased for around sixteen dollars in 1927. If you had power, an electric washing machine would set you back seventy-nine dollars.

FEBRUARY

TUESDAY, FEBRUARY 1

For three years the Southern Branch of the University of California had been conferring BA degrees. On this date the college formally changed to its name to the University of California at Los Angeles, more commonly referred to ever since as UCLA.

Two famous vacation resorts opened today, one on the seaside and the other in the desert. The first oceanside resort hotel in Hawaii, the Royal Hawaiian Hotel, opened in Waikiki, Honolulu, on the island of Oahu and was a success from the start. Still a luxury resort, the pink stucco structure in the Spanish-Moorish style is familiarly known as the "Pink Palace of the Pacific." On the same day, the first hotel in Death Valley National Park opened in the California desert. Boasting only twelve rooms, the Furnace Creek Inn was bought by the Pacific Coast Borax company and renamed the Inn at Death Valley, hoping to lure tourists to take the Tonopah and Tidewater Railroad to Death Valley. Over the decades more rooms, a swimming pool, and a dude ranch were added. Today the inn is the luxury resort known as the Oasis at Death Valley.

Dorothy Parker's revealing short story *Little Curtis* was printed in the February issue of the *Pictorial Review*. Unlike most of her stories set in contemporary New York, this one is a period piece set in a small town where the meticulous Mrs. Matson arranges everything in her life in a precise and orderly manner, including her young adopted son Curtis, whom she is obviously suffocating with demands for perfection. Although the story has the setting of a Booth Tarkington tale, the acid quality to the piece is very much in the Parker style.

The singing quartet known as the Smith Brothers today recorded the song "Hoosier Sweetheart" by Billy Baskette, Paul Ash, and Joe Goodwin on the Victor label. The ballad is an up-tempo song pleading for an Indiana girl to remain faithful to her lover.

SOME SPORTS FIGURES BORN IN 1927

Swimmer Greta Andersen
Baseball player Richie Ashburn (d. 1997)
Soccer player Walter Bahr (d. 2018)
Runner Josy Barthel (d. 1992)
Boxer Carmen Basilio (d. 2012)
Basketball player Ralph Beard (d. 2007)
Footballer George Blanda (d. 2010)
Basketball player Carl Braun (d. 2010)
Golfer Alice Bauer (d. 2002)
Baseball player Smokey Burgess (d. 1991)
Baseball player Jack Butler (d. 2013)
Rugby player Clive Churchill (d. 1985)
Baseball player Lou Creekmur (d. 2009)
Jumper Adhemar Ferreira da Silva (d. 2001)
Chess master Hein Donner (d. 1988)
Slalom racer Stein Eriksen (d. 2015)
Football player Fernie Flaman (d. 2012)
Baseball player Nellie Fox (d. 1975)
Golfer and tennis player Althea Gibson
　(d. 2003)
Cricketer Wally Grout (d. 1968)
Cricketer John Hayes (d. 2007)
Javelin champion Franklin "Bud" Held
Baseball player Bill Henry (d. 2014)

Boxer George Hunter (d. 2004)
Skier Trudi Jochum-Beiser
Sculler rower John Kelly Jr. (d. 1985)
Soccer player and manager Leonard Patrick
　"Red" Kelly (d. 1989)
Baseball manager Tommy Lasorda
Equestrian Liselott Lisenhoff (d. 1999)
Hockey player Calum MacKay (d. 2001)
Runner Dorothy Manley
Football player Gino Marchetti
Football player Joe Perry (d. 2011)
Baseball player Billy Pierce (d. 2015)
Sportswriter and author George Plimpton
　(d. 2003)
Race car driver Bill Rexford (d. 1994)
Tennis player Dick Savitt
Baseball player Carl Scheib (d. 2018)
Race car driver Archie Scott-Brown
　(d. 1958)
Sportscaster Vin Scully
Tennis player Frank Sedgman
Sportscaster Jim Simpson (d. 2016)
Golfer Shirley Spork
Football player Doak Walker (d. 1998)

Forrest Harrill Burgess, who would become All-Star baseball catcher, coach, and scout Smokey Burgess, was born today in Caroleen, North Carolina.

Sir George Higginson, a hero of the Crimean War, died today at the age of 100. The British general received many citations and medals during his seven decades of military service including the Legion of Honor from France.

WEDNESDAY, FEBRUARY 2

Mass murderer George J. Hassell today confessed to killing his wife and their eight children on December 5, 1926, in Farwell, Texas. Hassell not only led the police to where he had buried the bodies but gave graphic details on how he used a hammer, straight razor, shotgun, and axe to kill them. Police research later revealed that Hassell had previously committed murder, embezzlement, and military desertion. He was executed by electric chair in February 1928.

The stylish and most modern-looking playhouse on Broadway, the Ziegfeld Theatre, opened this night with the operetta *Rio Rita* produced by Florenz Ziegfeld. The playhouse was unique in that it had few right angles inside or on the exterior. Every surface was curved, including the windows, the walls, and even the stage. The main auditorium was a giant oval that featured a mural titled *The Joy of Living*, which was said to be the largest oil painting in the world. Not so modern was *Rio Rita*, which took the form of an operetta. Captain Jim (J. Harold Murray) of the Texas Rangers falls in love with the beautiful Rio Rita (Ethelind Terry) even though he knows she is also courted by the unappealing Mexican, General Esteban. Since Jim is on the hunt for the mysterious bandit called "The Kinkajou," Esteban tells Rita that Jim's prime suspect is her brother Roberto. This cools the romance between Jim and Rita until Jim proves "The Kinkajou" is none other than Esteban himself. The book by Guy Bolton and Fred Thompson was functional rather than inspired, but the score by Harry Tierney (music) and Joseph McCarthy (lyrics) was luscious, filled with such hit songs as the snappy "The Kinkajou," the rousing march "The Rangers' Song," the romantic duet "If You're in Love, You'll Waltz," and the adorable title number. Producer Ziegfeld made sure the production was as sumptuous as his new playhouse, and it thrilled the public for over a year. In 1929, *Rio Rita* was one of the earliest Broadway musicals to be filmed by Hollywood; the RKO movie was made with sound and in color.

The top ticket price to see the hit musical *Rio Rita* in the new, lavish Ziegfeld Theatre on Broadway was $5.50. One could get into a Manhattan movie palace for as little as twenty-five cents.

THURSDAY, FEBRUARY 3

A revolt against dictator General Carmona of Portugal and his government began today as rebels attacked the city of Oporto. The fighting went on for five days and over 120 people died. The rebels surrendered on the fifth day when heavy artillery was brought in and it looked like the entire city would be demolished. Carmona dealt harshly with the rebels, sending over six hundred of them to penal colonies in the Azores and Cape Verde. Carmona remained in power in Portugal for twenty-four more years.

Warner Brothers offered a lavish costume drama, *When a Man Loves*, starring John Barrymore in a romantic role that audiences expected from the leading man with the "great profile." Loosely based on Abbé Prévost's novel *Manon Lescaut*, the movie gave the familiar tragic tale a happy ending, which is probably the way Barrymore's many fans wanted it. He played the divinity student Fabien des Grieux whose thoughts of a religious life are changed when he rescues Manon Lescaut (Dolores Costello) from the lustful Comte Guillot de Morfontaine and falls in love with her. There is plenty of adventure before the two lovers escape on a small boat to freedom. *When a Man Loves*,

Warner Brothers released forty-three feature films in 1927, the largest number yet in their four-year history. Yet the studio was facing bankruptcy that year until *The Jazz Singer* opened on October 6.

directed with skill by Alan Crosland, is filled with romance and adventure and is still enjoyable moviegoing. The soundtrack score by Henry Hadley was recorded on the Vitaphone process and the music came from the speakers rather than from an orchestra in the pit. At the end of the film, the orchestra that recorded the soundtrack is seen briefly on screen and the premiere audience, realizing that they had been listening to a recording, was very impressed and broke out in applause.

FRIDAY, FEBRUARY 4

British motor car racer Malcolm Campbell had set a world record for land speed back in 1924 when he drove a 350 hp V12 Sunbeam up to 146.16 mph on Pendine Sands in Wales. Today he returned to the same site and, driving a Napier-Campbell Blue Bird, reached the speed of 174.883 mph. That record would be broken a month later by Henry Seagrave but Campbell would go on to set new land and water speed records in the 1930s.

SATURDAY, FEBRUARY 5

Tennis player Vincent Richards had been named the National Champion of 1926 by the United States Tennis Association. Today the organization took back his number one ranking because Richards had turned professional. The honor was then bestowed on amateur-status tennis ace Bill Tilden, whom tennis historians rate as one of the greatest American players of all time. Tilden himself turned professional in 1930.

Many consider the Civil War comedy *The General* to be Buster Keaton's best film, but when it opened today in New York City the critics were far from complimentary. In fact, most reviewers called the comedy long, tedious, unfunny, and in poor taste. It took years for *The General* to be recognized as the cinema classic that is so highly lauded today. Keaton coproduced, cowrote, codirected, and starred in the comedy about the Georgia railroad engineer Johnnie Gray (Keaton) who loves his fiancée Annabelle Lee (Marion Mack) almost as much as he loves his locomotive named *The General*. When the Civil War breaks out, Johnnie tries to enlist but the Confederate army needs him to run the locomotive for the war effort. Annabelle mistakenly thinks Johnnie is too cowardly to fight and breaks off the engagement. Later in the war, *The General* is kidnapped by the Union forces with Annabelle and other passengers aboard. In one of the cinema's greatest train chases, Johnnie uses various methods to pursue *The General* and eventually succeeds in recapturing it, being hailed a hero by the South and by Annabelle. In one of the most spectacular (and expensive) stunts in silent movies, the Union locomotive *The Texas* pursues the Confederates over a bridge that is on fire and the train plunges into the river below. The movie was based on a true story, which was written up as a memoir titled *The Great Locomotive Chase* by William Pittenger in 1863. United Artists purchased two retired locomotives from the Civil War era (and destroyed one on screen), which drove the film's planned budget from $400,000 up to $750,000. When *The General* did poor box office (just under $500,000 in its first national release), Keaton's clout in Hollywood dropped and for the rest of his long career he was no longer considered a major artist in the movie business. Not until a slightly revised and newly-scored version of *The General* was released in 1953 was the film proclaimed a comedy-adventure masterpiece. A non-comic film version of Pittenger's tale was made by the Disney Studio in 1956 and was titled *The Great Locomotive Chase.*

The ingenious comic actor Buster Keaton may have had a "stone face," but the rest of his body was agile and hilariously physical. He is pictured here in a tense moment in his comedy classic *The General. Continental Distributing / Photofest © Continental Distributing*

SUNDAY, FEBRUARY 6

The two-day Men's World Figure Skating Championship concluded today in Davos, Switzerland. Willy Böcki won the gold medal, Otto Preissecker the silver, and Karl Schäfer the bronze. All three were Austrian.

In Nicaragua, an army of fifteen hundred rebels today captured and burned the city of Chinandega. It took U.S. troops five days to recapture the city at the price of three hundred dead and five hundred wounded.

A noteworthy "race" film opened today in African American neighborhoods in New York City and then in other cities, an example of how movies were also part of the lively music, art, and literary scene in Harlem in 1927. Titled *The Scar of Shame*, it was produced by the Colored Players Film Corporation and featured an all-black cast. Alvin Hillyard is an educated "Negro" and a gifted musician so his family is not happy when he falls in love with Louise, a common girl whom he rescues from the bully Spike. Alvin marries her but Spike still pursues Louise, resulting in a shootout in which she is shot in the neck. Louise lives but is scarred for life and Alvin is sent to prison. While he is gone, Louise takes up with the gambler Eddie Blake. Alvin escapes from jail and, taking up a new identity, gets a job as a music teacher. He falls in love with Alice, one of his students, and when he and Louise meet again, he rejects her. This drives Louise to suicide and forces Alvin to tell Alice the truth about his past. *The Scar of Shame* is often a turgid melodrama but deals with some potent issues about the class system within the African American community.

MONDAY, FEBRUARY 7

The acclaimed British actress Mrs. Patrick Campbell, the original Eliza Doolittle in *Pygmalion* in 1914, had not appeared on the New York stage in fourteen years so anticipation was great when she opened in the comedy *The Adventurous Age* today on Broadway. She played a middle-aged mother who attempts a fling with a much younger man, much to the embarrassment of her grown children. The press thought the play hopelessly unfunny but noted that the sixty-two-year-old Campbell still had some vivacity in her acting. Audiences were not supportive and the comedy closed after two weeks.

TUESDAY, FEBRUARY 8

The Boy Scouts of America celebrated its seventeenth birthday today. The organization boasted over a million members, making it the largest youth organization in the nation. It was estimated that in 1927 one out of four boys at the age of twelve were Boy Scouts.

Emperor Taisho of Japan (known in the West as Yoshihito), who had died on December 25, 1926, at the age of forty-seven, was not given a funeral ceremony until today because of the massive scale and amount of preparation needed for the event. The funeral began at night and consisted of a four-mile-long procession in which twenty thousand mourners followed a herd of sacred bulls and an ox-drawn cart containing the imperial coffin. Some eighty thousand Japanese citizens lined the procession route, which was lit with iron lanterns. After an elaborate ceremony in the daylight, the emperor's coffin was then transported to his mausoleum in the western suburbs of Tokyo. Taisho was succeeded by his son Showa Hirohito who reigned until 1989.

WEDNESDAY, FEBRUARY 9

The Mailing of Firearms Act, formally known as the Miller Act of 1927, was signed today by President Coolidge, marking the strongest gun control legislation in the nation to that time. Taking effect on May 10, the new law prohibited the sending of revolvers, pistols, and other small arms through the U.S. mail. But the ban was easily avoided if one used private shipping companies. Over the years Congress considered closing this loophole, but nothing came of the effort. The law still stands, but of course in this day of the internet, eBay, and other sources, one can order handguns with practically no regulations that can be enforced.

In baseball news, the Cincinnati Reds today traded longtime center fielder Edd Roush to the New York Giants for first baseman George "High Pockets" Kelly. Roush began playing Major League Baseball in 1913 and continued until 1931. Kelly began in 1915 and retired in 1932. Both men were later inducted into the Baseball Hall of Fame, although Kelly's selection has always been regarded as controversial as the Veterans Committee, which ultimately voted him in, consisted of many former teammates and friends.

THURSDAY, FEBRUARY 10

The first Congress of Oppressed Nationalists, also known as the League against Imperialism, opened today in Brussels, bringing together delegates from thirty-seven countries under imperial rule. Among the delegates who would one day lead their people to independence were Jawaharlal Nehru from India, Ho Chi Minh from Vietnam, Mohammed Hatta from Indonesia, J. T. Gumede from South Africa, Léopold Sédar Senghor from Senegal, and Messali Hadj from Algeria. Also attending were European and American Leftist activists, such as Fenner Brockway, Arthur MacManus, Edo Fimmen, Reginald Bridgeman, and Gabrielle Duchêne, as well as intellectuals such as Henri Barbusse, Romain Rolland, and Albert Einstein.

Another conference of a very different nature was announced today. President Coolidge addressed a joint session of Congress and announced that he would invite the world's major powers to meet in Geneva in June for a Second Disarmament Conference to discuss further reductions of their navies. At the first conference, held in 1922, the Washington Naval Treaty had been signed by the United States, the United Kingdom, France, Italy, and Japan.

Ernst Krenek's German opera about an African American jazz musician, *Jonny spielt auf* (*Jonny Plays*), premiered in Leipzig today and was an immediate hit. It was performed over four hundred times throughout Germany and came to symbolize the artistic freedom of the pre-Nazi Weimar Republic. Once the Nazi Party came to power, the opera was banned. Krenek fled Germany in 1938 and settled in America, where he continued to compose and teach in the United States and Canada until his death in 1991.

FRIDAY, FEBRUARY 11

The U.S. Figure Skating Championships took place today in New York City, the seventh time the event was held. The Ladies Figure Skating competition resulted in the gold medal going to Beatrix Loughran, the silver to Maribel Vinson, and the bronze to Theresa Weld Blanchard. The gold medal in the Men's Figure Skating competition was awarded to Nathaniel Niles, the silver to Roger Turner, and the bronze to George Braakman.

Thomas Edison, America's most prolific and admired inventor, celebrated his eightieth birthday today with an intimate gathering at his New Jersey laboratory and then a dinner at the Robert Treat Hotel in Newark. Henry Ford was among the notables who attended and President Coolidge sent his congratulations in a letter.

One of the goriest crimes of the decade was committed today in Brooklyn. Four-year-old Billy Gaffney was kidnapped while playing near his apartment building and was never found. More than eight years later, convicted child murderer Albert Fish confessed to abducting, torturing, and killing Gaffney, then cooking and eating his body parts.

SATURDAY, FEBRUARY 12

The city of Shanghai was so important in world trade that several nations around the globe were making their presence known in the Chinese city. Today the first wave of the British expeditionary army landed in Shanghai, with many more to follow. Soon to arrive were military units from the United States, Japan, Italy, and France.

SUNDAY, FEBRUARY 13

Two Italian aviators and army officers, Lt. Col. Francesco de Pinedo and Lt. Col. Carlo del Prete, took off today in the Savoia-Marchetti S.55 flying boat *Santa Maria* and, in a series of flights, covered thirty thousand miles. Their route took them from Italy to Africa, then across the Southern Atlantic to South America, then north as far as Canada, and finally east to Rome. This was three months before Charles Lindbergh's nonstop flight across the North Atlantic. Pinedo and Prete made fifty stops and were sometimes forced to land on water and get towed to the nearest port. For one stretch of the journey, they even traveled by train with the *Santa Maria* on board. The trip took over four months, with 193 hours of flying time.

About one hundred people perished today when a series of twenty earthquake tremors in one hour shook Bosnia in an area along the Neretva River. Because the area was sparsely populated, the death toll was far less than if the quakes had hit elsewhere.

Hal Roach's newest Our Gang short, *Seeing the World*, was released today in theatres, and it was better constructed than many of the Rascals' comedies. A school teacher and the gang go to Europe and have misadventures in London, Rome, Venice, and the ruins of Pompeii. In Paris, when they climb the Eiffel Tower, Farina (Allen Hoskins) slips over the edge of the railing. The teacher desperately tries to save Farina, then wakes up and realizes the whole trip was a nightmare caused by the Rascals putting sleeping pills in his water glass.

Brooks Adams, the great-grandson of President John Adams, the grandson of John Quincy Adams, and the brother of philosopher and novelist Henry Adams, died today in Boston at the age of seventy-eight. Like other members of his illustrious family, Adams was a political scientist, historian, and author who theorized about trends in civilization in his many books and essays.

MONDAY, FEBRUARY 14

As a kind of Valentine's Day present to himself, Canadian businessman and sports enthusiast Conn Smythe purchased the Toronto St. Patricks hockey team today to keep it from being moved to Philadelphia. Smythe renamed the team the Toronto Maple Leafs, after the Maple Leaf Regiment that fought for Canada in World War I. The day before the purchase, the St. Pats had lost 1–0 to the Ottawa Senators, and were in last place in their division at 8–18–4. With their new name, the Maple Leafs played their first game on the day after the purchase in Windsor, Ontario, losing 5–1 to the Detroit Cougars (later the Detroit Red Wings).

A new record for the largest snowfall in a twenty-four-hour period was set today when a winter storm dumped 11.82 meters (38.78 feet) of snow on Japan's Mount Ibuki. The previous record of 8.18 meters (26.84 feet) was set in the Japanese town of Itakura one day earlier.

Boxer Jimmy Delaney defeated Maxie Rosenbloom, a future light heavyweight boxing champ, in a bout today in Cincinnati. During the fight, Delaney splintered a bone in his left elbow but ignored it, and ten days later in Buffalo he was matched against Benny Ross and lost. When his elbow got worse, Delaney sought medical treatment, but it was too late. Infection and blood poisoning had set in, and two operations and a blood transfusion failed to save him. Delaney died on March 4 at the age of twenty-six.

American artist Edward Hopper's renowned painting *Automat* was first shown to the public today as part of his second solo show at the Rehn Galleries in New York City. The painting depicts a lone, well-dressed woman sitting at a table in an automat gazing at her cup of coffee. *Automat* is a vivid example of Hopper's realistic yet ambiguous style. The oil painting was purchased in April for $1,200. Today it hangs in the Des Moines Art Center.

Alfred Hitchcock, who had been directing films in Europe since 1925, had his first international hit with *The Lodger: A Story of the London Fog*, which premiered in London today. The streets of London are not safe, because a serial killer known as the Avenger has been targeting blonde women. At the boarding house run by Mr. and Mrs. Bunting, a handsome but secretive young man, Jonathan Drew (Ivor Novello), rents a room, and the Buntings soon notice that he goes out most evenings. Their daughter Daisy is dating police detective Joe Chandler, who is working on the case of the Avenger, but she is drawn to Jonathan. Another murder convinces the jealous Joe that Jonathan is the Avenger, and when the boarder is out one night, Joe finds photos and news clippings about the murders in his room. He has Jonathan arrested and handcuffed but he escapes and is found by Daisy. He explains that his sister was the Avenger's first victim and he vowed to find the culprit and bring him to justice. A mob finds Jonathan and is about to take justice into their own hands when news arrives that the real Avenger has been captured. *The Lodger* is superior filmmaking in every aspect: the tight, suspenseful script, the superb acting, the dramatic cinematography and lighting, and Hitchcock's masterful direction, which one can recognize even this early in his career. The movie was a hit in Great Britain, then in Europe, and in 1928 it was a success in the States.

TUESDAY, FEBRUARY 15

The year 1927 was one of the worst ones on record for typhoons in the Pacific Ocean. Twenty-seven major storms developed north of the equator and took nearly 16,000 lives, particularly in China, Japan, and the Philippines. A typhoon today near Guam forced the freighter *Elkton* to capsize, drowning all of its crew and losing $1 million worth of sugar on board.

The worst storm in California history up to that time took place today when hurricane-force winds and rampant rains led to the deaths of twenty-four people. Thirteen of them were employees of California Edison Company who were buried alive when an avalanche covered them in their homes in the Sierra Nevada mountains.

Fog over the English Channel was so thick for the past five days that for the first time in half a century, boat and ferry travel across the Channel came to a halt.

Movie star Clara Bow was the iconic flapper of the Roaring Twenties, and Paramount's film *It* is perhaps the quintessential Jazz Age movie. Columnist Elinor Glyn had written a story about a young woman who possessed all the qualities of spirit, sex appeal, and freedom, a quality Glyn called "it." She helped adapt her story for the screen and there was no question of who should play the heroine. Bow already had "it," and the movie was built around her special talents. She played the working-class salesgirl Betty Lou Spence, who works in Waltham's Department Store and has a crush on the new manager, Cyrus Waltham Jr. He doesn't notice Betty Lou, but his friend Monty does and declares that she has "it" and helps bring the two together. Cyrus and Betty Lou have fun at Coney Island and enjoy the simple pleasures unknown to his upper-class set. What is developing into a serious relationship is waylaid when Cyrus mistakenly hears that Betty Lou has had a child out of wedlock. He considers making her his mistress until Betty Lou sets him straight about herself and teaches him a thing or two about the modern woman. *It* is a beautifully crafted comedy-drama in all departments, but it all comes down to Bow's vivacious performance. She was forever after known as the "It Girl."

Mary Pickford may have been America's sweetheart in Hollywood films of the 1910s and 1920s, but it was Clara Bow who epitomized the modern gal and dazzled moviegoers in the Jazz Age. Pictured here in the film *It*, she shows a department store heir (Antonio Moreno) how to have fun at Coney Island. *Paramount Pictures / Photofest © Paramount Pictures*

WEDNESDAY, FEBRUARY 16

Mao Zedong, better known later as Chairman Mao, delivered his *Report on an Investigation of the Peasant Movement in Hunan* to the Central Committee of China's fledgling Communist Party. In his report, Mao predicted "Within a short time, hundreds of millions of peasants will rise in Central, South, and North China, with the fury of a hurricane; no power, however strong, can restrain them." By the end of the year, Mao would lead the Autumn Harvest Uprising in China's Hunan and Jiangxi Provinces.

THURSDAY, FEBRUARY 17

The Ottoman Empire had severed diplomatic relations with the United States on April 20, 1917, after Congress had declared war against Germany on April 4. Diplomatic relations were reestablished today with the Ottoman Empire's successor state, Turkey. During World War II, Turkey remained neutral and retained diplomatic relations with the United States.

FRIDAY, FEBRUARY 18

The United States had always conducted its relations with Canada through the United Kingdom. Today, for the first time, direct diplomatic relations with Canada began as President Coolidge received the credentials of Charles Vincent Massey, the first Canadian minister to the United States, in a half-hour ceremony at the White House.

The popular evangelist Aimee Semple McPherson, who mesmerized audiences with her revivals in the 1920s, had found even wider notoriety when she mysteriously disappeared while swimming off the coast of California in 1926. She then reappeared five weeks later in Arizona and alleged that she had been kidnapped. The stunt and the subsequent trial for perjury (she was acquitted) made McPherson more famous than ever. Having announced that she would begin a "vindication tour" to rebuild her reputation, she arrived in New York City today for her first of a new round of rousing sermons. She packed each venue she played in the city and went on to preach across the nation until her death in 1944. Sinclair Lewis's novel *Elmer Gantry*, which featured a very thinly disguised version of McPherson, was released in March.

Musical radio broadcasts titled *Cities Service Concerts* had been offered in the New York City area since 1925 but today the NBC program went national. The one-hour variety show featured the NBC house orchestra and various singers as well as various kinds of music. Under different titles, the program continued until 1956.

SATURDAY, FEBRUARY 19

The two-day Women's World Figure Skating Championship concluded today in Oslo, Norway, where the Norwegian skater Sonja Henie won the gold medal. There was some controversy over the decision because three of the five judges were also Norwegian. But Henie was unquestionably an outstanding skater, winning more Olympic medals during her career than any other female figure skater. She also enjoyed a very successful Hollywood career in the 1930s and 1940s. The other winners at the 1927 Women's World Figure Skating Championships were Austrian Herma Szabo, who won the Silver medal, and Norwegian Karen Simensen, who won the bronze.

Solid carbon dioxide, or "dry ice," was discovered as far back as 1835 but no practical process for manufacturing the material was invented until 1925, by the Prest Air Devices company. Today the American Chemical Society, in a press conference in New York, announced that dry ice would become available worldwide as the result of a process that "converts solid carbon dioxide into a practical portable ice that is colder and melts slower than water ice." Dry ice was a milestone in transporting perishable foods because it took up less space than frozen water (1,200 pounds of dry ice could replace 17,000 pounds of regular ice) and left more room for goods.

Warner Brothers' landmark movie *Don Juan*, which had its New York City premiere in August 1926, was released to the public today and proved to be a big hit. Based on Lord Byron's 1821 poem and legends about the sixteenth-century Italian lover, *Don Juan* was a series of escapades involving Don Jose de Marana (John Barrymore) and various women and villains. The film's most famous scene is the climactic duel between Don Juan and Count Giano Donati (Montagu Love), made all the more thrilling by the vigorous music and the sound of steel striking steel. *Don Juan* is also known for its love scenes; there are over one hundred kisses in the movie, arguably a record that still stands. *Don Juan* was a risky experiment—the first feature film with synchronized music and sound effects—so Warner Brothers protected their investment by featuring John Barrymore as the title lover and hoping audiences would accept the innovative use of sound. There was no spoken dialogue but the soundtrack score came from the movie house speakers rather than from a live orchestra. More daring, one heard the clashing of swords, the sound of cannons, and other sound effects, all using the new Vitaphone process. Such techniques had been used in a few movie shorts but the studio's biggest concern was whether or not moviegoers would want to hear such sounds for a feature film. The reaction by audiences was so enthusiastic that Warner Brothers proceeded to put all their money into an even riskier experiment, *The Jazz Singer*.

Hollywood's other opening today, MGM's *The Demi-Bride*, is a sad reminder of the fate of many 1920s movies. The comedy starring Norma Shearer is believed lost, only some photo stills and posters surviving. The reviews from 1927 declared it a

Norwegian skater Sonja Henie won medals at the 1928, 1932, and 1936 Olympics, but she was already famous in 1927 because of her prowess on the ice as an eleven-year-old contestant at the 1924 Winter Olympics. When Henie went professional, she was featured in ice shows and in Hollywood feature films. *PA Images / Alamy Stock Photos*

LOST SILENT FILMS

According to the Library of Congress, approximately 75 percent of all the American silent films are now lost. The primary reason is that early movies were on nitrate film stock, which was highly flammable, and many were destroyed in fires. Yet, in many cases, silent films were considered worthless after sound came in and were thrown away by the studios. Among the many lost films from 1927 are:

Babe Comes Home (First National) Comedy featuring Babe Ruth as himself

Blake of Scotland Yard (Universal) Twelve-episode detective serial

The Broncho Twister (Fox) Tom Mix western

The Callahans and the Murphys (MGM) Irish comedy with Marie Dressler and Polly Moran

The Chinese Parrot (Universal) Charlie Chan adventure

The City Gone Wild (Paramount) Gangster film with Louise Brooks

The Conjure Woman (Micheaux) "Race" film based on C. W. Chesnutt novel

The Devil Dancer (Goldwyn Productions) Romantic drama with Gilda Gray and Clive Brook

Evening Clothes (Paramount) Comedy featuring Adolphe Menjou

The Fire Fighters (Universal) Action serial with Jack Dougherty

For the Love of Mike (First National) Drama starring Claudette Colbert, directed by Frank Capra

The Gateway of the Moon (Fox) Romance starring Dolores del Rio and Walter Pidgeon

Hats Off (MGM) Laurel and Hardy comedy short

Heebee Jeebees (MGM) Our Gang comedy short

Heroes of the Wild (Mascot Pictures) Western serial with Jack Hoxie

The House Behind the Cedars (Micheaux) "Race" film based on C. W. Chesnutt novel

London after Midnight (MGM) Horror film starring Lon Chaney

The Magic Flame (United Artists) Drama starring Ronald Colman

The Masked Menace (Pathé Exchange) Ten-part horror serial with Larry Kent and Jean Arthur

Melting Millions (Pathé Exchange) Adventure serial with Allene Ray and Walter Miller

The Mountain Eagle (Woolf & Freedman; UK) Melodrama directed by Alfred Hitchcock

Mumsie (Herbert Wilcox Productions; UK) War drama introducing Herbert Marshall

On Guard (Pathé Exchange) Ten-part melodrama serial with Cullen Landis and Muriel Kingston

The Potters (Paramount) Comedy starring W. C. Fields

Rolled Stockings (Paramount) Comedy with Louise Brooks

The Story of the Flag (UK) First feature-length British animated film

Sword of Penitence (Shochiku Kamata Studio; Japan) Director Yasujiro Ozu's first film

Taxi! Taxi! (Universal) Comedy featuring Edward Everett Horton

Tip Toes (British National; UK) Comedy featuring Dorothy Gish and Will Rogers

The Trail of the Tiger (Universal) Action serial with Jack Dougherty

Two Flaming Youths (Paramount) Comedy starring W. C. Fields and Chester Conklin

Yale vs. Harvard (MGM) Our Gang comedy short

See December 12 for silent films from 1927 that were believed to have been lost but were later rediscovered.

delightful romp set in Paris with Shearer as the wily Criquette, who blackmails the aristocratic Philippe Levaux (Lew Cody) into marrying her. It was directed by the prolific Robert Z. Leonard, his 49th of 109 feature film credits.

SUNDAY, FEBRUARY 20

Eight hundred more marines arrived at Corinto, Nicaragua, today to join the thousands of American soldiers in the Central American country, who were not having much success crushing the rebels. It was the United States military's first experience with a "jungle war" and, like Vietnam four decades later, it was not popular with the American public.

MONDAY, FEBRUARY 21

Franz Lehár's operetta *Der Zarewitsch* (*The Tsarevich*) premiered today at the Deutsches Künstlertheater in Berlin with tenor Richard Tauber as the title character, the son of Peter the Great. The romance between the Tsarevich and Sonja (Rita Georg) in Naples is cut short when Peter dies and the son must return to Moscow to rule Russia, a plot having similarities with the Sigmund Romberg operetta *The Student Prince* (1924).

Today was the second anniversary of the *New Yorker* magazine, which was founded by Harold Ross and first hit the stands on February 21, 1925. During its two years, the weekly magazine had become the most prominent literary journal in New York City if not the country. It was very cosmopolitan in nature yet mixed detailed reporting, intelligent reviews, sardonic commentary on life in the city, and humor (including cartoons) in a unique way. The cover of today's issue was the same as on the very first: artist Rea Irvin's caricature of the monocled dandy "Eustace Tilley." To this day, the *New Yorker* reprints a version of that cover each February.

TUESDAY, FEBRUARY 22

There were melodramas about the underworld aplenty on Broadway this year. One of the more successful ones was simply titled *Crime,* and it was exciting enough to run twenty-four weeks. Tommy Brown (Douglass Montgomery) and Annabelle Porter (Sylvia Sidney) are engaged to be married until some members of a gang led by Fenmore (Chester Morris) hold them up in Central Park and take the $130 they had saved to get married. In trying to get even, Tommy gets involved with gang leaders and is accused of murder, but he is saved by the sacrifice of Fenmore gone straight. *Crime* was well acted and staged and pleased the press and the public. Morris reprised his performance as Fenmore in the 1938 film version, which was titled *Law of the Underworld*.

WEDNESDAY, FEBRUARY 23

In Copenhagen working as a university lecturer and assistant to physicist Niels Bohr, Werner Heisenberg today wrote a fourteen-page letter to fellow physicist Wolfgang Pauli in which he described his concept in quantum mechanics that would later become known as the Heisenberg Uncertainty Principle.

The two-day World Figure Skating Pairs Championship concluded today in Vienna with Austrians Herma Szabo and Ludwig Wrede winning the gold medal. The silver medal went to Austrians Lilly Scholz and Otto Kaiser and the bronze was given to Else Hoppe and Oscar Hoppe from Czechoslovakia.

President Coolidge today signed the Radio Act of 1927, which created the Federal Radio Commission. Up to this point, the licensing of radio broadcasting fell under the jurisdiction of the Department of Commerce and a great deal of power was in the hands of Herbert Hoover, the secretary of commerce. The new FRC consisted of five people who would approve or deny licenses to broadcasters. It had no control over or regulation of content or censorship. Such aspects of radio control came later when the FRC was replaced by the Federal Communications Commission (FCC) in 1934.

THURSDAY, FEBRUARY 24

The use of movies as a news medium was demonstrated today when the Fox Film Corporation introduced its new product, *Movietone News*, which would allow moviegoers to see and even hear footage of recent events. At ten o'clock that morning, fifty news reporters were invited into Fox's New York studios for a filmed press conference. Four hours later, the same members of the press saw and heard themselves on the screen when Fox ran footage of the event.

Cecil B. DeMille had his own production company for a time and one of its films opened today, the western *White Gold*. When Arizona rancher Alec Carson brings his Mexican bride Dolores home, his father doesn't like her and tries to break up the marriage. He uses the itinerant farmhand Sam Randall to lure Dolores into infidelity, but the old man's plans go awry and Dolores ends up shooting Sam and is willing to pay the consequences. It is all more melodrama than western, but director William K. Howard aimed for reality and the movie is realistic down to the last detail, conjuring up the look and feel of the dusty Arizona ranch.

A new theatre opened on Broadway this evening and it was unusual in that it was a smaller house (only eight hundred seats) than the many large New York playhouses built during the decade. Briefly known as the Theatre Masque, it boasted a lovely Spanish interior and a subdued color pattern rather than a lot of gold gilt. The opening production, *Puppets of Passion*, closed inside of two weeks, followed by a mix of hits and flops. In 1938 it was renamed the John Golden Theatre, after a noted author and theatrical producer, and retains that name today.

In London, the drama *The Letter* by William Somerset Maugham opened to rave reviews and ran sixty weeks. Based on one of Maugham's short stories, the suspense play was unusual in that the audiences see Leslie Crosby (Gladys Cooper) shoot her lover in cold blood in the very first scene. The rest of the play is about her husband Robert (Nigel Bruce) and others in the British community in Singapore trying to learn the truth of what really happened. There was much applause for Cooper's performance as well as the play itself. The Broadway production opened later in 1927.

William Fuld, the so-called Father of the Ouija board, died today at the age of fifty-six when, while supervising the installation of a flagpole on the roof of his factory in Baltimore, he fell three stories. Although it is doubtful if Fuld actually invented the occult game board, he manufactured and marketed thousands of Ouija boards from the 1890s through the 1920s. His children continued to run the company until it was bought out by Parker Brothers in 1966. An accident also played a large role in the career of professional baseball player Charlie Bennett, who died today at the age of seventy-two in Detroit. Bennett was a catcher in the Major Leagues from 1879 until 1894 when he lost both legs in a train accident. He played on four teams but is most remembered for his eight seasons with the Detroit Wolverines. Bennett also holds the distinction of being catcher for the first perfect game in Major League Baseball history in 1880.

FRIDAY, FEBRUARY 25

In San Diego, California, a contract was signed today between Irish-American airplane manufacturer T. Claude Ryan and unknown airmail pilot Charles Lindbergh. The transaction, in which the Ryan Aeronautical Company would build a single-engine, single-passenger, high-wing monoplane jointly designed by Ryan and Lindbergh, did not make the news or attract any attention but it was the result of years of struggle by Lindbergh and the beginning of the aerial adventure of the decade. The building of the plane was instigated by the Orteig Prize, a $25,000 contest offered by French-born New York hotelier Raymond Orteig back in 1919 for the first aviator(s) to fly nonstop from New York to Paris or vice versa. Flying technology in 1919 was inadequate for such a flight, making the challenge a suicide mission. No one took up Orteig's offer. But as the years passed and aircraft construction got more sophisticated, Orteig announced the prize again in 1925 and this time there was a great deal of interest in the challenge. Several famous aviators from America and Europe made preparations by getting financing, building planes meant for long-distance flying, and testing them for the transatlantic flight. Among the notable flyers who participated in the competition were Richard E. Byrd, Clarence Chamberlain, Bert Acosta, François Coli, Charles Nungesser, Stanton Wooster, Noel Davis, and Lloyd Bertaud. By the time the contest was won by Lindbergh in May of 1927, six men had died in three separate crashes and several were injured in others. Lindbergh was by far the dark horse in the competition. The twenty-five-year-old aviation enthusiast hailed from Michigan and dropped out of college to attend a flight school. He worked as a barnstormer and an airmail pilot before the Orteig Prize became his goal. Financing the flight was problematic because Lindbergh was unknown and had no record of publicized stunts or flying achievements. Finally, two St. Louis businessmen took out a bank loan of $15,000, Lindbergh himself provided $2,000, and some donations totaled enough to proceed with the project. After touring the Ryan Aeronautical Company on February 23, Lindbergh signed a contract two days later. Unlike the other aviators planning the overseas flight, Lindbergh insisted that there be no copilot in order to save weight that was needed for fuel. He also insisted on a fuel-efficient single engine rather than dual propellers and that the fuel tank be placed in the front of the plane to improve the center of gravity. This meant the cockpit was unusually small and that the pilot had no front windshield, visibility being possible only from two side windows. Lindbergh remained in San Diego and participated in the design and the building of the plane, which he named *Spirit of St Louis*.

In the Soviet Union, the government put into force Article 58 (RSFSR Penal Code) which allowed the arrest and punishment without trial or even legal consultation of anyone involved in counterrevolutionary activities. This penal code, which would be revised and added to over the years, allowed the Communist Party to imprison or execute both notable Russians as well as unknown common people without the detrimental publicity associated with a trial.

The controversial McNary-Haugen Farm Relief Bill, which would subsidize American agriculture by raising the domestic prices of farm products and have the government buy the wheat and then store it or export it at a loss, had been voted down by Congress in 1924 and 1926 but it finally passed in 1927. Today President Coolidge vetoed the bill. Congress failed to override the veto and a law supporting domestic farm pricing would not be passed until 1933.

SATURDAY, FEBRUARY 26

Back in 1915, H. D. Pillsbury of Pacific Telephone and Telegraph and AT&T representative Col. H. E. Shreeve had spoken to each other during the first telephone conversation between San Francisco and New York. Today the same two men demonstrated the newest technology by speaking between San Francisco and London, a distance of 7,287 miles.

If Hollywood Central Casting was looking for someone to play the all-American hero, they couldn't have done better than the young, fair-haired, unassuming-looking airmail pilot Charles Lindbergh. He may have looked like a movie star, but "Lindy" was a brilliant pilot and navigator. *Photofest © Photofest*

SUNDAY, FEBRUARY 27

The Fourth Regiment of the United States Marines, consisting of twelve hundred men, arrived in Shanghai on the transport USS *Chaumont* today to protect American interests in the important Chinese seaport city. There would continue to be a U.S. Marine presence in Shanghai until 1941.

Hal Roach's comedy short *One Hour Married* was a clever vehicle for comedienne Mabel Normand. She played a bride whose husband is drafted into the U.S. Army one hour after the wedding ceremony. He is shipped off to France to fight in the Great War, so she disguises herself as a soldier and takes the next troop ship across the Atlantic, leading to comic complications that Normand exploits to the fullest. Sadly, *One Hour Married* was her last film. Suffering from the effects of drug abuse and tuberculosis, Normand left Hollywood and went into a sanatorium where she died three years later at the age of thirty-six.

MONDAY, FEBRUARY 28

The Military Inter-Allied Commission of Control, established by the Treaty of Versailles seven years earlier, was disbanded today. The Commission had overseen the occupation of Germany since the end of the war. France's marshal Ferdinand Foch declared that Germany's obligations under the Treaty of Versailles had been completed and the Commission closed its headquarters in Berlin.

Paramount's backwoods drama *Stark Love* was unusual on several fronts. It was filmed by director-writer Karl Brown in the Great Smoky Mountains, used real homes and natural light, was cast mostly with amateur locals who wore no makeup, and had a documentary look to it. In a secluded community in the North Carolina mountains, young Rob Warnick tries to better himself by leaving the valley for good but returns to rescue his sweetheart Barbara Allen from her brutal father. *Stark Love* was not a box-office success and was lost for many years. British film historian Kevin Brownlow discovered a copy in Prague in 1967 and two years later a restored version was shown in New York City. *Stark Love* is an important film not only as a significant silent movie but also as a visual record of Appalachian life in a community cut off from modern civilization.

The popular British painter and illustrator Sir Luke Fildes died today in London at the age of eighty-three. He first found fame illustrating newspapers, periodicals, and books. His drawing of Charles Dickens's empty chair in his study that appeared in *The Graphic* the day after Dickens died made him famous. Fildes later did portraits and other paintings, the most well-known in the United States being the evocative *The Doctor* (1891), which was later used by the American Medical Association to oppose nationalized health insurance in 1949.

࿇

MARCH

TUESDAY, MARCH 1

An underground gas and coal dust explosion today at a coal mine in Cwm, Wales, killed fifty-two men. There were fourteen hundred men employed at the Marine Colliery but fortunately when the explosion occurred only the night shift was working underground. The death toll would have been higher, but a manager on the site ordered the ventilation fan to be slowed down so that it wouldn't fan the flames of the fires burning below.

Spring training for both American League and National League Baseball began this week in warm southern locales, and fans eagerly looked forward to the news that came from the various sites. In the American League, the Athletics trained in Fort Myers, Florida; the Red Sox in New Orleans, Louisiana; the Senators in Tampa, Florida; the Indians in Lakeland, Florida; the Tigers in San Antonio, Texas; the White Sox in Shreveport, Louisiana; the Yankees in St. Petersburg, Florida; and the Browns in Tarpon Springs, Florida. The National League spring training found the Cardinals in Avon Park, Florida; the Cubs in Avalon, California; the Robins in Clearwater, Florida; the Giants in Sarasota, Florida; the Braves in St. Petersburg, Florida; the Phillies in Bradenton, Florida; the Pirates in Paso Robles, California; and the Reds in Orlando, Florida.

Railroad buffs were particularly pleased with Sterling Pictures' *Red Signals* since the trains often got more attention than the characters. A series of train wrecks on the Western Limited Railroad is clearly a matter of sabotage and the railroad's superintendent Mark Bryson investigates. The culprit is foreman Jim Twyler, whose gang is behind the wrecks, but it takes Bryson's brother Lee, disguised as a hobo, to go undercover and join the gang in order to get to the truth. For some romance, the telegraph operator Mary Callahan and Lee fall in love in between train wrecks. *Red Signals* has its entertainment values, but it is its documentation of trains in pre-Depression America that has a greater appeal to most modern audiences.

WEDNESDAY, MARCH 2

The management of the New York Yankees announced today that they had signed Babe Ruth for his eighth season with the team for a record-breaking contract of $70,000. (The second highest Yankee player was Herb Pennock at $17,500.) Before the season was over, the thirty-two-year-old Ruth would prove to be worth every penny of the then-unheard-of high salary. It was not only among Ruth's finest seasons but also a legendary year for the Yankees and a high point for American professional baseball.

Labeled by historians as the "last gold rush in the West," the discovery today of high-grade ore by teenagers Frank Horton Jr., and Leonard Taylor in Nevada attracted thousands of prospectors to the area near the community of Tonopah. The modern-day gold rush gave birth to the town of Weepah, Nevada, which sprang up overnight. It turned out the lode was not very large and the gold not of high quality, so within three months the rush was over. By August, Weepah was almost totally deserted, and it remains today as one of the many ghost towns in Nevada.

The largest-circulation humor magazine in America in 1927 was *Judge*, in which many of the best humorists were first published. In today's issue, young writer S. J. Perelman's comic piece "The Handy Girl around the House: How to Make a Sugar Papa" gave

BABE RUTH MID-CAREER

The 1927 Major League Baseball season was dominated by Babe Ruth, arguably America's most popular and famous athlete of all time. The Baltimore-born Ruth, known under various nicknames such as The Bambino and The Sultan of Swat, began playing in the major leagues in 1914 as a pitcher with the Boston Red Sox, but greater fame came when he was traded to the New York Yankees in 1920 and he started rewriting batting records. Ruth was an outfielder and a pitcher but it was as a batter that he dazzled fans until his retirement in 1935. Ruth pitched sparingly after his trade to the Yankees, as his value as a hitter outweighed his impressive pitching skills. He single-handedly ushered the long ball era into the game, forever changing the national pastime. The most beloved ball player in America had suffered a major setback mid-career. In 1925, weight problems, stomach ailments, and an excessive lifestyle caused him to miss many games that season, resulting in the Yankees finishing next to last. But by the 1926 season, Ruth was back on top, hitting forty-seven home runs, winning the Most Valuable Player Award, and leading the Yankees to the American League pennant. As the 1927 season approached, anticipation was extremely high for Ruth and the Yankees.

He was born George Herman Ruth Jr., but by 1927 the most famous baseball player in America was simply identified as The Babe, as well as other monikers. Babe Ruth played in the Major Leagues for twenty-two years, and none was greater than his 1927 season. *Photofest © Photofest*

wry instructions to enterprising women on how to snag and hang on to a wealthy "sugar daddy" for buying those little extras that a girl so much enjoys. At this point Perelman was also a cartoonist and many of his stylized cartoons also appeared in *Judge*.

The ever-ambitious Theatre Guild offered the first Broadway production of Luigi Pirandello's 1917 masterwork *Cosi e (se vi pare)*, which was billed as *Right You Are If You Think You Are*, and kept the Italian drama on the boards for six weeks. Like most of

Pirandello's works, the "parable" explored the questionable relationship between truth and illusion. Signor Ponza (Edward G. Robinson) chooses to believe what he wants about his wife and his mother-in-law rather than face the truth. The intriguing play was beautifully acted and staged and kept the audiences guessing long after the curtain fell.

THURSDAY, MARCH 3

One of the most controversial and talked about novels of the year, Sinclair Lewis's *Elmer Gantry* was published this month by Harcourt Trade Publishers. Although he had been a popular athlete in college and got every woman he went after, the self-centered Elmer Gantry abandons his hope of a legal profession and become an alcoholic. When he is accidentally ordained a Baptist minister, Gantry realizes there is money to be made and women to be seduced in the preaching field. He becomes a Methodist minister and then attaches himself to the traveling evangelist Sister Sharon Falconer, becoming her manager and lover. Gantry makes Sister Sharon famous, but when she dies in a fire in her new house of worship, he marries a rich woman and opens a congregation in the city of Zenith. Elmer Gantry is one of American literature's most unethical and narcissistic characters, but he mesmerizes the reader just as he seduces women and his congregations. Lewis worked with some traveling ministers while researching the subject for *Elmer Gantry* and based Sister Sharon on the then-famous preacher Aimee Semple McPherson. When the book was released it was castigated by religious leaders and was banned in Boston and other cities, but it sold very well. There was a stage version of the novel in 1928 and a popular film version in 1960 with Burt Lancaster as Elmer and Jean Simmons as Susan. There was a Broadway musical version in 1970 titled *Gantry* which closed on opening night and an opera version by Robert Aldridge and Herschel Garfein in 2007 that was more successful.

Winds at more than 125 mph hit the island of Madagascar today as a fierce cyclone brought with it an eight-foot-high storm surge that washed over the city of Tamatave. An estimated six hundred people perished and most of the ships in the harbor were picked up and carried inland.

For over twenty years archeologists had been excavating an area of Giza near the Great Pyramids of Egypt looking for the tomb of Queen Hetepheres I, the mother of Khufu, the builder of the Great Pyramid. In 1925 archaeologist George Andrew Reisner and his team found a shaft and for two years carefully dug down eighty-five feet, where they discovered some gold, furniture, and an alabaster sarcophagus. Today the sarcophagus was opened and was found to be empty. It is believed grave robbers centuries ago stole the mummy for its gold trappings yet it is still a mystery why the other valuable objects buried in the tomb were left behind.

The Welsh race car driver J. G. Parry-Thomas was killed in an auto crash today at the age of forty-two, the first driver to die while trying to break a land speed record. Parry-

Thomas set a world record of 171.02 mph (270 km/h) in 1926 but it was broken on February 4 by Malcolm Campbell on the Welsh beach Pendine Sands. When attempting to make a new speed record on the same beach, Perry-Thomas's car rolled over and he died of head injuries.

FRIDAY, MARCH 4

American chemist and second president of Johns Hopkins University Ira Remsen died in Carmel, California, today at the age of eighty-one. An eminent teacher and researcher, he is most known for accidentally discovering the artificial sweetener saccharin in 1880 with Constantin Fahlberg. Another noted American educator, Horace Wilson, died today at the age of eighty-four in San Francisco. After serving in the Civil War, Wilson was invited to Japan to teach English to the students at Tokyo Imperial University and stayed for twelve years. During that time, he introduced baseball to the Japanese students, and the game caught on across the nation. Wilson was elected to the Japanese Baseball Hall of Fame in 2003.

Today marked the beginning of the Seventieth U.S. Congress.

THE FEDERAL GOVERNMENT IN 1927

President: Calvin Coolidge
   (R-Massachusetts)
Vice President: Charles G. Dawes
   (R-Illinois)
Secretary of State: Frank B. Kellogg
   (R-Minnesota)
Secretary of the Treasury: Andrew Mellon
   (R-Pennsylvania)
Secretary of Commerce: Herbert Hoover
   (R-California)
Secretary of the Interior: Hubert Work
   (R-Colorado)

Secretary of Labor: James J. Davis
   (R-Pennsylvania)
Secretary of Agriculture: William Marion
   Jardine (R-Kansas)
Attorney General: John G. Sargent
   (R-Vermont)
Chief Justice: William Howard Taft (Ohio)
Speaker of the House of Representatives:
   Nicholas Longworth (R-Ohio)
Senate Majority Leader: Charles Curtis
   (R-Kansas)
Congress: 69th (until March 4), 70th
   (starting March 4)

SATURDAY, MARCH 5

The 1926–1927 college basketball season closed today in Omaha, Nebraska, with Notre Dame's Fighting Irish defeating Creighton University's Bluejays 31–17. It was a record-breaking season for Notre Dame, with nineteen wins and only one loss. College

COLLEGE BASKETBALL ALL-AMERICANS

The 1927 College Basketball All-American team, as chosen by the Helms Foundation:

Syd Corenman (Creighton)
George Dixon (California)
Vic Hanson (Syracuse)
John Lorch (Columbia)
Ross McBurney (Wichita)

John Nyikos (Notre Dame)
Bennie Oosterbaan (Michigan)
Gerald Spohn (Washburn)
John Thompson (Montana State)
Harry Wilson (Army)

Vic Hanson was chosen as the Helms Foundation Player of the Year.

basketball was significantly different in 1927. The major emphasis was on ball handling, passing, and defense, resulting in scores that seem low by today's standards.

General Motors today introduced the LaSalle, a smaller and more maneuverable luxury automobile that tried to compete with the best-selling Cadillacs and Packards on the market. The LaSalle, with a convertible coupe design, sold for $2,635.

The last of the fifty-six short stories featuring Sherlock Holmes, Arthur Conan Doyle's "The Adventure of Shoscombe Old Place," appeared in today's edition of *Liberty* magazine. The stablemaster at Shoscombe Old Place goes to Holmes because his employer, Sir Robert Norburton, has been acting very strangely and the future of the estate depends on the horse Shoscombe Prince winning the Derby. Holmes and Dr. Watson disguise themselves as anglers and explore the area, eventually discovering that Sir Robert's sister Beatrice had died but he kept it secret until after the Derby because their creditors would descend upon the family on hearing of her death. The story was included later in the year in the anthology *The Case-Book of Sherlock Holmes*.

SUNDAY, MARCH 6

The controversial British philosopher, pacifist, and agnostic Bertrand Russell today delivered his famous speech "Why I Am Not a Christian" at the Battersea Town Hall, sponsored by the National Secular Society. Declaring that religion is the outcome of fear and superstition, the address was widely debated and vilified. The speech was published as a pamphlet later in 1927 and remains in print in English and in translation in German and other languages.

San Francisco's Saint Peter and Paul Catholic Church in the city's Italian-American community was the target of five separate bomb attacks within one year's time in 1926 and 1927. Today the police spotted the radical anarchist and local anti-Catholic soap-box orator Celsten Eklund and another man in the process of lighting the fuse to a dynamite bomb in front of the church. The officers shot and mortally wounded both men. The identify of Eklund's accomplice was never determined.

While the 1927 influenza epidemic in Britain did not reach the high number of deaths that the infamous Spanish Flu epidemic of 1918 had, the fatalities were considerable. The flu reached its peak this week when one thousand Britons died from the epidemic. America was not spared the epidemic, but the number of deaths was minimal compared to those in Great Britain.

The landmark German film *Metropolis*, which had premiered two months earlier in Berlin, was shown in New York City today and the critical reaction varied widely. Some critics thought the expressionistic film was brilliant, while others thought it was visually interesting but dramatically unsatisfying. Eventually *Metropolis* would be acclaimed one of the greatest works of international cinema. Another premiere on that day is notable for launching one of the longest acting careers in the history of Hollywood. Six-year-old Mickey Rooney played the character Mickey Maguire for the first time in the First National short *Orchids and Ermine*, a charming romantic comedy in which he had only a supporting role. The story centered on hotel telephone operator Pink Watson, who falls in love with a valet who turns out to be a millionaire. Rooney played the feisty midget Maguire and had such a noticeable screen presence that the studio featured him in sixty-four subsequent "Mickey Maguire" shorts, including four in 1927.

MONDAY, MARCH 7

An earthquake measuring 7.6 on the Richter scale today struck Japan's Tango Peninsula. The tremors and subsequent fires killed over 3,000 people and destroyed the cities of Toyooka and Kinosaki. The quake was felt as far away as Tokyo.

Voting rights for African Americans continued to plague the South. In the case of *Nixon v. Herndon*, the United States Supreme Court today declared unconstitutional a 1923 Texas law that prohibited African Americans from voting in Democratic primary elections. The victory for African American physician Lawrence A. Nixon was short-lived, as Texas quickly passed a new law that gave political parties the right to set their own rules for voting in party primary elections. Such laws were not deemed unconstitutional until 1946.

TUESDAY, MARCH 8

Downhill skiing had long been a recreation and a competitive sport in Europe and Asia but was not taken seriously as a competition in America until the late 1920s. The first downhill skiing race on record in the United States took place today at Mount Moosilauke in New Hampshire and was won by Charles N. Proctor of Dartmouth College.

Ernest Thayer's famous poem "Casey at the Bat" was turned into a sixty-eight-minute comedy by Paramount and released on this date. While the poem covers one baseball game in Casey's career, the film shows how the hard-drinking Casey (Wallace Beery), with the help of shrewd talent scout O'Dowd, gets on the New York Giants team. Casey's sweetheart is milliner Camille (ZaSu Pitts) and her rival in the big city is chorus girl Trixie. She gets Casey drunk before the big game but the freckled teenage fan Spec gets him to the ballpark, where Casey strikes out and loses the game. O'Dowd, the team, and the fans turn against him, but when Casey arrives home, the faithful Camille welcomes him with loving arms. Much of *Casey at the Bat* is overdone slapstick, but the cast is in fine form, including awkward-looking Sterling Holloway in his screen debut.

WEDNESDAY, MARCH 9

In 1925 the Bavarian government had banned Adolf Hitler from speaking in public and participating in politics, considering him a political threat because of his rousing and inciting speeches. That ban was lifted in 1927, and today the thirty-eight-year-old Hitler gave his first of many speeches outlining his plans for a new Germany. He had already experienced an eventful but frustrating life by 1927, but before the year was out, his rise to power was imminent. Hitler had served in the Great War, had entered politics, and had joined the National Socialist German Workers Party (NSDAP). In 1923, he attempted to overthrow the government in the "Beer Hall Putsch" in Munich, for which he served some time in prison in 1924. He wrote *Mein Kampf* in 1925 and assumed leadership of the Nazi Party in 1926.

A drama comprised of African American characters and actors was not a common sight on Broadway, but the New Playwrights Theatre managed to present a few during the year. Em Jo Bashee's *Earth* was an expressionistic play set in the 1880s about Deborah, who has seen all six of her children die young. It has caused her to lose faith in both her Christian religion and her voodoo beliefs. When Deborah goes to a revival meeting held by the blind Brother Elijah, he declares she is a great sinner and responsible for a forest fire that has destroyed much of the county. The crowd rises up and lynches Deborah. The press commended the play and players but most singled out the traditional "Negro" hymns sung by the Hall Johnson Choir. *Earth* played for three weeks for the curious.

THURSDAY, MARCH 10

Zenith Radio Corporation today introduced automatic push-button tuning on its latest model of radio. This feature would be particularly useful when Zenith made car radios in the 1930s. Zenith's famous slogan, "The Quality Goes in before the Name Goes On," was first used in 1927.

An intimate musical revue titled *The New Yorkers* opened Off-Broadway on this night and stuck around for six weeks. The show spoofed people in the news and had songs by a handful of songwriters, most memorably composer Arthur Schwartz, who would go on to a distinguished career on Broadway.

FRIDAY, MARCH 11

The first armored car hold-up on record took place today in Bethel near Pittsburgh, Pennsylvania, when Paul Jaworski and the Flatheads Gang set off explosions to stop an armored car that was carrying the payroll for the Terminal Coal Company. The driver and two guards were seriously injured and the gang got away with over $100,000. Jaworski and the Flatheads pulled off other sensational robberies and murders before he was caught and executed in 1929.

Billed "The Cathedral of the Motion Picture," the Roxy Theatre in New York City opened to the public today with the Gloria Swanson melodramatic fantasy *The Love of Sunya*. The movie palace was the brainchild of showman Samuel "Roxy" Rothafel, who set out to build the largest theatre in the world, and he succeeded. The Roxy seated over six thousand patrons and had standing room for five hundred more. The five-story "rotunda," or lobby, had standing room for twenty-five hundred people waiting for the next showing. The orchestra pit had room for one hundred musicians, and backstage could accommodate three hundred performers. It took a staff of three hundred to run the Roxy, which on a sold-out night catered to ten thousand patrons. Opening night of the theatre featured a tap dance troupe, a newsreel, a mini-operetta, a chorus of Roxyettes, and then *The Love of Sunya*. The plot was complicated and messy. Swanson played Sunya Ashling, a singing student who is the reincarnation of an Egyptian maiden who was killed by an evil yogi centuries ago. The yogi is reincarnated as a gypsy fortune teller who must help Sunya in order to make amends for his past crime. Sunya is torn between the love for two men and finally makes her decision by looking into the yogi's crystal ball. While not one of Swanson's best performances, Sunya gives her the opportunity to wear luscious Art Deco gowns. The movie did modest business and, because it went way over budget, did not turn a profit. A similar fate awaited the Roxy Theatre. It was so huge and expensive to run that it was in financial trouble once the Depression hit. Different formats were tried over the decades, but the great movie palace closed its doors for good in 1960 and was demolished that same year to make way for an office building.

Irving Berlin's gentle ballad "Russian Lullaby" was introduced to the public when it was sung by baritone Douglas Stanbury as part of the opening night show at the Roxy

MOVIE PALACES

Some American movie palaces that opened in 1927 (* indicates still in operation):

Alabama Theatre* (Birmingham)
Albee Theatre (Cincinnati)
Belpark Theatre (Chicago)
California Theatre* (San Jose)
Carolina Theatre (Fayetteville,
    North Carolina)
Coronado Theatre* (Rockville, Illinois)
Florida Theatre* (Jacksonville)
Grauman's Chinese Theatre* (Los Angeles)
Jefferson Theatre (Beaumont, Texas)
Loew's Penn Theatre, today Heinz Hall*
    (Pittsburgh)

Marbro Theatre (Chicago)
Oriental Theatre* (Milwaukee)
Orpheum Theatre* (Sioux City, Iowa)
Palace Theatre* (Columbus, Ohio)
Palladium (New York City)
Paramount Theatre* (Seattle)
Roxy Theatre (New York City)
Saenger Theatre* (Mobile)
Saenger Theatre* (New Orleans)
Tivoli Theatre (Chicago)
United Artists Theatre (Los Angeles)
Varsity Theatre (Palo Alto)

For Broadway theatres built in 1927, see January 11.

The interior of the Roxy movie palace in New York City was impressive not only for its size (over six thousand seats) but also for its sleek Art Deco design. The demolition of the Roxy in 1960 was a major historical and architectural loss. *Courtesy of the Library of Congress, LC-G612-T01-19326*

Theatre today. The song is unusual in that it reveals Berlin's eastern European roots. The songwriter's boyhood in Russia is recalled in both the tender folk melody and the poignant lyric. "Russian Lullaby" was popularized by a 1927 record by Roger Wolfe Kahn and his Orchestra, followed by many other recordings.

SATURDAY, MARCH 12

Anti-British tension in China heightened today during a demonstration in Singapore observing the anniversary of the death of Sun Yat-sen, the founding father of the Republic of China. When the crowd stopped in front of a precinct station at Kreta Ayer, British officers fired on the demonstrators and six people were killed. Known as the Kreta Ayer Incident, it turned many more Chinese against the British colonial administration.

English author P. G. Wodehouse's short story *The Romance of a Bulb-Squeezer* was published in today's issue of the American magazine *Liberty*. The pub storyteller Mr. Mulliner tells a delightfully improbable tale about his cousin Clarence, who was a much-in-demand photographer. One doting father goes so far as to disguise himself as a spy and kidnap Clarence in order to get the photographer to do a portrait of his daughter. All ends well when Clarence falls for the girl and the father turns out to be a lord. The story was reprinted in the March issue of the *Strand Magazine* in England and then in the anthology *Meet Mr. Mulliner*.

United Artists' adventure film *The Beloved Rogue*, starring John Barrymore, was a romanticized biopic of French poet-rogue François Villon. It was a story first told in the novel *If I Were King* and then appeared on Broadway in 1901 and as a film in 1920 with William Farnum as Villon. Set in the fifteenth century, the celebrated French poet, lover, and rascal François Villon (Barrymore) is banished from the country by King Louis XI (Conrad Veidt) when Villon, made king for a day during the Feast of Fools celebration, insults Charles, the Duke of Burgundy. But Villon returns in secret and aids the poor of Paris, saves the aristocratic Charlotte de Vauxcelles from a forced marriage with Count Thibault d'Aussigny, survives torture and a death sentence, and wins the hand of Charlotte. *The Beloved Rogue* took plenty of liberties with history, the novel, and the play but it was all rousing fun with elaborate production values, efficient direction by Alan Crosland, and a deliciously hammy performance by Barrymore.

Hollywood's other entry today was the baseball comedy *Slide, Kelly, Slide* from MGM. Small-town hick Jim Kelly (William Haines) from Iowa becomes a pitcher-hitter for the New York Yankees and soon is hitting them out of the park. He falls in love with Mary, the daughter of the catcher Tom Munson, but fame inflates Jim's ego and he insults everyone and plays cruel practical jokes on his teammates. It takes the orphaned Mickey Martin to make Jim change his ways, win Mary's heart, and hit the decisive home run. Occasionally sentimental, often funny, and always fun, *Slide, Kelly, Slide* is one of the best sports movies of the era.

SUNDAY, MARCH 13

Generalissimo Chiang Kai-shek had run the Kuomintang, China's major political party, since the death of Sun Yat-sen in 1925. Some members of the party felt that Chiang was getting too powerful. Today the leadership of the Kuomintang voted to fire Chiang from most of his executive positions but retain him as commander of the expeditionary forces. Generalissimo Chiang ignored the demotion and made plans for a drastic takeover of the party.

Hal Roach Studios' comedy short *Duck Soup* was released today and marked an important Hollywood event: the first true Laurel and Hardy film. Oliver Hardy and Stan Laurel had already appeared in many silents and were even cast together in some, but *Duck Soup* was the first time they played the bumbling comedy team of Stan and Oliver that became an audience favorite. The short was based on a vaudeville sketch that Laurel's father had written for his son when Stan was beginning his career in England. The twosome play a pair of hobos who flee from a Forest Ranger looking for "volunteers" to put out a fire. They take refuge in the empty country home of Colonel Blood but soon Lord and Lady Tarbotham show up so Oliver poses as the butler Hives and Stan dresses up as the maid Agnes. They almost get away with it until the Colonel arrives and chases the duo off with a gun. They fall into the hands of the Forest Ranger who puts them to work putting out the fire. The twenty-minute comedy is superior Laurel and Hardy and they appear to have been working together for years. The short was so popular that Hal Roach quickly reteamed the comics in subsequent silent movies and they were just as successful with talkies. The title of the short and the celebrated Marx Brothers' *Duck Soup* (1933) being the same is not coincidence. Leo McCarey was assistant director on the Laurel and Hardy film and, believing no one remembered or cared about silent movies, used the title when he directed the Marx Brothers comedy six years later. As popular as the 1927 short was, it was lost for decades, as so many silent films were. Not until 1974 did a copy of *Duck Soup* show up in Belgium with French title cards inserted where the English ones were. Happily, a legendary Hollywood film is once again available for viewing and for laughs.

MONDAY, MARCH 14

Pan American Airways, Incorporated (PAA) was founded today by Air Corps Majors Henry H. Arnold, Carl A. Spaatz, and John H. Jouett as a counterbalance to the German-owned Colombian-German Air Transport Society, which had been operating in Colombia since 1920. The German company lobbied hard for landing rights in the Panama Canal Zone, saying that they wished to survey air routes to the United States. But the Air Corps viewed the plan as a German aerial threat to the canal. Pan Am, as it would be best known as later, changed names and management over the decades and was a major international carrier until its demise in 1991.

A mystery play that held its own on Broadway for fourteen weeks was *The Mystery Ship*, a whodunnit filled with clichés but enjoyable all the same. When a shot is heard and a man is murdered on board an ocean liner, a detective goes to work. The body mysteriously disappears and the suspects are many, but the detective eventually learns that there was no murder and the whole thing was a way to defraud the insurance company. The reviews were unenthusiastic, but producer Gustav Blum offered cut-rate ticket prices and a lot of publicity, and the show turned a profit.

TUESDAY, MARCH 15

A major financial disaster, known as the Shōwa Crisis, rocked Japan today. The day after Finance Minister Naoharu Kataoka mistakenly announced that the struggling Watanabe Bank had "collapsed," depositors panicked and tried to withdraw all of their money from the Tokyo bank. By the end of the week, two other banks had collapsed, followed by twelve more by the end of the month.

WEDNESDAY, MARCH 16

One of Ernest Hemingway's most famous short stories, "The Killers," was published in the March 1927 issue of *Scribner's Magazine*. The story features the author's hero Nick Adams for the first time as an adult. In a suburb of Chicago, the hit men Max and Al enter a lunchroom where they tie up the customer Nick Adams in the kitchen with the African American cook Sam. They then tell the proprietor George that they are waiting for the Swedish prizefighter Ole Andreson to arrive because they have been ordered to kill the boxer for a "friend." After waiting for some time, the two killers depart and George sends Nick to the boardinghouse where Andreson lives and to warn him. Nick finds Andreson fully dressed and lying on his bed. He does not panic at the news Nick brings and calmly remains in bed, saying there is nothing he can do about it and if death comes, he is ready. Nick returns to the lunchroom and tells George, who seems unconcerned one way or the other. In frustration and bewilderment Nick leaves Chicago for good. "The Killers" is told in blunt, simple prose with little description or character development. Yet the story has a minimalist power that intrigues and expresses Hemingway's fatalistic view of death. The story was included in the Hemingway collection *Men without Women* which was published in October. There have been three screen versions of "The Killers," in 1946, 1964, and 2009, each one expanding on the story to make a feature film.

THURSDAY, MARCH 17

The Teapot Dome scandal, which had brought down Warren Harding's administration in 1923, continued to be in the news. The scandal involved bribery and private deals with oil companies over petroleum fields located in Teapot Dome, Wyoming. Today a jury convicted Harry F. Sinclair, owner of Mammoth Oil Company (later Sinclair Oil), of contempt of Congress. After further trials and appeals, the multimillionaire Sinclair ended up serving only six months in prison in 1930.

The heavy cruiser HMAS *Australia*, ordered by the Royal Australian Navy in 1924, was launched today at Clydesbank, Scotland. The *Australia* was armed with eight eight-inch guns in four twin turrets and saw action in both the Atlantic and Pacific during World War II. It was decommissioned in 1954 and sold for scrap the following year.

The charming silent movie actor Charles Emmett Mack was on his way to a prodigious Hollywood career when he died today at the age of twenty-six in an auto accident. A native of Scranton, Pennsylvania, Mack danced in vaudeville then worked as a prop boy for D. W. Griffith before the famous director put him before the cameras and found he had screen presence. Mack appeared in seventeen silent movies and was on his way to a race track to film an auto racing scene for *The First Auto* (1927) when he died in a car collision.

FRIDAY, MARCH 18

Today Generalissimo Chiang Kai-shek and his Nationalist army arrived at the outskirts of the city of Shanghai. Known as the Northern Expedition, Chiang's plan was to conquer the northern provinces and bring China under one leadership. A garrison commander betrayed his city and gave Chiang the plans for Shanghai's defense.

A tornado swept through parts of Arkansas today killing twenty-six people. Hardest hit was the town of Green Forest, where sixteen people died, nearly one hundred were injured, and much of the town was leveled.

SATURDAY, MARCH 19

One of the most famous dogs of the twentieth century, the Siberian husky Balto, was rescued and celebrated today. The sled dog and his canine teammates had made international news in 1925 when they weathered a blizzard and delivered a serum to the Alaskan city of Nome, where a diphtheria outbreak was threatening the population. After the successful run, Norwegian Gunnar Kaasen, who drove the team, and the dogs became celebrities, making appearances in various cities and featured on the vaudeville circuit. But by 1927 the dogs were forgotten and Cleveland businessman George Kimble found them in a Los Angeles freak show where they were in poor health and abused. Kimble rescued Balto and six of his team members (Fox, Sye, Billy, Tillie, Moctoc, and Alaska Slim) and today they were given a parade and a hero's welcome in Cleveland, where they lived out their days at the city's zoo. When Balto died at the age of fourteen, his remains were mounted by a taxidermist and donated to the Cleveland Museum of Natural History, where the canine is still on view. There is also a famous statue of Balto in Manhattan's Central Park and his story was the inspiration for the 1995 Disney animated film *Balto*.

Civil unrest in Germany continued today as street fights between Communists and Nazis broke out in Berlin.

Leo Tolstoy's 1899 novel *Resurrection* was the basis of the movie of the same name that was released today by United Artists. The self-serving Russian Prince Dmitry Nekhludov (Rod La Rocque) seduces the maid Katusha (Dolores Del Rio) then abandons her. She loses her job, turns to prostitution, and one day murders a client who was beating her. At Katusha's trial, Dmitry sits on the jury that condemns her to prison in Siberia. His guilt drives him to visit her in jail, where he sees conditions of poverty never encountered by the upper classes, and his life is changed by the experience. He sets out to save her and, thereby, redeem himself. The beautiful Del Rio was the main attraction of *Resurrection*, though the film, directed and produced by Edwin Carewe, has solid acting and fine production values. Carewe also coproduced and directed the 1931 sound version starring Lupe Velez and John Boles.

SUNDAY, MARCH 20

The Albert Snyder murder case looked like a routine tabloid story at first but soon developed into one of the most sensational tales of the year, eventually inspiring two novels, a play, and several movies. Late on Sunday night, Albert Snyder, a forty-four-year-old art editor for the magazine *Boating*, was strangled with wire, then had his head bashed in with a window sash weight while in his bed in his Queens home. His wife Ruth Snyder was found unconscious in the next room. When the police arrived, Ruth said she was awakened in the night by the sound of two men with Italian accents in the next room. When she went to investigate, they attacked her in the dark and beat her unconscious. The presence of an Italian-language newspaper left in the room was the only tangible clue. The story made for a good newspaper headline but better copy soon followed. Investigation by police found that Ruth Snyder's story was full of holes. A physician who examined her found no bruises and no bump on the head that would render her unconscious. The police also questioned why Ruth, rather than her husband, went to check on the voices or why Albert Snyder never got out of bed once she was attacked. Also, the couple's nine-year-old daughter was asleep in the next room and heard nothing. Further investigation revealed that there were no signs of a break-in and that items supposedly stolen by the robbers were later found hidden in the house. Also suspicious, Ruth had recently convinced her husband to take out a life insurance policy for $48,000 with a "double indemnity clause" which paid twice the amount if death was from an unexpected act of violence. Clues in the house revealed that Ruth had a long-time lover, Judd Gray, who claimed to be in Syracuse the night of March 20 but his alibi could not be confirmed. Snyder and Gray were arrested on March 23 and when details of the case emerged, the story was hot news for weeks. At one point, Ruth claimed that the insurance scam and murder were Gray's ideas, then Gray revealed that Ruth had previously made seven attempts to kill her husband but failed each time, so she convinced him to kill Snyder for the insurance money. Because the victim had his head bashed in with a weight commonly called a window dumb-bell, the press and public jokingly referred to the crime as the Dumb-Bell Murder. The name also referred to how stupidly the crime was carried out. Anticipation for the trial in April kept the Albert Snyder murder frequently in the news. It also inspired Sophie Treadwell's play *Machinal* (1928), James M. Cain's novels *The Postman Always Rings Twice* (1934) and *Double Indemnity* (1943), Ron Hanson's 2011 novel *A Wild Surge of Guilty Passion*, and nine movies.

While the Robertson-Cole Pictures' adventure film *Tarzan and the Golden Lion* is not one of the better silent movies made about the jungle hero, it is the only film in which author Edgar Rice Burroughs participated in the production. He chose little-known actor James Pierce to play Tarzan and collaborated on the script, which was often very close to one of the Tarzan books. The natives have a diamond mine that the greedy Esteban Miranda covets, so he kidnaps Tarzan's sister, Betty, and forces her to show him where the diamonds are. Tarzan and his pet lion, Jad-bal-ja, capture Miranda, rescue Betty, and return her to overseer Jack Bradley, who loves her. Pierce never played Tarzan again, but he did fall in love with Burroughs's daughter Joan, and they were married for many years.

MONDAY, MARCH 21

With the help of Chinese Communist Party leader Zhou Enlai, Generalissimo Chiang Kai-shek and his Nationalist army took Shanghai today with little difficulty. The Nationalists took over the police stations and armories but obeyed Zhou's orders to not harm the many foreigners in the city.

The prolific French playwright and screenwriter Jacques Deval was represented on Broadway with the comedy hit *Dans sa candeur naïve*, which translators P. G. Wodehouse and Valerie Wyngate titled *Her Cardboard Lover*. Although Simone (Jeanne

Eagels) has divorced her husband, she still loves him and is afraid she'll go back to him. So, she hires the broke young gambler André (Leslie Howard) to distract her from returning to her ex. André does such a good job that the two fall in love and Simone happily forgets her former husband. The comedy was slight but very charming and the attraction was Eagels, who was an audience favorite and did not disappoint, giving a riveting performance. Unfortunately, Eagels was temperamental and hooked on drugs and alcohol. She started missing so many performances that the producers closed the play after twelve weeks, when it could have run longer. It was her last Broadway appearance. She died two years later at the age of thirty-five.

TUESDAY, MARCH 22

On Broadway, a musical and a thriller opened, but only the latter was successful. The musical was *Lucky*, and it boasted such talents as Jerome Kern, Otto Harbach, Bert Kalmar, and Harry Ruby providing the book and score. The plot they came up with was wanting, about the pretty pearl diver Lucky (Mary Eaton) in Ceylon who is a slave for her supposed father, Barlow, until the American Jack Mansfield is touring the island and falls in love with her. Producer Charles Dillingham's lavish, exotic production folded after eight weeks. *The Spider,* that night's mystery melodrama, pleased playgoers for a profitable nine months. During a mind-reading act in a vaudeville house, the young blindfolded man is able to identify objects from audience members. The act is cut short when a shot is fired and the young man is pronounced dead by a doctor in the audience. The police arrive and block all the exits to the theatre while the inspector investigates. There are plenty of suspects backstage and in the audience to keep the melodrama lively until it is revealed that the doctor, part of a drug ring, is the killer. *The Spider* was filmed as a talkie by Fox in 1931.

The distinguished American botanist Charles Sprague Sargent died today at the age of eighty-five, having run the Arnold Arboretum at Harvard University since 1872. Considered America's preeminent horticulturist for decades, hundreds of plants he identified carry *Sarg.* in their scientific name.

WEDNESDAY, MARCH 23

What historians have labeled the Nanjing Incident began today when the National Revolutionary Army (NRA) arrived at the Chinese port city then called Nanking and began attacking residents, particularly foreigners, and killing American professor John E. Williams, vice president of Nanjing University, and others. The NRA also took over the British, American, and Japanese consulates.

The French artist Paul César Helleu, known for his many portraits of high society ladies of the Belle Epoque period, died today in Paris at the age of sixty-seven. In America he is mostly remembered for his constellation-filled ceiling mural in New York City's Grand Central Station.

THURSDAY, MARCH 24

In Nanjing, American consul John K. Davis asked for military intervention as the riots, looting, and the killing of foreigners was rampant. The American destroyers USS *Noa* and USS *Preston* joined the British cruiser HMS *Emerald* in firing shells into the city and using machine guns to keep the Revolutionary troops off the streets.

Zoltán Kodály's Hungarian folk opera *Háry János* had premiered in Budapest in 1926 with success. He then wrote a six-movement *Suite from the Opera Háry János*, which was first performed today at the Gran Teatro del Liceo in Barcelona by the Orquestra Pau Casals conducted by Antal Fleischer.

FRIDAY, MARCH 25

A famous Japanese warship was commissioned into the Imperial Japanese Navy today. Although the *Akagi* was designed as a battleship, the importance of airplanes in warfare encouraged the naval command to redesign and outfit the ship as an aircraft carrier. The *Akagi* was active in the Second Sino-Japanese War in the late thirties and was one of the carriers used in the attack on Pearl Harbor. After assisting in Japan's conquest of several Pacific islands, the *Akagi* was severely damaged during the Battle of Midway in June of 1942. Deemed to be beyond repair, the carrier was scuttled so it would not fall into the hands of the Allies.

The Nanjing Incident entered its third day today. After a day of shelling the city of Nanjing, the United States and British military agreed to a one-day ceasefire if the National Revolutionary Army would allow the hundreds of foreigners in the city to be safely evacuated onto their ships. The NRA agreed and the foreigners departed, though the departing warships were fired upon as they sailed up the river to the sea. Casualty estimates from the Nanjing Incident are wildly inaccurate, depending on which nation was doing the reporting. The U.S. State Department announced the total number of deaths and injuries "at less than 100" while Chinese historians estimate that more than two thousand Chinese died from the bombardment and the French Communist newspaper *Communite* reported that seven thousand Chinese had been killed.

The Grand National horse race was run today for the eighty-sixth time at Aintree Racecourse near Liverpool, England. Jockey Ted Leader rode the eight-to-one favorite Sprig to victory. This was the first Grand National to be broadcast on BBC radio.

SATURDAY, MARCH 26

Generalissimo Chiang Kai-shek, commander-in-chief of the Cantonese armies, today arrived in Shanghai by gunboat from Hankou. He was able to take the city easily, thanks to the cooperation of the Communist forces inside Shanghai. Chiang was greeted upon his arrival by political and business leaders who offered him their financial backing if he would break off his alliance with the Communists.

The business mogul Alfred Hugenberg, who was leader of the German National People's Party and an early supporter of Hitler, today purchased the German film company UFA (Universum Film-Aktien Gesellschaft), the largest and most modern studio in the nation. Hugenberg's first directive was that the UFA devote its products to encourage nationalism. In the United Kingdom, the Ideal Film Company today merged with the Gaumont Film Company to form Gaumont-British Film Corporation, a major producer of movies and owner of movie houses.

In Hollywood, Lon Chaney was back in makeup as the title character in MGM's *Mr. Wu.* Although he has arranged an honorable marriage with a mandarin, Mr. Wu finds out his daughter Nang Ping (Renée Adorée) has been having an affair with Basil Gregory (Ralph Forbes), the son of a British diplomat, and is pregnant by him. In accordance with

Lon Chaney starred in fives movies released in 1927 and he looked very different in each one of them. Here he plays the aged Chinese patriarch in *Mr. Wu* comforting his daughter (Renée Adorée). *MGM / Photofest © MGM*

the ancient Chinese law that says such a dishonorable daughter must die by her father's hand, Mr. Wu kills his favorite daughter even as she pleads that he not harm her lover. Mr. Wu then resolves to take his revenge on Basil and the whole Gregory family but the ghost of Nang Ping appears to him, and so he lets Basil live. The movie is notable for Lon Chaney's performance and masterful makeup (in the prologue he plays the one-hundred-year-old ancestor of Mr. Wu) even if it does not rate among his very best films.

A very different star, baby-faced comic Harry Langdon, was the attraction in *Long Pants*, released today by First National Pictures. He played the pampered Boy, who reaches adulthood and is finally allowed to wear long pants. He is so pleased that he rides his bicycle about town showing off and comes across the sultry Vamp, who seems so much more exciting than his sweet fiancée, Priscilla. Mistakenly believing the Vamp likes him, the Boy pursues her and gets into all kinds of trouble with the police. Finally coming to his senses, he realizes Priscilla is the girl for him, and when he is released from jail, he marries her. Directed by Frank Capra, *Long Pants* is an implausible and odd comedy that seems almost surreal at times yet it is also brilliant in its way. Moviegoers in 1927 did not like it and the movie was a flop, beginning Langdon's decline in Hollywood.

SUNDAY, MARCH 27

The Jewish immigrant Anatol Josepho from Russia fled his homeland after the Russian Revolution and ended up in New York City with a few pennies and his Kodak Brownie camera. Long interested in photography, he came up with the idea of the automated photo booth, which he called the Photomaton. Josepho built and set up the first booth in September of 1925 in midtown Manhattan, and it was a success. Today he sold his invention to the newly created Photomaton Corporation and within a year he was a millionaire.

Henry Ford, the czar of automobile manufacturing, was in a car accident today. While driving his coupe on Michigan Avenue in Detroit, Ford was run off the road by a larger Studebaker and struck a tree. Although Ford was briefly hospitalized, news reports of the crash were kept from the press for several days. The accident was later investigated as a possible assassination attempt, but no substantial proof was found. Legend has it that the incident later prompted Ford to use safety glass in all his automobiles.

First baseman Joe Start, a leading figure in the early years of baseball, died today at the age of eighty-four. Dubbed "Old Reliable" for his consistently high batting average, Start began playing professional baseball with the Brooklyn Atlantics in 1862 and continued with various teams until retiring in 1886. William Healey Dall, an American naturalist and prolific author, died today at the age of eighty-one. He was famous for his expeditions into the interior of Alaska, earning him the title of Dean of Alaskan Explorations.

MONDAY, MARCH 28

One of the most beloved and popular playhouses in the Theatre District, the Majestic Theatre opened today on Broadway. Seating eighteen hundred patrons, the theatre, which is in the Louis XV style, has always been a favorite musical house and it has seen dozens of long-run hits over the decades, none bigger than *The Phantom of the Opera*, which has been running there since 1988. Ironically, the first show to play the Majestic was far from a success. *Rufus LeMaire's Affairs* was a musical revue in which producer Le-Maire assembled a fine cast but weak material. Long-legged Charlotte Greenwood kicked, band leader Ted Lewis offered some jazz, and the Albertina Rasch dancers went through their balletic routines, but it wasn't enough and the revue folded after seven weeks.

Alfred Klausmeyer, the cofounder and manager of the world's largest manufacturer of horse-drawn carriages from 1887 until 1915, died today at the age of sixty-six. In 1886, Klausmeyer and Anthony G. Brunsman formed the Anchor Buggy Company in Cincinnati and soon had sixty factories to keep up with the demand for their top-of-the-line carriages.

TUESDAY, MARCH 29

British car racing enthusiast Henry Seagrave today broke the land speed record when his 1,000 horsepower Sunbeam Mystery reached 203.79 mph on the sands of Daytona Beach, Florida. This broke Malcolm Campbell's world record, set a month earlier, by nearly thirty miles per hour. Seagrave continued to break land and water speed records until 1930, when he died trying to break a new boat speed on Lake Windermere in England.

Aviation was in the news throughout 1927 and feats of daring were plentiful. On this day, Australian polar explorer Hubert Wilkins and American bush pilot Ben Eielson flew farther north than any other plane ever had in order to explore the polar region north of Alaska. When they had engine trouble, Eielson was able to land the plane safely on a large floating icepack in the Arctic Ocean, the first time that had ever been accomplished. Wilkins and Eielson were able to repair the engine and then took off from the flat and managed to fly south to Alaska. The engine again failed and they were forced to land on an icy plain. The two then hiked ten days to get to Barrow, Alaska. The experience did not discourage the two men, and they continued to explore the polar regions, the next year being the first to fly from North America to Europe over the North Pole.

WEDNESDAY, MARCH 30

The Shōwa financial crisis, the worst financial panic in Japan's history, had ruined dozens of banks over the past two weeks. Today Japan's Diet passed an emergency banking law, called the Ginko Ho, to strengthen the financial standing of its banks. The new law raised considerably the amount of capital that banks were required to have in reserve in order to operate. Many small banks could not meet the requirements and over the next few years the number of banks in Japan fell from 1,417 to 680.

Two coal mine explosions occurred in two states today, in both cases trapping hundreds of miners underground until the next day. An explosion ripped through mine No. 3 of the Pennsylvania Coal and Coke company in Ehrenfeld, Pennsylvania, leaving nearly five hundred miners trapped below. Five died and the rest were freed the next morning. In Ledford, Illinois, eight miners were burned to death in a gas explosion nine thousand five hundred feet deep in the Saline County Coal Corporation mine No. 2. Some three hundred miners were trapped in other sections of the mine and were rescued the following day.

Ladislas Lazaro, one of the first Hispanic-Americans to serve in Congress, died today at the age of fifty-four. The Democrat from Louisiana was elected to the House of Representatives in 1913 and was still serving at the time of his premature death.

THURSDAY, MARCH 31

Vladimir K. Zworykin, the Russian-born American television pioneer, today received a British patent for an all–cathode ray television system. He had recently received his

New York City Police and Prohibition agents pour illegal alcohol down a sewer in Manhattan. The U.S. government also poured millions of dollars of liquor taxes down the sewer during 1927 alone. *Courtesy of the Library of Congress, LC-USZ62-123257*

THE GREAT EXPERIMENT

The Eighteenth Amendment, passed by Congress and signed by President Woodrow Wilson in 1920, was officially termed the Volstead Act but was often referred to as the Great Experiment. Most people called it Prohibition. As an experiment it was an utter failure and ended up increasing the consumption of alcohol rather than prohibiting it. The sale of beer, wine, and hard liquor was the fifth-largest industry in America before 1920, bringing in $2 billion a year, which was taxed and brought in $5 million a year. The booze business during Prohibition went into the hands of criminals, the government received no tax revenue, and drinking increased. In New York City, there were approximately fifteen thousand bars before 1920; during Prohibition the number of "speakeasies" was estimated at thirty-two thousand. The Eighteenth Amendment was not repealed until 1933.

doctorate from the University of Pittsburgh with a dissertation on improving the output of photoelectric cells. Zworykin went on to head television development at RCA and invented camera tubes that made "kinescopes" possible.

APRIL

FRIDAY, APRIL 1

Nearly two hundred thousand members of the United Mine Workers of America (UMWA) went on strike today when management and labor could not reach an agreement on pay rates. The strike was nationwide, but the impact was felt most in western Pennsylvania where forty thousand miners struck in the Central Competitive Field. The 1927 strike was one of the longest and most bitter strikes in Pennsylvania coal-industry history. All mining activity in the bituminous fields of western Pennsylvania was shut down until the coal companies used strikebreakers, private police, injunctions, and many other anti-union tactics. They also evicted twelve thousand miners and their families from company housing.

Today the Bureau of Prohibition, which had been part of the Bureau of Internal Revenue since the Eighteenth Amendment went into effect in 1920, was made a separate entity under the United States Department of the Treasury. Despite the name change, violation of the Volstead Act (Prohibition) was rampant and underfunded enforcement was unable to uphold the law.

Although there had been some British phonographs that changed records in different ways, today the Victor Talking Machine Company introduced "the automatic

A 1927 Victrola 2-60 portable record player costs forty dollars. It required no electricity and was powered by a spring motor operated with a crank. A phonograph record in 1927 cost thirty-nine cents.

orthophonic Victrola," which could be loaded with up to twelve records and then play them in sequence.

SATURDAY, APRIL 2

After the Nanking Incident, the British government today announced that its force of seventeen thousand soldiers in China would be increased by another five thousand men. The focus of the latest military strength was on the crucial city of Shanghai.

SUNDAY, APRIL 3

The state of Ohio, which had been in the Central Time Zone or Central Standard Time (CST) since 1883 when standardized time zones were first established, today was changed to the Eastern Time Zone or Eastern Standard Time (EST) by the Interstate Commerce Commission.

The Hal Roach comedy short *Slipping Wives* has a cast that includes Stan Laurel and Oliver Hardy, but it is not considered a Laurel and Hardy film. A housewife feels that her husband, Leon, is neglecting her, so she hires a dense handyman (Laurel) to pretend to make love to her, thereby making her husband jealous. Of course, the so-called lover is incompetent, and it takes the help of the butler (Hardy) to get the poor fellow out of the house when the jealous husband pulls a gun out and goes on a rampage during a dinner party. While Laurel and Hardy get to do some comic bits together, it is Laurel's befuddled handyman that is the comic heart of the film

The Indian activist Dr. B. R. Ambedkar today founded the weekly newspaper *Bahiskrit Bharat* (India Ostracized). Ambedkar and the newspaper championed the rights of the Dalits or "untouchable caste" in India.

The eminent British writer H. G. Wells, known for his keen eye on the future, was quoted in today's *New York Times Magazine* as saying radio broadcasting "is an inferior substitute for better systems of transmitting news and evoking sound. . . . I am afraid that the future of broadcasting . . . is a very trivial future indeed." Over the next few days, several rebuttals appeared in print, including one by Lee Deforest, the radio and

By the end of 1927, there were 732 radio broadcast stations in the nation. Only a small portion of these were network affiliates. On average, the household radio was on for two hours and twenty minutes each day.

television pioneer, who wrote, "No, H. G., radio is here to stay. It will become a more and more indispensable part of our daily and nightly home life. For radio has worked and is now working too profound a change in our national culture, our musical tastes, never to be cast aside."

MONDAY, APRIL 4

On Broadway, the drama *Spread Eagle* boasted a strong story and top-notch cast, and it received glowing reviews, yet, curiously, it managed to run only ten weeks. The American business mogul Martin Henderson (Fritz Williams) is so rich and powerful that he pays the Mexican general De Castro hundreds of thousands of dollars to start a revolution so that U.S. troops will have to go to Mexico and protect Henderson's interests in the Spread Eagle Mining Company. Henderson goes so far as to send his daughter's fiancé, Charles Parkman, to Mexico to manage the company, knowing Parkman will be shot, as previous company managers have been killed. Henderson uses his power with Congress to have the United States declare war on Mexico and troops are dispatched south. In the chaos, Parkman is shot but survives to return to the States and tell Henderson what he thinks of him and his megalomania. George Abbott directed the melodrama with a flare, using newsreel footage and radio broadcasts to trumpet Henderson's powerful political machine. Parallels with William Randolph Hearst's concocting a war with Spain in order to sell newspapers in 1898 were obvious.

Chicago mobster Vincent Drucci died today at the age of twenty-seven from gunshot wounds received during a struggle with police detective Dan Healy, who was attempting to arrest him. Drucci, nicknamed "the Schemer," was the leader of Chicago's North Side Gang and Al Capone's chief rival. The only major crime figure of the era to be killed by a policeman rather than another gangster, Drucci left an estate worth over half a million dollars and his lavish funeral, complete with a $10,000 silver casket and $30,000 worth of flowers, was attended by over one thousand mourners.

TUESDAY, APRIL 5

The Columbia Phonograph Company merged with the floundering United Independent Broadcasters today to form Columbia Phonographic Broadcasting System (CPBS). The merger gave the United Independent Broadcasters enough working capital to survive and start nationwide broadcasting by September 18. The company's name would later be shortened to the Columbia Broadcasting System (CBS).

The Austro-Hungarian-born American competition swimmer Johnny Weissmuller, who had won three gold medals at the 1924 Paris Olympics, set a new world record today swimming the 100-yard freestyle in less than a minute. He would best his time of fifty-one seconds in 1940 when he swam it in 48.5 seconds. During his amateur and professional swimming career, Weissmuller won fifty-two U.S. national championships and set more than fifty world records. He enjoyed an equally successful second career in Hollywood, playing Tarzan in twelve movies in the 1930s and 1940s.

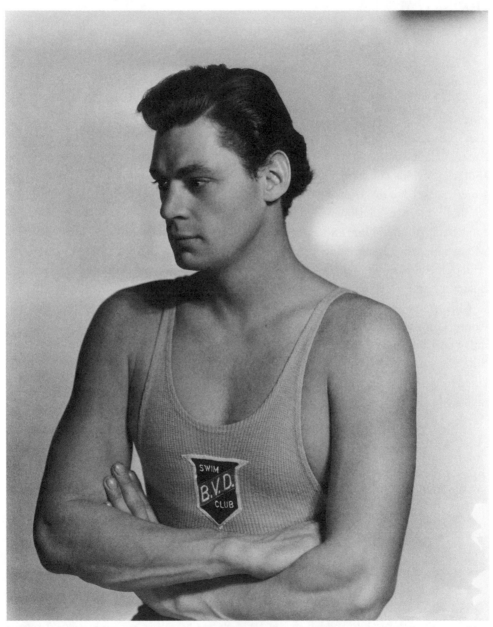

It didn't take much imagination on Hollywood's part to picture the record-breaking competition swimmer Johnny Weissmuller as a movie star. His acting may have been a little stiff, but he was ideal for playing the physically agile jungle-raised Tarzan. *MGM / Photofest © MGM*

WEDNESDAY, APRIL 6

An explosion today at the refinery of Producers and Refiners Oil Company in Parco, Wyoming, killed thirteen employees. The blast was so great that all the windows in the town of Parco were blown away.

When Webber College was founded today by Roger W. Babson and Grace Knight Babson in Babson Park, Florida, it was one of the nation's first business schools for women. The school was also the first private, not-for-profit college chartered under Florida's then new educational and charitable laws. Today the school is Webber International University.

> There were 975 institutions of higher learning in the States in 1927, including 153 junior colleges and 79 colleges for African Americans.

THURSDAY, APRIL 7

An early form of television was demonstrated today, sending an image with sound from Washington, D.C., to New York City. The Bell Telephone Company transmitted a thirty-line image at the rate of ten images per second using a rotating Nipkow disc system. The screen was only two by two-and-a-half inches in size but was big enough to show Secretary of Commerce Herbert Hoover in Washington speaking over a loud-speaker telephone to AT&T's president, Walter S. Gifford, and a group gathered in New York. After Hoover's speech, the first televised entertainment was broadcast: a performance by Irish vaudeville comedian A. Dolan, whose act included a blackface minstrel show number.

One of the greatest French silent films, Abel Gance's epic *Napoléon*, premiered today in Paris. The boy Napoleon first shows his talent for tactical warfare at boarding school where he turns a chaotic snowball fight into an organized assault. As a young lieutenant (Albert Dieudonné), he witnesses the horrors of the Reign of Terror in Paris and during the turbulent days of the revolution finds himself in and out of jail. During the Siege of Toulon, Napoleon demonstrates his skill as a leader of men and is made brigadier general. At this time, he meets and falls in love with Josephine de Beauharnais. They marry just as France is threatened by Italian military forces. Napoleon is made commander-in-chief of the French army and, in the movie's climax, leads a successful invasion of Italy. Abel Gance produced, wrote, and directed the historical epic, which in its original form ran over four hours. Gance used a variety of innovations in filming *Napoléon*, including split screen, multiple exposure, handheld camera work, point-of-view angles, fast cutting, and even some underwater camera shots. The climax of the movie was filmed

One of the great epics of the silent era is Abel Gance's ambitious French biopic *Napoleon*, with Albert Dieudonné (pictured) playing the renowned conqueror. Gance foresaw a series of six movies covering all of Bonaparte's life, but this 1927 film, covering the first twenty-eight years of his life, was the only one ever made. *MGM / Photofest © MGM*

with three cameras, creating a wide triptych that was presented by three projectors on three screens tinted with the colors of the French flag. *Napoléon* is a dazzling cinematic accomplishment that over the years has been restored and rediscovered with great enthusiasm. When the movie was first shown in London, it was cut down to three hours. The movie was not seen in the States until 1929, and that version was less than two hours. Not until British film historian Kevin Brownlow's restored version in the 1980s was Gance's masterpiece once again seen the way he intended. *Napoléon* was planned to be the first of six films about the complete life of the famous Frenchman, but the expense of making the first part made future installments impractical.

Sigmund Romberg's romantic operetta *The Desert Song*, which had opened on Broadway in November of 1926 and ran for 471 performances, had its London premiere today. Both critics and playgoers embraced the exotic musical set in the Sahara Desert, and it ran 432 performances. In 1929, *The Desert Song* became the first Broadway musical to be filmed with sound. Hollywood would remake the movie musical in 1943 and 1953.

FRIDAY, APRIL 8

Underwater cable communications, which were considered the fastest and most efficient form of transcontinental communication, were outshone today when the Amalgamated Wireless Company of Australia introduced wireless service between Sydney and London by beaming messages at the speed of light. Using shortwave radio, these messages traveled over 10,000 miles between the two cities.

The ever-controversial subject of Prohibition was demonstrated today in a debate held in the Roosevelt Club in Boston in which Dr. Nicholas Butler, president of Columbia University, declared the Eighteenth Amendment to be a total failure and its repeal should be on the Republican Party platform in the next election. Republican Senator William Borah defended Prohibition and argued that it had not been properly enforced.

SATURDAY, APRIL 9

Perhaps the most controversial crime and trial of the 1920s was the case of Sacco and Vanzetti, two Italian immigrants and anarchists who became symbols of sociopolitical oppression in America. The case remains a controversial one to this day and their guilt or innocence is still questioned, but the way justice was diverted and turned against them is more obvious. The story climaxes in 1927, and on this day Sacco and Vanzetti were sentenced to die for a crime that was nearly seven years old. On April 15, 1920, two men delivering the payroll for a shoe company in Braintree, Massachusetts, were robbed and gunned down by unknown persons who escaped in a stolen Buick. The car with the shotgun shells was found two days later. Both Nicola Sacco and Bartolomeo Vanzetti were suspected anarchists, and when confronted by the police, shells matching those of the stolen pistol used to murder the guards, as well as a similar revolver, were found on Vanzetti. Neither man had an alibi for the crime: Sacco was off work on the day of the shooting and Vanzetti was self-employed and could not be vouched for. Both men were arrested and charged with the murders on September 11, 1920. Adding to public prejudice was a series of bombings by anarchist groups, one of which killed thirty-eight people and wounded 134 others on Wall Street on September 16, 1920. The trial, which lasted from May 31 to July 14, 1921, was suspect in many ways. Witnesses for the prosecution claimed to have seen the defendants at the crime scene yet were contradictory in their descriptions and details. One witness, an Italian youth, admitted that he was rehearsed in what to say in court just as if he were in school. After both defendants were convicted of muder, a defense committee was formed to appeal, and over the next seven years it raised $300,000, the money used to have unbiased experts examine the evidence, in particular the gun and the shotgun shells. There was even an appeal to the Massachusetts Supreme Judicial Court, but the justices ended up concurring with the results of the trial. The controversy heightened in November 1925, when Celestino Medeiros, an ex-convict who was awaiting trial for murder, confessed that he committed the payroll robbery and the murders. Medeiros stated that Sacco and Vanzetti did not participate in the crime, that it was done by his gang, led by Joe Morelli. When the police followed up on the story, they found that Morelli looked a great deal like Sacco. Another appeal was made to the Massachusetts Supreme Court, and future U.S. Supreme Court justice Felix Frankfurter went so far as to write an article for the *Atlantic Monthly* criticizing the earlier denial and arguing for a retrial. But the court did not agree and the appeal was turned down on April 5, 1927. Four days later, Judge Webster Thayer again sentenced Sacco and Vanzetti to death and set the execution for August 23. Protests, demonstrations, letters from famous people, and walkouts would follow over the next four months.

Famed explorer and aviator Richard E. Byrd was the leading candidate to win the Orteig Prize for the first nonstop flight between France and the United States. With copilots Floyd Bennet and George Noville, Bryd made a practice flight today in their Fokker F-VIIb-3m named *America*. The plane crashed on takeoff, Bennett was seriously injured, Byrd and Noville were slightly injured, and the airplane was badly damaged.

The Brooklyn Celtics, the basketball team that changed its named from the Brooklyn Arcadians this season, won the U.S. professional basketball championship today, defeating the Cleveland Rosenblums 35–32, for a three-game sweep of the American Basketball League series.

British author P. G. Wodehouse's short story *It Was Only a Fire* was published in today's issue of the American magazine *Liberty*. The pub storyteller Mr. Mulliner relates

Nicola Sacco (far right) and Bartolomeo Vanzetti (center with mustache) are led handcuffed from the Norfolk County Courthouse in Dedham, Massachusetts, after being sentenced to death by Judge Webster Thayer for a robbery and murder that took place seven years earlier. *Firstrun Features / Photofest © Firstrun Features*

the tale of his Uncle William, who was in San Francisco during the great earthquake of 1906. He has fallen in love with the impressionable Myrtle Banks, but she wants to marry the braggart Desmond Franklyn who claims to be a brave wild game hunter. His proposal of marriage turned down by Myrtle, teetotaler William goes into a saloon and gets drunk for the first time in his life. Returning to his hotel room, the earthquake strikes and Williams assumes the falling ceiling and crumbling walls are all part of his drunken stupor and he sleeps through it. The next morning Myrtle finds that Franklyn was petrified by the quake and abandoned her but brave William is still there, so she agrees to marry him. The tale was printed as *The Story of William* in the May issue of the *Strand Magazine*

SUNDAY, APRIL 10

An evening of works by avant-garde American composer George Antheil tonight at Carnegie Hall was one long remembered as a night of chaos, excitement, laughter, and booing and hissing. The twenty-six-year-old Antheil rented the hall and assembled a variety of works, including his 1925 *A Jazz Symphony*, played by African American musicians, and his 1926 composition *Ballet Mécanique*, which combined classical instruments with such mechanized sounds as factory whistles, elevated trains, and airplanes. During the evening, a wind machine assaulted the audience and scattered their programs into the air and a siren refused to sound on cue, finally blasting out as the patrons were exiting the hall. The critics were vicious in their assessment of Antheil's music, which was being heard for the first time in America, and the composer never fully recovered from the humiliation. Ironically, Antheil's music was very influential to several modern composers, and his works are now consistently performed.

MONDAY, APRIL 11

The map of Europe changed today. The Royal and Parliamentary Titles Act 1927 took effect at midnight, making Ireland a separate Free Irish State. What was once called the United Kingdom of Great Britain and Ireland officially changed to the United Kingdom of Great Britain and Northern Ireland.

Sophie Tucker, who billed herself as the "Last of the Red Hot Mamas," today recorded two old favorites at the OKeh Records studio with Ted Shapiro's jazz dance band: "After You've Gone," a 1918 jazz standard by Turner Layton (music) and Henry Creamer (lyric), and "I Ain't Got Nobody (and Nobody Cares for Me)," a 1915 torch song by Spencer Williams (music), Roger Graham, and Dave Peyton (lyric).

The comedy-drama *The Second Man* opened on Broadway to laudatory reviews and launched the careers of playwright S. N. Behrman and actor Alfred Lunt. The young writer Clark Storey (Lunt) is a bit of a cad, living off the rich widow Mrs. Frayne (Lynn Fontanne) but toying with the affections of the young and impoverished Monica. When he tires of Monica, Clark tries to match her up with the scientist Austin. By the end of the play, both women discover the truth about Clark's character and drop him. Although all the cast members were praised, the greatest applause was for the up-and-coming Lunt, whose gift for high comedy and ability to play such subtle duplicity was outstanding. The critics were just as impressed by the clever script by Behrman, and *The Second Man* was the first of many sparkling comedies of manners he would write. The Theatre Guild produced the play, which ran a fruitful 178 performances. RKO's 1930 screen version was titled *He Knew Women* and starred Lowell Sherman in the Clark role. But much more than the title was changed, and the movie was a critical and box office failure.

TUESDAY, APRIL 12

The Shanghai Massacre of 1927, also known as the "April 12 Incident," occurred today. Generalissimo Chiang Kai-shek had employed the aid of Communist leader Zhou Enlai and his followers in taking over Shanghai a few weeks earlier. Wishing to please Western businessmen and strengthen his own power, Chiang betrayed the Communists with a surprise massacre. In the early hours of the day, Chiang ordered gang leader Du Yuesheng and hundreds of his followers to disguise themselves as workmen and enter the Zhabei District of Shanghai where the Communists had settled. Just before dawn, the slaughter began, leaving more than four thousand leftists killed and hundreds more captured, including Zhou Enlai, who later escaped. (It was Zhou Enlai who later became the prime minister of the People's Republic of China when Chiang and his Kuomintang party were driven out of mainland China in 1949.)

The Major League Baseball season officially began today with President Coolidge throwing out the first ball in Washington, D.C. The Washington Senators, lost to the Boston Red Sox 6–2. In Pittsburgh, future Hall-of-Famer Lloyd Waner made his major league debut playing left field for the Pittsburgh Pirates. His brother, future Hall-of-Famer

---

1927 MAJOR LEAGUE BASEBALL

American League:	National League:
Boston Red Sox	Boston Braves
Chicago White Sox	Brooklyn Robins
Cleveland Indians	Chicago Cubs
Detroit Tigers	Cincinnati Reds
New York Yankees	New York Giants
Philadelphia Athletics	Philadelphia Phillies
St. Louis Browns	Pittsburgh Pirates
Washington Senators	St. Louis Cardinals

In 1927 there were no Major League Baseball teams west of St. Louis. There were also no playoff games or Inter-League games, other than the World Series at season's end, when the American and National Leagues' champions met for the title.

1927 MINOR LEAGUE BASEBALL

American Association	International League	Pacific Coast League
Columbus Senators	Baltimore Orioles	Hollywood Stars
Indianapolis Indians	Buffalo Bisons	Los Angeles Angels
Kansas City Blues	Jersey City Skeeters	Mission Bells
Louisville Colonels	Newark Bears	Oakland Oaks
Milwaukee Brewers	Reading Keystones	Portland Beavers
Minneapolis Millers	Rochester Tribe	Sacramento Senators
St. Paul Saints	Syracuse Stars	San Francisco Seals
Toledo Mud Hens	Toronto Maple Leafs	Seattle Indians

There were many other Minor League teams but these three leagues were the most prominent.

Paul Waner, was in right field. The Pirates bested the Cincinnati Reds 2–1. Today was also the first game of the season for the New York Yankees. Because of the strong lineup of players, the team was eventually given the nickname Murderers' Row. The Yankees didn't exactly murder the Philadelphia Athletics, but they did beat them 8–3.

The Minor League Baseball season also began today. Although first started in 1901 as the National Association of Professional Baseball Leagues, the Minor Leagues were just coming into their own in the late 1920s. The national mania for baseball had been steadily growing over the years and teams and leagues had formed all over the country, from little towns and rural areas to cities of all sizes. While the National and American Leagues had the most money, the biggest stars, and the most notoriety, fans of professional baseball had many other alternatives to turn to. Hence, the rise of the popularity of Minor League Baseball. Some of these teams were actually owned by Major League teams who used them to develop and nurture promising players. These so-called "farm teams" were grooming the next generation of Major League celebrities. Baseball was, like so many things in the 1920s, big business, and the system of creating and delivering top-notch baseball was run in a very pragmatic and profit-aimed manner. What it all came down to for the public was a vast and widespread offering of professional baseball in America in 1927.

WEDNESDAY, APRIL 13

Today was the last day of the 1926–1927 National Hockey League season and the Stanley Cup Finals in which the Ottawa Senators beat the Boston Bruins for the prized trophy. The Senators, who won two games and tied two, took home the Stanley Cup for the fourth time since 1920, but it was their last victory. The original Senators would not win again.

THURSDAY, APRIL 14

The very first Volvo car rolled off the assembly line today in Gothenburg, Sweden. The name Volvo (Swedish for "I roll") was registered in 1911 as the trademark name for a company that produced ball bearings. By 1924 the company started plans for an automobile that could withstand the frigid temperatures of Scandinavia. Only 280 Volvo OV 4 cars were made in 1927; by 1930, Volvo's were becoming popular across Europe.

FRIDAY, APRIL 15

The Great Mississippi Flood of 1927, by far the most disastrous flood in the history of the nation before or since, technically began today when nearly fifteen inches of rain fell on New Orleans in less than twenty-four hours. In fact, the Great Flood, as it was called for many years, really began in the summer of 1926, when record rainfall was measured across the country, breaking records from California to Connecticut. Many rivers overflowed and remained higher than usual throughout the winter of 1926–1927. In the spring, the rains returned and the first signs of disaster appeared on the Northern reaches of the Mississippi River. Over the next 153 days, the Mississippi would cover over twenty-seven thousand square miles and would measure sixty miles across at some points. The number of lives lost was never accurately calculated, since many victims were the rural poor living in the flood zone. Estimates range from five hundred to triple that.

Babe Ruth hit his first home run of the season during the New York Yankees' game against the Philadelphia Athletics. Ruth hit the bases-empty homer against pitcher

---

NEW YORK YANKEES

Baseball historians nearly unanimously agree that the New York Yankees in the summer of 1927 was the greatest lineup of players in the history of the game. The complete roster consisted of: (future Hall of Famers in **bold**)

Pitchers: Walter Beall, Joe Giard, **Waite Hoyt**, Wilcy Moore, **Herb Pennock**, George Pipgras, Dutch Ruether, Bob Shawkey, Urban Shocker, Myles Thomas
Catchers: Benny Bengough, Pat Collins, Johnny Grabowski
Infielders: Joe Dugan, Mike Gazella, **Lou Gehrig**, Mark Koenig, **Tony Lazzeri**, Ray Morehart, Julie Wera
Outfielders: **Earle Combs**, Cedric Durst, Bob Meusel, Ben Paschal, **Babe Ruth**
Coaches: Art Fletcher, Charley O'Leary
Manager: **Miller Huggins**

The average yearly salary for this famous team was approximately $10,333 per player. If one deducts Babe Ruth's unheard-of salary of $70,000, the other players' average income was $7,850.

Thousands of square miles of Arkansas, Missouri, Illinois, Kansas, Tennessee, Kentucky, Texas, Louisiana, Mississippi, and Oklahoma lay underwater for months during the Great Mississippi Flood of 1927, still the most devastating natural disaster in the nation's history. *Courtesy of the Library of Congress, LC-DIG-npcc-16869*

Howard Ehmke during the first inning of the game, which the Yankees won 6–3. It would be the first of many during this historical season.

The popular French author Gaston Leroux died in Nice, today at the age of fifty-eight. While his 1910 novel *The Phantom of the Opera* is his most famous work, Leroux also wrote many detective stories and novels, including *The Mystery of the Yellow Room* (1907), an early classic example of the locked-room genre.

SATURDAY, APRIL 16

Today the first levee along the Mississippi River collapsed. At Dorena, Missouri, a dirt embankment twelve hundred feet long burst, and water equal to the surge of Niagara Falls broke through, creating a sound that was heard miles away. Other levees downstream were later washed away. The lower Mississippi swelled and rapid flooding followed in ten states. In Arkansas, 14 percent of the state was under water. Not until August would the waters start to recede.

The acclaimed German opera singer Rosa Sucher died today at the age of seventy-eight. Sucher was known as one of the finest interpreters of Richard Wagner's operas between 1871 and her retirement in 1903. Unfortunately, she made no recordings, so there are no archives of her singing prowess.

SUNDAY, APRIL 17

Actress Jean Arthur was not yet a star but was featured in nine movies in 1927, including today's comedy, *Horse Shoes*, released by Pathé Exchange. The star of the film was Monty Banks, who played the fresh-out-of-school lawyer Monty Milde. On the train for the big city, he and the pretty Miss Baker (Arthur) are mistaken by others as newlyweds because he has the berth above her. She turns out to be the daughter of Henry Baker, who has been hired by Monty to prove that John's brother William has forged a will disinheriting both father and daughter. Monty does some detective work, proves the will a forgery, and wins the hand of Miss Baker. Arthur is charming in the role, but her fame would not come until the arrival of the talkies, when audiences could enjoy her distinctively squeaky voice.

MONDAY, APRIL 18

A train robbery today near Limón in Mexico's Jalisco state left over one hundred fifty people dead. Armed bandits stopped a passenger train traveling from Guadalajara to Mexico City. In addition to stealing goods and shooting anyone who resisted, the bandits then set the wooden train cars on fire, causing most of the deaths.

Having wiped out the Communist faction during the Shanghai Massacre of April 12, Chiang Kai-shek today declared himself to be chairman of the National Government Committee and president of China with a new capital at Nanjing. The reigning government continued to operate at Beijing, but Chiang continued to purge the country of Communists in other provinces. In the Hunan Province alone, over four thousand peasants and workers were murdered in Chiang's efforts to root out Communists.

Young singer-songwriter Jimmie Rodgers traveled with his friend Otis Kuykendall to Asheville, North Carolina, and today performed on WWNC, Asheville's first radio station. Before the year was out, Rodgers cut six records and went on to become the first country music star.

George Jessel reprised his performance as Jewish singer Jakie Robin in a Broadway revival of *The Jazz Singer*, the 1925 play that he had starred in with great success. Warner Brothers tried to secure Jessel for a planned film version of the melodrama, but the star demanded too much money, so the studio contacted Al Jolson. Before the year was out, Jolson and *The Jazz Singer* would make cinema history.

TUESDAY, APRIL 19

The Boston Marathon was run today for the thirty-first year and, for the first time, used the internationally recognized marathon distance of twenty-six miles and 385 yards. The race was won by Clarence DeMar, finishing in two hours, twenty-five minutes, and forty seconds.

Having been convicted of obscenity charges for her 1926 play *Sex*, Mae West chose not to pay the fine and today began serving a ten-day jail sentence on Welfare Island (now known as Roosevelt Island), giving her further publicity and notoriety. She was released after eight days.

One of the biggest Broadway hits of 1925 was the swashbuckling operetta *The Vagabond King*, about the dashing poet-adventurer François Villon. The Rudolf Friml musical ran 511 performances in New York and then was a success touring the nation. The London production opened today and was also a hit, running 480 performances. Hollywood made screen versions of *The Vagabond King* in 1930 and 1956.

WEDNESDAY, APRIL 20

Tanaka Giichi, a general in the Imperial Japanese Army and leader of the Rikken Seiyūkai Party, became the new prime minister today. He would remain in power only two years. After the failed attempt to seize Manchuria in 1929, Giichi and his cabinet resigned and he died in September of that year.

THURSDAY, APRIL 21

The Art Institute of Chicago today opened a special one-month exhibit of work by students in the art classes at Hull House and other settlement houses in Chicago.

George Gershwin's *Rhapsody in Blue*, which had premiered in New York City in 1924, was recorded today by Paul Whiteman's Orchestra with Gershwin at the piano. This abridged "electrical" (as opposed to acoustical) recording ran nine minutes, about half the length of the original composition. Yet the recording was very popular, was reissued in the late 1930s on the Victor label, and in 1974 was inducted into the Grammy Hall of Fame.

Britain's King George V today opened the National Museum of Wales in Cardiff, having laid the foundation stone fifteen years before. The ceremony involved the king rapping on the massive doors with a mallet offered by the chief architect to gain admittance, then entering the museum dedicated to teaching "the world about Wales, and the Welsh people about their own Fatherland."

MUSEUMS

Some notable museums that opened in 1927 (listed by their current names):

Albacete Provincial Museum (Albacete, Spain)
Alferaki Palace (Taganrog, Russia)
Arkell Museum (Canajoharie, NY)
Children's Museum (Hartford, CT)
Colborne Lodge (Toronto)
Detroit Institute of the Arts
Esperanto Museum and Collection of Planned Languages (Vienna)
Ferens Art Gallery (Kingston upon Hull, UK)
Fogg Museum—new location (Cambridge, MA)
Galleria Giorgio Franchetti alla Ca' d'Oro (Venice, Italy)
General Phineas Banning Residence Museum (Los Angeles)
Henan Provincial Museum (Zhengzhou, China)
Henry Art Gallery (Seattle)
Honolulu Museum of Art
James Monroe Museum and Memorial Library (Fredericksburg, VA)

John and Mable Ringling Museum of Art (Sarasota, FL)
Mevlâna Museum (Konya, Turkey)
Museum of Asian Art of Corfu (Corfu, Greece)
Museum of Indian Arts and Culture (Santa Fe, NM)
National Museum of Wales (Cardiff)
Paula Modersohn-Becker Museum (Bremen, Germany)
The Reproductions Museum Bilbao (Spain)
Rijksmuseum Twenthe (Enschede, Netherlands)
Scottish War Museum (Edinburgh)
Speed Art Museum (Louisville, KY)
Taft Museum of Art (Cincinnati)
Turkmen Museum of Fine Arts (Ashgabat, Turkmenistan)
Usher Gallery (Lincolnshire, UK)
Walker Art Center (Minneapolis)
Wells Fargo History Museum (San Francisco)

See May 16 for notable works of art from 1927.

FRIDAY, APRIL 22

During the week after the Great Flood struck the Midwest, President Coolidge had declined to issue federal relief money for the hundreds of thousands left homeless and refused to call a special session of Congress to deal with the catastrophe. Today he finally announced that Herbert Hoover, the secretary of commerce, was appointed to head a Special Mississippi Flood Committee and asked the public to make "generous contributions" to the American Red Cross. Over $32 million was collected. Coolidge also allocated $10 million of federal money for the cause. Hoover, who had organized major relief efforts in Europe after World War I, wasted no time, and within days one hundred fifty tent cities were erected and in operation for the homeless. Unfortunately, living conditions for African American refugees were vastly inferior to those for white citizens. In fact, many were forced at gunpoint to do manual labor at the camps for no wages.

American composer Roger Sessions's Symphony no. 1 in E Minor premiered today in Boston with Serge Koussevitzky conducting the Boston Symphony Orchestra. The symphony, in three movements, is from the period in which Sessions was composing primarily in the neoclassical style.

SATURDAY, APRIL 23

An explosion rocked the city of Detroit this morning when the auto body plant of Briggs Manufacturing Company caught fire and exploded. Twenty-one workers were burned to death and more than one hundred were injured as the entire five-story, block-long structure was decimated. It was later determined that the fire started when a spark ignited the nitrocellulose fumes coming from the process of lacquering car bodies.

Today marked the publication of the first edition of the *Countryman* magazine, a British journal that is still in operation. Its offices housed in North Yorkshire, the magazine focuses on rural life in various forms. It started as a quarterly primarily for farmers, but over the years it has expanded its coverage and is now a monthly read by a wide audience in the English-speaking world.

In today's edition of the well-established *New Yorker* magazine, a poem by Dorothy Parker was published. Titled "Parable for a Certain Virgin," it is a sour portrait of the kind of man who flees from women and marriage, when in truth none want him.

In the humor magazine *Judge*, S. J. Perelman's farcical piece "That Old Gang o' Mine" appeared today, the author fondly recalling five friends going back to public school in Queens and how they all grew up to have disastrous or ridiculous lives.

SUNDAY, APRIL 24

Chinese Communist Party members, who had survived the April 12 Shanghai Massacre, met at Wuhan today and reelected Chen Duxiu as the party's secretary general. Chen was a philosopher and educator as well as a revolutionary socialist and had cofounded the Chinese Communist Party with Li Dazhao in 1921.

MONDAY, APRIL 25

Although Alaska would not become a state for another thirty years, the territory's branch of the American Legion held a contest in which schoolchildren in the territory submitted designs for an Alaskan flag, the winner getting a $1,000 prize. Today it was announced that the competition was won by the thirteen-year-old orphan Benny

Benson of Seward, Alaska, who based his design on the North Star and the eight gold stars of the Big Dipper against a dark blue field. The Alaska legislature adopted the design on May 2, and when Alaska became a state in 1959 the same design was used for the state flag.

The popular ditty "Sometimes I'm Happy" was one of the memorable songs introduced in the musical comedy *Hit the Deck!*, which opened today on Broadway and entertained audiences for a year. The sassy Loulou (Louise Groody) runs a coffee house on the docks at Newport but is prepared to give it all up to follow a sailor, "Bilge" Smith (Charles King). When Bilge ships out, Loulou follows him around the world. She finally persuades him to marry her, only to have him change his mind when she buys him a ship as a present and he learns she is an heiress. But Bilge changes his mind again after Loulou agrees to assign her inheritance to their children. Herbert Fields wrote the serviceable book, which was based on Hubert Osborne's 1922 play *Shore Leave.* The lively score by Vincent Youmans (music), Leo Robin, and Clifford Grey (lyrics) also included the spirited gospel number "Hallelujah," the questioning "Why, Oh Why?" and the rousing "Join the Navy." *Hit the Deck* was adapted into movies in 1930 and 1955.

Clara Bow and a not-yet-famous Gary Cooper are the people to watch in Paramount's romantic melodrama *Children of Divorce*, which opened today. Jean Waddington (Esther Ralston) and Ted Larrabee (Cooper) are childhood sweethearts, but, because they both come from divorced parents, Jean is worried that Ted will be unfaithful like his father was. Ted gets involved with the flirtatious Kitty Flanders (Bow), who is after Prince Ludovico de Saxe. The prince turns her down, Ted and Kitty join in a miserable marriage, Kitty commits suicide, and things look hopeful for Ted and Jean. The melodramatics in *Children of Divorce* get a bit thick, but the performances are strong enough to carry it all off.

The popular silent screen leading man Earle Williams died of bronchial pneumonia today in Hollywood at the age of forty-six. A major star at the Vitagraph Studios starting in the 1910s, Williams was voted America's favorite male star in 1915. The handsome actor usually played dashing and romantic heroes, often opposite Anita Stewart. Williams was working up until the time of his death, three of his movies being released in 1927.

TUESDAY, APRIL 26

Another setback, and a tragic one, occurred today regarding the Orteig Prize of $25,000 for the first aviator(s) to fly from New York to Paris. In a test flight for the transatlantic journey, Lieutenant Commanders Noel Davis and Stanton H. Wooster attempted a takeoff from Virginia's Langley Field in their Keystone Pathfinder monoplane *American Legion*. Because of the heavy load of fuel needed to cross the Atlantic, the plane was unable to climb high enough, and it crashed into some trees, killing both men.

WEDNESDAY, APRIL 27

Arguably the most sensational trial of the year began today in Long Island City, Queens, when Ruth Snyder and her lover, Judd Gray, were tried for the murder of her husband Albert Snyder on March 20. The well-publicized trial lasted until May 9.

The final game of Britain's 1927 Football (soccer, as we know it) Association Challenge Cup (the FA Cup) was played today in Wembley, London, with over 91,000 spectators on hand to see Cardiff City beat Arsenal 1–0. The winning goal was scored accidentally when Arsenal's goalie knocked the ball into the net while trying to gather it in. It was the fifty-second year of the FA Cup and the only time it was won by a non-English team. This final game was also the first to be broadcast on British radio.

London had a musical hit on this day, *Lady Luck*, which ran a profitable 324 performances and toured for two years but never came to New York. Yet much about the show was American: it was based on a 1917 Broadway musical flop, had American characters, and included two songs by Broadway songwriters Richard Rodgers (music) and Lorenz Hart (lyrics). The silly plot was about three Wall Street stockbrokers (Laddie Cliff, Cyril Ritchard, and Leslie Henson) who invest in the "Lady Luck" mine, which leads to some unlucky circumstances until the happy ending, when they hit pay dirt.

The politician and author Albert J. Beveridge died today in Indianapolis at the age of sixty-four. As a U.S. Senator from Indiana, the Republican Beveridge was a strong proponent of the Progressive Movement during Theodore Roosevelt's administration. After he retired from politics, Beveridge wrote biographies, his four-volume *The Life of John Marshall* (1916–1919) winning the Pulitzer Prize.

THURSDAY, APRIL 28

Construction and testing of the *Spirit of St. Louis* was completed today, and Charles Lindbergh, who had participated in the design and building of the single-engine monoplane, flew it for the first time in some test patterns over the Dutch Flats near San Diego.

The Chinese theoretician and political figure Li Dazhao was executed today, along with nineteen other Communists, at the Soviet Embassy in Beijing. He was thirty-nine years old. Li was one of the founders of the Chinese Communist Party and a political thinker who helped propel the populist revolution against foreign imperialism. Li took refuge from the Manchurian warlord Zhang Zuolin in the Soviet embassy, but Zhang and his men entered the embassy and had Li and his comrades hanged on the spot. Li was later proclaimed throughout China as a Communist martyr.

FRIDAY, APRIL 29

Two parishes in Louisiana were deliberately flooded in order to protect New Orleans, as a dynamite charge blasted the levee at Caernarvon. With the objective of relieving pressure from the Mississippi River on the larger city's flood walls, Governor Oramel H. Simpson obtained federal approval to evacuate residents, mostly African American farm families, of the parishes of St. Bernard and Plaquemines and then to destroy the flood wall.

The perennial song favorite "Side by Side" was recorded today by Paul Whiteman's Orchestra with vocals by the Rhythm Boys (Bing Crosby, Harry Barris, and Al Rinker). The freewheeling song about companionship was written by Harry MacGregor Woods, the composer of a handful of hits despite the fact that he had no fingers on his left hand. "Side by Side" was oft recorded throughout the Depression then enjoyed a revival in the 1950s with a disc by Frances Wayne.

Paramount had a surprise hit with its semi-documentary film *Chang: A Drama of the Wilderness*, which premiered today in New York. Directors Merian C. Cooper and Ernest B. Schoedsack went deep into the jungle of Northern Siam and followed the lives of the rice and cattle farmer Kru and his family as they struggled for survival. The family's major adversaries were the wild beasts that attacked them and their stock. The climax of the documentary is when a herd of angry elephants stampedes, trampling the family house and continuing on to destroy a nearby village. Cooper and Schoedsack had a script, and not everything in the movie was true documentary. Kru's wife was played by a local tribeswoman, some scenes were restaged if they were not effective enough, and the destructive climax was achieved by having baby elephants rampage through a miniature-sized village. On the other hand, none of the elephants, leopards, bears, and tigers were trained, and the filmmakers had to shoot footage at great peril and later fashion it into a story. *Chang: A Drama of the Wilderness* took eighteen months to film and was made under miserable conditions; it rained most of the time and codirector Cooper contracted malaria. Yet the resulting movie is a documentary triumph and one of the few films in the genre to be nominated for the Best Picture Academy Award.

SATURDAY, APRIL 30

One of the deadliest coal mining accidents in the history of American industry occurred today in Everettville, West Virginia, at the Federal No. 3 Coal Mine owned by the New England Fuel and Transportation Company. An explosion followed by a fire killed 111 coal miners with only a few survivors. It took two weeks to finally extinguish the fire and remove what bodies could be found.

Also today in West Virginia, the nation's first women's federal prison opened in Alderson. The Federal Industrial Institution for Women was built for women serving federal sentences of more than a year and was considered a model for prison reform at the time, offering activities such as farming, learning how to type and file, and cooking and canning vegetables and fruits. Because of its remote location, there were no high prison walls or armed guards. The first inmates, women prisoners from Vermont, arrived today. They were joined by another 174 women by the time the facility was formally opened on November 14, 1928. It continues today as the minimum-security Federal Prison Camp Alderson.

William Faulkner's second novel, *Mosquitoes*, was published by Boni & Liveright today. Set in the area around New Orleans, the novel centers on a four-day yacht excursion on Lake Pontchartrain. A group consisting of an artist, writer, art critic, three poets, a businessman, and a patroness of the arts are introduced in New Orleans, during the four days aboard the boat, and then in an epilogue once they return to the city. Though an early work, *Mosquitoes* already has many elements of Faulkner's style and themes. Critics at the time were not favorable in their opinions of the book, but once Faulkner became a major literary figure the novel was reexamined and better appreciated.

Starting a legendary tradition, Hollywood favorites Mary Pickford and Douglas Fairbanks Sr., became the first movie stars to put their handprints in cement at Grauman's Chinese Theater in Los Angeles, even though the movie palace would not open until May 18. There are different versions of how the tradition originated, most involving someone (owner Grauman, actress Norma Talmadge, construction foreman Jean Klosser, etc.) accidentally stepping into some wet cement. Today there are over two hundred footprints, handprints, and signatures in the courtyard in front of the movie palace. Also in film news, what is believed to be the first sound newsreel was introduced at the Roxy Theatre in New York by Fox Movietone News. The first four-minute installment of a series of news shorts showed cadets marching at the U.S. Military Academy.

German general Friedrich von Scholtz died today in Ballenstedt at the age of seventy-six. During the Great War he served as commander of the Twentieth Corps and the Eighth Army of the German Empire on the Eastern Front and later as commander of Army Group Scholtz on the Macedonian Front.

By 1927 there were over two thousand one hundred daily newspapers published in the United States. It is estimated they reached almost forty million readers.

MAY

SUNDAY, MAY 1

The Experimental Mechanised Force (EMF) was created today as a brigade of the British Army. It was the first military unit formed to research and develop better tanks and other weapons of armored warfare. The division was very controversial and pressure from the army and the navy forced the government to disband the program in 1929. Despite its brief existence, the EMF developed many mechanisms and ideas for armored vehicles that were used in World War II.

Imperial Airways, a British commercial company founded in 1924 that flew passengers from Great Britain to such far-flung destinations as South Africa and India, became the first airline in the United Kingdom to serve cooked meals onboard.

Henri Delaunay, a deputy on the board of the Fédération Internationale de Football Association, today proposed that the soccer football organization create the FIFA World Cup to honor the best senior men's national teams. The first such tournament was not held until 1930. Today the World Cup (as it is now called) is the most popular soccer tournament in the world and is viewed by more people than any other sporting event, even the Olympic Games.

Although the romantic melodrama *Lovers?* is lost today, it caused quite a ruckus in its day. It starred screen heartthrob Ramon Navarro and his frequent leading lady Alice Terry and was based on a popular Spanish play that was filmed before in 1920. Ernesto (Navarro) falls in love with Teodora (Terry), the wife of the diplomat Don Julian, causing a scandal in Madrid. Don Julian dies in a duel defending Teodora's honor, Ernesto is banished from Spain, and he and Teodora escape to Argentina. The Spanish government took offense at the way their country was portrayed in *Lovers?* so MGM promised to cut certain sections of the movie. But when the film was released today in New York and later in Europe without any of the guaranteed cuts, Spain banned all MGM films. The U.S. Department of State intervened, and all existing copies of *Lovers?* were destroyed. Film historians are still hoping a print has somehow survived because the reviews were favorable and the movie did very good business while it was available.

MONDAY, MAY 2

Today the winners of the Pulitzer Prizes in Letters and Drama were announced by Columbia University. The honorees were Louis Bromfield for his novel *Early Autumn*, Paul Green for his play *In Abraham's Bosom*, Samuel Flagg Briggs for his history book *Pinckney's Treaty*, Emory Holloway for his biography *Whitman*, and Leonora Speyer for her poetry collection *Fiddler's Farewell*.

An important and still controversial decision was made by the United States Supreme Court today. In the case of *Buck v. Bell*, Justice Oliver Wendell Holmes Jr. delivered the 8–1 majority opinion by the Court, upholding a Virginia law permitting compulsory sterilization of people with intellectual disability. The decision argued that "for the protection and health of the state," such actions did not violate the Due Process Clause of the Fourteenth Amendment to the United States Constitution. Holmes's tendentious conclusion to his decision was, "Three generations of imbeciles are enough." To this day, the Supreme Court has never expressly overturned *Buck v. Bell*.

Despite protests from the meat packing industry, the U.S. Department of Agriculture today began a one-year trial period of grading beef sold at retail. The designation of "choice" and "prime" grades were applied to those producers who requested the service. Although many in the industry prophesied that the program was unworkable, the one-year experiment was deemed a success and continued on, but on a voluntary basis. Mandatory grading of beef did not come until after World War II.

The International Economic Conference opened today in Geneva and continued for twenty-one days. Over fifty nations sent delegates to the conference to address international economic and trade issues. Sponsored by the League of Nations, the conference

THE SUPREME COURT

The Supreme Court Justices in 1927 and the year they were appointed:

William Howard Taft (1921)	Pierce Butler (1923)
Willis Van Devanter (1911)	George Sutherland (1922)
Oliver Wendell Holmes Jr. (1902)	Edward T. Sanford (1923)
James C. McReynolds (1914)	Harlan F. Stone (1925)
Louis D. Brandeis (1916)	

led to the Multilateral Trade Agreement, the most comprehensive and balanced international trade agreement approved to date. Although the United States was not a member of the League of Nations, it sent delegates to the conference.

The prominent British physiologist Ernest Starling died today of unknown causes on a boat off the coast of Jamaica at the age of sixty-one. Among Starling's many contributions to science were the first use of the word "hormone," the discovery of the hormone secretin, the Frank-Starling Law about how the heart pumps blood, information about how the kidney functions, and introduction of the science of endocrinology. Starling's textbook *Principles of Human Physiology* (1912) was often revised and went through twenty editions.

TUESDAY, MAY 3

When the British trawler *Gabriella* was stopped in New York harbor today, prohibition officials discovered 2,000 drums of alcohol valued at $1,200,000. It was the largest seizure of illegal goods in the U.S. up to that time.

The German aviator Ferdinand Scholtz set a record today for the longest time keeping a glider aloft. Without benefit of an engine, Scholtz was able to remain in the air fourteen hours and eight minutes.

Brother Major League Baseball pitchers Jesse and Virgil Barnes today found themselves in the unusual position of pitching against each other. The brothers had both played for the New York Giants between 1919 and 1923. Jesse Barnes now played for the Brooklyn Robins, and they faced each other in today's game, in which the Robins bested the Giants 7–6. A suspenseful game was played today between the Pittsburgh Pirates and the St. Louis Cardinals. The Pirates were behind until they scored a run in the eighth inning and two in the ninth to defeat the Cardinals 11–10. The victory moved the Pirates into an early season tie for first place in the National League.

Although it was butchered by the distributing company Pathé Pictures from ninety to forty-eight minutes and kept on the shelf for two years, Mack Sennett's comedy *His First Flame* is still a comic delight. It was the first feature-length movie starring the sad-faced comedian Harry Langdon, who had appeared in two dozen shorts. He played the naive and bumbling college grad Harry Howells, who falls in love with the striking beauty Ethel Morgan, but his woman-hating uncle, fire chief Amos McCarthy, proves to Harry that she is just a gold digger. Harry finds true love with Ethel's sweet sister Mary when he helps the fire brigade put out the flames at the Morgan home. Langdon's physical comedics throughout are superb and the truncated movie is still a joy to watch.

Broadway favorite Margaret Anglin was considered one of the finest actresses of tragedy on the New York stage and she proved it when she played the title role in Euripides's *Electra*. The Greek tragedy was presented for only two nights but was performed in the giant Metropolitan Opera House and quickly sold out. The press extolled Anglin's performance as well as the austere but riveting production. The producing Shubert Brothers offered one of their theatres for an open run of the production, but Anglin turned them down and went on to other projects.

Popular songwriter and performer Ernest Ball died today of unknown causes at the age of forty-eight, just minutes after he finished performing at the Yost Theatre in Santa Anna, California. Although he was not Irish, the prolific Ball wrote the music for some of the most beloved Irish-American ballads of all time, including "When Irish Eyes Are Smiling" and "Mother Macree," as well as such standards as "Will You Love Me in December as You Do in May?," "A Little Bit of Heaven," and "For Dixie and Uncle Sam." He began his career in vaudeville and was singing in his touring act "Ernie Ball and His Gang" when he died. Dick Haymes played Ball in the 1944 movie musical biography *Irish Eyes Are Smiling*.

WEDNESDAY, MAY 4

The former Mexican general Rodolfo Gallegos, who had joined the rebels in the state of Guanajuato, was shot dead today by pursuing federal forces at Los Organos. Gallegos had led an April 19 train robbery that massacred dozens of passengers.

British composer Gerald Finzi's Violin Concerto had its premiere today in London at the Queen's Hall with violinist Sybil Eaton and the British Women's Symphony Orchestra conducted by Malcolm Sargent. Critical reaction to the piece was not enthusiastic, and the concerto was not performed professionally again until 1999, when it was recognized as a superior piece of music.

Director Tod Browning, master of the macabre, and horror film favorite Lon Chaney reteamed for MGM's *The Unknown*, a classic tale of romance and freakishness. The armless knife thrower Alonzo (Chaney) works at the circus sideshow to hide from the police. He is a burglar who actually has arms but hides them because his deformed left hand is what the police are looking for. Alonzo loves Nanon (Joan Crawford), the daughter of the circus owner, Zanzi, and a romantic triangle develops with the evil strong man Malabar. Nanon has a phobia about being touched by any man, so Alonzo blackmails a surgeon into amputating his left arm. He then plots to kill Malabar during a circus performance, but Alonzo is trampled to death by one of the show horses. The armless Paul Desmuke was Chaney's double for the scenes in which Alonzo manipulates various objects with his mouth and torso but it is Chaney's powerful acting that carries the movie, his love and his vengeance both coming across as real and frightening. The only copies of *The Unknown* available were faded duplicates until a 35 mm print was located in Paris in 1968. Critics now rate the horror romance as a high point for both Browning and Chaney.

THURSDAY, MAY 5

To the Lighthouse, arguably Virginia Woolf's finest novel and certainly one of the great pieces of twentieth-century literature, was published today by the Hogarth Press in London. The novel, which relies on the characters' thoughts and reflections rather than dialogue, concerns members of the Ramsey family on two separate days. On the first day, the large Ramsey family and some guests are at a summer house on the Isle of Skye some years before World War I. Ten years later, after the war, some of the same characters are gathered at the same house and the differences in their outlook on life are explored. Tying the two days together is the talk of sailing a boat to the lighthouse on the first day and the actual ride finally happening on the second day. Woolf's prose has no one narrator but shifts point of view from character to character creating one of the most complex and revealing works of British fiction.

Because of the inflammatory nature of their gatherings and the incendiary quality of their speeches, the police banned the National Socialist German Workers' Party (Nationalsozialistische Deutsche Arbeiterpartei or NSDAP) from any activities in Berlin's metropolitan area.

French aviators Pierre de Saint-Roman and Hervé Mouneyres today attempted a transatlantic flight from Africa to South America but ended up on the list of many air casualties of 1927. The two flyers took off from Saint-Louis, Senegal, but never arrived in South America. Wreckage of an airplane believed to be theirs washed ashore in Brazil two months later.

FRIDAY, MAY 6

One of Hollywood's great tearjerkers, the romantic melodrama *7th Heaven* premiered today as a silent movie, but by the time it was distributed nationally in September it had sound effects and recorded music. It was the first teaming of Janet Gaynor and Charles Farrell, whose on-screen chemistry turned them into one of Hollywood's favorite couples; they went on to make ten films together. The story, based on an Austin Strong book and play, is about the Parisian sewer worker Chico (Farrell) and the beautiful but down-on-her-luck Diane (Gaynor), who is being chased by the police for a petty crime. Chico hides her from the cops, and the two fall in love. Although they have very little money, they wed and are happy in their seventh-floor apartment until Chico leaves to fight in the Great War. Diane patiently waits for him to return, then hears wrongly that Chico was killed in battle. Instead, he has been injured and is now blind. He manages to get back to Paris, where he and Diane are tearfully reunited. Beautifully filmed by Frank Borzage and with compelling performances by its two stars, *7th Heaven* was a major critical and commercial hit and put Fox Film Corporation in the Hollywood big

Besides being one of the most potent melodramas of its era, *7th Heaven* is notable for introducing one of Hollywood's favorite acting couples: Charles Farrell and Janet Gaynor. They played a struggling young married couple whose misfortunes did not leave a dry eye in the movie house. *Fox Film Corporation / Photofest © Fox Film Corporation*

leagues. The movie ended up earning $2.5 million, one of the top-grossing pictures of the decade. Also, Erno Rapee's recorded soundtrack score included a tune that was turned into the song "Diane" (lyric by Lew Pollock), which also became a bestseller in sheet music and records. Among the Academy Awards that *7th Heaven* later won in 1928 were Oscars for Gaynor, Borzage, and screenwriter Benjamin Glazer. The film was remade by 20th Century-Fox in 1937 with Simone Simon and James Stewart.

The Broadway singing comic Eddie Cantor, who had made his screen debut by reprising his stage hit *Kid Boots* in 1926, was the star of Paramount's *Special Delivery*. While silent movies could not capture Cantor's nasal voice and goofy singing, his pop-eyed expressions came across well. He plays mail carrier Eddie Beagle, who falls for the waitress Madge (Jobyna Ralston), whom he meets delivering mail at the diner Dutch Lunch. One of the regular customers at the diner who flirts with her is the suave stockbroker Harold Jones (William Powell), who turns out to be a racketeer. When Madge discovers the truth about him, Jones kidnaps her and it is up to Eddie to rescue her. Fatty Arbuckle, no longer allowed to appear on screen because of a past scandal, directed *Special Delivery* efficiently and it is a tight and funny little comedy.

SATURDAY, MAY 7

Chicago's 1910 ballpark Comiskey Park underwent an extensive addition in 1927 when both the left and right-field grandstands were expanded to include second tiers, thereby increasing the stadium's seating from thirty-two thousand to fifty-two thousand. During today's game between the New York Yankees and the Chicago White Sox, Yankee Lou Gehrig was the first player to hit a homer into the new right-field upper deck. Gehrig's ninth-inning grand slam helped the Yankees beat the White Sox 8–0. Comiskey Park was among several ballparks that expanded their seating in the late 1920s to accommodate the increased attendance at Major League Baseball games. This surge of interest began with the opening of Yankee Stadium in 1923 with its seating capacity of fifty-eight thousand.

The waterfront property Mills Field, a one-hundred-fifty-acre cow pasture located on the San Francisco Bay thirteen miles from the city's downtown, was dedicated today as Mills Field Municipal Airport in a ceremony headed by Mayor James Rolph Jr. The small airfield would be continually expanded over the decades and in 1954 was renamed San Francisco International Airport, today one of the busiest on the West Coast.

Great Britain's 1926–1927 soccer football season concluded today with Newcastle United as First Division champions.

MOST POPULOUS AMERICAN STATES

The six American states with the highest population in 1927:

New York (12.4 million)
Pennsylvania (9.5 million)
Illinois (7.5 million)

Ohio (6.4 million)
Texas (5.6 million)
California (5.5 million)

Two action adventure films opened today; one cost a bundle and lost it all, the other was made on a budget but was a box office hit. Cecil B. DeMille produced (but did not direct) *The Yankee Clipper* as a product of DeMille Pictures Corporation. Tensions between America and Great Britain are illustrated by a Yankee Clipper ship and a British vessel in a sea race from China to Boston to see which nation will get the lucrative Chinese tea trade. The American Captain Winslow (William Boyd) finds that a youth and a beautiful lady have stowed away onboard, adding complications and romance, while the clipper is also beset with a mutiny, a typhoon, and a shortage of drinking water. Winslow wins the race and the girl, which was of less importance than all the action scenes along the journey. One can see where all the money went, but when the film did only modest business DeMille's company floundered and then folded a few years later. Warner Brothers, on the other hand, had a much-needed hit with its adventure movie, *Tracked by the Police*, thanks to its canine star, Rin Tin Tin. In the parched Arizona desert, rival companies are trying to get contracts to build the Laguna Dam. The losing company attempts to sabotage the dam when it is completed, but Bob Owen (Jason Robards Sr.) and his German shepherd Satan (Rin Tin Tin) save the dam and catch the culprits after a thrilling train chase. The movie is often farfetched and even silly (Satan knows which levers to pull to stop the water flowing), but audiences loved Rin Tin Tin and *Tracked by the Police* made enough money to let Warners invest more money in its Vitaphone process and make *The Jazz Singer*.

SUNDAY, MAY 8

The French aviator Charles Nungesser, a decorated flyer from World War I considered Charles Lindbergh's chief rival in long-distance flying, today set off from Paris with navigator Captain François Coli in the Levasseur biplane *L'oiseau blanc* (The white bird) in an attempt to make the first nonstop airplane flight from Paris to New York, thereby winning the Orteig Prize of $25,000. The plane never arrived and was last seen approaching Cape Race, Newfoundland, at ten o'clock the next morning, still one thousand miles short of their destination. The *L'oiseau blanc*, Nungesser, and Coli were never found.

Virginia Woolf's short story "The New Dress" appeared in the May edition of *The Forum*, a New York journal. The story follows the thoughts of Londoner Mabel Waring as she attends a party given by Clarissa Dalloway and her insecurity as she sees herself in a mirror and realizes her new dress is all wrong. The story is believed to have been written as part of the novel *Mrs. Dalloway* in 1925 but was cut from the final version. *The New Dress* was later published in *A Haunted House and Other Stories* (1944).

The Denver oil mogul and philanthropist Colonel A. E. Humphreys, known as the King of the Wildcatters after discovering oil deposits in Texas, Wyoming, and Oklahoma, accidentally shot and killed himself today while packing his guns for a hunting trip. Rumors still circulate that the shotgun wound to the head was not an accident but suicide because Humphreys was about to be implicated in the Teapot Dome Scandal.

MONDAY, MAY 9

The sensational "Dumb-Bell Murder" trial ended today when a jury convicted Ruth Snyder and her lover-accomplice Judd Gray of the March 20 murder of her husband, Albert Snyder. The two were sentenced to death by electric chair. When Ruth Snyder was electrocuted on January 12, 1928, she was the first woman to be executed in Sing Sing prison since 1899. A photo of her moment of death was secretly taken by news photographer Tom Howard and published the next day in the *New York Daily News*.

> Although it was less than seven years old, by 1927 the *Daily News* had the largest circulation of all the New York City newspapers: 1,082,976 readers.

For over two decades there had been arguments in Australia over which of the country's two largest cities, Sydney or the current capital Melbourne, should be the capital city. In 1908 it was decided to create a new capital city that, like Washington, D.C., was independent and not part of any province. Construction of the planned, inland city of Canberra began in 1913 and today the Australian Parliament officially moved from Melbourne to its new Parliament House in Canberra. The Duke of York (future King George VI) opened Parliament after being introduced by Prime Minister Stanley Bruce. The opening was a pivotal moment for the duke who suffered from extreme stammering. But after working with Australian therapist Lionel Logue to help overcome his speech difficulties, the duke was able to deliver a brief speech without embarrassment.

Although it was written in 1926 by Roy Turk and Lou Handman, the song standard "Are You Lonesome Tonight?" was first recorded today by Charles Hart for Harmony Records. It was a version recorded by Vaughn De Leath on June 13 that made the song popular and it remained a favorite for decades. Of the many recordings over the years, none was more successful than an Elvis Presley version in 1960.

A series of tornadoes swept through six states in the south-central United States today, leaving over eight hundred people dead. Hardest hit was the town of Poplar Bluff, Missouri, where ninety-three people perished.

The sport of snooker, a form of billiards developed by British officers in India in the nineteenth century, became so popular in Britain in the twentieth century that various amateur competitions were held in different cities. The first professional competition, called the World Snooker Championship, concluded today in Birmingham, England. Professional billiards player Joe Davis won the competition that first year and every year until 1941, when the championship was suspended during World War II.

One of Edith Wharton's lesser-known novels, *Twilight Sleep*, published this month by D. Appleton & Company, remains a noteworthy satirical novel of the 1920s and a vivid record of such current topics as drugs, sexual mores, spiritualism, and the obsession with making money. The rich socialite and divorcee Pauline Manford fills her life with social committees, cosmetic treatments, making speeches, conferring with her guru, and entertaining and has little time for her husband, the ambitious lawyer Dexter, or her grown children. With unhappy marriages, futile efforts to find meaning in their lives, and unfulfilled dreams, the Manford family is imploding and Pauline's efforts to save everyone fail. *Twilight Sleep* was lauded by the press when it first came out and was very popular at the time but over the years has not remained as well known as several of Wharton's other novels.

TUESDAY, MAY 10

All eyes were on Detroit Tigers legend Ty Cobb today when he made his first appearance with the Philadelphia Athletics. The overflow crowd of thirty thousand packed Detroit's Navin Field to see Cobb play against his former teammates. In the first inning,

During his twenty-two years with the Detroit Tigers, outfielder Ty Cobb set ninety Major League Baseball records, including total runs, runs batted in, highest career batting average, at bats, stolen bases, batting titles, and career hits. Cobb found himself wearing a new uniform in 1927, when he played for the Philadelphia Athletics for two years before closing out his remarkable career. He is pictured here with Baseball Commissioner Judge Kenesaw Mountain Landis. *Photofest © Photofest*

with Eddie Collins on base, Cobb hit a double into the crowd and sent Collins home for the first run of the game. The Athletics went on to get five more runs, beating the Tigers 6–3.

Robert Lowery's popular hymn "Shall We Gather at the River?," which had been sung by church choirs since the 1860s, was recorded today by the Dixie Sacred Singers on the Vocalion label.

Andrea Gram, one of the greatest Norwegian artists of the late nineteenth and early twentieth centuries, died today in Stockholm at the age of seventy-four. She was best known for her portraits and her Scandinavian landscapes.

WEDNESDAY, MAY 11

The Academy of Motion Picture Arts & Sciences was officially incorporated today. The organization was the idea of MGM head producer Louis B. Mayer, who saw the Academy as an exclusive club of producers, actors, writers, technicians, and directors from different studios who would meet to deal with labor disputes within the movie industry. At that meeting, actor Douglas Fairbanks Sr. was elected as the first president of the Academy and actor-director-producer Fred Niblo was named first vice president. The Academy also bestowed its first honorary membership to Thomas Edison. The organization that night listed 230 members. It would not begin giving out awards until 1929.

> Moviegoing reached its peak attendance in 1927. There were 21,660 movie theatres nationwide and Hollywood produced 743 films for a record attendance figure of fifty-seven million. Radio and then the Depression would be major factors in a gradual decline in moviegoing thereafter.

Charles Lindbergh started to get some media attention today when he flew his plane *Spirit of St. Louis* overnight from San Diego and landed in St. Louis fourteen hours later. Because Lindbergh was the only entrant in the Orteig competition who planned to fly from New York to Paris without a copilot, the press labeled him "The Foolish Flyer." Yet the flight from San Diego set two new records: the first flight over the Rocky Mountains at night and the longest nonstop solo flight undertaken by an American.

It was the second day in a row for a baseball favorite to play against his former team for the first time. Second baseman Rogers Hornsby, who had played for the St. Louis Cardinals since 1915, was in his first season with the New York Giants. Today at the Polo Grounds, future Hall of Famer Hornsby hit a home run and five RBIs to give the Giants a 10–1 victory over the Cardinals.

Lillian Gish was the star of *Annie Laurie*, an MGM film set in the Scottish Highlands that was filled with action and romance. While the Scottish clans of Campbell and Macdonald are at war with each other, the Campbell chieftain tries to act as mediator and bring peace to the battling tribes. But all the forces of hatred are against him and the fighting intensifies. His daughter Annie Laurie (Gish) is in love with Ian Macdonald, but their romance is threatened by vengeance, kidnapping, and killing. The finale of the movie was filmed in an early form of Technicolor and the film cost a bundle to make. The box office take was modest and the studio lost a lot of money on the project. *Annie Laurie* is more highly esteemed today, particularly for Gish's performance and the impressive battle scenes.

The Spanish painter and sculptor Juan Gris, a pioneer in the Cubism movement, died today in Paris from cardiac and renal failure at the age of forty. He spent most of his artistic career in France where he developed "Crystal Cubism," the use of many geometric forms put together to make bold and impressionistic works of art.

THURSDAY, MAY 12

London's Scotland Yard police today raided the offices of the Soviet trade delegation, ARCOS (the All Russian Co-operative Society), looking for evidence of Russian espionage. Telephone lines were cut, the building was sealed, and the company's six hundred employees detained while the British police searched for and found top-secret documents that allegedly had been stolen from the War Office. The raid was considered a breach of the 1921 trade agreement with Russia, which had given diplomatic immunity to official trade agents of the USSR. Tensions between Great Britain and the Soviet Union were already major and this latest development heightened fears of war between the two countries. Today's raid would later result in severing diplomatic relations between the two governments.

Electrical inventor Philip F. Labre today applied for a patent for his "grounding receptacle and plug." In order to reduce electrical shock as a result of a short circuit, Labre added a third ground prong to the plug to be inserted into a third hole in the socket. The patent was granted in June of 1928 and Labre's three-pronged plug is still in use today.

FRIDAY, MAY 13

Postwar Germany, still struggling from the economic fallout from the Great War, today suffered another setback, which became known as "Black Friday" on the Berlin Stock Exchange. After a year of slow but steady growth, the equity market in Germany collapsed after Reichsbank president Hjalmar Schacht had attempted to stop price speculation by cutting advances to brokers. Instead, the Friday-the-thirteenth price drop ruined many businesses, and personal fortunes were lost. In essence, the Great Depression in Germany began on this day.

The first cricket match of the season for the Hampshire team was played today at Southampton against the Leicestershire team. The game was of particular interest to spectators because of Hampton cricketer Phil Mead, who was at the peak of his powers and the height of his popularity. Mead was arguably the greatest cricket player of his era. His career stretched from 1905 to 1936, during which time the left-handed batsman broke many records. He scored the most runs in the County Championship and the fourth-highest total in all first-class matches. For Hampshire he made 48,892 runs, the greatest number any batsman has scored for a single team. Mead also had over 1,000 runs in every season of first-class cricket except for his first, when he played in only one match. He was also a superior fieldsman, holding 675 catches. Mead was forty years old in 1927 and had an astonishing season on the Hampshire team.

SATURDAY, MAY 14

The Kentucky Derby, the first leg of the Triple Crown in thoroughbred horse racing, was held today for the fifty-third time at Churchill Downs in Louisville, Kentucky. Jockey Linus McAtee rode Whiskery to victory with a time of 2:06.

During a Major League Baseball game today at the Baker Bowl in Philadelphia between the Phillies and the St. Louis Cardinals, tragedy struck. After six innings, the Phillies were leading 12–3 and the Cardinals had one out in the seventh inning when the right field bleachers collapsed without warning. One man died of heart failure during the rush of the crowd that followed and some fifty spectators were injured. The collapse was blamed on rotted shoring timbers. The Phillies moved the rest of their games for the season to the Philadelphia Athletics' home field, Shibe Park, while the Baker Bowl was repaired and restructured.

With his name cleared of any wrongdoing and back in Major League Baseball, center fielder Tris Speaker was now playing for the Washington Senators. In his first game against his old team, the Cleveland Indians, Speaker was held hitless by pitcher George Uhle in four at bats. All the same, the Senators won the game 5–2.

While Charles Lindbergh and the *Spirit of St. Louis* were waiting at Roosevelt Field on Long Island for fair weather for his transatlantic crossing, his mother, Evangeline Lindbergh, arrived from Detroit to bid her son farewell and good luck. Lindbergh had risen in popularity since breaking records for his solo flight from St. Louis to New York, so plenty of reporters and photographers were on hand to capture what they hoped would be an emotional moment. They were greatly disappointed. Mother and son remained stone-faced as they shook hands and posed stiffly for photographs. When asked by a photographer to embrace for the camera, they refused, Mrs. Lindbergh explaining that they were from "an undemonstrative Nordic race." The *Evening Graphic* was not deterred. They photographed two clinching models and pasted the Lindberghs' emotionless faces onto the bodies for a cover picture in that night's edition. The press was beginning to find out that Charles Lindbergh was shy and reticent in public, something that would not change much even after he became the most famous man in the world.

Polish composer Karol Szymanowski's String Quartet no. 2, op. 56 was first performed today by the Warsaw String Quartet but aroused little interest. It was a performance in Paris a few months later that brought renown to the piece. In popular music, Ben Bernie's recording of "Ain't She Sweet," by Jack Yellen and Milton Ager, hit the number one spot on the singles chart today.

Paramount's romantic comedy *Rough House Rosie* is a lost Clara Bow film. Because it was based on a Nunnally Johnson magazine story, we know the plot: mischief-making Rosie Reilly (Bow) turns everything she tries into a comic disaster. When Rosie decides to go on the stage, she gets mixed up with some shady characters and finds herself in jail. When she tries to break into the upper-crust set, mayhem results. But when she is smitten with boxer Joe Hennessey, Rosie's seductive eyes and flashy smile distract Joe's opponent and Hennessey is the new champ.

SUNDAY, MAY 15

The bloody and controversial civil war in Nicaragua came to an end today. The Nicaraguan president, Adolfo Díaz, had requested President Coolidge to supervise elections that would be "free, fair, and impartial and not open to fraud or intimidation." U.S. envoy Henry L. Stimson acted as the intermediary for Díaz and approached the rebel leader José María Moncada. Today at Tipitapa, Nicaragua, Moncada agreed to the terms and his troops disarmed themselves. Election plans were made, and the voting took place in October of 1928, with Moncada winning the presidency.

MONDAY, MAY 16

The U.S. Supreme Court today ruled that criminals (including bootleggers) must pay income tax on their stolen property or face tax evasion charges. The case, *United States v. Sullivan*, presents a ruling that may seem laughable and impossible to enforce, for how many criminals are going to declare their profits to the Internal Revenue Service? Yet it was this ruling that finally brought down Al Capone in 1931.

New York Yankee outfielder Bob Meusel managed to steal second, third, and home all in one game today when the Yankees bested the Detroit Tigers 6–2. Meusel stole twenty-four bases for the season. In St. Louis's Sportsman's Park, forty-year-old Ty Cobb hit a home run in the seventh inning of a game in which his team, the Philadelphia Athletics, beat the St. Louis Browns 10–8. Since Cobb had hit his first Major League Baseball homer in 1905, he became the first player in history to hit home runs before his twentieth birthday and after his fortieth birthday.

The beloved comic actor Sam Bernard died today of apoplexy while on an ocean liner soon after departing from New York for Europe. He was sixty-four years old. The English-born entertainer grew up in the States and started out as a vaudeville comedian. Eventually Bernard starred on Broadway in comedies, musicals, and comic operettas, and he even made some silent films for the Triangle Film Corporation.

Today, six months after the death of French artist Claude Monet, a pair of oval rooms at the Musée de l'Orangerie in Paris displaying eight of his large paintings of water lilies were opened to the public. The rooms were designed as a permanent home for the paintings, which were lit by indirect natural light, as was intended by the artist. In 2006, the water lily paintings were moved to a similarly designed gallery on the upper floor of the Orangerie.

WORKS OF ART

Some notable art works completed or first exhibited in 1927:

Ansel Adams's photographic portfolio *Parmelian Prints of the High Sierras*

Ernst Barlach's bronze sculpture *Der schwebende Engel* (The floating angel)

Edwin Blashfield's painting *Spring Scattering Stars*

Pompeo Coppini's bronze sculpture *George Washington* (Portland, Oregon)

Salvador Dalí's painting *Apparatus and Hand*

Salvador Dalí's painting *Honey Is Sweeter Than Blood*

Salvador Dalí's painting *Three Figures*

Max Ernst's painting *Forest and Dove*

Max Ernst's painting *The Wood*

George Grosz's painting *Self-Portrait, Warning*

Edward Hopper's painting *Automat*

Edward Hopper's painting *Coast Guard Station, Two Lights, Maine*

Edward Hopper's painting *Drug Store*

Edward Hopper's painting *Two on the Aisle*

Karl Illava's bronze sculpture *107th Infantry Memorial* (Central Park, New York City)

Paul Klee's painting *Fish People*

Gaston Lachaise's bronze sculpture *Floating Figure*

Fernand Léger's painting *Nude on a Red Background*

Will Longstaff's painting *Menin Gate at Midnight*

L. S. Lowry's painting *Coming Out of School*

L. S. Lowry's painting *Dwelling, Orsdell Lane, Salford*

René Magritte's painting *The Enchanted Pose*

René Magritte's painting *The Menaced Assassin*

René Magritte's painting *One Museum Night*

René Magritte's painting *The Tiredness of Life*

Henri Matisse's bronze sculpture *Reclining Nude II*

Anne Marie Carl-Nielsen's bronze *Equestrian Statue of King Christian IX of Denmark* (Christiansborg Palace, Copenhagen)

Antonio Sciortino's bronze sculpture *Great Siege Monument* (Malta)

Lasar Segall's painting *Portrait of Mário de Andrade*

Charles Sheeler's photograph *Criss-Crossed Conveyors, River Rouge Plant, Ford Motor Company*

Stanley Spencer's painting *The Resurrection, Cookham*

Lajos Tihanyi's painting *Portrait of Tristan Tzara*

Henry Scott Tuke's painting *The Critics*

Rex Whistler's mural *The Expedition in Pursuit of Rare Meats* (Tate Gallery restaurant, London)

See April 21 for museums that opened in 1927.

TUESDAY, MAY 17

American aviator Lloyd W. Bertaud and his copilot, Clarence D. Chamberlin, were scheduled to take off today in the *Columbia* from Roosevelt Field for Paris in their attempt to win the Orteig Prize of $25,000. But arguments over demands and details with Charles A. Levine, owner of the plane and primary backer of the project, canceled the flight.

The town of Melville, Louisiana, with a population of 1,028 citizens, was washed away today when a levee on the Atchafalaya River collapsed. The town and its levee were later rebuilt and the population today is still around one thousand people.

In the longest Major League Baseball game of the season, the Chicago Cubs today beat the Boston Braves 4–3. It took them twenty-two innings to do so. The Cubs had twenty hits and the Braves fifteen in the marathon game, with future Hall-of-Famer Hack Wilson knocking in two of the Cubs' runs.

The aviation pioneer Major Harold Geiger died today when the Airco DH.4 de Havilland plane he was piloting crashed at Olmstead Field in Pennsylvania. He was forty-two years old. After graduating from the U.S. Military Academy in 1908, Geiger was one of the first to experiment with Army balloons and dirigibles before commanding historic airplane maneuvers for the military. At the time of his death, he was commandant of Phillips Air Field in Maryland.

WEDNESDAY, MAY 18

The deadliest act of mass murder at a school in American history to date, the Bath School disaster, occurred today in Bath Township, Michigan. Thirty-six schoolchildren and five adults were killed and dozens injured by dynamite charges placed underneath the school. The perpetrator was Andrew Kehoe, a local farmer who had served as treasurer of the township school board for a time. Kehoe planted the bombs under both the north and south wings of the school building, set to go off when 260 students and teachers were inside. He set a two-minute timer for each bomb then drove away in his truck. The explosives under the north wing detonated but a short circuit in one of the wires in the second bomb prevented the destruction of the south wing. It was soon discovered that Kehoe had murdered his wife earlier in the day and blew up his house and farm, killing all his livestock. About a half hour after the blast at the school went off, Kehoe killed himself and three other people by detonating a car bomb while sitting in his Ford truck. The site of the school today is the Bath School Memorial Park.

An earthquake in Gros Ventre, Wyoming, in 1925 formed a natural dam and created Slide Lake. Today a portion of the dam failed, creating a powerful flood that was six feet deep for at least twenty-five miles downstream. Six miles from the dam, the small town of Kelly was washed away, killing six people.

Cecil B. DeMille's biblical epic film *The King of Kings* premiered in Los Angeles today, marking the opening of the famous Grauman's Chinese Theatre. Both film and theatre were lavish and spectacular and audiences and critics were impressed with each. Sid Grauman, who had dazzled the public with Grauman's Egyptian Theatre in 1922, outdid himself with this nine-hundred-seat movie palace that featured bright colors in an elaborate Chinese design, giant dragons, oversized dogs acting as guardians, and its copper pagoda-like roof. The theatre today is known for the footprints, handprints, and signatures of stars in the concrete blocks in front of the entrance, a tradition that goes back to April 30, 1927. *The King of Kings* was also made on a large and grandiose scale. It was the second movie in producer-director DeMille's biblical trilogy, which began with *The Ten Commandments* (1923) and concluded with *The Sign of the Cross* (1934). All three embellished on the Bible versions and added lively new characters and scenes but were basically very reverent. *King of Kings* follows the life of Christ (H. B. Warner) during the last few weeks of his life, using the courtesan Mary Magdalene (Jacqueline Logan) as the thread to unite the story. The screenplay begins with her curiosity to seek out the carpenter she's heard about, and near the end of the film she asks forgiveness as God sends an earthquake and shows his wrath. The final scene, in which Jesus returns to the apostles after the resurrection, was shot in a two-color Technicolor, which was very impressive. (The opening credits and the first scene are also in color.) Many of the titles used throughout *King of Kings* come directly from the Bible, but it was veteran actress-writer Jeanie Macpherson who scripted the entire movie, which ran two hours and thirty-five minutes. It remains one of the best silent extravaganzas of the 1920s.

One of the many spectacular movie premieres at Grauman's Chinese Theatre in Los Angeles is captured here. Because of the signed foot- and handprints in the sidewalk in front, Grauman's is still a favorite tourist destination in Hollywood. *Photofest © Photofest*

MGM's 1961 epic *King of Kings* was not a remake but a film about the entire life of Christ (Jeffrey Hunter) although similarities could not be avoided.

Ernest Hemingway's short story "Italy—1927" was published in today's issue of the *New Republic*. Set in Fascist Italy two years after Benito Mussolini came to power, the tale relates a ten-day journey by two Americans that is marred by bad weather, lousy food, and unfriendly villagers. Retitled "Che ti dice la Patria?," the story was included in the Hemingway anthology *Men without Women* published in October.

The Ritz-Carlton Hotel opened in Boston today, an eighteen-story building designed by Strickland, Blodget & Law Architects. Room rates were $5 to $15 per night; $40 for suites. The three-hundred-room hotel had a strict dress code, did not allow unaccompanied women to dine in the restaurant, and checked names to see if they were in the Social Register before allowing guests to stay there. For many years, the Ritz-Carlton was considered the epitome of Boston snobbery and conservatism.

HOTELS

Some notable hotels and historic buildings that are now hotels that opened in 1927 (current names are used; * = still in operation):

Ace Hotel Downtown* (Los Angeles)
Astor House Hotel (Shanghai)
Barbazon Hotel for Women (New York City)
Berkeley City Club* (Berkeley, California)
Bonneville Hotel* (Idaho Falls)
Boston Park Plaza* (Boston)
The Carling Hotel (Chicago)
Casa Loma Hotel* (Tulsa)
Cassadaga Hotel & Psychic Center* (Cassadaga, Florida)
Cavalier Hotel* (Virginia Beach)
Chicago Hilton and Towers* (Chicago)
Crescent Hotel* (Beverly Hills)
DeWitt Clinton Hotel* (Albany)
Edgewater Hotel* (Winter Park, Florida)
Floridian Palace Hotel* (Tampa)
Fountain at La Hacienda Hotel* (New Port Richey, Florida)
Gage Hotel* (Marathon, Texas)
Garden of Allah Hotel (West Hollywood)
Grand Hotel Bohemia* (Prague)
Heathman Hotel* (Portland, Oregon)
Hollywood Historic Hotel* (Hollywood)
Hollywood Melrose Hotel* (Hollywood)
Hollywood Roosevelt Hotel* (Hollywood)
Hotel Kankakee (Kankakee, Illinois)
Hotel Monte Vista (Flagstaff, Arizona

Hotel New Grand* (Yokohama)
Hotel Principe di Savoia* (Milan)
Lake Lure Inn* (Lake Lure, North Carolina)
Lincoln Hotel (New York City)
Majestic Yosemite Hotel* (Yosemite Park, California)
The Mark* (New York City)
May Fair Hotel* (London)
Mayflower Park Hotel* (Seattle)
Millennium Knickerbocker Hotel* (Chicago)
Oasis at Death Valley* (Death Valley National Park)
The Parker House* (Boston)
Prince of Wales Hotel* (Waterton National Park, Alberta)
Ritz-Carlton Hotel* (Boston)
Riverside Hotel (Reno)
Royal Hawaiian Hotel* (Honolulu)
Savoy-Plaza Hotel (New York City)
Sherry-Netherland Hotel* (New York City)
Sofia Hotel* (San Diego)
Sprucewold Lodge* (Boothbay Harbor, Maine)
Taj Boston* (Boston)
Talbot Hotel* (Chicago)
Wyndham Duisburger Hof* (Duisburg, Germany)

The influential American dancer and choreographer Maurice Mouvet died today of tuberculosis at the age of thirty-eight in Lausanne, Switzerland. Internationally known simply as "Maurice," he was famous for introducing the sensual Apache dance and his own form of the tango in nightclubs, ballrooms, and theatres.

THURSDAY, MAY 19

Considered the first and still one of the best aviation movies, the World War I drama *Wings* was shown for the first time at the Texas Theatre in San Antonio before its New York City premiere in August. Much of the action-romance-war movie was filmed in and around San Antonio and director William Wellman, a veteran flyer from the Great War, offered his film to be shown to the locals first. The plot centered on small-town youths Jack Powell (Charles "Buddy" Rogers) and David Armstrong (Richard Arlen), who are rivals for the hand of Sylvia Lewis (Jobyna Ralston) and do not notice Mary Preston (Clara Bow), who is in love with Jack. When America enters the war, both men enlist and train together to be pilots with their new friend Cadet White (Gary Cooper). But David and Jack's illusions about glory are shattered when White dies in a plane crash during training. The two rivals become friends and are shipped off to France, and Mary also goes to Europe as an ambulance driver. She encounters Jack on leave in Paris, and he is so drunk she tries to put him to bed in his hotel room, only to be accused of prostitution by two MPs and sent back to the States. During the battle of Saint-Mihiel, David's plane is shot down behind enemy lines. He survives the crash and steals a German biplane to attempt to fly it back to his base but is gunned down by Jack, who thinks it is an enemy attack. Jack is proud of his feat until he finds out that it was David flying the plane. On his deathbed, David forgives the distraught Jack. Returning home a hero, Jack is still in grief and begs forgiveness from David's parents for accidentally killing their son. The Armstrongs blame the war, not Jack, and Mary is reunited with Jack, who finally realizes he loves her. *Wings* is outstanding cinema in all aspects, from the riveting acting to the breathtaking aerial photography. The film gave "It" girl Bow a substantial and serious role to play, and Cooper became a star even though his time on screen was brief. Yet the real star of *Wings* was Wellman, who practically invented the way to film air combat with this movie. He also came up with ingenious shots, such as the tracking of the troops, the aerial point of view of the pilots, and a stunning boom shot in which the camera seems to float through a crowded restaurant to focus on an inebriated Rogers. When the first Academy Awards were presented in 1929, *Wings* won the Best Picture Oscar, the only movie from the silent era to do so. The film cost about $2 million and took nine months to shoot but was a major hit at the box office. Despite its popularity, *Wings* was practically lost for a time, as the original negative was in such poor condition and copies were fading. *Wings* was meticulously restored in 1992 and has proven to be one of the American cinema's greatest accomplishments.

In London, the musical revue *One Damn Thing after Another* offered a score by the American songwriters Richard Rodgers (music) and Lorenz Hart (lyrics) but the rest

The first movie to win the Academy Award for Best Picture, *Wings* remains a cinema masterwork and still one of the best films about World War I. Shown here is airman Jack Powell (Charles "Buddy" Rogers) discovering that he has unknowingly shot down his best friend. *Paramount Pictures / Photofest © Paramount Pictures*

of the show was decidedly British. Jessie Matthews, London's favorite musical star, led the talented cast. The reviews were mixed, but audiences kept the show on the boards for thirty weeks. The score included the lovely ballad "My Lucky Star," but the hit of the revue was the beguiling "My Heart Stood Still." The song was soon all over town and became a particular favorite of Edward, the Prince of Wales. When he requested the orchestra to play it at a social gathering and the conductor didn't know the song, the Prince hummed the whole melodic line and the musicians joined in. *One Damn Thing after Another* did not transfer to Broadway, so Rodgers and Hart added "My Heart Stood Still" to their next New York show, *A Connecticut Yankee*.

After days of miserable weather out at Roosevelt Field, Wright Corporation's publicity head Richard Blythe suggested to Charles Lindbergh that they go into New York City and see the Broadway musical hit *Rio Rita* to take his mind off of the endless waiting. Blythe and Lindbergh arrived in Manhattan, but, before going into the Ziegfeld Theatre, Lindbergh made a telephone call to check on the weather forecast. The report said the skies over the ocean were clearing and the next day's weather looked promising. Lindbergh immediately returned to Long Island to make preparations and get some sleep at his hotel in Garden City. As it turned out, he didn't get a wink of sleep.

FRIDAY, MAY 20

The runway at Roosevelt Field was soft and muddy from the many days of rain, but the sky was clearing. Giving up any hope of sleeping, Charles Lindbergh left his hotel and by dawn was at the field. The fuel-heavy *Spirit of St. Louis* started down the runway at 7:52 a.m. but had difficulty leaving the ground. Finally, it gained altitude on the third try, just barely clearing some telephone wires near the end of the field. The *Spirit of St. Louis*, carrying a 5,150-pound load, banked to the left and headed north and out of sight to those gathered at the field. Because of the last-minute decision to begin the flight today, there were not many reporters on hand to see him off. But as soon as Lindbergh was on his way, word spread. Across New England and Nova Scotia many people watched the skies to view the plane passing overhead. Even the proceedings in Congress were interrupted by periodic reports of where Lindbergh was last spotted. Once the plane headed out to sea from Newfoundland there was no more visual communication. At the earliest, the *Spirit of St. Louis* might be spotted over Ireland in sixteen hours. The plane had no radio; Lindbergh thought it useless and excess weight. Excitement over the flight increased as the day went by. For months, the young unknown airmail flyer had been the long shot in the Orteig race, but as the more famous aviators literally dropped out of the running, Lindbergh was now the lone contestant. Yet lack of competition does not diminish his achievement that day. Lindbergh was an expert flyer but it probably took more will power to stay awake and alert than it took piloting skills. Where Lindbergh's genius lay was in his navigational skills. All long-distant fliers had a navigator on board to try and calculate where the plane was according to charts and estimates. Lindbergh did it alone using "dead reckoning" with a compass and a record of speed and time elapsed. Most flyers over large bodies of water reach landfall dozens if not hundreds of miles off course and then use land features to get to their destination. Lindbergh's navigational skills were such that he reached Ireland in the dark at the point where he had calculated. The same with Cap de la Hague in France. Soon he saw ahead the lights of Paris but did not know where the landing field of Le Bourget was located. So, he circled the city and noticed lines of light stretched out to one location. They were the headlights of ten thousand cars trying to get to Le Bourget to greet him. Thirty-three hours, thirty minutes, and twenty-nine seconds after lifting off in America, Lindbergh landed in France at 10:22 p.m. Paris time.

The Treaty of Jeddah was signed today between the United Kingdom and Sultan Ibn Saud, giving independence to what was then known as the Kingdom of Hejaz and Nejd. In the treaty, Saud agreed to cease the attacks on the adjacent British protectorates. In 1932, Nejd and Hejaz were joined and renamed Saudi Arabia by King Ibn Saud, the new nation's first monarch.

The American entrepreneur J. Willard Marriott started his rise to fame and fortune today not in the hotel business but with a nine-stool A&W Root Beer franchise in Washington, D.C. Marriott would eventually have a chain of A&W restaurants in several states. Not until 1957 did he branch out into hotels and found the worldwide Marriott Hotel chain.

SATURDAY, MAY 21

It was 5:21 p.m. in New York City when Charles Lindbergh landed the *Spirit of St. Louis* in Paris, and word reached America within minutes. The jubilation on both sides of the Atlantic was overwhelming. On the field at Le Bourget, thousands rushed the runway and swarmed around Lindbergh and his plane, carrying him away on their shoulders while others tore off pieces from the *Spirit of St. Louis* as souvenirs. Some control was finally maintained, and two French aviators rescued Lindbergh from being hurt, though his jacket, belt, and other items of clothing were stolen or ripped. It took

Charles Lindbergh poses on May 31, 1927, in front of the *Spirit of St. Louis*, a plane he codesigned and was as proud of as he was of winning the Orteig Prize. Today the *Spirit of St. Louis* is on display with another aviation treasure, the 1903 Wright Flyer, at the Smithsonian in Washington, D.C. *Courtesy of the Library of Congress, LC-USZ62-22847*

hours to get the dazed American to the U.S. Embassy in Paris, where he spoke with English-speaking reporters even though he had been up for sixty hours. After a brief hot bath, Lindbergh finally went to bed and slept for ten hours. In America, extra editions of newspapers came off the press as quickly as possible as church bells chimed and people celebrated in the streets. President Coolidge announced that June 11 would be Charles Lindbergh Day across America. Such excitement over one man was unprecedented. And it was just beginning.

The Preakness Stakes, the second jewel of thoroughbred horse racing's Triple Crown, was run today for the fifty-second time at the Pimlico Racetrack in Baltimore, Maryland. It was won by jockey Whitey Abel aboard Bostonian with the time 2:01.6.

In today's Major League Baseball game against the Chicago Cubs, the Brooklyn Robins used five different pitchers just in the eighth inning. That was a tie in the MLB record book at the time.

SUNDAY, MAY 22

The Gulang earthquake that rocked the Kansu Province of China today has been variously calculated as between 7.6 and 8.3 magnitude. The estimated number of fatalities is also variable, ranging from forty thousand to two hundred thousand. What is known is that 90 percent of the city of Gulang was leveled, a fourteen-mile fissure was created, and that the earthquake was felt over four hundred miles away.

Lieutenant Colonel Carlos Ibáñez del Campo, of the Chilean army, who had been acting president since May 10, was today elected the twentieth president of Chile. Because his only opponent was the Communist Elias Lafertte, who was in exile, Ibáñez received a reported 98 percent of the vote. Ibáñez served until 1931 and then was reelected in 1952 and was president for another six years.

The baseball season was still young, but Babe Ruth hit his tenth home run today when the New York Yankees played the Cleveland Indians. Ruth's slam to deep right field helped the Yankees beat the Indians 7–2.

While the sports comedy *Babe Comes Home* may not have been anything close to a classic, it did star Babe Ruth, so it's a shame that the movie is listed as lost today. Ruth played slugger Babe Dugan, who chews and spits so much tobacco that the laundress Vernie complains about how filthy his baseball uniform gets. Babe not only tries to placate Vernie but falls in love with her. She reforms his sloppy ways and he is a new man. Yet on the field Babe seems to have lost his touch. During a crucial point of an important game, Vernie tosses Babe a plug of tobacco and he happily chews away as he wins the game. Because Ruth was at the peak of his popularity, the First National movie did very well at the box office, though the critics pointed out that the great slugger was no threat as an actor. All the same, Ruth appeared in several film shorts in the 1930s and later did a cameo as himself in the Lou Gehrig biopic *The Pride of the Yankees* (1942).

MONDAY, MAY 23

The Bell Telephone Building in New York City was the site today for a demonstration of live television. The program was observed by over five hundred members of the American Institute of Electrical Engineers and the Institute of Radio Engineers

The Gaelic Athletic Association was founded in 1884 to promote Irish culture around the world, including various sports. Today the Kingdom of Kerry, defending soccer football champion of the Gaelic Athletic Association All-Ireland Championship, arrived in New York to begin its promotional tour of the United States.

Railroad magnate Henry E. Huntington died today in Philadelphia at the age of seventy-seven. As the owner of the Southern Pacific Railroad, Huntington used his fortune to develop and promote the city of Los Angeles and his name remains on many buildings and parks there. He was also an avid collector of art and rare books, most of which he bought through art dealer Joseph Duveen and book dealer A. S. W. Rosenbach. On his deathbed, Huntington summoned both Duveen and Rosenbach to his side and arranged for them to sell his collection worth $430 million. Legend has it that when the two dealers asked why Huntington summoned them at the last possible moment, he answered that he wanted to die like Jesus Christ, between two thieves.

TUESDAY, MAY 24

Wasting no time, Harmony Music Publishers released the sheet music for the song "Lucky Lindy" today and sales were brisk. Abel Baer (music) and L. Wolfe Gilbert (lyric) came up with the merry march ditty that celebrated Charles Lindbergh's transatlantic flight. It is believed to be the first of some 250 songs written about "Lindy"; it was certainly the most popular, selling thousands of copies of sheet music.

POPULAR SONGS

Some popular songs that were introduced in 1927:

"Adios Muchachos" (César Felipe Vedani, Julio Cesar Sanders)

"Ain't She Sweet" (Jack Yellen, Milton Ager)

"Among My Souvenirs" (Edgar Leslie, Horatio Nicholls)

"At Sundown" (Walter Donaldson)

"Back in Your Own Back Yard" (Billy Rose, Al Jolson, Dave Dreyer)

"The Best Things in Life Are Free" (B. G. De Sylva, Lew Brown, Ray Henderson)

"Bill" (Oscar Hammerstein, P. G. Wodehouse, Jerome Kern)

"Black and Tan Fantasy" (Duke Ellington, Bubber Miley)

"Bless This House" (Helen Taylor, May Brahe)

"Broken Hearted" (B. G. De Sylva, Lew Brown, Ray Henderson)

"Can't Help Lovin' Dat Man" (Oscar Hammerstein, Jerome Kern)

"Changes" (Walter Donaldson)

"Chlo-e (Song of the Swamp)" (Gus Kahn, Neil Moret)

"Creole Love Call" (Duke Ellington, Joe King Oliver)

"Dew-Dew-Dewey Day" (Al Sherman, Charles Tobias, Howard Johnson)

"Diane" (Ernie Rapee, Lew Pollack)

"Did You Mean It?" (Abe Lyman, Sid Silvers, Phil Baker)

"The Doll Dance" (Nacio Herb Brown)

"Everywhere You Go" (Larry Shay, Joe Goodwin, Mark Fisher)

"Fifty Million Frenchmen Can't Be Wrong" (Willie Raskin, Billy Rose, Fred Fisher)

"Four or Five Times" (Marco H. Hellman, Byron Gay)

"Funny Face" (Ira Gershwin, George Gershwin)

"Girl of My Dreams" (Sunny Clapp)

"Good News" (B. G. De Sylva, Lew Brown, Ray Henderson)

"Hallelujah" (Leo Robin, Clifford Grey, Vincent Youmans)

"He Loves and She Loves" (Ira Gershwin, George Gershwin)

"Hoosier Sweetheart" (Billy Baskette, Paul Ash, Joe Goodwin)

"Ice Cream" (Howard Johnson, Billy Moll, Robert King)

"I'll Take Care of Your Cares" (Mort Dixon, James V. Monaco)

"I'm Gonna Meet My Sweetie Now" (Benny Davis, Jesse Greer)

"I'm Looking Over a Four Leaf Clover" (Mort Dixon, Harry MacGregor Woods)

"In a Mist" (Bix Beiderbecke)

"It All Belongs to Me" (Irving Berlin)

"I've Danced with a Man, Who's Danced with a Girl, Who's Danced with the Prince of Wales" (Herbert Farjeon)

"Just Imagine" (B. G. De Sylva, Lew Brown, Ray Henderson)

"Just Like A Butterfly (Caught in the Rain)" (Mort Dixon, Harry Woods)

"Keep Sweeping the Cobwebs Off the Moon" (Sam Lewis, Joe Young, Oscar Levant)

"The Kinkajou" (Joseph McCarthy, Harry Tierney)

"Let a Smile Be Your Umbrella (On a Rainy Day)" (Irving Kahal, Francis Wheeler, Sammy Fain)

"Life upon the Wicked Stage" (Oscar Hammerstein, Jerome Kern)

"Lindbergh (The Eagle of the U.S.A.)" (Al Sherman, Howard Johnson)

"The Lonesome Road" (Gene Austin, Nathaniel Shilkret)

"Lucky in Love" (B. G. De Sylva, Lew Brown, Ray Henderson)

"Lucky Lindy" (L. Wolfe Gilbert, Abel Baer)

"Make Believe" (Oscar Hammerstein, Jerome Kern)

"Mary, (What Are You Waiting For)" (Walter Donaldson)

"Me and My Shadow" (Billy Rose, Al Jolson, Dave Dreyer)

"Miss Annabelle Lee" (Lew Pollack, Sidney Clare, Harry Richman)

"Mississippi Mud" (James Cavanaugh, Harry Barris)

"My Heart Stood Still" (Lorenz Hart, Richard Rodgers)

"My One and Only" (Ira Gershwin, George Gershwin)

"Ol' Man River" (Oscar Hammerstein, Jerome Kern)

"Plenty of Sunshine" (B. G. De Sylva, Lew Brown, Ray Henderson)

"Rain" (Eugene Ford, Carey Morgan, Arthur Swanstrom)

"Rio Rita" (Joseph McCarthy, Harry Tierney)

"Rosy Cheeks" (Seymour Simons, Richard A. Whiting)

"Russian Lullaby" (Irving Berlin)

"Sam the Old Accordion Man" (Walter Donaldson)

"Shaking the Blues Away" (Irving Berlin)

"Side by Side" (Harry MacGregor Woods)

"Sometimes I'm Happy" (Leo Robin, Clifford Grey, Vincent Youmans)

"The Song Is Ended (But the Melody Lingers On)" (Irving Berlin)

"Soon" (Ira Gershwin, George Gershwin)

"Strike Up the Band" (Ira Gershwin, George Gershwin)

"Struttin' with Some Barbecue" (Lillian Hardin Armstrong)

"'S Wonderful" (Ira Gershwin, George Gershwin)

"Thinking of You" (Bert Kalmar, Harry Ruby)

"Thou Swell" (Lorenz Hart, Richard Rodgers)

"The Varsity Drag" (B. G. De Sylva, Lew Brown, Ray Henderson)

"What Does It Matter?" (Irving Berlin)

"Why Do I Love You?" (Oscar Hammerstein, Jerome Kern)

"You Are Love" (Oscar Hammerstein, Jerome Kern)

"Your Land and My Land" (Dorothy Donnelly, Sigmund Romberg)

See July 1 for music compositions, operas, and ballets from 1927.

Prime Minister Stanley Baldwin told the House of Commons today that the United Kingdom intended to terminate diplomatic relations with the Soviet Union because of evidence of espionage by Soviet diplomats and Russian infiltration leading to underground agitation. The Commons approved Baldwin's resolution three days later by a vote of 357 to 111.

WEDNESDAY, MAY 25

Lt. James H. Doolittle of the U.S. Army today became the first person to perform an aviation maneuver that was previously thought to be impossible. Since 1912, adventurous aviators had been trying to perform an "outside loop"; at least two pilots had been killed in the attempt. At Wright Field in Dayton, Ohio, Doolittle flew his Curtis B-1B Hawk to ten thousand feet then turned the nose of the plane downward, reaching a speed of 289 mph. When he was at six thousand feet, Doolittle flew back upward to his original altitude and completed the circle. Although he did many stunts and made important innovations in flying, Doolittle is most remembered for his daring raid on Tokyo in 1942.

The anticlerical Cristero Rebellion, which had been raging in Mexico since 1926, today claimed the lives of two noted priests, Cristobal Magallanes, fifty-seven years old, and Agustin Caloca Cortés, twenty-nine years old. Both were arrested by government secularists on May 21, were accused of inciting rebellion, found guilty without a trial, and today were shot by a firing squad at Colotlán. Magallanes and Cortés were canonized as Roman Catholic saints by Pope John Paul II in 2000.

THURSDAY, MAY 26

Automobile pioneer Henry Ford today watched the last Model T Ford roll off the assembly line at his factory in Highland Park, Michigan. It was car number 14,689,525 since the model was introduced in 1909 and first made the automobile affordable for the average person. Ford car dealers across the United States all received a telegram today saying that the factories were being retooled to make way for the new Model A, which would be introduced in December.

After six days of being hailed by tens of thousands of Parisians everywhere he went and receiving the esteemed French Légion d'honneur from President Gaston Doumergue, Charles Lindbergh returned to Le Bouget field to check on how the repairs were coming on the *Spirit of St. Louis*. Pleased with the progress, Lindbergh then borrowed a French Nieuport fighter plane, a kind of aircraft that he had never flown before, and took it for a spin, doing stunts and loops to the horror of the officials, who were afraid the most famous man in the world would kill himself.

Broadway star Al Jolson today signed with Warner Brothers to play the title role in the studio's experimental "talkie" *The Jazz Singer*. George Jessel, who had originated the role in the 1925 Broadway play, was scheduled to reprise his performance on screen, but he walked away from the project when he was denied extra money after learning that *The Jazz Singer* was not going to be a silent movie. Once Jolson was signed, production was scheduled to begin in July.

FRIDAY, MAY 27

The Dole Air Race was announced today by James D. Dole, the "Pineapple King," who was inspired by Charles Lindbergh's transatlantic flight and wanted to encourage air traffic to Hawaii where he and his company resided. Also known as the Dole Derby, the competition was indeed a race. Qualified fliers would depart from Oakland, California, on August 16 and the first plane to arrive in Honolulu would receive a prize of $25,000. The second flyers to reach Honolulu would win $10,000. What seemed like a grand and exciting venture ended up being something of a tragedy. Eighteen airplanes applied for entry and eleven qualified, but three of those crashed before the race ever started, leaving three flyers dead. Of the eight competitors who remained, two crashed on take-off and two were never heard from again. Yet another plane went missing when it went searching for the other two lost participants. Only two planes made it to Honolulu (the *Woolaroc* flown by Arthur C. Goebel and the *Aloha* piloted by Martin Jensen) and they won the prizes. By the time the race was over, ten flyers had died. Yet the Dole Air Race did open up the field for transpacific flights and made the territory of Hawaii seem much more accessible to Americans.

French composer Henri Sauguet's ballet *La chatte* had its premiere today at the Theatre Sarah Bernhardt in Paris presented by the Ballet Russe. George Balanchine choreographed the ballet about a young man whose kitten is transformed into a beautiful girl who retains some feline qualities, such as chasing mice.

SATURDAY, MAY 28

English batsman Walter Hammond today scored his one thousandth cricket run of the season, which was only twenty-two days old. By the end of the season he had tallied 2,969 runs. By the time Hammond retired in 1947, he was considered one of the best batsmen in the history of cricket.

Before he wrote children's books, E. B. White began contributing articles to the *New Yorker* magazine in 1926 and continued to do so for six decades. In today's issue of the magazine, his article "Eviction" was a wry report on the changes being made on Park Avenue as some establishments disappeared to make way for the widened boulevard.

Two superior American films opened on this day and enjoyed some success, yet, sadly, neither movie exists in its entirety today. Warner Brothers' *A Million Bid* was a drama starring Dolores Costello as Dorothy Gordon, who marries the wealthy Geoffrey Marsh (Warner Oland) to please her greedy mother. Dorothy loves the brain surgeon Dr. Robert Brent (Malcolm McGregor) and, after Marsh's yacht sinks in a storm and he is presumed dead, Dorothy survives and is treated back to health by Brent. They fall in love and wed, but their happiness is threatened when Brent is asked to treat an amnesia victim, whom Dorothy recognizes as Marsh. Brent restores Marsh's memory, but, seeing how happy Dorothy is in her life with Brent, he pretends not to remember his past marriage and walks away. *A Million Bid* was directed with skill by the prolific Michael Curtiz (who had already directed over sixty films in Europe and Hollywood by 1927 and went on to direct over one hundred more) and the performances by Costello and Oland (in his pre–Charlie Chan days) are first rate. Most of the movie survives and a copy is kept in the Library of Congress. Also kept there is what remains of the Fox comedy *Cradle Snatchers*, which was based on a very popular 1925 Broadway play. Fed up with their husbands' philandering, three housewives decide to get even by hiring three college boys to pose as their young lovers. The scheme backfires when the wives and the lads start to take a serious liking to each other. In the end, the husbands see the error of their ways and spouses are reunited as the boys go back to college. *Cradle Snatchers* was one of the early directorial efforts of Howard Hawks and his command of fast-paced comedy is already evident. For many years the movie was thought lost, but five and a half of the seven reels were discovered by Peter Bogdanovich in the mid-1970s.

The Russian artist Boris Kustodiev died today of tuberculosis in Leningrad at the age of forty-nine. He was most known as a portrait painter and stage designer throughout Europe and in his native country. Kustodiev was also a successful book illustrator.

SUNDAY, MAY 29

Italy's Fascist dictator, Benito Mussolini, and king, Victor Emmanuel III, joined Spain's Crown Prince Alfonso and some sixty thousand soccer football fans for the first game in the new Stadio Littoriale (also known as the Stadio Renato Dall'Ara) in Bologna. The Italian team defeated the Spanish players 2–0.

Stan Laurel is the comic centerpiece of the Hal Roach short *Eve's Love Letters*, and it is odd seeing him without his partner, Oliver Hardy. The young wife Eve is being blackmailed by Mr. X who has love letters from her and wants a bundle of money not to show them to her husband Adam. Eve enlists the help of her butler Anatole (Laurel) to break into Mr. X's house and find the letters. Adam follows them, suspecting Eve is having an affair, and Mr. X returns unexpectedly, so things get crazy, including having Anatole dress up like a woman and trying to seduce the husband out of the house.

MONDAY, MAY 30

The fifteenth annual Indianapolis 500 was run today at the Indianapolis Motor Speedway and the winning racer was George Souders, a twenty-four-year-old driving his first major auto race. Souders won by eight laps, the largest margin since 1913, and averaged 97.545 mph. He was the first driver to win the full 500-mile race solo, without help from a relief driver or a riding mechanic.

Over one hundred thousand Britons greeted Charles Lindbergh when he flew the *Spirit of St. Louis* from Brussels to Croydon airport in London today. The crowd was so enthusiastic that they rushed the police line and filled the runway so Lindbergh was not able to land until order was restored. After he was on the ground, the young flyer was taken to Buckingham Palace, where he was congratulated by King George V and Queen Mary. It was Lindbergh's hope to tour Europe then fly back home across the Atlantic, but President Coolidge had already dispatched the naval cruiser USS *Memphis* to England to bring Lindbergh and his plane back to Washington in time for Charles Lindbergh Day in America.

Baseball fans at the Chicago Cubs-Pittsburgh Pirates game today were in for a rare treat. In the first game of a doubleheader, Cubs shortstop Jimmy Cooney made an unas-

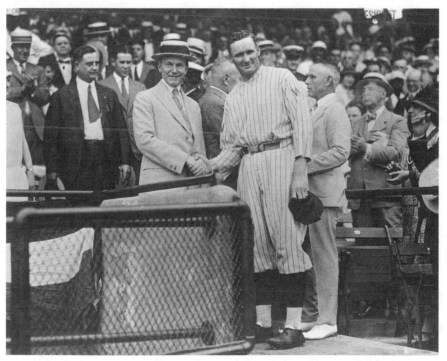

The 1927 Major League Baseball season was the last for celebrated pitcher Walter Johnson, seen here shaking hands with President Calvin Coolidge at Griffith Stadium in Washington, D.C. Johnson's entire twenty-one-year MLB career was with the Washington Senators, and by the time he retired, he had broken many pitching records, including the most shutouts and strikeouts. *Courtesy of the Library of Congress, LC-USZ62-32732*

sisted triple play. It was only the sixth time in Major League Baseball history that such a feat was accomplished.

Record-breaking pitcher and future Hall of Famer Walter Johnson, playing for the Washington Senators, today pitched his 110th shutout. It was also his last. Johnson retired at the end of the season with 417 wins and 3,509 strikeouts, becoming Washington's manager. He played his entire twenty-one-year career with the Senators then managed for Washington and Cleveland from 1929 to 1935.

Igor Stravinsky's opera *Oedipus Rex* premiered today at the Theatre Sarah Bernhardt in Paris as an oratorio. Jean Cocteau wrote the French-Latin libretto based on Sophocles's tragedy. Considered one of Stravinsky's more neoclassical works, *Oedipus Rex* is sometimes performed as a fully staged opera, other times as a concert oratorio. Regardless, it is considered one of the finest musical works of the twentieth century.

In London, the renowned actress Peggy Ashcroft made her London debut in the play *One Day More*. Although Ashcroft would appear in films and on television throughout her career, she continued to act on the London stage through 1982.

TUESDAY, MAY 31

Lightning struck twice in a row in baseball history this week. After Chicago Cub Jimmy Cooney made an unassisted triple play the previous day, Detroit Tiger Johnny Neun repeated the feat during today's game against the Cleveland Indians. Two unassisted triple plays on consecutive days has never been repeated. In fact, baseball fans would have to wait until 1968 to witness the next unassisted triple play by Washington Senators shortstop Ron Hansen. There have been only fifteen unassisted triple plays in MLB history, a feat rarer than a pitcher throwing a perfect game.

Nineteen-year-old Jimmie Foxx, who had quit high school to play Major League Baseball for the Philadelphia Athletics two years earlier, hit his first home run today. By the time he retired in 1945, Foxx had slated 534 home runs, a record second only to Babe Ruth at the time. Foxx was elected to the Hall of Fame in 1951.

The first radio beacon to airplanes was inaugurated today at College Park, Maryland. Dr. George Burgess, director of the U.S. Bureau of Standards, demonstrated how the radio signals were sent to aircraft for the purpose of guiding them to their landing destination, around threatening weather patterns, and away from other airplanes. The installation at College Park was the first of a planned network of stations situated two hundred miles apart from each other.

Since 1924, the Neighborhood Playhouse in lower Manhattan had offered an annual musical revue titled *Grand Street Follies*, a satiric alternative to Florenz Ziegfeld's lavish Broadway *Follies* shows. The 1927 edition of *Grand Street Follies* opened downtown on April 19 and was so well received it moved uptown to Broadway on this day. The show spoofed everything from Calvin Coolidge to current theatre stars, and audiences enjoyed it enough to let the revue run 148 performances.

JUNE

WEDNESDAY, JUNE 1

Alvan T. Fuller, the governor of Massachusetts, under pressure from so many protests about the Sacco and Vanzetti case, today appointed an Advisory Committee of three men to look into the trial and to see if justice had been served. There was an immediate backlash, many finding a history of bias in some of the committee members. Consequently, few were surprised when the committee later agreed with the trial's verdict.

The Federal Radio Commission today announced dates by which radio stations were required to begin broadcasting on their assigned AM radio frequency. The nation's 694 radio stations had to switch to their assigned frequency no later than 3:00 a.m. Eastern time on June 15 or have their licenses taken away.

> The year 1927 is the first in which radio became a major part in the lives of many Americans. By the end of the year it was estimated that one-third of all households had a radio.

Teenage sleuths Frank and Joe Hardy, two of the most popular of all juvenile heroes in American fiction, made their first appearance today when Franklin W. Dixon's young adult novel *The Tower Treasure* was published by Grosset & Dunlap. High school students Frank and Joe, the sons of detective Fenton Hardy, investigate a "red headed" criminal, and their pursuit brings them to the Tower Mansion, where a stash of money is said to be hidden in "the old tower." After a few blind alleys and encounters with characters in disguise, the brothers discover hidden money and jewels and return them to the rightful owners. Like most of the subsequent Hardy Boys books, *The Tower Treasure* is straightforward, fast moving, and very appealing to teen readers, particularly boys. The pseudonym Franklin W. Dixon is listed as the author for the books, but the series was the brainchild of editor Edward Stratemeyer, who hired various ghostwriters over the years. *The Tower Treasure* was actually written by Leslie McFarlane, the author of nineteen of the first twenty-five Hardy Boys mysteries. Given how popular the books are, it is surprising that Hollywood never brought them to the big screen, but the Hardy Boys have made many appearances on television over the years, most memorably on Disney's television show *The Mickey Mouse Club* in 1956.

The infamous Lizzie Borden died of pneumonia today at the age of sixty-six in Fall River, Massachusetts, taking with her to the grave the truth of what happened thirty-five years earlier. On the morning of August 4, 1890, Andrew and Abby Borden were hacked to death by multiple hatchet wounds. Andrew's daughter (and Abby's stepdaughter) Lizzie was arrested and tried for the double murder. There was so much contradictory evidence in the case that Borden was acquitted, but no other suspects were pursued. Although she was ostracized by the community, Borden continued to live quietly in Fall River for the rest of her life. To this day speculation over whether Lizzie Borden did or did not kill her parents continues.

THURSDAY, JUNE 2

American aviation entrepreneur Juan Trippe today founded the Aviation Corporation of America after securing the backing of financiers Cornelius Vanderbilt Whitney and W. Averell Harriman. The trio raised $250,000 in startup capital from the sale of stock to launch the first major airline, Pan American World Airways.

The Chinese scholar and poet Wang Guowei committed suicide today by drowning in the Kunming Lake as the revolutionary army made its way into Beijing. The influential historian, linguist, literary critic, and poet was forty-nine years old.

FRIDAY, JUNE 3

The handsome Swedish screen actor Einar Hanson, who was becoming the new Rudolph Valentino since that actor's death in 1926, died in a car crash today near Santa Monica, California. He was only twenty-nine. Hanson had acted opposite Pola Negri, Clara Bow, Greta Garbo, and other stars since coming to Hollywood in 1925 and he made six movies that were released in 1927.

SATURDAY, JUNE 4

Both Charles Lindbergh and his famous plane, *Spirit of St. Louis*, departed Europe today aboard the naval cruiser USS *Memphis*, which President Coolidge had sent to bring the aviator hero home. That same day, Coolidge was on the U.S. presidential yacht *Mayflower*, stationed off of Cape Henry, Virginia, watching a massive naval review, one of the most elaborate in American history. Nearly one hundred aircraft carriers, submarines, battleships, destroyers, and other U.S. Navy vessels sailed past the president. Legend has it that Coolidge was quite bored with the magnificent display and left after watching only twenty minutes of the review. Another version of the story says that Coolidge got seasick and left to lie down in a bed below deck.

The Ryder Cup matches, an international match play golf event, was played this year for the first time. The two-day event concluded today at the Worcester Country Club in Worcester, Massachusetts, with the USA team beating the Great Britain team 9½ points to 2½ points. Samuel Ryder, an English entrepreneur and golf enthusiast, founded the prize but was in such ill health that he was not able to attend the first competition named after him. The Ryder Cup matches are still held every two years.

The prolific stage and screen actor Robert McKim died in Hollywood today at the age of forty, three weeks after suffering a cerebral hemorrhage while performing in a vaudeville show. McKim worked in legitimate theatre and vaudeville, making his screen debut in 1915. Over the next dozen years, he acted in ninety-nine feature films.

SUNDAY, JUNE 5

Arthur Barry, arguably the most successful "gentleman thief" in history, was arrested today at the train station in Ronkonkoma, New York. Barry had started his career as a thief at the age of fifteen, and by the time the thirty-one-year-old American was finally caught, it is estimated that he had stolen jewelry items worth more than $5 million. His victims were always wealthy, and he often used his charm as a ladies' man to gain entrance to their homes. Barry escaped from prison in 1929 but was recaptured in 1932, then released from jail in 1949.

The French Tennis Championships (today known as the French Open) concluded today in Paris. It was the thirty-second anniversary of the event and the first time that a foreign woman, Kornelia Bouman, won the women's singles event, and she became the first, and only, Dutch woman to win a Grand Slam singles title. Frenchman René Lacoste bested American Bill Tilden in the men's singles; Frenchmen Henri Cochet and Jacques Brugnon defeated Jean Borotra and Lacoste in the men's doubles; South Africans Irene Peacock and Bobbie Heine won the women's doubles over British players Peggy Saunders Mitchell and Phoebe Holcroft; and in the mixed doubles competition, French players Marguerite Broquedis and Borotra defeated Spaniard Lilí de Álvarez and Tilden.

MONDAY, JUNE 6

American aviator Clarence D. Chamberlain had not been allowed to participate in the competition for the Orteig Prize because of a court injunction on his plane *Miss Columbia*, and Charles Lindbergh then became the first to make a transatlantic flight. Today, with the injunction lifted, Chamberlain set off from Roosevelt Field in *Miss Columbia* with copilot Charles A. Levine to not only cross the Atlantic but break Lindbergh's distance record. Their planned destination was Berlin, but they were forced to land in Eisleben, Germany, one hundred miles short of their goal, because of a damaged propeller. All the same, they created a new record: a nonstop flight of 3,905 miles in forty-four hours and thirty-five minutes.

The rising young British actor John Gielgud received further attention today when he opened in the London production of Eugene O'Neill's expressionist play *The Great God Brown*. It was his first appearance in an American play and his portrayal of the tormented hero was highly praised. The next year Gielgud would make his Broadway debut.

Universal's ten-part western serial *Whispering Smith Rides* began running in theatres on this date. All the episodes are believed lost and only a trailer for the series survives. J. P. McGowan played the cowboy hero Whispering Smith; Wallace MacDonald was his nemesis, Jim Macklin; Rose Blossom as Bobbie Van Tine provided the love interest; and Merrill McCormick provided the laughs as "Deaf" Leffingwell.

TUESDAY, JUNE 7

The 1920s fad of pole-sitting was popularized by Alvin "Shipwreck" Kelly in 1924 when he climbed and sat on a pole outside a Philadelphia department store for thirteen hours and thirteen minutes as a publicity stunt. Other pole-sitting feats followed, and today Kelly climbed up the fifty-foot-high flagpole at the St. Francis Hotel in Newark, New Jersey, to break his own record. He sat on a stool atop the pole for twelve days and twelve hours.

The Russian revolutionary Pyotr Voykov, who had participated in the murder of the Romanov royal family in 1918, was serving as the Soviet ambassador to Poland when he was assassinated today in Warsaw. The assassin was Boris Kowerda, the eighteen-year-old son of a White Russian monarchist, who said he killed Voykov in retaliation for the murder of Tsar Nicholas II and the Russian Imperial Family. A Polish court sentenced Kowerda to life imprisonment, but he was paroled in 1937 and spent the rest of his seventy-nine years in the United States.

WEDNESDAY, JUNE 8

Babe Ruth wasn't the only Yankee totaling up home runs this season. Today second baseman Tony Lazzeri hit three homers in one game, guaranteeing a victory over the Chicago White Sox, 12–11.

The announcement by U.S. secretary of state Frank B. Kellogg that, as of December 1, all Canadians working in the United States needed to obtain immigrant visas, was met with disfavor by the Canadian government, which expressed its concerns today in a formal letter of protest. For many years, thousands of Canadian citizens commuted to jobs in the United States every day. Kellogg ordered the border restrictions because liquor was legal in Canada and efforts were being made to stop the flow of alcohol into the United States.

THURSDAY, JUNE 9

An early version of the musical synthesizer, the Clavier à Lampes, was demonstrated today by its French inventor, Armand Givelet, at the Trocadero Theatre in Philadelphia. Givelet, an engineer and physicist, sought a way of solving the problem of broadcasting music over the radio because of the amount of static that resulted from microphones. Givelet's solution was to build an electronic organ that could be directly plugged into the transmitter without using microphones. The resulting instrument, the Clavier à Lampes, was a monophonic vacuum-tubed keyboard instrument. After introducing the instrument in Paris, Givelet took his invention to America, where he gave concerts on it, the first one today in Philadelphia.

Federico Garcia Lorca, Spain's greatest playwright of the twentieth century, had his first success when his biographical drama *Mariana Pineda* premiered at the Teatre Goya Theatre in Barcelona today. The heroine of the play is the nineteenth-century liberal who was executed for her political ideas. Ironically, Lorca was also executed for his political beliefs in 1936.

The famous suffragette Victoria Woodhull, the first woman to run for president of the United States, died in England today at the age of eighty-eight. In 1872, although women did not yet have the vote and Woodhull was a few months shy of the minimum age of thirty-five to be a presidential candidate, she was the Equal Rights Party candidate in the election. Her running mate was the African American spokesman Frederick Douglass. Throughout her busy and controversial life, Woodhull was also a stockbroker, a newspaper editor, an advocate of free love and abortion, and a labor organizer.

FRIDAY, JUNE 10

Nanna Popham Britton had been Warren Harding's secretary and mistress while he was serving in the U.S. Senate, and she had a daughter by him in 1919. Harding supported Britton and their daughter Elizabeth Ann, but when he died in 1923 Harding's wife Florence stopped payments. So, Britton wrote her tell-all book *The President's Daughter* to earn money to support herself and her daughter. No reputable publisher would take on the book, so it was picked up by the Elizabeth Ann Guild, a group dedicated to helping unwed mothers. The book was scheduled for release but today all copies of the book and the printing plates were confiscated by New York City police after a complaint by the Society for the Suppression of Vice. After much debate in the newspapers and even in Congress, the books and plates were returned to the printer but *The President's Daughter* was not released until 1928. It was an immediate bestseller and possibly the first in a long line of scandal-based autobiographies. Not until 2015 DNA testing on Britton's descendants was it proved that Elizabeth Ann was indeed Harding's daughter.

SATURDAY, JUNE 11

Today was declared Charles Lindbergh Day across America by President Coolidge and the nation had rarely seen anything quite like it. Early that morning, the U.S.S. *Memphis* sailed up the Potomac River to the Washington Navy Yard with Lindbergh and the *Spirit of St. Louis* on board. The *Memphis* was joined by four destroyers and eighty-eight planes and two dirigibles in flight above them. In addition to the thousands on hand to welcome "Lucky Lindy" home, the new National Broadcasting Company covered the event with the first coast-to-coast broadcast. It is estimated that every radio in America was tuned in to the festivities of the day. Mrs. Lindbergh was reunited with her son, and the two rode into the District of Columbia in an open-top Pierce-Arrow as over a million cheering Americans lined the streets. President and Mrs. Coolidge and members of the Cabinet greeted Lindbergh at a platform set up near the Washington Monument where speeches were given and Coolidge presented him with the Distinguished Flying Cross. Lindbergh was the first person to receive the medal, which had been created in 1926. When it was finally time for the young hero to talk, he said a few halting words of thanks then was silent. It turned out that "Silent Cal" had met his like.

The fifty-ninth running of the Belmont Stakes today in Belmont Park, Elmont, New York, saw jockey Earl Sande ride the thoroughbred Chance Shot to victory with a time of 2:32.6.

Babe Ruth hit his nineteenth and twentieth home runs of the season today when the New York Yankees bested the Cleveland Indians 6–4. Both homers came against left-handed pitcher Garland Buckeye. By the end of the season, Ruth would triple that twenty count.

British humorist P. G. Wodehouse's short story "Came the Dawn" was published in today's issue of the American magazine *Liberty*. Lancelot Mulliner wants to be a poet and marry the smart and lovely Angela rather than take over the family pickle business, but both his father and Angela's father put a stop to it. His uncle, the raconteur Mr.

Mulliner, tells the story, which ends with the good-looking Lancelot being signed to go to Hollywood and appear in the movies. "Came the Dawn" was reprinted in England in the July issue of the *Strand Magazine* and in the anthology *Meet Mr. Mulliner*.

Vaudeville and Broadway comic and juggler W. C. Fields was already an established star on the silent screen by 1927 and was in three feature films that year, but only one has survived: Paramount's *Running Wild*. Fields played the hen-pecked Elmer Finch, who is bossed around at work and at home, only his daughter Elizabeth showing him any familial affection. Under a trance induced by a stage hypnotist in a vaudeville show, Elmer turns from mouse to lion and puts both his family and his boss in their place. The spell eventually wears off, but by then Elmer has mastered the ways of being the master of his house, and everybody seems to like him better for it. Gregory LaCava was the astute director and Fields, sporting a tiny mustache in his silent days, is surprisingly funny even without dialogue.

SUNDAY, JUNE 12

The distinguished Italian scientist Guglielmo Marconi, the inventor of wireless radio, today married the Countess Maria Cristina Bezzi-Scali in Rome. Marconi had been married for twenty-two years to Beatrice O'Brien Marconi and they had four children, but he was able to get the marriage annulled so that he could marry Maria Cristina. The ceremony was a lavish one with full military honors and attended by the Italian high society, as well as dictator Benito Mussolini.

Today was the second day in a row that the Brooklyn Robins defeated the Pittsburgh Pirates. Interestingly, the score for both games was the same: 11–10.

The American serial killer Earle Nelson, dubbed "The Gorilla Murderer" and "The Dark Strangler" by the press, was arrested today in Winnipeg, Manitoba, Canada, after killing over twenty women during a period of a year and a half. Nelson's killing spree began in 1926 in California then moved to the Midwest before going to the East Coast and ending up in Canada. Nelson is arguably the first known sex murderer of the century, his killings including rape and necrophilia. He was tried and executed by hanging in Winnipeg in January of 1928.

Hal Roach's comedy short *Love 'em and Weep* cast Stan Laurel in the leading comic role while Oliver Hardy has a small supporting part. The successful businessman Titus Tillbury is not happy when his old flame Peaches tries to crash a dinner party his wife Aggie is throwing. He enlists the help of his hapless assistant Romaine Ricketts (Laurel) to keep her away, but his efforts lead to comic complications that are not surprising but funny all the same. Roach remade the farce as a talkie in 1931 as *Chickens Come Home* with Laurel reprising his performance and Hardy playing the husband.

MONDAY, JUNE 13

The ticker-tape parade on Wall Street in New York City today honoring Charles Lindbergh was watched by over four million people and millions more listened to coverage of the event on the radio. A banquet that night was given for Lindbergh at a Long Island estate with New York City's mayor Jimmy Walker and New York governor Al Smith among the guests.

President and Mrs. Coolidge, along with staff and reporters, left Washington by train today for a three-month stay in South Dakota while renovations were made at the White House. The extended summer vacation was spent at the State Game Lodge at the foot of Mount Harney near Rapid City. When Coolidge had presidential business to attend to, he did so in a classroom at Rapid City High School.

TUESDAY, JUNE 14

Reinhold Glière's ballet *The Red Poppy* premiered today at the Bolshoi Theatre in Moscow, choreographed by Lev Lashchiline and Vasily Tikhomirov. The libretto by Mikhail Kurilko is set in contemporary China, where a Soviet sea captain rescues some starving Chinese laborers from a cruel harbormaster. The captain is aided by a Chinese girl who gives him a red poppy, a symbol of love, before she is killed for her efforts. *The Red Poppy*, considered the first Communist-themed ballet, ran over one hundred performances in Moscow and was subsequently staged in many Russian cities.

A dinner given at the Commodore Hotel in honor of Charles Lindbergh is thought to be the largest and most lavish ever given in New York City. About thirty-seven hundred guests consumed three hundred gallons of turtle soup, six thousand pounds of chicken, two thousand pounds of fish, eight hundred quarts of ice cream, and twelve thousand pieces of cake.

A popular British author of comic prose, Jerome K. Jerome died today in Northampton, England, from a cerebral hemorrhage at the age of sixty-eight. He wrote plays, essays, and novels in the comic vein and is best known for his satiric travelogue *Three Men in a Boat* (1889), one of the finest works of British comedy of the nineteenth century.

WEDNESDAY, JUNE 15

The Buddhist monk Dashi-Dorzho Itigelov died today in Buryatia, Russia, at the age of seventy-five. Although he was influential in the palace of the royal Romanovs and was named the Hambo Lama of the Buddhist order, Itigelov would be forgotten today if not for his strange history after his death. Dying in the lotus position, his body was placed that way into a pine box by his fellow monks, as were his wishes. Before dying, Itigelov also instructed the monks to exhume his body after thirty years had passed. They did so and found the body still in the lotus position and with no signs of decay. The Buddhist monks kept their discovery secret and reburied Itigelov. The body was exhumed again officially in 1973 and 2002 and it still remains intact. Today the self-preserved body of Itigelov is a sacred Buddhist treasure, even the Russian president Putin visiting the famous monk in 2013.

THURSDAY, JUNE 16

Raymond Orteig, who had sponsored the Orteig Prize for the first person to fly nonstop across the Atlantic Ocean, today presented Charles Lindbergh with the award and a check for $25,000 at a reception at the Hotel Brevoort in New York.

The Chicago Cubs' 7–2 victory today over the Philadelphia Phillies made for a twelve-game winning streak, bringing the team to within one game of first place in the National League. This was the first season in which the Cub's home ballpark was called Wrigley Field; it was named Weeghman Park when it opened in 1914 and was known as Cubs Park from 1920 to 1926. The Cubs still play in the revered ballpark, which has since seen six renovations and expansions.

FRIDAY, JUNE 17

The thirty-first U.S. Open, the prestigious golf competition, concluded today at the Oakmont Country Club in Oakmont, Pennsylvania. Sixty-two players out of a field of 148 made the cut and in the final round Scottish-American golfer Tommy Armour defeated British player Harry Cooper in an eighteen-hole playoff to win the first of his three major titles. The winner's share for the tournament was $500. The Silver Scott, as Armour was dubbed, went on to win the PGA Championship in 1930 and the Open Championship in 1931.

With the civil war temporarily resolved in Nicaragua and domestic and financial stability restored, a small portion of the thousands of American soldiers occupying the country sailed today from the port city of Corinto to return to the United States.

John R. Thompson, dubbed the Father of Fast Food, died today at the age of sixty-two. He is sometimes credited with coming up with the word "cafeteria" and the cafeteria-style of restaurant that catered to patrons in big cities who had limited time for lunch. Thompson opened his first restaurant in Chicago in 1893; there were over one hundred Thompson Restaurants in forty-two states by 1927.

Scottish-American golfer Tommy Amour, dubbed the Silver Scott, won more championships in his day than anyone else. His amateur career began in 1920 and he had many trophies to his name by the time he went professional in 1925. The year 1927 saw him win the U.S. Open, Long Beach Open, El Paso Open, Oregon Open, and the Canadian Open. *Courtesy of the Library of Congress, LC-USZ62-108418*

SATURDAY, JUNE 18

The U.S. Postal Service today issued the first stamp in honor of a living person. The first printing of a ten-cent airmail stamp with a picture of the *Spirit of St. Louis*, in honor of Charles Lindbergh's flight to Paris, went on sale in four locations: St. Louis, Detroit, Washington, and Lindbergh's boyhood hometown of Little Falls, Minnesota. Eventually fifteen million copies of the dark blue airmail stamp were printed. The popularity of the stamp was a turning point in mail delivery in America. By the end of 1927, the use of airmail doubled, the applications for airmail pilot's licenses tripled, and the number of airmail planes in service quadrupled. Also in Lindbergh news today, the young aviator was promoted to the rank of colonel in the Air Corps of the Officers Reserve Corps of the U.S. Army.

The Finnish runner Paavo Nurmi, who had won five gold medals at the 1924 Paris Olympics, today broke a world record by running the 2000-meter course in 5:24.6.

SUNDAY, JUNE 19

The 1925 Broadway musical hit *Tip-Toes* featured a terrific score by the Gershwin brothers, but the plot was weak, so Hollywood wasn't interested in a screen version. But British National Films was and hired American stars Will Rogers and Dorothy Gish for a silent treatment which they titled *Tip Toes*. The location was moved from Florida to London and some of the story was the same. Down on their luck music hall performers Tip Toes Kaye (Gish) and her Uncles Hen (Rogers) and Al (Nelson Keys) check into a swanky hotel and try to pass Tip Toes off as an heiress, hoping to catch a rich husband. She and Lord William Montgomery fall in love, but the happy ending is delayed by a series of complications caused by the foolish Hen and Al. The London film critics were not approving of *Tip Toes* and when it opened on this day in the States, the reviews were not enthusiastic. How accurate those commentators were is hard to say since the film is believed lost.

MONDAY, JUNE 20

The Geneva Naval Conference, also known as the Second Disarmament Conference, opened today in Geneva. Called by President Coolidge to discuss further reductions of the navies of the world's powers, the conference opened with representatives of the United States, the United Kingdom, and Japan discussing further limitations on the building of warships, including a prohibition against submarines. But other issues arose, negotiations broke down, and the conference was an utter failure, adjourning on August 24 with no agreement. Historians looking back note that the Geneva Naval Conference was hastily and poorly prepared and suffered from the superior attitude of the American and British admirals. If anything, the conference caused hostilities and led to a naval arms race.

French statesman Aristide Briand, who had already served as prime minister of France ten times and won the Nobel Peace Prize in 1926, today visited the U.S. Embassy in Paris and presented his proposed treaty to outlaw war. Later known as the Kellogg-Briand Pact, it would be signed by France, Germany, and the United States in 1928.

"Mississippi Mud," the jazzy Southern dance song encouraging one to beat one's feet in the oozing mud, was recorded on the Victor label today for the first time, sung by the Rhythm Boys (Bing Crosby, Harry Barris, and Al Rinker) with Paul Whiteman's Orchestra. Barris and James Cavanaugh wrote the foot-stomping song, which Whiteman and the Rhythm Boys recorded again in 1928 featuring Bix Beiderbecke on cornet. They all reprised the number in the film *King of Jazz* (1930).

TUESDAY, JUNE 21

A hazing incident today at the Kings County Hospital Center in Brooklyn unveiled a strong element of anti-Semitism at the revered institution and made national news. Three Jewish interns were taken from their beds in the middle of the night and bound and gagged. After being dunked in ice cold water the three Jews were threatened with further reprisals if they didn't withdraw from the traditionally "Christian" institution. Dr. Mortimer D. Jones, superintendent of Kings County Hospital, stated that there was no anti-Semitism at the hospital, but an outside investigation and the testimony from some of the nurses revealed that the perpetrators were a group of fellow interns. The victims pressed charges and six of the attackers were later expelled.

Less than a month after *A Million Bid* opened, Dolores Costello and Warner Oland were again featured in another Warner Brothers melodrama, *Old San Francisco*. Oland played the cruel boss Chris Buckwell of the Tenderloin District who persecutes the Chinese immigrants even though he himself, unknown to others, is part Asian. The greedy Buckwell tries to buy the land of Don Vásquez, who refuses, and Buckwell has Vásquez killed. Vásquez's daughter Dolores (Costello) reveals Buckwell's blood lineage and vows to avenge her father's death, but the 1906 San Francisco earthquake does the job for her, killing Buckwell and many others. Warner Brothers released *Old San Francisco* with a music and sound effects soundtrack using the Vitaphone process but it is lost. The movie survives and it holds up despite a current of racism that runs through it.

WEDNESDAY, JUNE 22

Residing in South Dakota for the summer while repairs and renovations were made to the White House, Calvin Coolidge had a local mountain named after him. The state legislature today voted unanimously to rename Lookout Mountain, at 5,971 feet high, Mount Coolidge, in honor of the president.

Two giants in American aviation met today when Charles Lindbergh shook hands with Orville Wright at Wright Field in Dayton, Ohio. It was part of Lindbergh's cross-country tour, during which he was swamped with throngs of well-wishers wherever he went. The shy, emotionless aviator rarely waved or smiled and sometimes he refused to participate in another parade or honorary dinner. It was becoming clear that the most famous man in the world did not enjoy being famous.

Doubleday put together several short stories by Don Marquis about Archy, a cockroach, and Mehitabel, an alley cat, and published the anthology as *archy and mehitabel.* The two fictional characters were created by Marquis in 1916, when he worked as a columnist for the *Evening Sun* newspaper in New York City. The cockroach and alley cat appeared in hundreds of humorous verses and short stories in Marquis's daily column, The Sun Dial. Supposedly, Archy had been a free verse poet in a previous life and now pounded out poetry on Marquis's typewriter when the human wasn't in the office. Because Archy could not reach the shift key, all his verses were in lower case without punctuation. Archy's best friend was the alley cat Mehitabel, and the two often had comic adventures together, which Archy then wrote about. Other recurring characters included the lady-killer tom cat Big Bill, the theatre cat Tyrone T. Tattersal, and the unseen human The Newspaperman, who was Marquis himself. Although they were nonhuman, Archy and Mehitabel had very human attitudes and emotions and they were often able to satirically comment on people's behavior and foibles. The two characters remained popular long after Marquis died in 1937. The 1927 collection was followed by other anthologies, and the characters have shown up on a record album, a Broadway musical titled *Shinbone Alley* (1957), and an animated feature film in 1971.

THURSDAY, JUNE 23

The English professional cricketer Wilfred Rhodes today became the first person to play in one thousand first-class cricket matches. The right-handed all-rounder was fifty years old when he played for Yorkshire against Nottinghamshire in today's match.

New York Yankee first baseman Lou Gehrig hit three home runs in today's Major League Baseball game against the Boston Red Sox. The Yankees beat the Red Sox 11–4. Gehrig went on to hit forty-seven homers with 173 runs batted in before the season was over.

Manufacturers of expensive cars had always offered their customers a variety of colors and styles. Today General Motors CEO Alfred P. Sloan announced that mass-produced cars should also be visually appealing and created the "Art and Color Section" department in the company. Headed by Harley Earl, the new department's goal was to bring style and color to GM products.

The Julian Petroleum Company, which had swindled over $150 million from forty thousand investors, had been investigated and production halted on May 5. Today a grand jury in Los Angeles issued an indictment of fifty-five persons on charges of conspiracy, bribing judges and officials, and fraudulent promotion and sales.

The very successful businessman Wilson B. Hickox, while on a trip to New York, died at the age of forty-three in his room at the Roosevelt Hotel after drinking a cocktail. Although Hickox purchased it from a top-grade bootlegger, he died of alcohol poisoning. He was one of 11,700 people who died from such poisoning in 1927. Many others were rendered blind, crippled, paralyzed, or comatose. Hickox's death was not big news but was used by anti-Prohibition advocates to illustrate how the government was killing its citizens by putting alcohol in the hands of profiteers with no health requirements.

The stage, television, and film director-choreographer Bob Fosse was born today in Chicago.

FUTURE DIRECTORS

Some notable stage and film directors and choreographers born in 1927:

Kenneth Anger	Lee Philips (d. 1999)
Frank Dunlop	Stuart Rosenberg (d. 2007)
Bob Fosse (d. 1987)	Herbert Ross (d. 2001)
Gerald Freedman	Ken Russell (d. 2011)
Lucio Fulci (d. 1996)	Paul Sills (d. 2008)
Adrian Hall	Hiroshi Teshigahara (d. 2001)
Robert Moore (d. 1984)	Howard Zieff (d. 2009)
Marcel Ophüls	

FRIDAY, JUNE 24

The Iron Guard (Garda de fier), a far-right political party known officially as the Legion of the Archangel Michael (Legiunea Arhanghelul Mihail), was founded today in Romania by Corneliu Codreanu. The fascist movement was extremely nationalist, anti-Semitic, and anti-Communist, and it promoted Eastern Orthodox Christianity. Because its party members wore predominantly green uniforms, they were familiarly called the Greenshirts. The Legion was a powerful force in Romania and oversaw the murder of thousands of Jews before it was disbanded in 1941.

SATURDAY, JUNE 25

Much lauded when it premiered on this day in New York City, Paramount's *The Way of All Flesh* starred Emil Jannings in an Oscar-winning performance. The melodrama is not based on the 1903 British novel of the same title by Samuel Butler but is an original tale about a happily married husband and father, the Milwaukee bank clerk August Schiller (Jannings), who is transporting $1,000 to Chicago but is cheated out of the money by a seductive woman and her cronies. When one of the thugs falls and is run over by a train, it is assumed the victim is Schiller and his family mourns his passing. Twenty years later Schiller is a tramp walking the streets, and he begs for some money at his own home, where no one recognizes him. But his now-grown son gives the tramp a dollar, and Schiller walks away content to see that the boy he provided violin lessons for is now an acclaimed musician. Victor Fleming was the astute director but it is Jannings who got all the praise. Unfortunately, only two fragments of *The Way of All Flesh* survive today, enough for film historians to witness Jannings's moving performance.

SUNDAY, JUNE 26

The Comet 7P/Pons-Winnecke, which had been discovered by Jean Louis Pons in 1819 and was later rediscovered by Friedrich August Theodor Winnecke in 1858, approached within 3.7 million miles of Earth today, the closest a comet had come to the planet in the twentieth century.

Arguably the most famous roller coaster in America, the Coney Island Cyclone, which is still in operation, opened for business today. The wooden coaster was deemed the world's largest and fastest roller coaster when it opened at New York City's Coney Island as part of the theme park Astroland. The ride lasted just under two minutes, but it reached the speed of 60 mph. After four decades of continuous use, the Cyclone was refurbished in 1975 and continues to be ranked among the best roller coaster rides in the world.

The Washington Irving Memorial, honoring one of America's earliest authors, was unveiled today in Irvington, New York, in the Hudson River Valley close to where the writer lived and where many of his stories take place.

The French impressionist painter Armand Guillaumin died today in Orly, France, at the age of eighty-six. He was a friend of Vincent Van Gogh but, unlike that unfortunate artist, Guillaumin won an artist's competition that brought money and recognition. He was able to quit his government job and paint full-time, later becoming friends with Paul Cézanne and Camille Pissarro, who had a strong influence on his work. Guillaumin is most known for his impressionist landscapes depicting southern France.

MONDAY, JUNE 27

Herbert Hoover's road to the White House unofficially began today in a very effective manner. Over four thousand people (some three thousand of them African Americans) gathered in Pine Bluff, Arkansas, to thank the secretary of commerce for his relief work during the aftermath of the Great Mississippi Flood. The gathering, in which a hundred African American women sang "Swing Low, Sweet Chariot" for Hoover, was in essence a rally carefully planned by the shrewd politician.

Warner Brothers' sentimental *The First Auto* was about the new technology at the turn of the century, the transition from horse-drawn vehicles to automobiles, but the movie was also about cinema technology. The film had a recorded music soundtrack, sound effects, and three spoken words using the Vitaphone process. It is far from a talkie but is innovative in its own small way. The story is about livery stable owner Hank Armstrong (Russell Simpson) who is not happy when his son Bob (Charles Emmett Mack) takes up the newfangled sport of auto racing. As more and more people buy cars, Hank eventually goes out of business and Bob goes to Detroit, where cars are made and witnesses the famous race car driver Barney Oldfield break the speed record in a Ford 999. Bob returns to his hometown of Maple City to woo his sweetheart Rose Robbins and participate in the county's first auto race. Hank sabotages one of the race cars to explode upon starting then finds out too late it is the auto his son is to drive. Bob barely survives the explosion and Hanks changes his attitude, going into car manufacturing with his son. *The First Auto* has a certain amount of authenticity, such as using restored cars from the turn of the century and having ace driver Oldfield play himself. Roy Del Ruth directed with a sure but heavy hand, and the melodrama still has its powerful moments. Sadly, there is an ironic and tragic backstage aspect to the film: actor Mack died in a car crash before filming was completed and a double was used for his remaining scenes.

Beloved torch singer Ruth Etting today recorded the heartfelt ballad "At Sundown" for Columbia Records; the disc was a hit and she sang the song throughout the rest of her career. Walter Donaldson wrote the entrancing song about the coming of night and it had been introduced earlier in the year by Cliff Edwards at the Palace Theatre in New York.

TUESDAY, JUNE 28

Experienced pilots and Army Air Force lieutenants Lester J. Maitland and Albert F. Hegenberger took off from Oakland, California, today in an Atlantic-Fokker C-2 transport plane nicknamed the *Bird of Paradise.* Their destination was Honolulu, Hawaii, which was 2,407 miles away. Maitland and Hegenberger encountered cloudy weather and radio signal failures but used dead reckoning and a compass and arrived in Hawaii after twenty-five hours and fifty minutes, becoming the first persons to fly from the U.S. mainland to the Hawaiian Islands. Two other pilots, Ernest L. Smith and Captain C. H. Carter, had set off from Oakland a few hours after Maitland and Hegenberger but had to turn back when a crack developed in the windshield.

The murals known as *The Building of Britain,* a series of eight historical paintings by various artists, was unveiled today in St. Stephen's Hall of the Palace of Westminster in London. The paintings illustrated pivotal moments in British history, such as King

Alfred defeating the Danes in 877, King Richard I setting off on a crusade in 1189, King John signing the Magna Carta in 1215, Queen Elizabeth I commissioning Sir Walter Raleigh to set sail for America in 1584, and the Union of Scotland and England in 1707.

The Danish artist Otto Bache died today in Copenhagen at the age of eighty-seven. Bache was a realistic painter who did portraits and animals, but he is most known for his detailed scenes from events in Danish history.

WEDNESDAY, JUNE 29

A total eclipse of the sun took place today, putting northern Europe and Asia in darkness for a short time soon after sunrise. The moon's shadow covered the United Kingdom for the first time in 203 years. Such a phenomenon did not occur again until 1999.

Richard E. Byrd (center) and Clarence Chamberlain (right) were celebrated aviators when Charles Lindbergh (left) was still an airmail pilot. But after his famous transatlantic flight, Lindbergh quickly outshone them. All the same, he was thrilled when he finally got to meet his idols. Here the three great flyers pose in front of the *Spirit of St. Louis. Courtesy of the Library of Congress, LC-USZ62-113392*

The distinguished explorer and aviator Commander Richard E. Byrd and his crew (Bert Acosta, George O. Noville, and Bernt Balchen) took off today from Roosevelt Field in New York in the Fokker Trimotor airplane *America* in an attempt to duplicate Charles Lindbergh's transatlantic flight to Paris. The flyers managed to cross the ocean successfully, but in France cloud cover prevented them from locating Paris. Running out of fuel, the *America* crashed into the sea within two hundred meters of the beach at Ver-sur-Mer. All three survived the water landing, and Byrd lived on to achieve many notable feats during his lifetime, such as being the first man to reach both the North and South Poles.

While filming MGM's Klondike adventure movie *The Trail of '98* (1928) on location in Alaska, four stuntmen were killed when they were washed away by the rapids of the Copper River. Two of the bodies were never found. Ironically, on the same day, stand-in Ethel Hall was killed in the Merced River in Yosemite National Park while shooting the Tom Mix western *Tumbling River* (1927). She was standing in for leading lady Dorothy Dwan when her boat overturned and Hall hit her head on a boulder.

THURSDAY, JUNE 30

Most scientists mark today as the birth date of quantum chemistry. German physicists Walter Heitler and Fritz London submitted their paper "Wechselwirkung neutraler Atome und homöopolare Bindung nach der Quantenmechanik" (Interaction of neutral atoms and homo-polar bonding according to quantum mechanics) for publication in the German scientific journal *Zeitschrift für Physik*. The article was the first application of wave mechanics to the theory of chemical bonding.

AFRICAN AMERICAN RADIO PIONEER

The twenty-five-year-old African American Floyd Joseph Calvin became the first host of a black radio talk show in America. Calvin was a writer and special features editor for the *Pittsburgh Courier*, the most widely circulated black newspaper in the country after the *Chicago Defender*. In 1927, Calvin hosted a periodic radio talk show, sponsored by the *Courier* and broadcast on radio station WGBS. Titled *The Courier Hour*, it was the first radio program ever sponsored by a black newspaper and the first radio talk program targeting an African American audience.

⚜

JULY

FRIDAY, JULY 1

The sixtieth anniversary of the Dominion of Canada was celebrated today with two notable events. Centre Block, the main building of the Parliament of Canada on Parliament Hill in Ottawa, officially opened. It had been rebuilt after a 1916 fire. Also, today marked the first coast-to-coast radio network broadcast in Canada. At the beginning of 1927, only 46 percent of Canadians listened to the radio. By the end of the year, that percentage rose to 76.

Boeing Air Transport introduced its single-engine mail plane the Boeing 40A today which had room for two passengers in addition to the pilot. Intended for use by the U.S. Post Office, the Boeing 40 models would eventually offer more passenger service and become part of United Airlines.

The last of Thomas Edison's acoustic recordings was made today in New York City. Throughout the 1920s, the inventor had experimented with acoustical recording techniques but he never managed to perfect the system. Recorded today was the ditty "Dew-Dew-Dewey Day" by Al Sherman, Charles Tobias, and Howard Johnson. The song was later used by candidate Thomas Dewey in the 1948 presidential election.

Hungarian composer Béla Bartók's Piano Concerto no. 1 premiered today at the fifth festival of the International Society for Contemporary Music in Frankfurt with Bartók as the soloist and Wilhelm Furtwängler conducting. The piece is in three movements and calls for a full orchestra but it is the percussive piano work that is most dominant. The concerto came after a three-year period in which Bartók wrote very little and this piece created a rebirth of interest in his work.

CLASSICAL MUSIC

Some notable music compositions, operas, and ballets first performed in 1927:

Béla Bartók's Piano Concerto no. 1

Béla Bartók's String Quartet no. 3

Havergal Brian's Symphony no. 1, *The Gothic*

Frank Bridge's *Enter Spring* (Rhapsody for Orchestra)

John Alden Carpenter's String Quartet

Pierre-Octave Ferroud's opera comique *Chirugie*

Pierre-Octave Ferroud's Sérénade pour orchestre

Gerald Finzi's Violin Concerto

André Fleury's organ composition Allegro symphonique

Reinhold Glière's ballet *The Red Poppy*

Karl Amadeus Hartmann's Two Sonatas for Unaccompanied Violin

Leoš Janáček's *Glagolitic Mass*

Dmitri Kabalevsky's Piano Sonata no. 1 in F Major

Albert Ketèlbey's orchestral "tone picture" *By the Blue Hawaiian Waters*

Zoltán Kodály's *Suite from the Opera Háry János*

Józef Koffler's Musique Quasi una Sonata for Piano, op. 8

Ernst Krenek's opera *Jonny spielt auf* (Jonny plays)

Franz Lehár's operetta *Der Zarewitsch* (*The Tsarevich*)

Bohuslav Martinů's jazz ballet *La revue de cuisine*

Darius Milhaud's Concerto no. 1 for Violin and Orchestra, op. 93

Darius Milhaud's Sonatina for clarinet and piano, op. 100

Darius Milhaud's *3 Caprices de Paganini* for Violin and Piano, op. 97

Carl Nielsen's orchestral rhapsody *An Imaginary Trip to the Faroe Islands*

Dane Rudhyar's piano composition *Paeans*

Henri Sauguet's ballet *La chatte*

Arnold Schoenberg's String Quartet no. 3

Roger Sessions's Symphony no. 1 in E Minor

Dmitri Shostakovich's Symphony no. 2 in B Major, op. 14

Igor Stravinsky and Jean Cocteau's opera *Oedipus Rex*

Karol Szymanowski's String Quartet no. 2, op. 56

Anton Webern's String Trio, op. 20

See May 24 for popular songs from 1927.

SATURDAY, JULY 2

For the Independence Day holiday weekend, more New Yorkers than ever were expected to spend the holiday at beaches on Long Island and New Jersey. Anticipating record crowds, starting today the Pennsylvania Railroad ran 235 additional trains to Long Island and the New Jersey Shore.

The forty-seventh Wimbledon Championships concluded today after thirteen days of tennis competition at the All England Lawn Tennis and Croquet Club in Wimbledon, London. Henri Cochet won the Men's Singles over fellow Frenchman Jean Borotra after losing the first two sets, 4–6 and 4–6, then winning the next two 6–3, 6–4, and taking the match 7–5. The Men's Doubles was won by Bill Tilden and Frank Hunter and Hunter won the Mixed Doubles with Elizabeth Ryan. Helen Wills became the first American player in twenty years to win the Women's Singles, besting the Spanish champion Lilí de Álvarez in straight sets, 6–2, 6–4. Wills and Ryan took the trophy for Women's Doubles.

Jane Eads, a reporter for the *Chicago Herald and Examiner*, today became the first airline passenger when she traveled on a Boeing Air Transport Model 40 that flew from Chicago to San Francisco. Those to fly notable distances previously were pilots or navigators.

Having made such a strong impression in a small but memorable role in *Wings*, Gary Cooper was given his first leading role in the Paramount western *The Last Outlaw*. He plays the new sheriff, Buddy Hale, whose first job is to find the murderer of the previous sheriff. The culprit is Ward Lane, the brother of Janet Lane, whom Buddy has fallen in love with. But Lane is shot by one of his accomplices, the two remaining villains are killed by a cattle stampede, and Buddy gets Janet and becomes mayor of the town. It is a routine western at best, but Cooper's strong screen presence and solid acting point to a long and successful movie career.

Champion boxer Jack Dempsey was struck with a crippling blow outside the ring today when his brother Johnny Dempsey, living in Schenectady, New York, murdered his wife Edna then shot himself. Jack Dempsey had to go to Schenectady to identify the bodies, and the experience haunted him for the rest of his life.

SUNDAY, JULY 3

The beach and amusement parks on Coney Island today boasted a record number of one million visitors. It is estimated another five hundred thousand vacationers were in nearby Rockaway and Staten Island.

Acclaimed African American pitcher Satchel Paige today made his debut with the Birmingham Black Barons in a Negro League game in Detroit. The twenty-one-year-old Paige was sold to the Barons by the Chattanooga White Sox, where he began his professional career the year before. A victim of time and age, Paige would not make his debut in Major League baseball until 1948, shortly after the color barrier was broken. Past his prime at the age of forty-two, Paige nevertheless played from 1948 to 1953, and again in 1965 at the age of fifty-nine. His professional baseball career also included playing in Cuba, the Dominican Republic, Mexico, Venezuela, and other countries, making Paige's career, in the opinion of many, one of the longest and greatest in the history of the sport.

MONDAY, JULY 4

The Fourth of July being his birthday, President Coolidge celebrated by dressing up in full regalia as a cowboy and posing for the press. The outfit, complete with ten-gallon hat, chaps, boots, and spurs, was a gift from the state of South Dakota in honor of the president's fifty-fifth birthday. With the outfit came a horse named Kit, but he turned out to be a bit too frisky for the non-rider Coolidge. He did love the outfit and often wore it during the rest of his three-month summer vacation in the Black Hills. It should be pointed out that Coolidge was just as thrilled dressing up in the full-fledged attire of a Native American chief on occasion. The press took photos, America laughed, and Coolidge was pleased.

Yankee Stadium was packed with seventy-four thousand baseball fans today when the New York Yankees played the Washington Senators. It was a record attendance number for a non-World Series game. The large crowd watched the Yankees clobber the Senators 21–1 with Lou Gehrig and Tony Lazzeri each homering and knocking in five runs.

The *Golden Eagle*, the first monoplane Lockheed Vega manufactured by the Lockheed Corporation, made its inaugural flight today when pilot Eddie Belande took off from Mines Field in Los Angeles. The Lockhead Vega had a cruising speed of 120 mph and could reach 137 mph, making it a favorite of later record-breaking aviators such as Wiley Post and Amelia Earhart.

Joseph Goebbels, leader of the Nazi Party in Germany since 1926, was publisher of the newspaper *Der Angriff* (*The Attack*), which put out its first issue today. The paper, whose motto was "For the oppressed against the exploiters," began as a weekly publication with aggressive language and severe anti-Semitic views. As the Nazis gained power, it became a daily newspaper that reached a peak circulation of over three hundred thousand in 1944.

The Indonesian National Party (Perserikatan Nasional Indonesia), which sought independence from the Netherlands, was formed today by the twenty-six-year-old engineer Kusno Sosrodihardjo, better known as Sukarno, and members of the Algemeene Studie Club. In 1945, Sukarno would become the first president of independent Indonesia.

Calvin Coolidge enjoyed dressing up as both a cowboy and a Native American chief and having his picture taken and published in the newspapers. Here he poses with photographers who came to South Dakota to film him showing off the gaucho outfit that was given to him for his birthday by the state of South Dakota. *Courtesy of the Library of Congress, LC-USZ62-29740*

Neil Simon, one of America's most successful playwrights and screenwriters, was born today in New York City.

TUESDAY, JULY 5

In New York City, the *Herald Tribune* reported that some three hundred people were injured from fireworks on the previous day's celebrations in the city and that the fire brigades responded to over three hundred fires, most caused by fireworks. The paper also ran a report by the National Museum of Safety stating that 4,044 Americans died in the War for Independence but, between 1895 and 1927, some 4,500 Americans died in Independence Day fireworks celebrations.

After losing fifteen games in a row, the Boston Red Sox finally had a victory today when they beat the Philadelphia Athletics 6–5.

Northwest Airlines, which was founded in 1926, began carrying passengers today. Businessman Byron Webster's plane ticket from Minneapolis to Chicago meant a journey of more than twelve hours with stops in the Wisconsin cities of LaCrosse, Madison, and Milwaukee before arriving in Chicago the next morning at 2:30 a.m. Northwest would become one of the largest airlines in the United States before being merged with Delta Air Lines in 2010.

Traditionally, the summer heat closed many Broadway playhouses and productions suspended performances until the cooler weather returned in September. On the other hand, Broadway offered some new works each summer, including several lighthearted musical revues, and 1927 was no exception. Eight such revues opened in June, July, and August, and a few were lucky enough to show a profit. On this day, *Padlocks of 1927* opened and delighted audiences with its sassy sense of humor. The show's title referred to New York district attorney Wales and his fight against salacious stage shows. He got the city to pass the Padlock Act, which gave the D.A. power to close down any offending theatre for an entire year. The new law was rarely enforced and was a joke among the theatre community. The producing Shuberts capitalized on the law in *Padlocks of 1927* and hired the risqué hostess Texas Guinan, known to New York nightclubbers for her slangy style and the way she greeted each audience with "Hello, suckers!" The cast also included singer Lillian Roth, comic Jay C. Flippen, and hoofer George Raft, but it was Guinan who was the draw, ad-libbing and kidding the celebrities in the audience.

The renowned German biochemist Albrecht Kossel died from an attack of angina pectoris today in Heidelberg, Germany, at the age of seventy-three. Kossel was a pioneer in the study of genetics and discovered nucleic acids that make up biological cells. He was awarded the Nobel Prize for Physiology or Medicine in 1910.

NOBEL PRIZES

The winners of the Nobel Prizes in 1927:

Physics: American atomic physicist Arthur Holly Compton
Literature: French essayist and philosopher Henri Bergson
Chemistry: German organic chemist Heinrich Otto Wieland
Physiology or Medicine: Austrian neurophysicist Julius Wagner-Jauregg
Peace Prize: French negotiator and peace advocate Ferdinand Buisson and German
  negotiator and pacifist Ludwig Quidde

WEDNESDAY, JULY 6

The Church of England Assembly today approved a revised version of the nearly four-hundred-year-old Book of Common Prayer. After much debate, the governing assembly voted 517 to 133 in favor of the proposed revision. By law, any changes to the book had to be approved by both Houses of Parliament so the proposed version was sent there where the debate was reignited in December.

The song of domestic bliss "My Blue Heaven," by Walter Donaldson (music) and George A. Whiting (lyric), was recorded today by Paul Whiteman and his Orchestra, vocals by the Rhythm Boys (Bing Crosby, Al Rinker, and Harry Barris), and became a popular seller. But it was eclipsed in 1928 by a recording by Gene Austin and the Victor Orchestra that sold over five million copies.

THURSDAY, JULY 7

Since its founding in 1901, Henry Ford's weekly magazine, the *Dearborn Independent*, had often hinted at or openly expressed anti-Semitic views as well as negative comments about organized labor. A recent article in the paper resulted in a libel lawsuit brought by Aaron Sapiro, an activist and organizer of a Jewish farm cooperative. Ford settled out of court, but part of the agreement was an apology, which was widely published today. Such lawsuits continued, and by December Ford stopped publishing the *Independent*.

James Joyce's collection of thirteen poems titled *Pomes Penyeach* was published today by Shakespeare and Company. The poems had been composed by the Irish writer between the years 1904 and 1924 but not published until he collected them under the title, which is a pun, "pomes" suggesting the French word *pommes* (apples) and "penyeach" a Joycean neologism suggesting that by buying a dozen poems/apples you get an extra one free. The most famous poems in *Pomes Penyeach* include "Tilly," "On the Beach at Fontana," and "A Flower Given to My Daughter."

After a good deal of persuasion, British music enthusiast Christopher Stone convinced the BBC to let him do a radio program of American popular songs and American-influenced jazz with some ad-libbed commentary by himself. The show was first broadcast today and was a success. Stone is considered the first British disc jockey. Elman B. Meyers was the first American disc jockey of sorts, playing recorded songs with commentary on a New York radio station as early as 1911.

FRIDAY, JULY 8

The German general Maximilian Hoffman died today at the age of fifty-eight at a spa in Bavaria. Considered by historians as one of the most skillful military leaders of World War I, Hoffman was made chief of staff soon after the war broke out, and he spearheaded the defeat of the Russian Army on the Eastern Front in 1914.

SATURDAY, JULY 9

Heavy rain in the Saxony region of Germany caused the Elbe River to swell and led to flash floods that killed approximately two hundred people. Hardest hit was the village of Berggießhübel where ninety-three people drowned when a seven-foot-high wall of water swept through the streets of the town.

For several years the Federal Trade Commission had been investigating Hollywood's practice of "block booking," in which film distributors required movie houses to rent a package of films that included both popular and less appealing movies. Today the FTC outlawed the use of block booking, issuing a cease and desist order to Paramount Pictures, one of the prime offenders. Hollywood pretty much ignored the new law and block booking continued without penalty. Not until 1935 were more severe measures taken to stop the practice.

British writer P. G. Wodehouse saw his short story *Pig-hoo-o-o-o-ey* published today in the States before it appeared in print in his native country. The comic tale was in today's issue of the American magazine *Liberty* and is memorable for introducing Lord Emsworth's prize pig, the Empress of Blandings. In the story, Emsworth is distraught because the Empress is bound to win at the Shropshire Agricultural Show, but she has stopped eating since the pigman Wellbeloved has been thrown in jail for being drunk and disorderly. Only when Emsworth learns the call of "pig hoo-o-o-o-ey" does the Empress regain her appetite and win the competition. The story was later published in England in the August issue of the *Strand Magazine*.

In today's Major League Baseball game between the Detroit Tigers and the New York Yankees, Detroit first baseman Johnny Neun had five base hits and five stolen bases. It was the first time since 1914 to have at least five of each in one game. Neun's prowess contributed greatly to the Tigers' victory over the Yankees, 14–4.

Screen idol John Gilbert got to play against type in MGM's *Twelve Miles Out*, a sea adventure with a bit of romance thrown in. Rival bootleggers Jerry Fay (Gilbert) and Red McCue (Ernest Torrence) are flourishing during Prohibition. When Jerry has a speedboat loaded with rum and is pursued by the Coast Guard, he takes refuge in the seaside home of Jane (Joan Crawford). She threatens to call the cops, so Jerry kidnaps her and takes her aboard his ship. McCue and his crew hijack the boat, resulting in a drinking competition between the two men that gets deadly. Jerry is wounded but recaptures his boat and plans to take Jane back home but by now she has fallen in love with him and she nurses Jerry to health and happiness.

> The average admission ticket to the movies in 1927 cost sixty cents. Movie palaces cost much more but small neighborhood cinemas cost considerably less.

The American theatre lost two notable actors today. The comedy favorite John Drew Jr. died in San Francisco at the age of seventy-three. A senior member of the celebrated Drew-Barrymore family, he performed in all kinds of comedies, from Shakespearean works to modern plays. Drew was the uncle of John, Lionel, and Ethel Barrymore and the great-great-uncle to contemporary actress Drew Barrymore. Less famous but a familiar figure on Broadway, Gregory Kelly died of a heart attack in New York City today. He was only thirty-six years old. He had appeared in some hit comedies before his premature death. Kelly was married to actress Ruth Gordon, who outlived him by fifty-eight years.

SUNDAY, JULY 10

Kevin O'Higgins, Ireland's vice president and minister of justice, was assassinated today while walking to mass in Dublin. He was shot six times by three anti-Treaty members of the IRA—Timothy Coughlan, Bill Gannon, and Archie Doyle—in retaliation for O'Higgins's participation in the executions of seventy-seven IRA prisoners during the Irish Civil War of 1922. The three assassins were never apprehended, although Coughlan was killed the next year by an undercover policeman. The thirty-five-year-old O'Higgins was both revered and hated in Ireland, some proclaiming him a hero, others comparing him to Mussolini.

The eighteen-year-old Moroccan War (also known as the Rif War) ended today when General José Sanjurjo of Spain declared the pacification of Spanish Morocco. The rebellion, led by Rifian leader Abd el-Krim, was put down by the Spanish with the help of French troops and the Republic of the Rif was dissolved.

The French artist Louise Abbéma, who was instrumental in getting women artists taken seriously by critics and the public during La Belle Epoque, died today in Paris at the age of seventy-three. Abbéma was a versatile painter, sculptor, printmaker, book illustrator, and designer whose work was exhibited at the Paris Salon several times as well as at the World Columbian Exposition in Chicago in 1893 and the Exposition Universelle in Paris in 1900. She received many awards and citations during her lifetime and also wrote regularly about art for French journals. Today Abbéma is considered a pioneer in the women's art movement.

MONDAY, JULY 11

A massive earthquake with its epicenter in the northern section of the Dead Sea today killed over two hundred fifty people in an area then called Mandatory Palestine. The city of Jericho was hardest hit, but there was severe damage also in Jerusalem, Nablus, Tiberias, Salt, and Ramla. The quake was so powerful that the River Jordan was emptied and remained that way for twenty-one hours.

The first "convenience store" opened today in Dallas, Texas. John Jefferson Green began selling eggs, milk, and bread from one of the Southland Ice Company's sixteen ice house storefronts in Dallas, not only allowing customers to purchase essentials without having to travel far but also remaining open longer hours than a traditional grocery store. Green's idea developed into the Southland Corporation which in 1946 changed the stores' name to 7-Eleven because they were open from seven in the morning until eleven o'clock at night. Today there are over sixty-four thousand 7-Eleven stores in eighteen countries.

Newcomer Ethel Waters was the highlight of the African American revue *Africana*, which opened on Broadway today, the critics saluting her dancing as well as her singing. The notices were favorable, but with so many "Negro" revues this season, competition was tough and the show ran only nine weeks.

TUESDAY, JULY 12

In today's baseball game in which the New York Yankees shut out the Cleveland Indians 7–0, Yankee favorite Babe Ruth hit his thirtieth home run of the season, as well as his seventy-seventh and seventy-eighth runs batted in (RBIs). Lou Gehrig knocked in his league-leading 101st run during the same game. Gehrig would eventually have the most RBIs with 173, with Ruth closing the gap at 165 by season's end.

Dorothy Parker's caustic short story "The Sexes" was published in today's issue of the *New Republic*. A conversation between a contemporary man and woman becomes an argument because she will not say what she means and he is not smart enough to know why. The story is still remarkably relevant.

WEDNESDAY, JULY 13

A delegation from the National Women's Party presented themselves at Coolidge's "summer White House" in Rapid City, South Dakota, to get his support for an Equal Rights Amendment to the Constitution. Since many women in America were not in favor of such a law, it was easy for Coolidge to turn down the delegates.

The influential Turkish architect known as Mimar Kemaleddin ("Kemaleddin the Architect") died today in Ankara of a cerebral hemorrhage at the age of fifty-seven. His career began in the final years of the Ottoman Empire and continued into the age of the Republic, leading a new form of design known as the First Turkish National Architectural Movement. Kemaleddin designed several tombs, shrines, mosques, hotels, train stations, and other structures throughout Turkey. He was also a noted restorer of buildings, most memorably the Dome of the Rock in Jerusalem.

THURSDAY, JULY 14

In his second attempt to fly from Oakland, California, to Honolulu, pilot Ernest L. Smith took off today with navigator Emory Bronte in the monoplane *City of Oakland*

and nearly succeeded. After flying over twenty-six hours, the plane ran out of fuel and Smith made a forced landing, ending up in a tree on the Hawaiian island of Molokai. Because he did not make it to Honolulu, Smith was disqualified from the Dole Air Race and its $25,000 prize.

One of the most discussed books of the twentieth century, Hermann Hesse's *Der Steppenwolf*, was published today by S. Fischer Verlag in Germany. The novel is autobiographical and psychological and reflects the author's personal and spiritual crisis during a period of his life when he suffered severe depression and considered suicide. Harry Haller, the novel's middle-aged protagonist, lives a hollow existence. He was once a highly respected intellectual, but now he only views the world with bitterness and disgust, retreating from the world by day and at night visiting taverns. Part of Haller is wolf-like, a savage beast who travels alone; the other part is still human, searching for companionship, society, and even love. *Der Steppenwolf* was first translated into English in 1929 and has remained a much analyzed and respected novel ever since, though Hesse (who died in 1962) himself always claimed that *Steppenwolf* was greatly misunderstood.

FRIDAY, JULY 15

Known in Austria as the July Revolt of 1927 or the Vienna Palace of Justice Fire, riots broke out in the capital city when a jury found three members of the right-wing veterans' organization *Frontkampfer Vereinigung* not guilty for killing a member of the leftist organization and mortally wounding an eight-year-old boy in the town of Schattendorf on January 30. This "Schattendorf Verdict" led to a general strike that soon turned into a full-scale riot with the burning of the Palace of Justice (Justizpalast) and the police firing into the crowd and killing eighty-nine protestors. The fighting was so violent that over six hundred police as well as over six hundred demonstrators were injured.

Twenty-five-year-old American golfer Bobby Jones successfully defended his champion status today during the sixty-second British Open at the Old Course at St. Andrews, Scotland. On the last day of the three-day competition, Jones shot 73 and 72 for a 285 total, the second of his three victories at the celebrated golf tournament. Frenchman Aubrey Boomer and Englishman Fred Robson tied for second place.

The Irish politician Countess Markievicz (née Constance Gore-Booth) died today of complications related to appendicitis in Dublin at the age of fifty-nine. A founding member of several Irish Free State organizations, Markievicz was the first woman to be elected to the British House of Commons. After Irish independence from the United Kingdom, she became the Irish Free State's Minister for Labour.

American Bobby Jones was not only one of the top professional golfers of the twentieth century, but also a cofounder of the Masters Tournament, and he introduced many innovations in how golf competitions were organized and run, ideas that have been utilized by professional golf tournaments around the world. *Photofest © Photofest*

SATURDAY, JULY 16

The first recorded use of dive bombing occurred today during the Battle of Ocotal in Nicaragua. In the middle of the night, Augusto César Sandino and a few hundred rebels attacked the American garrison at Ocotal, which was manned by only thirty-eight American marines and forty-seven Nicaraguan civil guards. USMC Captain Gilbert Hatfield and his vastly outnumbered men held the garrison throughout three assaults. When word of the attack reached Major Ross E. Rowell at the Marine Corps airbase at Managua, he led a squadron of five De Havilland DH-4 biplanes that flew to Ocotal and dived as low as three hundred feet to drop bombs on the rebels. Sandino and the rebels were surprised and astonished by the unheard-of maneuver and fled. Some three hundred rebels, or Sandinistas as they were thereafter called, were killed, and only one U.S. marine died in the battle. Although the conflict at Ocotal was an American victory, it was the beginning of Sandino's five-year war against the U.S. occupation of Nicaragua.

Twenty-three-year-old Theodor Geisel had his first cartoon published in today's issue of the *Saturday Evening Post*. As a college student he had started using his mother's maiden name, Seuss, and came up with the nom de plume Dr. Seuss, which appeared in print today and for the rest of his very long career.

S. J. Perelman, writing in the humor magazine *Judge*, lampooned the latest dance fads named after animals (he calls one the "The Grizzly Hug") in today's piece "Dance Madness at Coney Island."

SUNDAY, JULY 17

The Tour de France, the one-month-long bicycle race with twenty-four stages that starts and ends in Paris and covers 3,349 kilometers along the borders of the country, was held for the twenty-first time this year and ended today. The winner was Nicolas Frantz of Luxembourg, who had come in second in 1926 and who would win again in 1928.

MONDAY, JULY 18

Playing against his former team, Philadelphia Athletics center fielder Ty Cobb hit a home run today against the Detroit Tigers. No one seemed to be aware of it at the time, but it was Cobb's four thousandth hit of his Major League career. Cobb was the first player to ever amass that many hits and is still one of only two to do so. His lifetime total of 4,189 hits remained a record until broken by Pete Rose in 1985. On the same day, New York Giants right fielder Mel Ott hit the first home run of his Major League Baseball career, an inside-the-park homer, in a game against the St. Louis Cardinals. Ott would chalk up 511 homers before he retired in 1947.

An international furor was started today when German president Paul von Hindenburg spoke at the dedication of the war memorial at Tannenberg and in his speech denied that Germany had initiated the Great War. His statement not only contradicted Article 231 of the Treaty of Versailles but also fueled anti-German feelings around the world. The eighty-year-old Hindenburg insisted that Germany entered the war as "the means of self-assertion against a world full of enemies. Pure in heart, we set off to the defense of the Fatherland and with clean hands the German army carried the sword."

TUESDAY, JULY 19

Although Spain had been using a design approved by King Charles III in 1760 for its national flag, it was never officially adopted by the government until today. The flag, with a coat of arms against a yellow field between two red stripes, was used for only four more years. When the Second Spanish Republic came to power in 1931, the flag was changed, as it would be several more times until the present day.

Celebrated humorist James Thurber, who was hired by *New Yorker* magazine editor Harold Ross earlier in the year, was promoted to the popular "Talk of the Town" column today and started writing short and usually sly reports on the doings of Manhattan. Thurber would eventually take over the column, then start doing short stories in 1928 and cartoons in 1930. Before his death in 1961, Thurber's contribution to the *New Yorker* is estimated at one thousand articles, stories, and cartoons.

The Senegalese religious leader Amadou Bamba died today at the age of seventy-four. Throughout his life, the Muslim Bamba was a pacifist and preached, wrote poems, and meditated, while Senegal remained under French colonial rule. In 1883 he founded the Mouride brotherhood and soon had many followers. The French government exiled Bamba to Ghana in 1895 and then Mauritania in 1907 but once it was determined that he was not going to lead a rebellion, he was allowed to return to Senegal. Bamba began the building of the Mouride mosque at the holy city of Touba in 1926. When it was completed in 1963, it was the largest mosque in sub-Saharan Africa.

Having been arrested after the Shanghai Massacre on April 12, the young Chinese Communist leader Zhao Shiyan was executed today by the Nationalists. He was only twenty-six years old. Today in China, Zhao is honored as a Communist martyr.

WEDNESDAY, JULY 20

King Ferdinand I of Romania, who had been on the throne since 1914, died today from cancer at the age of sixty-one at his palace in Sinaia. Ferdinand had not sided with the Central Powers during the Great War, instead fighting against the Germans.

Consequently, after the war the size of Romania was greatly enlarged to include Transylvania and other lands. On the death of the King, his five-year-old grandson was named the new monarch and given the name King Michael I. Until the boy came of age, Romania was to be governed by three regents. Ferdinand's son Carol, who had renounced his claim to the throne and was living in Paris, changed his mind and returned to Romania and proclaimed himself King Carol II. He reestablished ties with Germany, supported the Nazi Party, and even passed anti-Semitic laws in Romania. By 1940 Carol was virtually a Fascist dictator and was forced by the government to abdicate the throne and go into exile. Michael I was reinstated as the King of Romania, but he turned out to be the last monarch, abdicating the throne to the Communists in 1947. He lived to the age of ninety-six, dying in Switzerland in 2017.

> The most popular camera in 1927 for the amateur shutterbug was Kodak's Box Brownie Camera which cost $2.29.

THURSDAY, JULY 21

A record crowd of ninety thousand packed Yankee Stadium today to see the up-and-coming twenty-five-year-old boxer Jack Sharkey face the thirty-two-year-old former heavyweight champion Jack Dempsey to determine who would be the challenger in a September bout against champion Gene Tunney. Sharkey was the six-to-five favorite and was winning after six rounds. But in the seventh, Dempsey struck two low-body blows to Sharkey, who unwisely turned toward referee Jack O'Sullivan to complain of a foul. When Sharkey turned his head, Dempsey struck him in the jaw with a short left hook and knocked him out.

FRIDAY, JULY 22

The famous Italian soccer football team Associazione Sportiva Romamerger, better known as A.S. Roma or just Roma, was created today by merging three soccer clubs: Roman FC, SS Alba-Audace, and Fortitudo-Pro Roma SGS.

Ernest Hemingway's celebrated short story "Fifty Grand" first appeared in the July issue of the *Atlantic Monthly*, then in October was included in the Hemingway anthology *Men without Women*. The welterweight champ Jack Brennan is training in New Jersey for a boxing match against the challenger Jimmy Walcott but, bothered with money and family worries and unable to sleep, Jack tells his trainer Doyle that he doesn't think he has a chance of beating Walcott. After some strangers approach Jack and have words with him in his room, Jack tells Doyle to put his money on Walcott because he is going to throw the fight. Jack himself has bet $50,000 on Walcott but once in the ring he gets carried away and nearly defeats Walcott. Only by punching him below the belt and the move declared foul does Jack lose the match. "Fifty Grand" is an unusual Hemingway story in that it is narrated by Doyle, a character in the tale, rather than the author's usual third person, objective style.

SATURDAY, JULY 23

The infamous British officer Reginald Dyer, labeled the "Butcher of Amritsar," died today after a series of strokes in Somerset, England, at the age of sixty-two. While serving as a temporary brigadier general in the British Army in India in 1919, he ordered his troops to fire into a crowd of protesters in Amritsar, killing hundreds of unarmed civilians. Dyer was recalled from India and allowed to resign with a considerable pension, which caused further tension between India and Great Britain. The Amritsar Massacre is considered a significant event in the waning of British rule in India.

Dorothy Parker's short but potent poem "Frustration" was printed in today's issue of the *New Yorker* magazine. The speaker reflects on the ways one could kill off all unwanted and irritating associates but, having no lethal weapon, must be satisfied with wishing them all in hell. "Frustration" is among the most bitter of all Parker's poems.

The 1895 Civil War melodrama *The Heart of Maryland* by David Belasco was a giant hit in its day and had made a stage star of Mrs. Leslie Carter. There had been screen versions in 1915 and 1921 but Warner Brothers' thought there was still life in the old tale so today the studio released its adaptation starring Dolores Costello. The screenplay made many changes in the story of a family split by their allegiances to the North and the South, but the movie retains the play's most famous scene in which the heroine Maryland (Costello) climbs into the church belfry and keeps the bell from sounding the alarm to the troops by holding on to the clapper and swinging with it back and forth. Despite Costello's popularity (she starred in five films in 1927), *The Heart of Maryland* was not a box office success. Fox had more luck with its comedy *Paid to Love*, which boasted no big-name stars. The American banker Peter Roberts (J. Farrell MacDonald), in a Balkan duchy on business, befriends the crown prince Michael (George O'Brien) and acts as matchmaker, introducing him to the cabaret dancer Gaby (Virginia Valli). The prince and the commoner fall in love but several complications stand in the way of their marriage until Gaby is made a duchess. Howard Hawks directed the romantic comedy with panache and the performances are delightful. *Paid to Love* is among the many silent films that were believed lost for many years and then rediscovered in the 1970s.

SUNDAY, JULY 24

The Menin Gate Memorial to the Missing, a monument to nearly ninety thousand soldiers of Great Britain and the Commonwealth who went missing in action in the three Battles of Ypres in the Great War, was dedicated in Ypres, Belgium, today. The structure is a triumphal arch with a barrel vaulted ceiling with the names of 54,900 soldiers who were missing in action engraved on stone panels. Another 34,888 names are inscribed at a memorial at the nearby Tyne Cot cemetery. Each evening at eight o'clock, except during the German occupation of Belgium in World War II, the local Last Post Association temporarily closes the road going through the arch and buglers play the British cavalry call "Last Post."

When Babe Ruth hit his thirty-first home run today in a game between the New York Yankees and the Chicago White Sox in Comiskey Park, he achieved the distinction of having hit a homer in every ballpark in the American League.

Harriet Beecher Stowe's *Uncle Tom's Cabin* was presented on Broadway as a musical in 1924. Titled *Topsy and Eva*, the two characters were portrayed by the popular Duncan Sisters, who also wrote some jazz-flavored songs mixed with some old numbers. The plot centered on the relationship between the loving Eva St. Clare (Vivian Duncan) and the odd but cheerful slave Topsy (Rosetta Duncan in blackface) on a plantation in the old South. The Duncans recreated their performances in a screen version that was released today. Even without the sound of their singing, the sisters captivated their audiences. The film survives and is a valuable record of vaudeville and minstrel shows but very little of *Uncle Tom's Cabin* survives the adaptation. The two heroines are pictured from their birth (a black stork delivers Topsy) through their childhood to a happy ending in which Eva lives thanks to the prayers of Topsy and the other slaves. Interestingly, Uncle Tom is played by the African American actor Noble Johnson and, compared to the dancing, frolicking Duncans, his performance is rather subdued and realistic. Legend has it that the film pioneer D. W. Griffith directed portions of the film but was not credited. Despite its racist aspects, *Topsy and Eva* is a surprisingly enjoyable movie.

Two notable suicides occurred today on opposite sides of the Pacific Ocean. In Tokyo, the Japanese author Ryūnosuke Akutagawa took his own life with an overdose of barbiturates. He was only thirty-five years old. Akutagawa wrote over 150 short stories and defined the new style of Japanese literature in the twentieth century. He also influenced Western writers who were inspired by his brilliant character development and plot lines. His most famous story is "Rashomon" which has been adapted in several languages for film, the stage, and opera. Today the Akutagawa Prize is a highly revered literary award in Japan. The other suicide occurred in San Francisco where Maurice E. Crumpacker, a Republican member of the U.S. House of Representatives for Oregon, jumped into San Francisco Bay and drowned. He was forty years old. Both Akutagawa and Crumpacker had been showing signs of mental anguish and instability in the days before their deaths.

Since the income tax reduction of 1926, most Americans in 1927 found themselves tax free. With a tax exemption of $3,500 for a married couple and most annual incomes below that amount, 98 percent of workers paid no income tax at all.

MONDAY, JULY 25

A system for remote control of railroad signals from a central location, invented by Sedgwick N. Wight, was first used today for a forty-mile stretch of the New York Central Railroad between Walbridge and Berwick, Ohio. The same basic centralized traffic control system is still in use on railroads around the world.

The historic Prince of Wales Hotel in Waterton National Park, Alberta, Canada, opened to the public today. Built by the Great Northern Railway to encourage Americans to cross the border to the exclusive, chalet-style hotel during Prohibition, it was named after the then Prince of Wales, heir to the British throne. It was designated a National Historic Site of Canada in 1995.

TUESDAY, JULY 26

In China, the Central Executive Committee of the Kuomintang Party today passed a resolution refusing to allow Communists to be members of the country's Nationalist Party. The committee also went so far as to call for the outlawing of the Chinese Communist Party.

The Ford Motor Company today announces that its earnings for the first six months of 1927 were $129 million, the largest semiannual income on record for a manufacturing company. This number is even more impressive when one considers that the popular Ford Model A was not put on the market until December of 1927.

Hollywood writer and agent June Mathis died of a heart attack today in New York City while watching a Broadway show. She was forty years old. Mathis was one of the most successful women in the film business, having discovered Rudolph Valentino and written the screenplays for some of his most popular movies. She wrote over 100 scripts for different studios before her premature death.

WEDNESDAY, JULY 27

Only eight weeks after Charles Lindbergh landed in Paris in the *Spirit of St. Louis*, his autobiography *We* was published today by G. P. Putnam's Sons in New York. The 319-

page illustrated book is not an accounting of his life but of the preparation and execution of his famous transatlantic flight. The title refers to the team of Lindbergh and his plane, though some say that Lindbergh meant it to stand for his St. Louis backers and himself. *We* was an immediate bestseller and remained so for over a year. With its translation into many different languages, *We* sold over six hundred fifty thousand copies the first year, earning him $250,000, ten times the amount of the Orteig Prize. Lindbergh would go on to write or cowrite fourteen other books.

A typhoon that had battered the Philippines for four days and then moved west into southeastern China finally dissipated today. It left behind floods along the Jiulong River that drowned ten thousand people, mostly in mountainous areas near Zhangzhou. The flooding also left another one hundred thousand people homeless.

During today's reenactment of Custer's Last Stand in a Montana amphitheater before ten thousand spectators, a team of horses panicked and charged through the crowd and out of the arena heading toward an open-air automobile where President and Mrs. Coolidge were sitting and watching the show. The horses were about twenty feet from the car when they veered away. Amazingly neither the Coolidges nor other spectators were injured.

The American freighter SS *Carl D. Bradley*, for twenty-two years the longest (639 feet) and largest (10,028 tonnage) ship on the Great Lakes, made its maiden voyage today, traveling from Lorain, Ohio, to Rogers City, Michigan. For most of its life, the *Carl D. Bradley* carried limestone and other heavy cargo. Caught in a storm on Lake Michigan in 1958, the freighter sank, with all but two of its thirty-five crew members lost.

British artist Solomon Joseph Solomon died today in Birchington, England, at the age of sixty-six. A distinguished painter of portraits and scenes from mythology and the Bible, Solomon was a member of the Royal Academy who illustrated books and authored the influential tome *The Practice of Oil Painting and Drawing* (1914). Yet perhaps his greatest contribution was the development of camouflage during World War I, convincing the military to use his designs for camouflaging watch towers and tanks as well as using camouflage netting to hide artillery and troop stations.

THURSDAY, JULY 28

A summer pleasure ride aboard the excursion boat *The Favorite* ended in tragedy today. About seventy-five people were cruising from Chicago's Lincoln Park to the Municipal Pier when a heavy squall rose up on Lake Michigan half a mile from land. The passengers moved to the leeward side of *The Favorite* seeking shelter from the storm, causing the vessel to capsize. Twenty-seven people, including sixteen children, drowned. Eleven of the survivors were said to be rescued by Olympic medal-winning swimmer Johnny Weissmuller, who was swimming in Lake Michigan training for the Chicago Marathon.

FRIDAY, JULY 29

One of the most controversial moments in the modern history of the Russian Orthodox Church occurred today when Sergei Stragorodsky, patriarch of the Russian Orthodox Church since 1925, issued the "Civil Fatherland Declaration" that obliged Orthodox clergy to proclaim loyalty to the Soviet government. Many worshippers refused to comply with the edict, particularly bishops and priests, who chose to emigrate. This resulted in a synod of Russian bishops in Karlovtsi in Yugoslavia, who set up a Russian Orthodox Church in Exile and disavowed all links with the Mother Church in Soviet Russia.

Also controversial was the Trade Disputes and Trade Unions Act of 1927, which came into effect in the United Kingdom today after receiving approval by King George V. The act was in reaction to the General Strike of 1926, which had crippled the nation by closing factories and most forms of transportation. The new law put criminal penalties on secondary action, including sympathy strikes against the government. The Labor Party started working immediately to have the act repealed but it took until 1946 to do so.

SATURDAY, JULY 30

Although a reigning king of England had never yet visited Canada, two future kings arrived in Quebec today on the liner RMS *Empress of Australia* to begin a month-long tour of the Dominion to honor Canada's Diamond Jubilee. Joining British prime minister Stanley Baldwin were members of the royal family who were first and second in line for the throne: the Prince of Wales, who would become King Edward VIII, and the Duke of York, who would be King George VI. During their stay, the two princes dedicated Union Station and the Princes' Gate in Toronto and the Peace Bridge over the Niagara River.

SUNDAY, JULY 31

Music historians point to this date as the birth of country music as a mainstream art form. Ralph Peer of the Victor Talking Machine Company spent the month of July in Bristol, Tennessee, recording local musicians and singers. During these "Bristol Sessions," records were made of Henry Whitter, the Alcoa Quartet, the Teneva Ramblers, Uncle Eck Dunford, Jimmie Rodgers, and others. On the last day of the month, singer A. P. Carter; his wife, Sara, on autoharp; and his sister-in-law, guitarist Maybelle, showed up from Maces Springs, Virginia. Never having cut a record before, the Carter Family was paid fifty dollars by Peer to record six songs, including "Wabash Cannonball," "Keep on the

Sunny Side," "Will the Circle Be Unbroken," and "Wildwood Flower." The recordings were not only popular but marked the first time such country songs were heard by many Americans across the nation. The original Carter Family made records for the next three decades and the trio was the first group later inducted into the Country Music Hall of Fame. The descendants of the Carter Family are still performing today.

Claudette Colbert had a featured role in First National's *For the Love of Mike*, and the critics pointed out her beauty and notable screen presence. Unfortunately, the movie is lost. The plot centered on the foundling Mike Lyon, who is abandoned as a baby in the Hell's Kitchen section of New York and raised by the Irish street cleaner Patrick O'Malley, the Jewish tailor Abraham Katz, and the German deli owner Herman Schultz. As an adult, Mike (Ben Lyon) falls in love with the Italian neighbor girl Mary (Colbert), who convinces him he should grant his three fathers' wishes and go to college. At Yale, Mike is a first-rate athlete, but he gives into the temptations of drink and gambling. Deep in debt, Mike agrees to throw the crucial Yale-Harvard rowing match to satisfy the gamblers' demands. But when Mary arrives with his three fathers to watch the match, Mike does not go through with the plan, wins the race, gets to marry Mary, and the three fathers settle with the gamblers. *For the Love of Mike* was one of director Frank Capra's early feature film assignments.

Sir Harry Johnston, the British explorer who traveled extensively throughout Africa during the 1880s and 1890s, died today in Nottinghamshire, England, at the age of sixty-nine. Johnson was also a linguist who spoke several African languages, an artist who recorded on paper scenes from nature and tribal life, and an author who penned over forty books on African subjects. The prominent amateur golf champ Walter Travis died today in Denver at the age of sixty-five. The Australian-born golfer came to America as a young adult in 1886 and in 1898 participated in his first U.S. Amateur tournament. He won the championship in 1900, 1901, and 1903, and the British tournament in 1904, all in the pre-professional era. Travis made many other contributions to the sport, such as writing books and founding magazines on golf, popularizing the use of the Schenectady Putter, and developing and designing several notable golf courses, many of which are still in use today.

The population of the United States, as recorded in July of 1927, was 119 million. That same year, the population of China was over 484 million.

AUGUST

MONDAY, AUGUST 1

Today's date is considered the birthday of the Communist Chinese People's Liberation Army, still celebrated in China as Army Day. Historians call it the Nanchang Uprising and the beginning of the Chinese Civil War between the Nationalists and the Communists. In order to counterattack the purges the Nationalists were making on Communist settlements, Zhou Enlai, He Long, and other leftist revolutionaries led twenty thousand Communists in an attack on the city of Nanchang. They took and held the city for five days even as the Nationalists lay siege on Nanchang with heavy artillery. On August 5, the Communists escaped from the city and took refuge in the Jinggang Mountains, where they prepared for further assaults.

Comic character actors Wallace Beery and Raymond Hatton were teamed in a handful of silent films, including Paramount's slapstick comedy *Fireman, Save My Child*, which was released today. Beery and Hatton play firefighters Elmer and Sam, who spend more time tending to the spoiled Dora, the daughter of Chief Dumston, than to putting out fires. The girl pulls the fire alarm whenever she needs help or attention so Sam and Elmer eventually ignore one of her alarms, only to learn it is a real fire. All ends well, but only after a lot of pratfalls and other broad physical comedy. Opening the same day in the States was the British historical romance *Madame Pompadour*, which starred American actress Dorothy Gish as the mistress of France's King Louis XV. She may belong to the king, but Madame loves Rene Laval (Antonio Moreno), who has been thrown in jail for his antiroyalist politics. Using her influence, Madame has Rene freed and made her personal bodyguard, adding romantic and political complications. The British National Films production was lavish and eye-catching but a little on the dull side, so it was not a box office hit on either side of the Atlantic.

TUESDAY, AUGUST 2

In his usual quiet and unobtrusive way, President Coolidge made it clear today he would not run for reelection in 1928. During his extended vacation in Rapid City, South Dakota, Coolidge requested press members to report to Central High School at noon. There the reporters found him in a classroom sitting at the teacher's desk. He asked each member of the press to file past the desk and as they did so he handed them a slip of paper that read, "I do not choose to run for President in nineteen twenty-eight." When asked if he would care to comment further, Coolidge replied, "No" and left the room. The surprise announcement had been timed so that the news would not be made public until after the close of trade on that day's stock markets. To this day, historians argue about the reasons why Coolidge did not run when it was clear he would have easily been reelected. Some believe he saw the crash coming; others point out that he was never happy living in Washington. And there is also the possibility that Coolidge was still suffering from depression since the death of his young son Calvin Jr., in 1924. From the moment of Coolidge's decision, it was clear to many that Secretary of Commerce Herbert Hoover was the most likely candidate to take his place.

Allez-Oop was the carefree title of a Broadway revue that found an audience in the hot days of summer. Much of its success could be attributed to two favorite comic actors, Charles Butterworth and Victor Moore, both of whom were known for their low-key but very funny antics. Both the press and the public were enthusiastic enough about them and their show that *Allez-Oop* ran fifteen weeks.

President Calvin Coolidge (left) and his Secretary of Commerce Herbert Hoover were very different kinds of men. While Coolidge was laid back and passive, Hoover was a take-charge leader who was politically ambitious. He took over projects that Coolidge avoided, so it was natural that Hoover would eventually take up his job as well. *Courtesy of the Library of Congress, LC-DIG-hec-35160*

WEDNESDAY, AUGUST 3

Fifteen miners were killed when there was an explosion deep inside the West Kentucky Coal Company's Mine Number 7 at Clay, Kentucky. The disaster occurred one day before the tenth anniversary of an explosion, on August 4, 1917, at the same mine. That disaster killed sixty-two coal miners.

THURSDAY, AUGUST 4

Three days after the Carter Family had cut their debut single, Jimmie Rodgers recorded in the same studio in Bristol, Tennessee, his first two country songs: the yodeling lullaby "Sleep, Baby, Sleep" and "The Soldier's Sweetheart."

The concept of a "rebroadcast" was introduced today when Dallas radio station WFAA in Dallas decided to replay NBC Radio's June 11 broadcast of Charles Lindbergh's parade in Washington. They were able to do this because a phonograph record had been made by the RCA Victor company of the original broadcast.

The pioneer country music singer, musician, and composer Jimmie Rodgers was not only the genre's first nationally known country and western star, he also performed folk and blues and introduced yodeling to American popular music. Rodgers died in 1933 at the age of thirty five, but the Father of Country Music inspired and influenced dozens of later artists. *Photofest © Photofest*

The French pioneer photographer Eugène Atget died today in Libourne, France, at the age of seventy. His passing was little noted in the press because Atget did not find fame until years after his death. His photos were of a documentary nature yet were often more surrealistic than realistic. One of his life-long projects was to photograph as many streets and buildings in Paris as he could before modernization had destroyed them. The later French surrealist artists were greatly influenced by Atget's use of double exposure, blurred figures in a streetscape, and time-exposure photographs.

FRIDAY, AUGUST 5

In order to protect the United Kingdom from the possibility of the British pound being devalued against the U.S. dollar, today the U.S. Federal Reserve Board cut the prime lending rate at the same time that British chancellor of the exchequer Winston Churchill placed Britain back on the gold standard. It was an unusual step for a major economic power to change its policy to come to the aid of a secondary currency.

SATURDAY, AUGUST 6

Rolla H. Harger, a professor of biochemistry and toxicology at the Indiana School of Medicine, today demonstrated how breath contained in a balloon could be dispersed into sulfuric acid and then accurately measured to calculate blood alcohol content. Harger later patented his device and called it the Drunkometer, an early version of the breathalyzer used by police today. Also invented and demonstrated today was the negative feedback amplifier, an important breakthrough in electronics. American electrical engineer Harold Stephen Black spent years developing a way to get rid of the distortion when two electronic signals moved in a linear way. The negative feedback amplifier eliminated the linear configuration and made long distance communication clearer and static free.

United Artists' *College*, starring Buster Keaton, had its premiere in San Francisco today. He played the bookish college student Ronald, who looks down on sports until he realizes all the co-eds, including his heart's desire Mary, are smitten with the jocks on campus. Ronald attempts to join various team sports, including baseball and track, but fails miserably. He finally makes the rowing team but the coach puts a sleeping potion in Ronald's drink to get him eliminated. The plan backfires when another rower drinks the potion, and Ronald bungles his way through the race and actually wins it. The jealous athlete Jeff, who has been kicked out of school, kidnaps Mary and brings her to his dorm room, knowing she too will be expelled if found there. But Ronald pole vaults up and in through the window saving Mary's honor and winning her heart. *College* is well constructed and produced but it is Keaton who makes the movie worth watching.

SUNDAY, AUGUST 7

The Peace Bridge, an international bridge connecting Canada and the United States across the Niagara River, was officially dedicated today. The 5,800-foot-long steel bridge, which extends from Buffalo, New York, to Fort Erie, Ontario, had opened to the public on June 1, but it was today's ceremony that drew a host of notables. From Great Britain, future kings Edward, Prince of Wales, and Prince George, Duke of York, were joined by the British prime minister, Stanley Baldwin. From the United States, Vice President Charles G. Dawes, Secretary of State Frank B. Kellogg, and New York governor Al Smith were in attendance. Canadian prime minister William Lyon Mackenzie King and Ontario premier Howard Ferguson were also present. About a hundred thousand Americans and Canadians gathered on each end of the bridge and the ceremony was given a live broadcast in both countries, listened to by an estimated fifty million people.

For twenty years, Florida rum smuggler James Horace Alderman had been one of the most notorious criminals in coastal waters, earning such titles as the King of the Rum Runners and the Gulf Stream Pirate. Since Prohibition had started, he had become even more infamous for his smuggling of all kinds of alcohol. Today he was intercepted by a Coast Guard cutter in the waters between Bimini and Florida. The encounter turned violent and Alderman killed a Prohibition agent, a Coast Guardsman, and a machinist. Alderman was tried, found guilty, and hanged in August 1929.

Politician and military figure Major General Leonard Wood died today in Boston at the age of sixty-six. During his impressive career he served as chief of staff of the U.S. Army, governor-general of Cuba, and governor-general of the Philippines. He was also a politician who nearly won the Republican nomination for president in 1920 and a commander in the Apache Wars, the Spanish-American War, the Philippine-American War, and World War I.

Pope Cyril V of Alexandria, patriarch of the Coptic Orthodox Christian Church since 1874, died today in Egypt at the age of ninety-six. He served as pope longer than any other in the Coptic religion.

MONDAY, AUGUST 8

The first stock market in the Philippines, the Manila Stock Exchange, was founded today by five American businessmen. Some years later the Makati Stock Exchange was formed, and in 1994, the rival markets would merge to create the Philippine Stock Exchange.

A German cinema classic, *Dr. Mabuse, der Spieler* (*Dr. Mabuse: The Gambler*), was first released in Berlin in 1922 but was not seen in the United States until its New York City premiere on this date. Loosely based on a novel by Norbert Jacques, the two-part movie dramatizes several deeds of the diabolical Mabuse (Rudolf Klein-Rogge), who uses his gang of thugs, psychic manipulation, kidnapping, hypnotism, and various disguises to control the Berlin underworld, in particular the gambling racket. He is eventually brought down by the state prosecutor, Norbert von Wenk, but survives to return in several movie sequels. Fritz Lang was the ingenious director who experimented with nighttime photography, superimposed images, and other special effects. The two parts of *Dr. Mabuse: The Gambler*, running four and a half hours, encapsulate the chaotic state of Weimar Germany in the 1920s and had little appeal to American moviegoers. Not until the 1970s would it be embraced in America as a cinema classic.

Retired professional baseball player Billy Gilbert died of apoplexy today in New York City at the age of fifty-one. He played second base for four different teams (Milwaukee Brewers, Baltimore Orioles, New York Giants, and St. Louis Cardinals) between 1901 and 1909, and was on the Giants team when they won the World Series in 1905.

TUESDAY, AUGUST 9

British actor Robert Shaw was born today in Westhoughton, Lancashire, England.

FUTURE ACTORS AND ACTRESSES

Some notable actors and actresses born in 1927:

Tom Bosley (d. 2010)	Pat McCormick (d. 2005)
James Broderick (d. 1982)	Roger Moore (d. 2017)
Pat Carroll	Lois Nettleton (d. 2008)
Jack Cassidy (d. 1976)	Patrick O'Neal (d. 1994)
Michael Constantine	Geoffrey Palmer
William Daniels	Estelle Parsons
Peter Falk (d. 2011)	Brock Peters (d. 2005)
Robert Guillaume (d. 2017)	Sidney Poitier
Rosemary Harris	Barbara Rush
Dickie Jones (d. 2014)	George C. Scott (d. 1999)
Robert Keeshan (d. 2004)	Robert Shaw (d. 1978)
Alan King (d. 2004)	McLean Stevenson (d. 1996)
Phyllis Kirk (d. 2006)	Jerry Stiller
Harvey Korman (d. 2008)	Carl "Alfalfa" Switzer (d. 1959)
Janet Leigh (d. 2004)	Clint Walker (d. 2018)
Gina Lollobrigida	Virginia Weidler (d. 1968)

See October 28 for singers born in 1927.

WEDNESDAY, AUGUST 10

President Coolidge wore full cowboy regalia today when he dedicated Mount Rushmore on the site where the monument was to be built in South Dakota. After promising national funding for the carving of the massive project, the president handed sculptor Gutzon Borglum a set of stone carving tools, and Borglum climbed to the top of the mountain and began drilling where George Washington's head would one day be. Actual work on the memorial would not begin until October 4.

Celebrated writers Dorothy Parker, John Dos Passos, and Edna St. Vincent Millay were among those gathered in front of the State House in Boston to protest the impending execution of Sacco and Vanzetti. Governor Fuller also received letters from such esteemed persons as Albert Einstein, H. G. Wells, Upton Sinclair, Eleanor Roosevelt, and George Bernard Shaw.

King Sisowath of Cambodia, monarch of the French protectorate since 1904, died today in Phnom Penh at the age of eighty-six. The Buddhist king was succeeded by his son, Sisowath Monivong.

THURSDAY, AUGUST 11

Éamon de Valera had been active in Irish independence for decades, having participated in the 1916 Easter Rising, the War of Independence, and the Irish Civil War, as well as founding the Irish independence party, Fianna Fáil. Today de Valera took his seat in the parliament of the Irish Free State, the Dáil Éireann, even though it would require him to sign an oath of allegiance to the king. Legend says that de Valera solved this ethical dilemma by covering the written oath with one hand while applying his signature with the other hand.

FRIDAY, AUGUST 12

The *Bardo Thodol*, an ancient Tibetan text intended to guide one through the consciousness one has after death and in the interval between death and rebirth, was published today for the first time in the United States by Oxford University Press. Translator Dr. Walter Y. Evans-Wentz titled the work *The Tibetan Book of the Dead* because of the parallels he found with the Egyptian *Book of the Dead*. The *Bardo Thodol* was composed in the eighth century by Padmasambhava, written down by his student Yeshe Tsogyal, buried in the Gampo Mountains in Tibet, and later discovered by Karma Lingpa in the fourteenth century.

SATURDAY, AUGUST 13

Actor Lon Chaney, always on the lookout for challenging roles, played a mentally deficient Russian peasant in MGM's *Mockery*. Set during the Russian Civil War following the revolution, the Siberian drifter Sergei (Chaney) helps the disguised Countess Tatiana escape the Bolsheviks and is later rewarded with a job in her household. But Sergei eventually gets the revolutionary fever and temporarily turns against the countess until his loyalty leads him to give his life for her. Opening to mixed notices, *Mockery* was not a box office success. The movie was believed lost until a print was discovered in the 1970s and many now consider Chaney's performance as one of his best.

The very popular author James Oliver Curwood died today in Owosso, Michigan, of an infection and blood poisoning from an insect bite he got during a fishing trip in Florida some months before. He was forty-nine years old. Curwood's adventure novels usually took place in some kind of wilderness and many of them were bestsellers, making him one of the most successful writers of fiction in the 1910s and 1920s. His books also were adapted into eighteen movies. Interest in Curwood's fiction was revived in 1988 when his 1916 novel *The Grizzly King* was made into the popular French film *The Bear*.

SUNDAY, AUGUST 14

Herbert Lord, who had been director of the U.S. Bureau of the Budget (now the OMB) since 1922, had managed for there to be a surplus in the federal budget every year since Coolidge was inaugurated in 1924. Today Lord announced that the current surplus was more than two billion dollars. He proudly gave the precise figure of $2,392,909,074.38.

La Coupe de l'Europe Centrale (Central European Cup), better known as the Mitropa Cup, was one of the first major European championships for soccer football clubs. It was founded this year and today began its first tournament with eight teams drawn from the top finishers and the cup winners of the national soccer football leagues of Austria, Hungary, Yugoslavia, and Czechoslovakia. The Czechoslovakian team Sparta Praha defeated the Austrian team Rapid Wien in the two-game final to win the first Mitropa Cup.

In today's issue of the *Saturday Evening Post*, RCA head David Sarnoff wrote a prophetic article about how television would change the way Americans learn about news and how they would see as well as hear about the events of the day. Some of his predictions were a bit extreme, such as Americans attending night school using television and mothers getting advice from health clinics on how to care for their young children.

Hungarian director and later producer Alexander Korda arrived in Hollywood in 1926 and First National gave him his first assignment, the melodrama *The Stolen*

Bride (released today) because the tale was set in Hungary. During the Great War, the Hungarian countess Sari (Billie Dove) falls in love with the working-class Franz Pless (Lloyd Hughes), a soldier in the Hapsburg army. Class differences make marriage out of the question, so Franz kidnaps the more-than-willing Sari and, after a lot of plotting and complications, the lovers are permanently united. *The Stolen Bride* is not Korda at his best, but he gets a splendid performance out of Dove; the two made three more movies together.

MONDAY, AUGUST 15

Furor over the upcoming execution of Sacco and Vanzetti turned violent today. In the middle of the night, a bomb exploded in the East Milton, Massachusetts, home of Lewis McHardy, one of the jurors who had convicted the two men of robbery and murder back in 1920. Miraculously, McHardy, his wife, and three children survived with only cuts and bruises.

Richard Barthelmess was a favorite leading man in 1920s Hollywood, and his acting in First National's *The Patent Leather Kid* later earned him an Oscar nomination. A cocky prizefighter is known as the "Patent Leather Kid" (Barthelmess) because of his well-groomed, slicked-down hair. When America enters the Great War, the Kid is more interested in fighting in the ring than on the battlefield even though his girlfriend, dancer Curley Boyle (Molly O'Day), tries to appeal to his sense of patriotism. The Kid gets drafted and sent to France and Curley signs up as a nurse. Amid the horrors of war, the Kid has a change of heart and rallies his fellow soldiers to attack. This act of bravery leaves the Kid near death and only Curley's pleading with a doctor not to give up on him saves the boxer's life. Although he is permanently crippled, the Kid manages to rise and salute the American flag in the movie's tearful finale. In addition to Barthelmess's powerful performance, the film boasts some compelling scenes directed by Alfred Santell. *The Patent Leather Kid* ranks with the best silent films about World War I.

Elbert H. Gary, the key founder and first president of the United States Steel Company, died today in New York City at the age of eighty. He brought Andrew Carnegie, Charles M. Schwab, and J. P. Morgan together to form the steel trust in 1901. He also planned and built the city of Gary, Indiana, in 1906 as a model community for his steelworkers. Gary had so much influence on the economy that news of his death was delayed until the Stock Exchange closed to avoid a panic. Alabama politician B. B. Comer also died on this day in Birmingham at the age of seventy-eight. During his political career he served as governor of Alabama and as a Democratic senator, but he is most remembered for the education and railroad reforms in his state and his building of roads and textile mills and setting aside land for conservation purposes.

TUESDAY, AUGUST 16

The much-anticipated Dole Air Race began today in Oakland, California, with eight airplanes poised to fly twenty-four hundred miles to Honolulu, Hawaii. The first plane to arrive would win the $25,000 from James D. Dole and the Dole Pineapple Company. The second-place prize was $10,000. Three of the participating planes had crashed during pre-race drills and three flyers were already dead. More deaths were to follow. Over seventy-five thousand people gathered to watch the eight airplanes take off, even though there was heavy fog and rain. Two of the planes, the *El Encanto* and the *Pabeo Flyer*, crashed on takeoff, probably because of the weight of the gasoline needed to make the long flight. The *Dallas Spirit* and the *Oklahoma* managed to lift off, but soon had to return to Oakland because of an overheated engine and ripped fabric over the fuselage. The *Golden Eagle* and the *Miss Doran* took off and were never seen or heard of again. Only two of the airplanes made it to Hawaii.

One of the most impressive home run hits by Babe Ruth occurred today during a Major League Baseball game in which the New York Yankees bested the Chicago White Sox 8–1 in Comiskey Park. Ruth's hit off of pitcher Tommy Thomas cleared the roof of the right field grandstand by a considerable margin. Had Ruth hit that same homer in Chicago's Wrigley Field, it is estimated that the ball would have reached Lincoln Park Golf Course and theoretically might have hit some golfers.

Irving Berlin (center with sheet music) became America's most popular songwriter with "Alexander's Ragtime Band" in 1911 and held that position for over four decades. He wrote many songs for the *Ziegfeld Follies* in the 1910s and 1920s. Here he poses with some of the chorus girls in rehearsal for the *Ziegfeld Follies of 1927*. *Photofest © Photofest*

For the twentieth consecutive year, Florenz Ziegfeld offered his latest *Follies*, opulent musical revues that were considered the classiest shows on Broadway. As in most previous years, the *Ziegfeld Follies of 1927* was the most expensive production of the season, a record $289,000. Ziegfeld started the series with *Follies of 1907* but by 1911 he had attached his name to the title. While a great deal of emphasis was placed on spectacular sets and costumes, the *Follies* also had major stars, often four or more headliners in one show. The edition that opened today was unusual in that it had only one top-billed star, comic Eddie Cantor, who was in so many sketches and musical numbers that he had trouble sustaining his energy, and after 167 performances he quit the show. The production was selling out and could have run longer, but without Cantor there was no show. Ziegfeld was furious and brought the comic up on charges before Actors Equity. The union took Ziegfeld's side, but it was too late to revive the elaborate production. Irving Berlin wrote most of the songs, but only one of his became a hit, the vibrant "Shaking the Blues Away" performed by Ruth Etting. Also memorable were the dazzling sets, designed by Joseph Urban, which included a verdant bamboo jungle with fabricated creatures and a palatial white setting with nineteen ladies in white playing white pianos and other white instruments. *Ziegfeld Follies of 1927* may not go down as one of the best in the series, but it was done with impeccable taste and high entertainment value. The show lost so much money that it was the last *Follies*. Ziegfeld tried to resuscitate the *Follies* in 1931, but by then the Depression had bankrupted him, and he died the next year leaving debts totaling hundreds of thousands of dollars.

The song "My Blue Heaven," a warm ballad about domestic happiness by Walter Donaldson (music) and George A. Whiting (lyric), had been written in 1924 and had been heard on the radio, but it got a major boost when Eddie Cantor sang it in this year's *Ziegfeld Follies.* Thanks to various recordings, within a year it would become one of the most popular songs in America.

Major League third baseman Jerry Denny died today in Houston at the age of sixty-eight. He played on seven National League teams during his thirteen seasons from 1881 to 1894. Denny was the last non-pitcher in Major League Baseball to play his entire career without using a fielding glove. The meatpacking millionaire J. Ogden Armour died of heart failure in London today at the age of sixty-three. He inherited the Armour meat packing company from his father in 1901 and turned it into the largest food industry in America and a giant on the international market as well. At one point, Armour was the world's richest man, but in 1921 the company lost $130 million in a postwar slump. Still, he was worth $21 million at the time of his death.

WEDNESDAY, AUGUST 17

In Honolulu, at the finish line for the Dole Air Race, the *Woolarac*, piloted by Arthur C. Goebel and navigated by William V. Davis Jr., landed after just over twenty-six hours in the air and won the first prize of $25,000. The *Aloha*, piloted by Martin Jensen and navigated by Paul Schluter, took a little over twenty-eight hours and arrived to claim the second prize of $10,000. The celebratory nature of the Dole Air Race was dampened by the fact that ten fliers lost their lives in the competition.

THURSDAY, AUGUST 18

The Dutch ship S.S. *Sapoerea*, caught in a tropical cyclone in the Philippine Sea, today recorded what was the lowest barometric pressure yet measured at sea level: 26.185 inches or 88.673 kilopascals.

The German painter and sculptor Sascha Schneider died today in present-day Poland from a diabetic seizure at the age of fifty-six. The Russian-born artist is most remembered for his stylized male nudes and was an early advocate of homoeroticism.

FRIDAY, AUGUST 19

A significant landmark in Adolf Hitler's rise to power occurred today, the first day of the three-day rally by the Nazi Party in Nuremberg. The rally included a torchlight procession, a march of twenty thousand uniformed Nazi Party members and one thousand Hitler Youth, a dedication of banners, and several speeches. Hitler's speech was the climax of the rally, in which he stirred up the crowd with a vision of a new and powerful Germany. Many subsequent rallies would be held at Nuremberg, each one larger than the last. Several would also be filmed for propaganda purposes. The 1927 rally was the first to be so documented, resulting in the film *Eine Symphonie des Kampfwillens* (*A Symphony of the Will to Fight*).

SATURDAY, AUGUST 20

Franklin D. Roosevelt, who had suffered from polio since 1921, first visited Warm Springs, Georgia, in 1924 and found that the water improved his mobility. In 1926 he bought the property and today he signed over $140,995 of his own money to establish the Georgia Warm Springs Foundation and construct a rehabilitation facility. Eventually FDR had the property further developed, including the building of his "Little White House," which is where he died in 1945.

P. G. Wodehouse's story "The Bishop's Move" was published in today's issue of *Liberty* magazine. The genial storyteller Mr. Mulliner recounts a tale about how his nephew Augustine Milliner got to be vicar of Steeple Mummery. He helped the Bishop of Stortford and the Headmaster of Hardchester when the two old classmates accidentally took an overdose of the Mulliner potion Buck-U-Uppo and, behaving like schoolboys again, get into some mischief covering the statue of their old nemesis, Lord "Fatty" Hemel, with pink paint. The story also appeared in the September issue of the British *Strand Magazine* and was included in the anthology *Meet Mr. Mulliner*.

The gangster film genre is thought of as a product of the 1930s, but Paramount's *Underworld*, which opened in New York City today, is a silent classic in the field and is still thrilling entertainment. The complex plot centers on rival mobsters "Bull" Weed (George Bancroft), "Buck" Mulligan (Fred Kohler), "Rolls Royce" Wencel (Clive Brook), and the hard-hearted moll "Feathers" McCoy (Evelyn Brent), who is mixed up in their lives. When Weed and Mulligan partake of a drunken spree in which Weed passes out, Mulligan tries to seduce Feathers, but Weed comes to in time to kill Mulligan. He is charged and convicted of murder and sentenced to die. Feathers and Wencel help Weed's gang try to break him out of prison on the night before his execution, but their plot fails and Weed escapes on his own. Thinking Feathers and Wencel have betrayed him, Weed goes after them for revenge. But before he can gun them down, Weed learns the truth and surrenders to the police. Paramount had little faith in *Underworld* and released it in just one theatre in Manhattan. All the same, word got out, and by August it was a nationwide hit. Some film historians point to *Underworld* as the first film noir because of the way Josef von Sternberg filmed it with long shadows and atmospheric lighting. Today *Underworld* ranks among the best gangster movies to come out of Hollywood.

SUNDAY, AUGUST 21

Thousands of protesters rallied at Union Square in New York City on the eve of the scheduled execution of Sacco and Vanzetti. After some speeches were delivered, about two thousand people paraded down Fifth Avenue but the protest march was dispersed by the police. In Boston, an estimated twenty thousand people gathered in Boston Common to protest the impending executions.

The Pan-African Congress met today for the fourth time since its initial gathering in 1919 in Paris. Today's conference met in New York and continued to find peaceful ways for decolonization in Africa and in the West Indies. Among the resolutions made at the Congress were demands to end colonial rule and racial discrimination, to denounce imperialism, and to seek human rights and the equality of economic opportunity.

MONDAY, AUGUST 22

Forty minutes before they were scheduled to go to the electric chair, Sacco and Vanzetti, along with Celestino Medeiros, who had confessed to the murders for which the two men were condemned, were given a twelve-hour reprieve by Governor Fuller. The delay was due to the Massachusetts Supreme Court, which was still considering retrying the case. On the same day, a conservatively estimated seventy thousand workers nation-wide walked off their jobs in support of Sacco and Vanzetti. The Industrial Workers of the World (IWW) called for a three-day nationwide walkout to protest the execution. In Colorado, the United Mine Workers were particularly sympathetic. In the Walsenburg district, 1,132 miners stayed off the job and only 35 went to work.

The celebrated French director Jean Renoir made thirty-five feature films during his forty-year career. The only one that is lost is the silent drama *Marquitta*, which premiered today in Paris. Marquitta is a street singer who becomes the mistress of Prince Vlasco until he finds that she has stolen a valuable piece of jewelry. Years later, the prince is deposed and living in poverty and Marquitta returns to care for him, explaining that it was her father who stole the jewel. The third directorial effort by Renoir, *Marquitta* is one of the most sought-after of all lost silent films.

The renowned ornithologist Louis Agassiz Fuertes died today at the age of fifty-three after his car was hit by a train at a railroad crossing at Unadilla, New York. The prolific bird artist was considered the most important American ornithologist after his predecessor John James Audubon.

TUESDAY, AUGUST 23

When the Massachusetts Supreme Court decided not to retry the case of Nicola Sacco and Bartolomeo Vanzetti, the execution took place at Charlestown State Prison near Boston soon after midnight. Preceding them in the electric chair was Celestino Medeiros, who was executed for an unrelated murder but who had sworn that he had committed the 1920 robbery and murders. All three men were put to death by state executioner Robert G. Elliott. On May 17, 1928, Elliott's home was bombed, but he survived. On September 27, 1932, the home of trial judge Webster Thayer was bombed, destroying his house and injuring his wife and housekeeper. Thayer lived thereafter at his Boston club with around-the-clock guards. He died in 1933.

The Egyptian revolutionary leader Saad Zaghlul died today in Cairo at the age of sixty-eight. He founded and led the nationalist Wafd Party in 1919 and by 1924 was prime minister of Egypt.

WEDNESDAY, AUGUST 24

Protests and riots took place in several cities around the world on the news that Sacco and Vanzetti had been executed. Demonstrations turned violent in London, Paris, Geneva, Tokyo, Amsterdam, Berlin, and Johannesburg.

During night maneuvers off of Jizosaki Lighthouse in the Shimane Prefecture, the Japanese battle cruiser *Jintsū* accidentally struck the starboard side of the destroyer

Warabi. The impact cut the destroyer in two and it sank with ninety-two crew members on board. The captain of the *Jintsū*, in disgrace, later committed suicide.

The most publicized divorce trial of 1927 was that of moviemaker Charles Chaplin and actress Lita Grey Chaplin. During the trial, Chaplin's many affairs with different women were revealed with sensational details. In fact, the court transcript was later published and copies were sold in the thousands. The trial ended today with the judge insisting on a settlement of $625,000 to Mrs. Chaplin and a $200,000 trust fund for their two sons. It was a record for the highest divorce settlement up to that time.

After the Soviet Union, the United States had the highest divorce rate in the world in 1927.

Today Irving Berlin finished writing the song "Puttin' on the Ritz" and had it copyrighted as an unpublished song. The slangy number was not published until two years later and was then introduced in the film *Puttin' on the Ritz* in 1930. It has proven to be one of Berlin's most durable songs, heard in many movies and recordings by various artists over the years. Modern movie audiences mostly know "Puttin' on the Ritz" as the number sung and danced by Dr. Frankenstein (Gene Wilder) and the Monster (Peter Boyle) in *Young Frankenstein* (1974).

The German-born architect Ludwig Mies van der Rohe, one of the most influential designers of the twentieth century, today received a patent for processing the mass production of steel chairs and tables that were minimalist, lightweight, and durable.

The multi-talented Venezuelan figure Manuel Díaz Rodríguez died today at the age of fifty-six in New York City, where he was being treated for a throat infection. Rodríguez was an author, historian, government official, journalist, minister of education, diplomat, and a leading figure in the modernismo movement in Latin America.

THURSDAY, AUGUST 25

The twenty-five-year-old American pilot Paul R. Redfern set out today to outdo Charles Lindbergh. His plan was to fly his Stinson Detroiter solo, nonstop, from the port of Brunswick, Georgia, to Rio de Janeiro, Brazil, a distance of more than four thousand six hundred miles. This was not only longer than Lindbergh's transatlantic feat but also farther than anyone had ever attempted in one flight. Redfern was spotted by a Norwegian freighter a few hours after he took off then was never seen or heard from again. Remnants of his plane were discovered in British Guyana in 1936.

In 1927, Cole Porter was still a struggling songwriter trying to get his songs heard on Broadway. Today in London the musical *Up with the Lark* opened, and it had one

Porter song in the score, the jubilant "I'm in Love Again." Fame would not come to Porter until 1928 with his first Broadway success, *Paris*, which introduced his first hit song "Let's Do It (Let's Fall in Love)."

FRIDAY, AUGUST 26

A hurricane off the coast of Nova Scotia today took the lives of 184 people, mostly fishermen caught out at sea when the storm hit. Also a victim of the hurricane was the American racing schooner *Columbia*, which sank off of the coast of Sable Island, along with its entire crew of twenty-two.

SATURDAY, AUGUST 27

The Kellogg-Briand Treaty, also known as the Paris Pact, was signed today by fifteen countries in the Quai d'Orsay Palace in Paris. Named after its authors, U.S. secretary of state Frank B. Kellogg and French foreign minister Aristide Briand, the treaty was a denunciation of war and called for the peaceful settlement of disputes between nations. While such an agreement did not stop wars, it was a gesture by powerful nations to seek alternatives to bloodshed. Eventually sixty-four countries signed the pact.

A group of five women from the province of Alberta, who would become known as the Famous Five, today petitioned the Supreme Court of Canada for the right of women to serve in the Senate of Canada, arguing that the law stated "persons" were eligible and that women were persons. Although the petition by the women (Emily Murphy, Irene Parlby, Nellie McClung, Louise Crummy McKinney, and Henrietta Muir Edwards) was denied by the nation's high court, they won a victory in the British Privy Council in 1929. The ruling allowed for Canadian women to not only serve in the Senate but to have the same rights as men in politics.

Parks College, the first federally certified aviation school, opened today in St. Louis. The institution was founded by pilot and flight instructor Oliver Parks. Today named the Parks College of Engineering, Aviation and Technology, it is part of St. Louis University.

Clara Bow was the star of Paramount's romantic drama *Hula*, which opened with her swimming nude in a Hawaiian stream. Bow played the free-spirited Hula Calhoun, the daughter of a pineapple plantation owner, who is wooed by Harry Dehan (Arnold Kent). But Hula is attracted to the British engineer Anthony Haldane (Clive Brook), who is there to construct a dam on the property. The fact that Haldane is married does not stop Hula from pursuing him, going so far as performing a sensual hula dance for him. She has to blow up part of a dam, but Hula ends up getting her man. One viewing of *Hula* today will explain the popularity of Bow in the 1920s.

Walt Disney's series of fifty-six "Alice" cartoon shorts came to an end today with the release of *Alice in the Big League.* Lois Hardwick played the live-action Alice who cavorted with animated creatures in animated settings. Disney abandoned the series to begin work on his "Oswald the Lucky Rabbit" shorts.

Ernest Hemingway's very short and potent story "Hills Like White Elephants" was published today in the August edition of the literary magazine *Transition.* Consisting mostly of dialogue, the story is a good example of Hemingway's talent for presenting a tense subtext under a somewhat mundane conversation. On a hot day at a Spanish train station, an American man and his lover, "Jig," are drinking as they wait for their train. He tries to convince her to get an abortion (though he never comes right out and uses the word) and she reluctantly agrees. Then he insists that he doesn't want her to go through with it if she doesn't want to. She gets testy, they argue a bit, he goes inside to get another drink, and the story ends with the two back together and her insisting that everything is fine. The title comes from a simile that the man makes about the scenery, though the hills might also symbolize the problem that the two cannot ignore. "Hills Like White Elephants" was included in the Hemingway collection *Men without Women* which was published in October.

SHORT STORIES

Some notable short stories first published in 1927:

Arthur Conan Doyle's "The Adventure of Shoscombe Old Place"
Arthur Conan Doyle's "The Adventure of the Veiled Lodger"
Sherwood Anderson's "Another Wife"
Dorothy Parker's "Arrangement in Black and White"
Dashiell Hammett's "The Big Knockover"
Zona Gale's "Bill"
P. G. Wodehouse's "Came the Dawn"
H. P. Lovecraft's "The Colour out of Space"
Ernest Hemingway's "Fifty Grand"
Erle Stanley Gardner's "For Higher Stakes"
J. P. Marquand's "Good Morning, Major"
Erle Stanley Gardner's "Grinning Gods"
DuBose Heyward's "The Half Pint Flask"
Ernest Hemingway's "Hills Like White Elephants"

H. P. Lovecraft's "The Horror at Red Hook"
P. G. Wodehouse's "It Was Only a Fire"
Ernest Hemingway's "Italy—1927"
P. G. Wodehouse's "Jeeves and the Yule-Tide Spirit"
Ernest Hemingway's "The Killers"
Dorothy Parker's "Little Curtis"
Virginia Woolf's "The New Dress"
Erle Stanley Gardner's "On the Stroke of Twelve"
H. P. Lovecraft's "Pickman's Model"
P. G. Wodehouse's "The Romance of a Bulb-Squeezer"
Dorothy Parker's "The Sexes"
Agatha Christie's "The Tuesday Night Club"
Zona Gale's "Yellow Gentians and Blue"

See September 15 for other 1927 literature.

SUNDAY, AUGUST 28

After two days of being on view at Langone Funeral Home in Boston's North End, where the bodies of Nicola Sacco and Bartolomeo Vanzetti were visited by over ten thousand mourners, a funeral procession through Boston attracted some two hundred thousand people. At one point near the State House, police tried to block the procession and there was a scuffle. But the hearses eventually reached Forest Hills Cemetery, where a brief eulogy was given and the bodies were cremated. The funeral of the two anarchists was not the end of their story. Protests continued, American embassies were bombed, pamphlets and books were written, and judicial reforms were made in Massachusetts and other states. The trial and the evidence are still studied by experts, but the truth about Sacco and Vanzetti continues to be a matter of debate. On August 23, 1977, the fiftieth anniversary of their execution, Massachusetts governor Michael Dukakis declared it Nicola Sacco and Bartolomeo Vanzetti Memorial Day. He could not pardon them, but he proclaimed, in both English and Italian, that the two men were not fairly tried or convicted.

A western serial by Pathé Exchange titled *Hawk of the Hills* began running today in theatres and there was a new episode each week for ten weeks. The hawk of the title was the half-breed Native American Hawk, who led his tribesmen in raids against prospectors in the California hills. When the prospector Clyde Selby strikes gold, the Hawk tries to kidnap his daughter Mary, and the government agent Laramie aids in the rescue. It took several cliffhangers before justice (and the serial) was done. On the same day, Hal Roach offered Stan Laurel and Oliver Hardy in the comedy short *With Love and Hisses*. An Army Reserve troop is partaking of a weekend camp where a series of misadventures occur, most memorably Sergeant Banner (Hardy) and his men bathing in a lake with addle-brained Cuthbert Hope (Laurel) assigned to watch their uniforms. When Hope decides to go swimming and Banner tosses away his cigarette, everyone's clothes go up in flames. Captain Bustle and some lady companions come by and the naked platoon members are forced to hide behind a billboard. The troop also has an unpleasant encounter with a hornets' nest resulting in enough stings to cause swollen buttocks. Such broad comedy would become more structured and refined in the later Laurel and Hardy efforts.

MONDAY, AUGUST 29

Naturalist Carl Schwachheim, who for a year had been excavating the area near Folsom, New Mexico, today made one of the most important archeological discoveries of the century. He found a man-made spearhead that was imbedded in the skeletal remains of a bison that lived during the last Ice Age. This artifact was the first concrete proof that humans had arrived in North America thousands of years earlier than previously believed.

A typhoon that had developed in the South China Sea today moved ashore at Guangdong in southern China, its waves killing five thousand people and destroying twenty thousand homes and four hundred boats.

George and Ira Gershwin's musical comedy *Strike Up the Band* opened in Long Branch, New Jersey, today on its tryout tour. The title number was an audience favorite, but the rest of the show was in trouble and it closed in Philadelphia in September. The musical was totally revised in 1930 and the title song was finally heard on Broadway where *Strike Up the Band* was a hit.

TUESDAY, AUGUST 30

To mark the sixtieth anniversary of the 1867 independence of Canada, the Princes' Gates, consisting of a stone archway, pillars, and a statue of the Winged Victory, were dedicated in Toronto today by Prince Edward (later King Edward VIII) and Prince George (later King George VI). The neoclassical structure, which serves as the gateway to Exhibition Place, was originally to be called the Diamond Jubilee of Confederation Gates, but when it was learned that royalty was coming for the dedication, the name was changed to the Princes' Gates.

Today was the conclusion of the forty-first U.S. Women's National Tennis Championship, in which American Helen Wills Moody bested British player Betty Nuthall. Beginning with this win, Moody held the top position in women's tennis for a total of nine years (1927–1933, 1935, and 1938). During her career she won thirty-one Grand Slam tournament titles (singles, women's doubles, and mixed doubles), including nineteen singles titles.

WEDNESDAY, AUGUST 31

The British aristocrat Lady Anne Savile, whose marriage to a Bavarian prince brought her the title Princess Anne of Löwenstein-Wertheim-Freudenberg, had been a flying enthusiast for some years and had broken some short-distance flying records over the previous thirteen years. Today she attempted to duplicate Charles Lindbergh's transatlantic flight in reverse by flying from England to Canada. With pilot Leslie Hamilton and navigator Frederick F. Minchin, the sixty-three-year-old princess took off in her large Fokker F.VII monoplane *Saint Raphael* from Uphaven in Wiltshire and headed for Ottawa. The plane was last seen by a steamer off the coast of Ireland later in the day. No trace of the *Saint Raphael* or its three occupants was ever found.

Wild West star William F. Carver died today in Sacramento, California, at the age of seventy-six. The dentist-turned-plainsman took up a career in sharpshooting and was featured in Buffalo Bill Cody's Wild West Show before forming his own show in the 1880s. When business started to fall off, he invented a horse diving act which was soon copied across the nation.

SEPTEMBER

THURSDAY, SEPTEMBER 1

Today marked the end of government-run airmail service. Congress had voted back in 1925 to take airmail delivery out of the hands of the U.S. Post Office and place it in the hands of private contractors. The last federal delivery of airmail took place today as the Postmaster General completed transition of the service from government-owned airplanes to individual airline companies. One of these was National Air Transport, which got the lucrative contract for mail delivery between Chicago and New York. The company would later grow and be divided into three airlines, one of them United Airlines.

A tough-as-nails melodrama, *Burlesque*, opened on Broadway and thrilled playgoers for eleven months. A young and unknown Barbara Stanwyck played Bonny, who is married to Skid Johnson (Hal Skelly), the two working together in a second-class burlesque company in which Skid is the leading comedian. Bonny worries about Skid, who is a heavy drinker, takes hurtful pratfalls as part of his act, and has his eye on a cute showgirl who is about to leave for a Broadway musical. To make Skid jealous, Bonny openly flirts with a rich rancher who has been buying tickets to their show every night. Skid is unconcerned, and when an offer comes for Skid to appear in the same Broadway show as the chorus girl, he takes it. In no time he is having an affair with the showgirl, so Bonny sues for divorce and agrees to marry the rancher. Just before the divorce becomes final, Skid goes on a binge and loses his job. When a friend offers to produce a musical featuring Bonny and Skid, the two recognize how much each needs the other. The play was written by George Manker Watters and Arthur Hopkins, who also produced and directed the gritty, realistic production. The reviews for *Burlesque* were laudatory and Stanwyck was particularly praised. The melodrama was filmed in 1929 as *The Dance of Life* and again in 1948 as the Betty Grable musical *When My Baby Smiles at Me*. A 1946

Broadway revival of *Burlesque* with Bert Lahr as Skid and Jean Parker as Bonny, and with Hopkins once again directing, ran for over a year.

The jazz standard "Chlo-e (Song of the Swamp)" was recorded for the first time in September although it had been added to the Broadway revue *Africana* for a while. The narrative song, in which one looks for a lost love in a "dismal swampland," was written by Neil Moret (music) and Gus Kahn (lyric) and the Columbia recording was made in Los Angeles with vocalist Douglas Richardson. There have since been dozens of recordings, including a very popular parody version by Spike Jones and His City Slickers in 1945.

Charles Coghlan, the first prime minister of Southern Rhodesia and still holding the position since 1923, died of a cerebral hemorrhage today at the age of sixty-four. Born and educated in what is today South Africa, Coghlan was active in developing Southern Rhodesia first as governor then as premiere (later changed to prime minister).

The American stage actress Amelia Bingham today died of heart disease and pneumonia in New York City at the age of fifty-eight. The temperamental leading lady often played feisty Irish girls or strong-willed society women. Bingham made her Broadway debut in 1893 and was active on the New York stage until 1926.

FRIDAY, SEPTEMBER 2

A Major League Baseball record was broken today when New York Yankee Babe Ruth hit a home run off of Philadelphia Athletics pitcher Rube Walberg. It was the 400th homer of Ruth's career; he was the first player in MLB to reach that number.

MGM's *The Garden of Allah* was not the first screen version of Robert Hichens's exotic, romantic 1904 novel and it wasn't the last. The tale of the monastic Fr. Adrien (Iván Petrovich), who falls under the spell of the beautiful Domini Enfilden (Alice Terry) and runs off with her to the desert, was first filmed in 1916 with Tom Santschi and Helen Ware and again in 1936 with Charles Boyer and Marlene Dietrich. This version was shot in France with actual desert locations in North Africa so the movie looks authentic even if the acting and the story seem a bit dated today.

SATURDAY, SEPTEMBER 3

A bloody rampage in Youngstown, Ohio, made national news today. Unemployed mill worker Tony de Capua went on a shooting spree, killing his wife, his four daughters, his two grandchildren, and a neighbor. He also shot and wounded his daughter-in-law, a passerby, and a city policeman who managed to return fire and overpower de Capua. Ruled incompetent to stand trial, de Capua was sent to the Ohio Hospital for the Criminally Insane in Lima.

With the Pittsburgh Pirates and the St. Louis Cardinals tied for first place in the National League, today's two-game sweep over the Cardinals put the Pirates in first place, where they remained for the rest of the season.

For the first and only time all season, the New York Yankees were shut out today when the Philadelphia Athletics bested them 1–0. Only the 1932 Yankees and the 2000 Cincinnati Reds would go a full season without being shut out.

The pioneering African American artist Hale Woodruff, known for his expressive and sometimes abstract murals, left New York City today to study in Paris at the Academie Scandinave and the Academie Moderne thanks to an award by the Harmon Foundation. Woodruff returned to the States in 1931 and began his notable career by founding an art school at Atlanta University.

One of H. P. Lovecraft's most popular short stories, "The Colour out of Space," appeared in the September issue of the science fiction magazine *Amazing Stories*. A surveyor from Boston narrates the tale about how he explored a remote area in Massachusetts that the locals called the "blasted heath." It is discovered that a meteorite crashed to Earth on this location many years ago and has affected the people, animals, and vegetation, causing abnormal and grotesque growth, and erratic behavior and insanity. Also, a very inhuman-like alien creature has taken residence in the area and either destroys or scares off any remaining people. "The Colour out of Space" was included in Edward O'Brien's anthology of *The Best American Short Stories* (1928) and has inspired several movies.

SUNDAY, SEPTEMBER 4

The 1927 LEN European Aquatics Championships were concluded today in Bologna, Italy, for the second year, and for the first time women's events were included. The competition included swimming, diving, and water polo. Germany was the runaway victor with sixteen gold, silver, and bronze medals. Sweden came in second, taking home seven medals.

Mickey's Circus was the first of sixty-four comedy shorts to star Mickey Rooney as Mickey Maguire. Rooney had introduced Maguire as a midget in *Orchids and Ermine* back in March, but he now played a tough and adventurous kid, this time concocting a circus using the local dogs. The short was believed to be lost until 2014 when a print was discovered in the Netherlands.

MONDAY, SEPTEMBER 5

Universal Studios today introduced Walt Disney's cartoon character Oswald the Lucky Rabbit in the film short *Trolley Troubles*. During the six-minute short, Oswald tries to drive his trolley car but various animals keep jumping on board and he eventually loses control of the trolley when it races down a hill. The cartoon was immediately popular and Disney was contracted to make twenty-five more in the series. When Disney left to start his own studio in 1928, Universal retained the rights to the character of Oswald so the animator had to come up with a new character. The result was Mickey Mouse.

A long-forgotten stage musical titled *The Sidewalks of New York* opened in New York today with twenty-four-year-old Bob Hope making his Broadway debut in a small role. He did a comedy routine with his vaudeville partner George Byrne as part of the loosely plotted musical. *The Sidewalks of New York* ran fourteen weeks; Hope's career lasted sixty-seven more years.

The movie theatre mogul Marcus Loew, founder of the Loews Theatres chain of cinemas and cofounder of Metro-Goldwyn-Mayer, died today of a heart attack at the age of fifty-seven. Loew began his career managing nickelodeons then moved on to vaudeville theatres and then movie houses. It was his business plan to merge Samuel Goldwyn's company with that of Metro Pictures and producer Louis B. Mayer in 1924, thus creating MGM Studios. Also dying at the age of fifty-seven today was Wayne B. Wheeler, a leader in the American temperance movement. As a leader of the Anti-Saloon League, he put pressure on Congress to pass the Eighteenth Amendment in 1920, which brought on Prohibition.

TUESDAY, SEPTEMBER 6

One of the quintessential 1920s musical comedies, *Good News!* opened on Broadway today and introduced a bouquet of song hits, including the perennial favorite "The Best Things in Life Are Free," the snappy "The Varsity Drag," the romantic duet "Lucky in Love," the dreamy ballad "Just Imagine," and the vivacious title number. The famous score was by Ray Henderson (music), Lew Brown (lyrics) and B. G. De Sylva (lyrics), who cowrote the book with Laurence Schwab. It was not Broadway's first collegiate musical but it was one of the best. Tom Marlowe (John Price Jones), the star of football-crazy Tait College's team, may not be able to play if he fails his astronomy exam. Connie Lane (Mary Lawlor) agrees to tutor Tom, since she loves him even though she suspects he really loves another girl. Tom passes, Tait wins, and Connie gets Tom. The reviews were like valentines and the show ran nineteen months in New York and toured extensively. It then became a popular favorite with schools and summer theatres for decades. *Good News!* was filmed twice by MGM, in 1930 and 1947.

American aviator Lloyd W. Bertaud had set some records as an airmail pilot but was kept from competing for the Orteig Prize, which was won by Charles Lindbergh in May. All the same, Bertaud was determined to make the transatlantic flight, so today he, fellow airmail pilot James DeWitt Hill, and Philip Payne took off in the Fokker monoplane *Old Glory* from Maine for Rome. The flight was sponsored by newspaper tycoon William

Randolph Hearst to help sell copies of his *New York Daily Mirror*. *The Old Glory* was last seen that night by the steamship *California* off of Cape Race, but a few hours later the ocean liner *Transylvania* picked up an S.O.S. signal from the plane. Some wreckage of the *Old Glory* was found six hundred miles northeast of Newfoundland a week later, but the bodies of the three fliers were missing.

New York Yankee Babe Ruth hit a home run today during a doubleheader against the Boston Red Sox that was reputedly the longest ever hit at Fenway Park. The Yankees won the first game 14–2 and the Red Sox won the second 5–2. As for Ruth, he chalked up his forty-fifth, forty-sixth, and forty-seventh homers of the season.

Also in baseball news today, Lave Cross, third baseman and catcher for twenty seasons, died of a heart attack today in Toledo, Ohio, at the age of sixty-one. Between 1887 and 1907, Cross played for ten different teams and was captain of the 1902 and 1905 AL champion Philadelphia Athletics. He was also one of the first ten baseball players to collect 2,500 hits.

WEDNESDAY, SEPTEMBER 7

The Autumn Harvest Uprising, led by Mao Zedong, broke out today in the Chinese Hunan and Jiangxi Provinces. The insurrection established a short-lived Hunan Soviet presence. Mao led a small peasant army against the Kuomintang, China's major political party, and the landlords of Hunan. The uprising was defeated by Kuomintang forces and Mao was forced to retreat to the Jinggang Mountains on the border between Hunan and Jiangxi. The Autumn Harvest Uprising was the first armed insurrection by the Communists in China, and it inspired Mao and Red Army founder Zhu De to develop a rural-based strategy based on guerrilla tactics, paving the way to the Long March of 1934.

Many media historians point to this date as the birth of television. Twenty-one-year-old inventor Philo Farnsworth today demonstrated to friends and lab assistants in his San Francisco laboratory the first completely electronic television system. An earlier version of mechanical television, using a rotating disk, had been created by John Logie Baird in 1926, but it limited the picture to ten frames per second and a thirty-line image. Farnsworth's system used a scanning electronic tube to convert an image into electromagnetic waves that were then transmitted from one room in his laboratory to a receiver in another room, where the image was displayed. Farnsworth perfected his invention and in 1928 demonstrated it to the press for the first time.

Stage favorite Mary Boland was known for her comic characters on Broadway, but she turned to a very serious drama with *Women Go on Forever*, in which she played Daisy Bowman, who runs a working-class boarding house. The convoluted plot included Daisy's unfaithful lover, who is murdered; her blind son, who marries an ugly matron thinking she is beautiful; and a boarder on the run from the police, who is gunned down in the final scene. The melodrama may have been a contrived mess, but Boland was deemed excellent and she helped keep *Women Go on Forever* running for fifteen weeks. The drama was filmed in 1931 with Clara Kimball Young playing Daisy.

Gaylord Wilshire, a colorful character who was a developer, politician, socialist speaker, and a medical quack, died today in New York City at the age of sixty-six. His land development in Los Angeles included today's Wilshire Boulevard. For a time, he was famous for his Wilshire Ring, a metal circular rod through which electricity passed. Sitting inside the ring was said to reduce one's weight. Also known as the I-On-A-Co, the Wilshire Ring was sold by the thousands at the price of $58.50 each (it cost only $5.75 to manufacture) until the American Medical Association and Better Business Bureau declared the device a fraud, the public lost interest, and Wilshire ended up destitute by 1927.

THURSDAY, SEPTEMBER 8

The Cessna-Roos Aircraft Company was incorporated today when aviator and airplane builder Clyde Cessna partnered with manufacturer Victor Roos. The goal of the company was to make small, well-built, and affordable planes. Roos dropped out of the corporation after a month and in December the company was renamed the Cessna Aircraft Company.

After three months of occupying China's Shandong Province, Japanese troops began to withdraw from the city of Jinan. Ten years later, the Japanese would return and seize Shandong during the Second Sino-Japanese War.

The feather-light musical *The Girl Friend*, with a fine score by Richard Rodgers (music) and Lorenz Hart (lyrics), was a hit in 1926 and ran nine months. Today the London version opened and it was even more successful, running a full year. But the New York and London versions of *The Girl Friend* barely resembled each other. The West End producers threw out the original story about a bicycle race and replaced it with a bedroom farce set in a hotel suite. The two best songs from the Broadway production, the entrancing "The Blue Room" and the Charleston-like title number, were retained and two older Rodgers and Hart numbers, "Mountain Greenery" and "What's the Use of Talking?," were interpolated into the British score. The London version was not only successful in the West End but also on tour and in Sydney, Australia, and even Budapest.

FRIDAY, SEPTEMBER 9

The Ku Klux Klan was possibly more active and influential in Indiana during the 1920s than in any Southern state. Politicians and judges in high places were members and for years illegal dealings had supported and protected the Klan. Today, Indiana governor Edward L. Jackson and Indianapolis mayor John L. Duvall, both members of the Klan, were indicted, along with Indiana Klan leader George V. Coffin, Klan counsel Robert I. Marsh, and several other members who were accused of conspiracy to commit a felony and bribery. Governor Jackson was acquitted by a hung jury but left office in disgrace.

Nicaraguan rebels, led by Augusto Sandino, today ambushed a group of American marines who were marching near the U.S. base at Las Flores. The American military leaders in Nicaragua were still learning about jungle warfare and guerrilla fighting, which they had never encountered before.

The legendary jazz musician Bix Beiderbecke today recorded his own jazz composition, "In a Mist," in New York City for the OKeh label. Although most known for his cornet playing, Beiderbecke played his piece on the piano for the recording.

Universal would become the studio associated with classic horror films in the 1930s but the tradition goes back to the 1920s, as witnessed by today's premiere of the comic-horror movie *The Cat and the Canary*. The millionaire Cyrus West mistrusts his relatives, so when he dies in his castle on the Hudson River, his instructions are that his will not be opened until twenty years have passed. Two decades later his heirs are summoned to hear the will read by the family lawyer, Roger Crosby. The bulk of the estate goes to Annabelle West (Laura La Plante), but, because the eccentric West feared there was a strain of insanity in the family, she must be examined by Dr. Ira Lazar to see if she shows any signs of unsound mental behavior. If so, the estate goes to someone named in a sealed envelope. Adding to the tension, it is announced that a dangerous lunatic known as the Cat is loose on the estate grounds. The night is full of screams, clutching claws, and other devices meant to drive Annabelle insane. The lawyer Crosby is murdered, but, with the help of the timid would-be heir Paul Jones, Annabelle discovers the culprit is the handsome Charles Wilder, who broke into the safe and therefore knew his name was in the second envelope and took on the role of the Cat. The movie was based on the 1922 Broadway hit of the same name, but changes were made, in particular the way German director Paul Leni filmed the tale in the style of German expressionism. It was his first Hollywood assignment and made quite an impression on the critics and moviegoers, becoming a box office hit for Universal. There have since been five subsequent screen versions of *The Cat and the Canary* in different languages and with different titles. The most known is Paramount's 1939 adaptation starring Bob Hope and Paulette Goddard.

Perhaps no other Major League Baseball player did more to bring Italian Americans into the ballparks than Yankee second baseman Tony Lazzeri. He was the idol of the Italian immigrants, who saw his fame and success as an inspiration. Today was declared Tony Lazzeri Day at Yankee Stadium, and thousands of fans of Italian descent came and called out "Poosh 'Em Up Tony," imploring him to hit one out of the ballpark, during the game between the Yankees and the St. Louis Browns. While the Yankees won 9–3, Lazzeri would go 0–3 but added his ninety-third RBI on a sacrifice fly.

SATURDAY, SEPTEMBER 10

The 1927 International Lawn Tennis Challenge, which is now known as the Davis Cup, concluded today at the Germantown Cricket Club in Philadelphia. This year, twenty-one teams entered from the Europe Zone while four from the America Zone participated. France defeated Japan in the Inter-Zonal playoff then today bested the United States, which had won the previous six years. It was the first Davis Cup for France.

The controversial Dr. Morris Fishbein, editor of the *Journal of the American Medical Association* (*JAMA*) and secretary of the AMA, was often in the news for his attacks on midwifes, medical fads, gland treatments, and in particular chiropractics, which he made strong efforts to outlaw. In today's issue of *JAMA*, Fishbein took issue with the American obsession with losing weight, calling it "the menace of an anemic nation." Fishbein stated that "If the false gospel of unscientific dieting continued to prevail for a few generations, the United States would become a nation of undersized weaklings and anemics, lacking in both physical and mental force."

Paramount's antiwar drama *Barbed Wire* pleaded for understanding between Britain and Germany, but anti-German sentiments were still so strong in Britain that the movie was criticized there even as it was praised in the United States. It is a World War I POW film in which the French farm girl Mona (Pola Negri) falls in love with the German prisoner-of-war Oskar (Clive Brook), making her an outcast in the town. When a French sergeant tries to rape Mona, Oskar attacks him and the German is charged with assault. Mona defends Oskar at his trial and is branded a traitor by the town. The war ends and Mona's brother returns blinded from his battle wounds and makes a plea for peace, helping Mona and Oskar get married. Directed by Rowland V. Lee, *Barbed Wire* is realistically acted and presented. Many of the POWs were played by actual German war veterans who had been imprisoned in camps during the war. Reviews in America were favorable and, with Negri's popularity, *Barbed Wire* was a box office success. Released on that same day was Hal Roach's comedy short *Sugar Daddies*, which featured Stan Laurel and Oliver Hardy, though they were not sold as a comedy team. In fact, neither of them was the leading character. That was the oil tycoon Cyrus Brittle (James Finlayson) who, in an alcoholic spree, gets married and then finds that his in-laws are trying to bump him off to inherit his money. Laurel played Brittle's lawyer and Hardy was his butler, and the two of them help the hunted millionaire to escape by leading a merry chase through a dance hall and an amusement park. The twenty-minute farce is not Laurel and Hardy at their best, but one can see their teamwork and sense of comic rapport developing.

SUNDAY, SEPTEMBER 11

At a science conference that began today at Lake Como, Italy, the Danish physicist Niels Bohr presented a lecture titled "The Quantum Postulate and the Recent Development of Atomic Theory" in which he introduced the word "complementarity" and described the foundation for understanding atomic structure and quantum theory.

With extensive renovations and remodeling of the White House complete after three months' work, President Coolidge and his family ended their summer residence in South Dakota and returned to Washington today.

After losing twenty-one games in a row to the New York Yankees, the St. Louis Browns finally beat the Yankees today with a score of 6–2. During the game, Babe Ruth hit his fiftieth home run of the season.

The final volume of Marcel Proust's seven-volume masterpiece *À la recherche du temps perdu* was published in Paris by Gallimard. Its title commonly translated as *In Search of Lost Time* or *Remembrance of Things Past*, the mammoth work is considered one of the most influential pieces of literature of the twentieth century. The sprawling novel follows the thoughts, recollections, and experiences of an unnamed narrator from early childhood through adulthood during World War I. Like the entire novel, the final volume, titled *Le Temps retrouvé* (*Time Regained* or *Finding Time Again*), uses the concept of involuntary memory whereby the past intrudes upon the narrator because of something he sees or hears. Proust died in 1922 when only four of the volumes had been published. This last novel was first translated into English in 1931.

MONDAY, SEPTEMBER 12

The country of Panama had addressed to the World Court the question of ownership of the Panama Canal recently. Although the United States was not a member of the League of Nations, Secretary of State Frank B. Kellogg communicated with the League today and warned that his country would not abide by any ruling of the World Court over ownership of the Panama Canal Zone.

Although he himself was not a college graduate, the Christian evangelist Bob Jones Sr. today opened Bob Jones College in Panama City, Florida, with eighty-eight students and nine faculty members. The goal of the school was to offer a Fundamentalist alternative to secular education, which taught liberal religious ideals. Under Jones's son, Bob Jones Jr., the school struggled and changed locations a few times before settling in Greenville, South Carolina, and becoming Bob Jones University.

Three new productions opened on Broadway today and two of them were hits. George M. Cohan wrote and produced the farce *Baby Cyclone*, which had a slim and contrived plot but delighted playgoers all the same. Gene Hurley (Spencer Tracy) hates the way his wife (Nan Sunderland) pampers and talks baby talk to her Pekinese pup Baby Cyclone, so he steals the dog and sells it to the first woman he runs across on the street. Mrs. Hurley throws a tantrum when she finds out, and the passing stockbroker Joseph Meadows (Grant Mitchell) hears her screams and brings Mrs. Hurley home to protect and comfort her. Then Meadows's fiancée Lydia (Natalie Moorehead) shows up with Baby Cyclone, which she just bought from a man on the street. Both women fight over who gets the Pekinese and it takes three acts to unravel the many comic complications. The critics could not help but recommend the silly farce, and there were compliments for the little-known young actor Tracy. *Baby Cyclone* ran six months and was filmed by MGM in 1928. The night's other offering, the operetta *My Maryland*, ran nearly twice as long. Sigmund Romberg composed the luscious music for this musicalization of Clyde Fitch's 1899 Civil War play *Barbara Frietchie*, and the book and lyrics were by Dorothy Donnelly. The romantic triangle between Marylander Barbara (Evelyn Herbert); her Confederate suitor, Jack Negly; and her Yankee sweetheart, Captain Trumbull climaxed with Barbara choosing Trumbull and proudly waving the Union flag when the Confederate army marches into her town of Frederick, Maryland. An officer orders Barbara shot, but Stonewall Jackson admires Barbara's bravery so much he pardons her. The score was full of entrancing operetta songs, most famously "Silver Moon," "Won't You Marry Me?," and "Your Land and My Land." *My Maryland* was Donnelly's last musical. Having collaborated with Romberg on such hits as *Blossom Time* (1921) and *The Student Prince* (1924), she was one of the most successful female lyricists and librettists of her era. She died of pneumonia during the run of *My Maryland* at the age of forty-seven.

An outstanding English movie, Gaumont British Pictures' *Hindle Wakes* premiered in London today but was not seen in the United States until November of 1929 because it was felt to be too British. The annual celebration in Lancashire known as "Wakes Week" gives laborers and schoolchildren time off for a well-deserved summer holiday. In the fictional Lancashire town of Hindle, the working girls Fanny Hawthorn and Mary Hollins go to Blackpool for the holiday and meet up with Allan Jeffcote, the son of the factory owner in Hindle. Allen convinces Fanny to steal off with him to a resort in Wales and Mary promises to mail a postcard from Blackpool later in the week so Fanny's parents don't know about the Wales tryst. Mary dies in a boating accident, the postcard is never mailed, and Fanny and Allen's illicit trip is discovered by both sets of parents. Everyone agrees that Allen must marry Fanny except Fanny herself, who declares her right to sow her wild oats and moves out of her home to live her own life. Based on a 1912 British play, *Hindle Wakes* was filmed four times and caused controversy each time. This 1927 version is considered the best and is still first-class entertainment. Since the title made no sense to Americans, the film was retitled *Fanny Hawthorne* when it eventually was released in the States.

TUESDAY, SEPTEMBER 13

The New York Yankees easily won the American League pennant today by defeating the Cleveland Indians in both games of a doubleheader by identical scores of 5–3. Babe Ruth hit his fifty-first home run against Willis Hudlin and his fifty-second off

Joe Shaute. During the month of September, Ruth hit an amazing seventeen home runs, still a record today. Also impressive was Yankee pitcher Waite Hoyt, who won his twentieth game. By season's end, Hoyt won twenty-two games, more than any other Yankee.

An undersea earthquake combined with a typhoon created a ten-foot-high tsunami that washed away buildings along the coast of the Japanese island of Kyushu and carried boats two miles inland. Nearly six hundred people perished, and flooding in the city of Ōmura destroyed five thousand houses, leaving fifteen thousand people homeless. The storm also ruined hundreds of acres of rice fields, causing prices to increase.

Heinrich Himmler, who had recently been appointed deputy of the Schutzstaffel (SS) by Adolf Hitler, today created the Sturmabteilung (Stormtroopers), an elite, loyal, and racially pure group of two hundred SS members with their own distinctive uniform.

Today Gene Austin recorded the song "My Blue Heaven," which would become the bestselling record of 1928, selling over five million copies. The song of simple domestic happiness by Walter Donaldson (music) and George A. Whiting (lyric) was ideal for the gentle crooner Austin, and it was the hit song of his career.

WEDNESDAY, SEPTEMBER 14

Of the four notable deaths on this date, the one to get the most coverage was that of the American innovative dancer and international celebrity Isadora Duncan. She is known for her new style of free and natural dancing, exotic costumes, many lovers, her dance schools in various countries, and her becoming a Soviet citizen late in life. On this date Duncan was killed in a freak car accident in Nice, France. Her long scarf that was wrapped around her neck with one end flowing in the breeze got tangled in the axel of the automobile and strangled her to death. She was either forty-nine or fifty years old. Also dying on this day was the avant-garde German poet Hugo Ball, aged forty-one, who was an important figure in the Dadaist movement; British doctor and scientist Sidney Rawson Wilson, aged forty-five, who died while experimenting with the effects of nitrous oxide on his body; and Joseph M. Quigley, who had been the chief of police in Rochester, New York, since 1909 and was the inventor of the "silent policeman," a portable traffic signal that could be set up in the middle of an intersection.

THURSDAY, SEPTEMBER 15

Aviator William S. Brock and Detroit businessman Edward F. Schlee, who had set off from Harbour Grace, Newfoundland, on August 27 in their Stinson SM-1 monoplane *The Pride of Detroit* to become the first persons to fly around the world, today abandoned their ambitious plans. The pair had gone halfway around the globe making scheduled stops for refueling, when a storm forced them to land in Omura, Japan. The next leg of their route was across much of the Pacific Ocean to Midway Island, but friends and family members convinced them not to risk their lives with such a journey. Schlee and Brock traveled back to the United States on a ship and were greeted as heroes all the same.

Willa Cather's atypical but captivating novel *Death Comes for the Archbishop* was published today by Alfred A. Knopf. The story is the saga of a French bishop, Jean Marie Latour, and his attempts to establish a diocese in New Mexico Territory in the nineteenth century. With his friend the vicar Joseph Vaillant, the bishop travels a year to get from the end of the railroad line in Cincinnati to New Mexico Territory recently acquired by the United States. The two encounter fictional and historical characters along the way, convert some of the Native Americans, escape murder by bandits, visit and encourage priests already working in remote areas, and eventually build churches and create a diocese. Old and worn out, Latour dies with some satisfaction with the life he has led. Cather based the novel on two historical figures, Jean-Baptiste Lamy and Joseph Projectus Machebeuf, who were pioneers in getting the Catholic Church a foothold in the American Southwest. *Death Comes for the Archbishop* is very different from Cather's other works, which focus on life in the Midwest. Yet the novel is ranked highly among her works and American literature in general.

LITERATURE

Some notable works of literature that were first published in 1927:

Franz Kafka's novel *Amerika*

Don Marquis's anthology of short stories *archy and mehitabel*

Countee Cullen's collection of poems *The Ballad of the Brown Girl*

Amy Lowell's collection of poems *Ballads for Sale*

Agatha Christie's novel *The Big Four*

Kwee Tek Hoay's novel *Boenga Roos dari Tjikembang* (*The Rose of Cikembang*)

Thornton Wilder's novel *The Bridge of San Luis Rey*

Anita Loos's novel *But Gentlemen Marry Brunettes*

Arthur Conan Doyle's anthology *The Case-Book of Sherlock Holmes*

Theodore Dreiser's anthology *Chains: Lesser Novels and Stories*

Cornell Woolrich's novel *Children of the Ritz*

Julien Green's novel *The Closed Garden*

Mourning Dove's novel *Co-ge-we-a, The Half-Blood: A Depiction of the Great Montana Cattle Range*

B. Traven's novel *Der Schatz der Sierra Madre* (*The Treasure of the Sierra Madre*)

Warwick Deeping's novel *Doomsday*

H. P. Lovecraft's novel *The Dream Quest of Unknown Kadath*

Rosamond Lehmann's novel *Dusty Answer*

Sinclair Lewis's novel *Elmer Gantry*

Yury Olesha's novel *Envy*

Langston Hughes's poetry collection *Fine Clothes to the Jew*

Joseph Roth's novel *Flight without End*

Zane Grey's novel *Forlorn River*

David Garnett's novel *Go She Must!*

James Weldon Johnson's poetry collection *God's Trombones*

Mazo de la Roche's novel *Jalna*

D. H. Lawrence's novel *John Thomas and Lady Jane*

Warwick Deeping's novel *Kitty*

Jaime de Angulo's novel *The Lariat*

Paul Morand's novel *The Living Buddha*

P. G. Wodehouse's short story collection *Meet Mr. Mulliner*

Ernest Hemingway's short story anthology *Men without Women*

William Faulkner's novel *Mosquitoes*

Edna Ferber's novel *Mother Knows Best*

T. F. Powys's novel *Mr. Weston's Good Wine*

Sherwood Anderson's poetry collection *A New Testament*

Upton Sinclair's novel *Oil!*

Edna Ferber's novel *Old Charleston*

Philip MacDonald 's novel *Patrol* (aka *The Lost Patrol*)

Booth Tarkington's novel *The Plutocrat*

Vilhelm Moberg's novel *Raskens*

Ze'ev Jabotinsky's novel *Samson the Nazerite*

Baroness Orczy's novel *Sir Percy Hits Back*

Will James's novel *Smoky the Cowhorse*

Fannie Hurst's short story collection *Song of Life*

Hermann Hesse's novel *Steppenwolf*

Samuel Hopkins Adams's novel *Summer Bachelors* (under pseudonym Warner Fabian)

Henry Williamson's novel *Tarka the Otter*

François Mauriac's novel *Thérèse Desqueyroux*

Virginia Woolf's novel *To the Lighthouse*

Franklin W. Dixon's young adult novel *The Tower Treasure*

Edith Wharton's novel *Twilight Sleep*

Dorothy L. Sayers's novel *Unnatural Death* (*The Dawson Pedigree* in the United States)

Halldór Kiljan Laxness's novel *Vefarinn mikli frá Kasmír* (*The Great Weaver from Kashmir*)

See August 27 for 1927 short stories.

FRIDAY, SEPTEMBER 16

Crooner Gene Austin, who wrote the lyric for Nathaniel Shilkret's music for the folk-like ballad "The Lonesome Road," recorded the song today with the Victor Orchestra, and it was a hit. It is estimated that the bluesy number has had over two hundred different recordings over the years.

The city of San Francisco practically shut down today in anticipation of a visit by Charles Lindbergh. Schools, businesses, and other activities were abandoned as thousands waited at the airport in the rain. When Lindbergh flew in, in the *Spirit of St. Louis*, the crowd went wild. Thousands lined the streets as Lindbergh's motorcade went to City Hall, where there were speeches and awards. The only reason the shy, reticent Lindbergh made such appearances was to promote aviation in America.

SATURDAY, SEPTEMBER 17

An aerial sightseeing excursion turned deadly today when a Fokker F.VII operated by Reynolds Airways crash-landed, killing seven people and injuring five others. It was the deadliest plane crash to date. Penny-a-Pound Pleasure Trips offered twenty-minute plane rides from Hadley Field near South Plainfield, New Jersey, charging one cent per pound of each passenger. When the airplane was five hundred feet in the air, the engine stalled and the eleven-passenger Fokker crashed into an orchard. Reynolds Airways of New Brunswick, Fokker Aircraft Corp., Atlantic Aircraft Corp., General Motors, and owner Richard Reynolds were later sued for $1.8 million.

The 1927 U.S. National Tennis Championships (now known as the U.S. Open) concluded today at the West Side Tennis Club in Forest Hills, New York. It was the forty-seventh year for the competition, which is considered the fourth and final Grand Slam of tennis each year after the competitions in Australia; France; and Wimbledon, England. Frenchman René Lacoste beat American Bill Tilden in the Men's Singles with scores of 11–9, 6–3, and 11–9. The Women's Singles was won by American Helen Wills over British player Betty Nuthall with victories of 6–1 and 6–4. Tilden and fellow American Frank Hunter defeated Americans Bill Johnston and R. Norris Williams for the Men's Doubles; British players Kitty McKane Godfree and Ermyntrude Harvey won the Women's Doubles over Nuthall and American Joan Fry; and for the Mixed Doubles competition, American Eileen Bennett and Frenchman Henri Cochet bested American Hazel Hotchkiss Wightman and Lacoste. Tennis historians looking back on Wimbledon and the Australia, French, and U.S. Open of 1927 rate the year as having some of the finest players and most dazzling matches in the annuls of the sport.

The Washington State Cougars defeated the Willamette Bearcats 32–6 in the first game of the 1927 college football season.

COLLEGE FOOTBALL ALL-AMERICANS

The 1927 College Football All-American Team, as chosen by consensus of various organizations and writers:

Larry Bettencourt (center) St. Mary's
Red Cagle (halfback) Army
John Charlesworth (center) Yale
Morley Drury (quarterback) USC
Ed Hake (tackle) USC
Jesse Hibbs (tackle) Penn

Herb Joesting (fullback) Minnesota
Tom Nash (end) Georgia
Bennie Oosterbaan (end) Michigan
Clipper Smith (guard) Notre Dame
Bill Webster (guard) Yale
Gibby Welch (halfback) Pitt

An unsigned satiric piece in today's issue of the *New Yorker* magazine was titled "Polo in the Home," which was written by James Thurber, one of his earliest contributions to the magazine.

SUNDAY, SEPTEMBER 18

While college football seemed to get all the attention in 1927, there were professional gridiron teams, and interest in them was growing. The American Professional Football

Association (APFA) was founded in 1920 with ten teams from four states. The organization was renamed the National Football League (NFL) in 1922. The 1927 NFL season began today with twelve teams in the league. (There were twenty-two the previous season but the league decided to eliminate the financially weaker teams.) Five African American players participated in the 1926 season (including future Hall-of-Famer Fritz Pollard), but none played during the 1927 season. In today's game, the Green Bay Packers defeated the Dayton Triangles 14–0. The other teams in the NFL that season were the Buffalo Bisons, Chicago Bears, Chicago Cardinals, Cleveland Bulldogs, Duluth Eskimos, Frankfort Yellow Jackets, New York Giants, New York Yankees, Pottsville Maroons, and Providence Steam Roller.

William S. Paley had recently bought out the struggling United Independent Broadcasters, Inc. and, combining it with Columbia Records, renamed the company the Columbia Phonographic Broadcasting System (later known as CBS). The new company went on the air today with a network of sixteen radio stations in eleven U.S. states. It was the third national network, after NBC's Red Network and Blue Network. Broadcasting from Newark, New Jersey, the 2:00 p.m. show featured music from the Howard L. Barlow Orchestra. Later in the day, Donald Voorhees conducted dance music and Deems Taylor conducted the Metropolitan Opera presentation of Taylor's *The King's Henchman*.

MONDAY, SEPTEMBER 19

Austrian composer Arnold Schoenberg's String Quartet no. 3 was first performed today in Vienna by the Kolisch Quartet. The piece is in four movements and is a vivid example of Schoenberg's use of the twelve-tone technique. The first recording of the sentimental but heartfelt ballad "Among My Souvenirs" was made today by the Kit-Cat Band, but the song did not catch on until Paul Whiteman's recording was made on November 22, which became a giant hit in 1928.

Two gripping plays opened on Broadway this day, a courtroom melodrama and a crime drama. Bayard Veiller's *The Trial of Mary Dugan* was indeed a trial, all the action taking place in a realistic courtroom setting and the procedures of justice fairly accurate. Mary Dugan (Ann Harding) has been accused of killing her lover, Edgar Rice, after she was found in her apartment standing over his dead body with a bloody knife. Her attorney, Edward West, does such a poor job interrogating the witnesses that a young man in the court rises, announces he is Mary's brother Jimmy, a lawyer from California, and has come East to aid his sister. Jimmy uncovers the true facts in the case, and it turns out the attorney West is the murderer. The press praised the taut drama and the skillful acting, encouraging patrons to keep the play on the boards for over a year. *The Trial of Mary Dugan* was filmed in 1929 with Norma Shearer and in 1941 with Laraine Day. Less melodramatic was *Four Walls* by George Abbott and Dana Burnett, which looked at crime psychologically. After five years in prison, Benny Horowitz (Muni Weisenfreund) is released and vows to free himself from a life of crime by removing the "four walls" that have entrapped his mind and spirit. Benny goes straight, but one night he comes across an old gang member beating up a girl on a rooftop. In the struggle to rescue her, Benny pushes the gangster from the roof and he dies. The girl offers to tell the police Benny wasn't there but he gives himself up to the law, freeing himself from his psychological "four walls." All the reviewers agreed that newcomer Wisenfrend from the Yiddish theatre was an outstanding actor and encouraged audiences to see his performance. They did so for over four months. Wisenfrend was quickly picked up by Hollywood, where he was renamed Paul Muni and had a distinguished screen career. *Four Walls* was filmed in 1928 with John Gilbert and Joan Crawford.

The Danish artist Michael Ancher died today in Skagen, Denmark, at the age of seventy-eight. Ancher was mostly a realistic painter who confined his subjects to the fishermen and other people in his home village of Skagen.

TUESDAY, SEPTEMBER 20

The Beauval Indian Residential School near the Canadian village of Beauval, Saskatchewan, caught fire in the middle of the night while thirty-seven students and eight Roman Catholic nuns were sleeping. Flames blocked the exits from the boys' wing of the building but the girls were able to escape. By morning, it was discovered that nineteen boys between the ages of seven and twelve died as well as one of the nuns.

The Command to Love was a German play translated by Americans about a Frenchman played by a British actor and set in Spain, truly an international night on Broadway. English actor Basil Rathbone, starting to make a name for himself on the New York stage, played the French ladies' man Gaston, the Marquis du Saint-Luc, who is coerced by the French ambassador to Spain to go to Madrid and flirt with the wives of influential Spaniards in order to get certain treaties signed. Gaston begrudgingly cooperates and is quite a success with the women at the Spanish court, even falling in love with Manuela (Mary Nash), the wife of the minister of war. Gaston's influence gets an important treaty passed, then he returns to France, a sadder but a better Frenchman. The flirtations in the play were considered indecent by some of the press and word got around that the police might close the play. This boosted business so much that *The Command to Love* ran seven months.

According to a report by the Internal Revenue Service, the standard of living in America in 1927 was the highest in the world. The per capita income for an employed person in the U.S. was $2,010; the average per capita was $770.

WEDNESDAY, SEPTEMBER 21

Although the Canary Islands had been conquered by the Spanish in 1402, not until to-day were they formally incorporated into the Kingdom of Spain. The two major islands, Tenerife and Gran Canaria, which had been rivals for control of the Canaries for many years, were turned into separate provinces.

As odd it may seem to us today, Hollywood made silent films of popular stage operettas. Even without the songs, some of these theatre works played well on screen. Perhaps the finest example is MGM's romantic *The Student Prince of Old Heidelberg.* The 1924 Broadway musical hit was based on a 1901 German play and had a ravishing score by Sigmund Romberg (music) and Dorothy Donnelly (lyrics) but the screen version had an original soundtrack score that was played by a full orchestra in some theatres. The plot is a solid one. Crown Prince Karl Heinrich (Ramon Navarro) is in line for the throne of a small European kingdom, so he lives in seclusion in the castle and is getting an education from his tutor, Dr. Juttner (Jean Hersholt). Juttner convinces the king to let the prince study at the tutor's old alma mater at Heidelberg, so the two head for the university there. The prince quickly falls in love with Kathi (Norma Shearer), the niece of an inn owner, and she loves him. But their joy is quickly destroyed when news arrives that the king has died and the prince must return to be crowned king. Although he is betrothed to a princess, the prince still loves Kathi and returns to Heidelberg to bid her one last farewell, then he returns to his duty. Ernst Lubitsch directed the period piece with style, and the production values were outstanding. Navarro and Shearer make a lovely couple and the movie is still moving and beautiful to look at.

In 1926 the Gershwin brothers and British star Gertrude Lawrence scored a major hit on Broadway with the musical *Oh, Kay!* The show was chock full of hit songs, including "Clap Yo' Hands," "Maybe," "Do Do Do," and "Someone to Watch over Me." Yet Lawrence's beguiling performance as Lady Kay, who gets mixed up with some rum runners on Long Island, was equally responsible for letting *Oh, Kay!* run nearly nine months. On this day the London production opened with Lawrence reprising her Kay but with a British supporting cast and the show was nearly as successful in the West End, running seven months. In 1928, First National Pictures made a silent screen version of *Oh, Kay!* with Colleen Moore in the title role. Even without the Gershwin songs, the movie was deemed very entertaining by the critics; unfortunately, the film is believed lost.

THURSDAY, SEPTEMBER 22

One of the most famous and controversial matches in the history of professional boxing occurred today at Chicago's Soldier Field when former heavyweight champion Jack Dempsey sought to regain the title that he had lost to Gene Tunney the year before. A crowd of 104,943 fans watched and another ninety million people listened to Graham McNamee's radio broadcast of the fight. Spectators at Soldier Field included many celebrities, ranging from movie stars to Al Capone, who bet $50,000 on Dempsey to win. For six rounds Tunney was using Dempsey as a punching bag, but fifty seconds into the seventh, Dempsey briefly knocked Tunney unconscious with six consecutive punches. In ten seconds, he would regain his crown. But Dempsey made the mistake of not immediately following an order by referee Dave Barry to move to the farthest corner of the ring away from Tunney for the count. Thus, Barry had to walk Dempsey there while timekeeper Paul Beeler started to count. He had already reached five when Barry rushed over and restarted the count at one. Before Beeler reached the count of nine, Tunney regained consciousness and got to his feet after having been down for fourteen, possibly eighteen, seconds. Tunney returned to action and during the eighth round knocked Dempsey down. The unanimous decision of the judges was that Tunney won, but Dempsey fans thought he was cheated. The Tunney v. Dempsey bout became known as "The Long Count," and is still argued to this day.

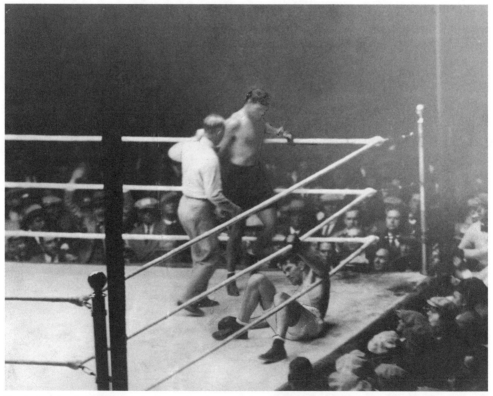

Boxing enthusiasts still argue about the "long count" match between heavyweights Jack Dempsey (in dark trunks) and Gene Tunney on September 22, 1927, in Chicago. With over 100,000 spectators and nationwide radio coverage, it was the most famous boxing event of the era. *Everett Collection Historical / Alamy Stock Photos*

FRIDAY, SEPTEMBER 23

High on every film critic's list of the greatest of Hollywood silent films is Fox's *Sunrise*, which premiered today in New York City. A farmer, only identified as the Man (George O'Brien), has a young Wife (Janet Gaynor) and a child, but he has an affair with a vacationing Woman from the city (Margaret Livingston). He wants to return to the city with the Woman, so she convinces him to drown his Wife. The Man and his Wife set off by boat for the city, but when the time comes to drown her, he cannot bring himself to do so. They continue on to the city where they see a young couple getting married, and the Man begs his Wife to forgive him. She does and together they have a marvelous day getting their photo taken, going to a carnival, and dancing. Returning home in their boat that night, a storm arises and the Man ties two bundles of reeds to his Wife to act as a life preserver. In the darkness and the storm, the boat capsizes and two are separated. The Man survives and awakes on shore, but efforts to find his Wife fail. The Woman assumes he drowned the Wife as planned, but when she goes to him, the Man starts to choke her. Then news comes that the Wife has washed up on the shore and is still alive. Happily reunited, the Man and Wife embrace and the Woman returns to the city as the sun rises. German director F. W. Murnau, known for his expressionistic films in Europe, was brought to Hollywood by producer William Fox to make *Sunrise*, and the result is an innovative movie with many surreal touches and fanciful elements. Cinematographers Charles Rosher and Karl Struss contributed their own unique look with forced perspective, distorted images, and challenging tracking shots. *Sunrise*, subtitled *A Song of Two Humans*, also featured a complete synchronized musical soundtrack, although title cards were used and there was no dialogue. Enthusiastic critical reception was repeated by the Academy of Motion Picture Arts and Sciences which named it "Best Unique and Artistic Picture" and gave Oscars to Gaynor, Rosher, and Struss.

Opening the same night in Los Angeles was United Artists' comedy *Two Arabian Knights*, which, oddly enough, took place during World War I. The American soldiers Sgt. Peter O'Gaffney (Louis Wolheim) and W. Daingerfield Phelps III (William Boyd) escape from a German POW camp during a snowstorm by wearing white robes to camouflage themselves. The two men are friendly antagonists, and their misadventures together include being recaptured and mistaken for Arab prisoners, stowing away on board a cargo ship headed to Arabia, and rescuing the Princess Mirza (Mary Astor) from drowning and from an arranged marriage to the ruthless Shevket Ben Ali. The freewheeling comedy was produced by Howard Hughes and directed by Lewis Milestone, who won an Oscar for his efforts. *Two Arabian Knights* was popular with the press and the public, yet the movie was believed lost for many years. After the death of Hughes in 1976, a print was found among his collection.

P. G. Wodehouse's short story "Portrait of a Disciplinarian" was published in today's issue of the American magazine *Liberty*. Although Frederick Mulliner is an adult,

F. W. Murnau's beguiling movie masterpiece *Sunrise* moves from a dark murder plan to a romantic affirmation of marital love without ever losing its dreamy, surreal tone. The Academy of Motion Picture Arts and Sciences was just as beguiled, giving the film an Oscar for Artistic Quality of Production. *Fox Film Corporation / Photofest © Fox Film Corporation*

he is still terrified of his old Nanny from childhood. Forced to take tea with her and the pretty Jane Oliphant, who has turned down his marriage proposal, Frederick is reduced to a blubbering schoolboy. Not until Nanny punishes them both by locking them in a cupboard do the couple reconcile their differences. The tale was later printed in the October issue of the *Strand Magazine* and appeared in the anthology *Meet Mr. Mulliner*.

SATURDAY, SEPTEMBER 24

When the New York Yankees beat the Detroit Tigers today 6–0, it was the team's 106th victory.

On a busy Saturday in college football, there were four shut-out games. USC beat Occidental 33–0; Army bested Boston University 13–0; Pittsburgh defeated Thiel College 42–0; and Texas A&M trounced Trinity 45–0.

Liberty magazine's pretentious club for writers was satirized in today's issue of the *New Yorker* magazine. James Thurber wrote the wry piece titled "The Literary Meet."

ALGONQUIN ROUND TABLE

One of the most famous gatherings of the 1920s was the Algonquin Round Table, a group of writers, actors, critics, and publishers who met irregularly for lunch at the Algonquin Hotel in Manhattan. Sometime calling themselves the "Vicious Circle," the members were famous for their insults, witticisms, and word games. The group began informally in 1919 and continued for a decade with some new members joining and some old ones dropping out when their careers took them to Hollywood or other far-flung places. The Algonquin Round Table was going strong in 1927 when its members included columnist Franklin Pierce Adams; humor writer, critic and sometime actor Robert Benchley; sportswriter Heywood Broun; playwright Marc Connelly; playwright and novelist Edna Ferber; playwright and wit George S. Kaufman; comic actor Harpo Marx; poet, short-story writer, and critic Dorothy Parker; Broadway producer Brock Pemberton; Harold Ross, the founder and editor of the *New Yorker* magazine; playwright Robert E. Sherwood; Broadway publicist John Peter Toohey; and acerbic wit and critic Alexander Woollcott. The last of the glory days for the Vicious Circle were in 1929 before the Stock Market crashed and many of the members found work outside of New York City.

SUNDAY, SEPTEMBER 25

The Rhine River overflowed its banks in the principality of Liechtenstein today, flooding all of the lowlands (der Unterland) and destroying most of the nation's farms. Overnight, Lake Constance in Switzerland rose fifteen feet. Volunteers from across Europe came to the aid of the little nation, a notable occasion of international relief in peacetime.

First National's sports drama *The Drop Kick* was a box office smash thanks to the popular actor Richard Barthelmess who had recently starred in the studio's boxing movie *The Patent Leather Kid*. College football star Jack Hamill (Barthelmess) is the best friend of Coach Brad Hathaway even though he dated the coach's wife Eunice before they were married. When the coach commits suicide, Jack is suspected as the reason because he and Eunice were reunited at the prom. But it is finally revealed that Brad had stolen money from the football fund to pay his many bills and couldn't face being found out. Jack dumps Eurnice, returns to his fiancée Cecily Graves, and wins the big football game. Playing the small role of a football player in the movie is twenty-year-old John Wayne.

Sailors, Beware! was another Hal Roach comedy short featuring Stan Laurel and Oliver Hardy before they were considered a comedy team. Cab driver Chester Chaste (Laurel) brings Madame Ritz and her small child to the docks where they board a steamship without paying the cab fare, so Chester follows them. On board, purser Cryder (Hardy) helps find the Madame and her son, who turns out to be a midget crook, the two of them planning a jewel robbery.

MONDAY, SEPTEMBER 26

Among the many 1927 aviation feats besides Charles Lindbergh's famous Atlantic crossing was the first attempted around-the-world flight by French aviators Dieudonné Costes and Joseph Le Brix. They set off today from Paris in a Breguet 19GR named *Nungesser-Coli* with a planned route that went south to Africa, crossed the South Atlantic to Argentina, north through South America to the United States, east across the Pacific to Japan, then on to India and Greece and back to France. Although they were forced to cross most of the Pacific by boat, Costes and Le Brix broke several distance records on their six-month journey.

It was a busy night on Broadway with six new productions and the opening of a new playhouse, the now-revered St. James Theatre. It was actually called the Erlanger Theatre when Abraham Erlanger built it and retained that name until 1932, when it was renamed after the famous London playhouse long known as the St. James Theatre. Although it had sixteen hundred seats, the press commented on how intimate the Georgian-style playhouse felt. The opening production was the musical *The Merry Malones*, which George M. Cohan wrote, produced, and starred in. Molly Malone (Polly Walker) loves the rich aristocrat Joe Westcott (Alan Edwards) but her father (Cohan) strongly objects. So, Joe plans to get disinherited by his wealthy family, plans that Mr. Malone tries to waylay until the happy ending. No hit songs came from Cohan's score, but the spectacular production (an entire subway car was recreated on stage for one scene) and the box office appeal of Cohan himself kept *The Merry Malones* running for six months. Running two months longer, thanks to another star, was the musical *Manhattan Mary*, which was a vehicle for stage comic Ed Wynn. He played the waiter Crickets, who helps Mary Brennan (Ona Munson) get a job in the latest *George White's Scandals*. White produced *Manhattan Mary* and played himself on stage, even doing some of his legendary hoofing in the second act. But the real attraction was Wynn, who did some of his expected ad-libbing, telling stories that had nothing to do with the plot, and generally pleasing his fans playing the "Perfect Fool."

Two hit plays were also among the night's offerings. Most memorable was William Somerset Maugham's drama *The Letter*, which was still running in London. For the New York production, the renowned Katharine Cornell played the woman who shoots a man and then lies about it to everyone, including her husband, saying it was self-defense when in truth the man was her lover who tried to walk out on her. Critics approved of both the play and Cornell's performance and *The Letter* ran three months then went on a successful road tour. *The Letter* is most remembered today for the 1940 screen version with Bette Davis as the conniving heroine. The comedy *The Shannons of Broadway* by James Gleason managed to run over twice as long as *The Letter* thanks to a delightful cast telling a simple story. Struggling vaudevillians Emma (Lucile Webster) and Mickey Shannon (Gleason) end up stranded in a small New England town where the only hotel is about to be foreclosed on by the local miser. The Shannons invest in the hotel and turn it into a popular stopping place for traveling actors, who often do their acts in the lobby. The whole town comes to life thanks to the Shannons, but show business calls and the couple sells the hotel to an investor to keep it out of the miser's hands. *The Shannons of Broadway* was filmed by Universal as *Goodbye Broadway* in 1938 with Alice Brady and Charles Winninger as the vaudeville couple.

TUESDAY, SEPTEMBER 27

Ten years after the Russian Revolution, a power struggle was going on in the Soviet Union since the death of Lenin in 1924. Leon Trotsky, one of the original revolutionaries behind the October 1917 revolt, had served in various political capacities in the Communist Party. But Joseph Stalin saw Trotsky as a threat and systematically took away Trotsky's political positions. Today Trotsky was expelled from the Comintern, the Communist International organization that advocated world Communism.

Prospectors working for the Benquet Consolidated Mining Company today discovered a gold vein in the Gran Cordillera Mountains on the island of Luzon in the Philippines. A gold rush resulted that changed the economy of the islands. By 1929 there were ninety-four mining companies in the area; by 1933, there were nearly eighteen thousand companies; by 1939, the Philippines was one of the leading gold producers in the world.

Twin ceremonies to mark the groundbreaking for the George Washington Bridge over the Hudson River took place today in Washington Heights in Manhattan and at Fort Lee, New Jersey, the two locations to be connected by the 4,760-foot-long structure. There were also speeches given on the steamer *DeWitt Clinton* which was anchored at the mid-point of the Hudson. Construction began within a month and the bridge was completed in 1931. Carrying over 103 million vehicles each year, the George Washington Bridge is estimated to be the busiest motor vehicle bridge in the world.

British author P. G. Wodehouse introduced the delightful character of Mr. Mulliner in a short story published in the *Saturday Evening Post* and the *Strand Magazine* in 1925, followed by his return in other magazine stories. Today the collection *Meet Mr. Mulliner* was released in the United Kingdom by publisher Herbert Jenkins and the character found an even wider readership. Mr. Mulliner is a pleasant raconteur who is usually found in the pub parlor of the Angler's Rest quietly listening to the patrons' conversation. At one point he politely interrupts the talk and tells a story related to the topic. The tale usually involves some relative of his and is a comic story with a nonsensical moral to it. *Meet Mr. Mulliner* was later published in the United States in March of 1928 by Doubleday and Doran and the character found many new fans in America. Mr. Mulliner would appear in forty stories by the time Wodehouse retired the character in 1967.

The Old West gunslinger Frank M. Canton, who during his colorful life was both a lawman and an outlaw, died today in Edmond, Oklahoma, at the age of seventy-eight. Born Josiah Horner in Indiana, he was involved in the Johnson County War, had a famous shootout with cattle rustler Bill Dunn, robbed banks in Texas, and served as a deputy U.S. marshal in Oklahoma.

WEDNESDAY, SEPTEMBER 28

Scribner's today published S. S. Van Dine's *The Canary Murder Case* which went on to break all records for detective fiction. It was Van Dine's second book featuring detective hero Philo Vance and is considered a classic example of a puzzle mystery. The beautiful singer Margaret Odell, known as "the Canary," is murdered in her apartment and there are plenty of suspects. There were many men in Odell's life and it seems that several of them visited her the evening of the murder. Vance solves the case by breaking the alibi of the murderer. *The Canary Murder Case* was filmed by Paramount in 1929.

THURSDAY, SEPTEMBER 29

One of the deadliest storms ever to hit St. Louis, Missouri, came today in the form of a tornado that ripped through the center of the city leaving a seven-mile path of destruction in five minutes. The midday storm hit seven schools filled with students; at Central High School, five students died. In all, the tornado left seventy-nine people dead and over five hundred injured.

When Babe Ruth hit his fifty-eighth and fifty-ninth home runs in today's game between the New York Yankees and the Washington Senators, he tied his own yearly record of fifty-nine home runs in 1921. The Yankees beat the Senators 15–4.

One of the most impressive sculptural works in New York City's Central Park was unveiled today. The 107th Infantry Memorial is a dynamic bronze figural group depicting seven larger-than-life-sized World War I foot soldiers in battle. The piece was sculpted by Karl Illava, who was a sergeant in the honored regiment that consisted of members of the New York Army National Guard.

The acclaimed Dutch physiologist Willem Einthoven died today in Leiden, Netherlands, at the age of sixty-seven. He invented the first successful electrocardiogram in 1903 and was awarded the Nobel Prize in Medicine in 1924.

FRIDAY, SEPTEMBER 30

Today marked a new record for Babe Ruth and Major League Baseball. The Washington Senators were playing the New York Yankees and the score was tied 2–2 in the eighth inning with a runner on third. Ruth hit his sixtieth home run of the season off of pitcher Tom Zachary for a Yankees 4–2 victory. Ruth's record of sixty home runs in a season would stand for thirty-four years until Roger Maris, also a Yankees right fielder, would hit sixty-one in 1961.

Babe Ruth broke so many Major League Baseball records that often the only records left to be broken were his own, as with his achieving sixty home runs in one season during a game between the New York Yankees and the Washington Senators on September 30, 1927. *Photofest © Photofest*

The average cost of a quart of milk in 1927 was fourteen cents. A gallon costs forty-five cents.

OCTOBER

SATURDAY, OCTOBER 1

The Pittsburgh Pirates won the National League pennant today with their 9–6 victory over the Cincinnati Reds. The New York Yankees played their last regular season game today and beat the Washington Senators 4–3, officially winning the American League pennant. The Yankees had won 110 of the 154 games they played this season. Since Pittsburgh had been in first place in its league for some time, it was clear early on that the contestants in the 1927 World Series would be the Pirates and the Yankees.

The University of Michigan in Ann Arbor celebrated the opening of its new stadium today by defeating Ohio Wesleyan 33–0. Officially called Michigan Stadium, the venue is better known as The Big House because it was the largest stadium in the nation when it opened and it still is today. Seating capacity in 1927 was 70,000 but over the years it has been expanded and today it can hold 107,601 spectators.

SPORTS STADIUMS

Some notable sports stadiums that were built in 1927 (* = still in operation):

Detroit Olympia	Kyle Field* (College Station, Texas)
Estadi Olímpic Lluís Companys* (Barcelona)	Michigan Stadium* (Ann Arbor)
Gator Bowl Stadium (Jacksonville, Florida)	The Palestra* (Philadelphia)
Grotenburg-Stadion* (Krefeld, Germany)	Rice Stadium (Salt Lake City)
Kenan Memorial Stadium* (Chapel Hill, North Carolina)	Stadio Renato Dell'Ara* (Bologna, Italy)

Among the other college football games played this day were USC over Santa Clara 52–12; Notre Dame defeating Iowa's Coe College 28–7; and two shutout games, Army v. Detroit Mercy 6–0 and Yale v. Bowdoin 41–0.

The college football season for the Western Conference (later the Big Ten) teams opened today with Minnesota beating North Dakota 57–10; Michigan besting Ohio Wesleyan 33–0; Illinois defeating Bradley 19–0; and four other shutout games: Pittsburgh v. Grove City College 33–0; Nebraska v. Iowa State 6–0; Georgia v. Virginia 32–0; and Texas A&M v. Southwest Texas 31–0.

Paramount spent a bundle on *The Rough Riders*, hiring hundreds of extras, building a military encampment outside of San Antonio, and re-creating the storming of San Juan Hill in Cuba during the Spanish-American War. But the script was an inaccurate and romanticized version of Colonel Teddy Roosevelt (Frank Hooper) and his horse patrol known as the Rough Riders. There is a melodramatic subplot about the monied draftee Stewart Van Brunt (Charles Farrell) and his sweetheart Dolly (Mary Astor). More interesting is the character of the earthy scoundrel Hell's Bells (Noah Beery). The expensive movie fared so poorly with preview audiences that scenes were reshot and edited and the film was then released under the title *The Trumpet Call*. Since all that remains of *The Rough Riders* today are sections of the battle scenes, it is impossible to say if the changes were an improvement or not. In either case, the movie was a box office failure. Also losing money on its release but surviving today and widely praised is the British movie *The Ring*, directed by and (most unusual) written by Alfred Hitchcock. Set in the world of professional boxing in England, the film has a conventional romantic triangle involving undefeated fairground boxer "One Round" Jack Sander, the world heavyweight champ Bob Corby, and the pretty Mabel. She marries Jack but loves Bob, and there is a lot of fuss leading up to the climactic bout between the two pugilists. What makes *The Ring* noteworthy are the masterful Hitchcock touches, such as cross cutting to create suspense and adding bits of ironic humor during tense moments. The film received laudatory reviews when it opened, but oddly it was not a hit for the new company British International Pictures. Today it is ranked very highly by film critics and Hitchcock fans. The day's third opening of note was MGM's melodrama *Body and Soul*,

When the University of Michigan opened its football stadium in Ann Arbor in 1927, it was the largest outdoor sports venue in America. It still is. The structure of The Big House, as it is called today, is unusual in that the playing field and much of the spectator section is below ground level. *Courtesy of the Library of Congress, LC-USZ62-127311*

with a strong yet creepy performance by Lionel Barrymore. He played Dr. Leyden, a sadistic surgeon who turned to drink and was forced out of town. He goes to a village in the Swiss Alps, where he becomes obsessed with the inn servant Hilda. Leyden tricks the girl into marrying him then treats her poorly. When her affections turn to the young skier Ruffo, Leyden arranges for the youth to have an accident. Leyden offers to save Ruffo's life if Hilda will give up the young man. She agrees, and he cruelly brands her with a burning iron to mark her as his. For a happy ending, an avalanche strikes and kills Leyden thereby reuniting Ruffo and Hilda.

SUNDAY, OCTOBER 2

Ernest Hemingway's second anthology of stories, *Men without Women*, was published today by Charles Scribner and Sons. Although the collection met with mixed critical notices, the book contains some superior Hemingway stories, most memorably "Fifty Grand," "Now I Lay Me," "Che ti dice la Patria?," "The Undefeated," "The Killers," "In Another Country," and "Hills Like White Elephants." The subject matter for the fourteen stories is varied, including bullfighters, troubled relationships, the Great War, boxing, and death.

The 1927 Minor League Baseball season ended officially today, although there were a few post-season games throughout the following week. In the American Association, the Toledo Mud Hens came in first, winning 101 games and losing 67. Second place went to the Kansas City Blues (99–69) in a tie with the Milwaukee Brewers (99–69). The other teams and their season tallies of wins and losses were: Columbus Senators (60–108), Louisville Colonels (65–103), Indianapolis Indians (70–98), Minneapolis Millers (88–80), and the St. Paul Saints (90–78). The Buffalo Bisons (112–56) came in first place in the International League, followed by the Syracuse Stars (102–66) in second and the Newark Bears (90–77) in third. The other leagues teams were the Toronto Maple Leafs (89–78), Baltimore Orioles (85–82), Rochester Tribe (81–86), Jersey City Skeeters (66–100), and the Reading Keystones (43–123). The Pacific Coast League first-place winner was the Oakland Oaks with 120 wins and 75 losses. Second place went to the San Francisco Seals (106–90) and the Sacramento Senators (100–95) came in third, followed by the Mission Bells (86–110), Portland Beavers (95–95), Hollywood Stars (92–104), Los Angeles Angels (80–116), and the Seattle Indians (98–92).

Although he was born on May 12, German President Paul von Hindenburg's eightieth birthday was celebrated across Germany today. Because of Hindenburg's inflammatory remarks made on September 18 about Germany not being responsible for starting the Great War, the president received few congratulations from international heads of state.

The Swedish chemist and physicist Svante Arrhenius died today in Stockholm at the age of sixty-eight. He won the Nobel Prize in Chemistry in 1903 for his discovery of the greenhouse effect, outlined in his 1896 paper "On the Influence of Carbonic Acid in the

Air upon the Temperature of the Ground." Southern politician Austin Peay, governor of Tennessee since 1922. died today in Nashville from a cerebral hemorrhage at the age of fifty-one. He instituted many improvements in his state and helped establish the Great Smoky Mountains National Park. In 1925, Peay signed the Butler Act, which prohibited the teaching of evolution in Tennessee schools. This led to the famous Scopes Trial that same year. Austin Peay State University was named in his honor in 1929.

MONDAY, OCTOBER 3

One of H. P. Lovecraft's best horror stories, "Pickman's Model," was published in the October issue of *Weird Tales* magazine. Set in the crime-ridden North End of Boston, the tale is told in the first person by Great War veteran Thurber about the artist Richard Upton Pickman, whose paintings are so ghoulish that he is expelled from the Boston Art Club. Pickman takes Thurber on a tour of his studio hidden deep in the slums of Boston where each painting is more hideous than the last. The most horrifying piece is a painting depicting a dog-human creature devouring a person. There is a photo attached to the painting and when Pickman rushes out of the room and fires a series of gunshots, Thurber grabs the photo and sees in it that the canine monster is not a product of Pickman's imagination but a real thing. Pickman disappears and Thurber tells the story to a man named Eliot. Interestingly, Pickman later shows up as one of the ghouls in Lovecraft's novel *The Dream Quest of Unknown Kadath*.

When former Mexican president Álvaro Obregón announced that he would run again in the 1928 election, two rival candidates came on the scene: General Francisco Serrano and General Arnulfo Gomez. The current president, Plutarco Elías Calles, today ordered Serrano's arrest and execution. As General Serrano and twelve of his men traveled on the road between Cuernavaca and Mexico City, they were intercepted and killed by General Claudio Fox and his soldiers. Obregón's other rival, General Arnulfo Gomez, would be executed on November 5. With no competitors left, Obregón easily won the election, only to be assassinated before he took office in 1928.

Henrik Ibsen's 1882 controversial drama *An Enemy of the People* was first presented on Broadway in 1895. A revival of the Norwegian drama opened today with venerated stage actor Walter Hampden playing the hero who tries to warn his village about pollutants in the local water. Hampden also did the English translation and produced and directed the production. Both critical and public plaudits for the revival allowed *An Enemy of the People* to run sixteen weeks, still the longest run on record for that Ibsen work.

TUESDAY, OCTOBER 4

Work began today on Mount Rushmore, one of America's most known and iconic memorials. Sculptor Gutzon Borglum and his crew began the blasting of granite in prepara-

NATIONAL PARKS

There were eighteen National Parks in America in 1927. Today there are fifty-eight. The National Parks in 1927 and the year they were established:

Yellowstone (Idaho, Montana, Wyoming) 1872
Sequoia (California) 1890
Yosemite (California) 1890
Mount Rainier (Washington) 1899
Crater Lake (Oregon) 1902
Wind Cave (South Dakota) 1903
Mesa Verde (Colorado) 1906
Glacier (Montana) 1910
Rocky Mountain (Colorado) 1915

Hawaii Volcanoes (Hawaii) 1916
Haleakala (Hawaii) 1916
Lassen Volcanic (California) 1916
Denali (Alaska) 1917
Acadia (Maine) 1919
Grand Canyon (Arizona) 1919
Zion (Utah) 1919
Hot Springs (Arkansas) 1921
Bryce Canyon (Utah) 1924

tion for carving the head of George Washington. The likeness of Washington would be ready for dedication on July 4, 1934, and the entire quartet of presidents would not be completed until 1939.

Margaret Bevan was elected today the lord mayor of Liverpool, England. She was the first woman mayor in Great Britain.

Some smart thinking and quick action today saved a mining town in Canada from becoming a disaster claiming many lives. A nickel mine in Worthington, Ontario, had been in operation since 1893 and was very productive until October 3, 1927, when a mine foreman noticed strange movements in the earth. He ordered all the workers out of the mine, then, seeing how extensive the cracks in the mine shafts were, had all the citizens of Worthington evacuate the town. At 5:30 a.m. on October 4, the mine not only collapsed, it took with it the mine buildings, several houses, railroad tracks, and the surrounding area, leaving a giant gaping hole, which today is a lake. The structures were not rebuilt, and today Worthington is a much-visited ghost town that is mostly underwater.

The African American concert pianist and composer John William Boone died today at the age of sixty-three. A brain fever when he was six months old necessitated the removal of both of Boone's eyes yet he grew up to study music, compose ragtime and other kinds of music, and give over seven thousand concerts across North America.

WEDNESDAY, OCTOBER 5

In the first game of the World Series, two errors by the Pittsburgh Pirates led to three unearned runs as the New York Yankees won the game 5–4 in Pittsburgh. Babe Ruth went 3 for 4 and scored two runs, while Lou Gehrig knocked in two of the runs with a triple and a sacrifice fly.

One of the handful of plays from 1927 that is still regularly performed is *Dracula*, the Hamilton Deane and John Balderston stage adaptation of Bram Stoker's 1897 novel, which opened on Broadway today. This version takes place entirely in England, with Count Dracula haunting a local asylum and matching wits with Dr. Van Helsing. The script was tested in a tour of Great Britain before opening in London on February 14, 1927. Perhaps the greatest of the many thrills this production of the horror tale provided was its leading man, Bela Lugosi, whose Romanian accent was both alluring and dangerous. Broadway producer Horace Liveright saw the London hit and secured the rights to present it in New York with Lugosi reprising his celebrated performance. *Dracula* was an immediate hit on Broadway, running nearly nine months, and this version has been revived several times in New York City, most memorably a 1977 production featuring Frank Langella that ran two and a half years. Lugosi reprised his Dracula in the famous Universal film in 1931. There have been countless adaptations of Stoker's story and different Draculas on stage, screen, and television over the decades, but there is still something unique about this original film.

Samuel L. Warner, who cofounded Warner Brothers Studio in 1910, died today of pneumonia in Los Angeles at the age of forty. He was not only the chief executive officer of the company, but also the force behind the effort to secure the technology for talking movies. Ironically, he died the day before his studio released the first talking feature film.

THURSDAY, OCTOBER 6

If one movie can claim to have changed the history of American film, that movie would be *The Jazz Singer*, which premiered today and was an immediate hit. Commonly known as the first talking feature film, the Warner-Vitaphone production is actually a silent movie with the human voice added for the songs only. Yet however one categorizes it, the movie is a major landmark and is still surprisingly effective. Young Jakie Rabinowitz (Bobby Gordon) lives on Manhattan's Lower East Side and is a concern to his parents (Warner Oland and Eugenie Besserer), especially when the youth is caught singing jazz and ragtime in a local saloon. Jakie refuses to study to be a cantor like his father and four generations of Rabinowitzes before him, so he runs away from home and, under the name Jack Robin, goes into show business. The years pass and, with the love and encouragement of dancer May (May McAvoy), Jack (Al Jolson) finds success, singing in nightclubs and returning to New York to be in a Broadway show. He hears his father is dying so he goes to the local synagogue and sings the Yom Kippur service in the old man's place. Jack then opens on Broadway and, with his mother sitting in the front row, sings "My Mammy" to her. *The Jazz Singer* was based on Samson Raphaelson's 1925 play, which had starred George Jessel on Broadway. Unlike the stage work, the action in the film glides through the immigrant neighborhoods and opens up the story to present the neighbors and other characters who influence Jakie's life. Although much of the movie is dated, there are still marvelous things to enjoy. Director Alan Crosland shot the exteriors on location in New York City and the depiction of the neighborhoods, the smoky saloons and nightclubs, and the backstage of the theatres has a tawdry realism to it. The plotting is solid; character development is not complex but clear; and of course, there is the riveting presence of Al Jolson. In both the silent and sound sections of the movie, the stage entertainer manages to grab one's attention and hold it with confident gusto. In the more serious scenes he avoids melodramatics and lets a simple frown or the turn of the head say it all. It was Jolson's first feature film and he embraced the camera like a silent film veteran. The script called for sound to be used only when the actors started singing, either the songs or the Hebrew chants. Yet Jolson was accustomed to inserting phrases and brief comments in his stage performances so when he did the same on film the audience actually heard his speaking voice as well as his singing. Jack tells the applauding patrons in a San Francisco nightspot "Wait a minute! Wait a minute! You ain't heard nothing yet!" before he breaks into "Toot, Toot, Tootsie," and there is a lovely section when Jolson ad-libs some words of affection to his mother while he sits at the piano and sings "Blue Skies." That is about all the dialogue that is heard in the movie but it was enough to start a revolution. Most of the songs used in *The Jazz Singer* were numbers already familiar to audiences, including

Warner Brothers didn't think that moviegoers wanted to hear screen actors talk, but the studio knew audiences wanted to hear Broadway star Al Jolson sing. Yet when Jolson ad-libbed a speech to his mother (Eugenie Besserer) in this scene from *The Jazz Singer*, the history of movies changed. *Warner Bros. Pictures / Photofest © Warner Bros. Pictures*

"My Gal Sal," "Dirty Hands, Dirty Faces," and "Waiting for the Robert E. Lee." The birth of the movie musical also meant the beginning of selling popular songs by way of Hollywood. The Warner Brothers gambled everything on the newfangled process of Vitaphone and Jolson's singing. Nearly bankrupt before the picture opened, *The Jazz Singer* saved the studio and changed the course of film history. The same studio remade *The Jazz Singer* in 1953 with Danny Thomas, and a third version in 1980 updated the story and featured rock singer Neil Diamond.

The Pittsburgh Pirates' sloppy play contributed to the New York Yankees winning the second game of the World Series. An error, a wild pitch, and a hit batsman all contributed to Yankee runs, as they cruised to a 6–2 win, with eleven hits and George Pipgras's complete game three-hitter in his first World Series appearance.

The Cincinnati lawyer and bootlegger George Remus made national news today when he shot and killed his wife Imogene Holmes in public on the day that their divorce was to be finalized. In fact, both parties were on their way to the courthouse in separate cars when Remus had his driver force Holmes off the road in Eden Park. In view of several people sitting in the Spring House Gazebo, Remus fired a shot into Holmes's abdomen as their daughter looked on.

FRIDAY, OCTOBER 7

The twenty-six-year-old Langston Hughes, an African American student at Lincoln University in Pennsylvania, who had seen his poetry published and win some minor awards, incited some controversy this week with the publication of his collection of poems entitled *Fine Clothes to the Jew* put out by Alfred A. Knopf. The black press thought the poems were harsh and painted a negative picture of African Americans living in Northern cities. The title refers to down-and-out "Negroes" who are so desperate for money that they pawn their very best clothes at the Jewish-owned pawn shops. The poetry anthology did not sell well, but years later, once Hughes was established as one of the finest African American poets, *Fine Clothes to the Jew* was reconsidered and highly praised.

Tommy Loughran, nicknamed the Phantom of Philly, became the light heavyweight boxing champion of the world today when he beat Mike McTigue in fifteen rounds at New York's Madison Square Garden. Later in his career, Loughran fought as a heavyweight and acted as a boxing referee.

A three-run home run by Babe Ruth capped off a six-run seventh inning as the New York Yankees bested the Pittsburgh Pirates 8–1 in the third game of the World Series. Lou Gehrig also hit a double and a triple, knocking in two runs at Yankee Stadium, while Herb Pennock pitched a three-hitter for the win.

The Kimberly-Clark paper mill in Appleton, Wisconsin, suddenly collapsed today, trapping over thirty employees under the rubble. Nine workers died and eighteen were injured.

THE HARLEM RENAISSANCE

The 1920s was a period of exciting African American art, music, literature, fashion, theatre, and social movements that, in retrospect, has been termed the Harlem Renaissance. At the time, many called it the *New Negro Movement*, named after the 1925 anthology of essays by philosopher, educator, and writer Alain Locke, considered the Dean of the Harlem Renaissance. This blossoming of African American talent was not limited to the Harlem section of New York but also flourished in Paris, the Caribbean, and in several large American cities. Critics point to the period between 1924, with the first edition of *Opportunity: A Journal of Negro Life*, and 1929, when the Stock Market crashed, as the high point of the Harlem Renaissance. Most of the outstanding African American artists of the movement, from Duke Ellington, Bessie Smith, Ma Rainey, and Eubie Blake in music to writers, such as Countee Cullen, Zora Neale Hurston, Langston Hughes, Claude McKay, and James Weldon Johnson, were all active and thriving in 1927 and appealed to many white and black Americans.

After eight attempts, Mercedes Gleitzer today became the first English woman to swim the English Channel. Gleitzer later became the first person to swim the Straits of Gibraltar between Europe and Africa and to swim the one hundred miles around the Isle of Man.

An all-around British athlete and sportsman, John Shillington "Jack" Prince died today in Los Angeles at the age of sixty-eight. He began his career as a cricketer then went professional as a bowler. Prince found more fame as a racehorse rider and a race car and motorcycle driver but he also broke records as a bicyclist. He built tracks for bicycle, motorcycle, and sprint car racing as well.

The avant-garde French artist Paul Sérusier died today in Morlaix, France, at the age of sixty-two. He was a pioneer in the field of abstract art and was one of the group of artists known as Les Nabis along with Paul Gauguin, Pierre Bonnard, and Edouard Vuillard.

A name more familiar to drinkers of Irish stout around the world, Guinness, was in the news today when Edward Guinness, the First Earl of Iveagh, died in London at the age of seventy-nine. The heir of the famous Guinness brewing company ran the family business from 1868 to 1889, when he retired to do philanthropic work, collect art, serve in the House of Lords, and finance medical research and exploration, such as the 1907 British Antarctic Expedition. When he died, Guinness's estate was worth 13.5 million pounds, a record at the time.

The average life expectancy for an American male in 1927 was fifty-three years.

OCTOBER

SATURDAY, OCTOBER 8

The twenty-fourth World Series came to an exciting end today when the New York Yankees completed a four-game sweep of the Pittsburgh Pirates. It was the first sweep ever by an American League team over the National League. Babe Ruth's fifth-inning home run gave the Yankees a 3–1 lead, but Pittsburgh tied later in the game. In the bottom of the ninth inning, Yankee Earle Combs walked, Mark Koenig beat out a bunt, and Ruth was intentionally walked to fill the bases. Two outs later, a wild pitch rolled far enough away for Combs to score the winning run, resulting in a final score of 4–3. Ruth knocked in a total of seven runs during the series, bringing the stellar Yankees season to a close. It was the second Yankees championship; they had won the World Series in 1923. The team would go on to win twenty-five more.

In Negro League Baseball, the Colored World Series concluded today as well. Luther Farrell of the Atlantic City Bacharach Giants pitched a rain-shortened seven-inning no-hitter against the Chicago American Giants, winning the game 3–2, and winning the Series five games to three with one tie.

In college football today, Texas A&M recorded its third shutout of the season with its 18–0 victory over Sewanee. Other shutout games included Pittsburgh v. West Virginia 49–0; Notre Dame v. Detroit Mercy 20–0; Minnesota v. Oklahoma State 40–0; Michigan v. Michigan State 21–0; and Illinois v. Butler 58–0. In other notable games, USC edged Oregon State 13–12 while Missouri did likewise with Nebraska 7–6; and Army defeated Marquette 21–12. In a battle of the Bulldogs, Georgia beat Yale 14–10.

Just as the Sandinista War in Nicaragua was the first time dive bombers were used, another military tactic was introduced today, this time by the rebels. Sandinista guerrillas shot down a U.S. Army Air Corps biplane near Jicaro, then waited for the Americans to rescue the two pilots who survived the crash. When the rescue party arrived, the rebels ambushed and killed four members of the Nicaraguan Guardia Nacional and wounded some of the U.S. Army forces. The maneuver is believed to be the first ever tactic of using downed aircrew as bait to ambush rescue forces. The two downed pilots were captured and later executed by the Sandinistas.

With more and more single women working as secretaries in offices, lots of possibilities for screen romances opened up. The Paramount comedy *Figures Don't Lie* is one of them. Mrs. Jones (Blanche Payson) is convinced that her husband "Howdy" Jones (Ford Sterling) is having a fling with his attractive secretary, Janet Wells (Esther Ralston). But Janet is attracted to the smart-aleck insurance sales manager Bob Blewe (Richard Arlen). He's so fresh with her, however, she plays hard to get. Bob finally wins Janet's heart at the same time he saves Jones from bankruptcy. During a scene at the company picnic at the beach, Ralston got to show off her own lovely figure, indicating the title was not just about ledger numbers. Unfortunately, only a poster and some publicity photos with Ralston in a bathing suit survive; the film is believed lost. Opening the same day and surviving to be enjoyed today is the Laurel and Hardy comedy short

The Second Hundred Years. The two comics play convicts who dig a tunnel only to end up in the warden's office. So, they dress up like painters, walk out of the prison, then steal some fancy duds from some dignitaries. Forced to play the roles of such important people leads to comic complications, ending with the two of them driven in a limousine back to the prison to take a tour.

A memorable short story by Dorothy Parker appeared in this day's issue of the *New Yorker* magazine. It was titled "Arrangement in Black and White." At a posh party where an African American singer is the guest of honor, a wealthy white woman attempts to demonstrate her lack of prejudice, but in making conversation with the singer, she manages to offend the man and the other guests.

SUNDAY, OCTOBER 9

Film idol Ramon Navarro played many dashing heroes in his career, few more delectable than the Spanish captain José Armando in MGM's *The Road to Romance* released nationwide today. When the beautiful maiden Seranida (Marceline Day) is kidnapped by Caribbean pirates and will be forced to marry the evil judge Don Balthasar (Roy D'Arcy), Armando disguises himself as a buccaneer and lives among the island inhabitants until he finds the right opportunity to rescue Seranida and engage in a swashbuckling duel with Balthasar. Loosely based on the British novel *Romance* by Joseph Conrad and Ford Maddox Ford, *The Road to Romance* was given a Latin setting that added to Navarro's allure and helped make the movie a success.

MONDAY, OCTOBER 10

In another chapter in the Teapot Dome scandal, today the Supreme Court ruled that the oil leases in the scandal had been corruptly obtained. The Court had invalidated the Elk Hills lease in February and today ruled by unanimous decision that the 1922 lease of rights to Wyoming's Teapot Dome oil field, granted by then secretary of the interior Albert Fall in return for personal favors, was invalid.

Broadway had an unlikely hit when the Theatre Guild offered the drama *Porgy* and it ran twenty-eight weeks. The African American Porgy (Frank Wilson) is a crippled beggar who lives and works in the Charleston, South Carolina, tenement district called Catfish Row. He loves the beautiful but weak-willed Bess (Evelyn Ellis), who is the mistress of the vicious Crown (Jack Carter). When Crown kills a man in a crap game and flees, Bess goes to live with Porgy. On Crown's return, Porgy fights with him and kills him. Porgy is taken to jail, and while he is there Bess is lured away by the drug peddler Sportin' Life. Released from jail and finding Bess gone, Porgy leaves Catfish Row to seek her out. Although the playwrights Dorothy and DuBose Heyward were white, they lived in Charleston and were very familiar with the African American community there. The press declared *Porgy* to be a bold and powerful work and also applauded the strong cast. Although today the play is overshadowed by the later folk opera version *Porgy and Bess* (1935) by the Gershwins, *Porgy* remains one of the greatest of all American folk dramas. That same night a very different kind of entertainment opened, the musical comedy *5 O'Clock Girl* which was billed as a "fairy tale in modern dress." Patricia Brown (Mary Eaton), who works at the Snow Flake Cleaners, has been in telephone correspondence with a young man whom she phones every day at five o'clock when she gets off work. When she finally meets her telephone lover, he turns out to be the monied Gerald Brooks (Oscar Shaw), so Patricia pretends to be rich as well. The disguise doesn't last long but causes enough complications before arriving at a happy ending. Bert Kalmar and Harry Ruby wrote the tuneful score which included the hit song "Thinking of You." *5 O'Clock Girl* was unpretentious fun and entertained audiences for thirty-five weeks.

The aviation pioneer Gustave Whitehead died today of a heart attack in Bridgeport, Connecticut, at the age of fifty-three. The German-born Whitehead immigrated to the U.S. in 1893 and experimented with airplane designs and made gliders and kites. He supposedly built and flew a steam-powered airplane in Pittsburgh in 1899 (three years before the Wright Brothers' first flight), but the plane crashed and left Whitehead in the hospital for several weeks. The details about the feat, and other early Whitehead flights, remain controversial. Later in his career, when flight had been mastered by the Wrights, Whitehead designed, manufactured, and flew airplanes and invented several modifications in engine and propeller design.

TUESDAY, OCTOBER 11

New York Yankees first baseman Lou Gehrig was today named the American League's Most Valuable Player (MVP). Although Babe Ruth had been the Major League Baseball season's most outstanding athlete, he had won MVP in 1926 and the rules at the time did not allow winners in consecutive years. All the same, the twenty-four-year-old Gehrig certainly deserved the award. He had a tremendous season, batting .373 and leading the league with 173 RBIs and fifty-two doubles.

Stage actress and amateur pilot Ruth Elder took off today from New York's Roosevelt Field in a Stinson "Detroiter" airplane dubbed *American Girl* in an attempt to become the first woman to duplicate Charles Lindbergh's transatlantic crossing to Paris. Her copilot was the experienced George Haldeman and their route over the North Atlantic was charted to avoid existing storms. But mechanical problems with the fuel line caused Elder and Haldeman to ditch the plane when they were only 360 miles from landing in Europe. The two pilots were rescued by an oil tanker, but the plane caught fire and sank into the sea. While many claimed Elder was just a publicity seeker, she and Haldeman did

Born Heinrich Ludwig Gehrig in New York City, the Iron Horse, as Lou Gehrig was later called, was one of the greatest Major League Baseball players of the twentieth century. The first baseman played his entire seventeen-year professional career for the New York Yankees, from 1923 until 1939, when he was struck down by amyotrophic lateral sclerosis (ALS), better known today as Lou Gehrig's disease. *Photofest © Photofest*

establish a new over-water endurance flight record of 2,623 miles. Also, Elder was an active feminist and wanted to prove that a woman could accomplish whatever a man could. Returning to New York by ship, the two pilots were honored with a ticker tape parade in Manhattan. The flight made Elder famous, and she was dubbed the "Miss America of Aviation." She later gave talks promoting aviation, advocated women pilots, participated in air races, and even had a brief movie career. There was a resurgence of interest in Elder in the twenty-first century with Malene R. Laugesen's children's book *Flying Solo: How Ruth Elder Soared into America's Heart* and the 2016 novelized version of her life, *Crossing the Horizon* by Laurie Notaro.

Another bold woman made the news today when Mona McLellan (pseudonym of Dorothy Cochrane Logan) arrived at Folkestone, England, after swimming the English Channel and reportedly breaking Gertrude Ederle's 1926 record with a new time of thirteen hours and ten minutes. "McLellan" was awarded a $5,000 prize from the British newspaper *News of the World*. Five days later, Logan revealed to the press that her Channel swim had been a hoax and she had only swum four hours and did the rest of the crossing by boat. Returning the prize money, Logan told *News of the World* that the stunt was designed to demonstrate the lack of monitoring or verification of record-breaking attempts. Some believe Logan did not plan to reveal her deception and only made the announcement when she was found out. Either way, she was fined for perjury.

Character actor Frank Craven wrote and starred in the Broadway comedy *The 19th Hole*, which opened to mixed notices but became a modest hit all the same. Vernon Chase (Craven) is a respected author but gets little respect from his overbearing wife Emmy (Mary Kennedy). When the couple summers in the suburbs, Vernon gets addicted to golf and, after several mishaps, ends up winning a tournament and some appreciation from his wife. The paper-thin comedy was well acted and held the boards for fifteen weeks.

WEDNESDAY, OCTOBER 12

Wilbur Wright Field, an airfield outside of Dayton, Ohio, was established in 1919. After the city of Dayton added 750 acres to the field and built some permanent brick buildings, it was dedicated today as Wright Field, honoring both of the Wright Brothers, who hailed from Dayton. The field was used by the United States Army Air Corps for training and testing of aircraft. It is now part of Wright-Patterson Air Force Base.

THURSDAY, OCTOBER 13

Lionel Barrymore was the first of the famous stage family to turn to the movies and by 1927 he had appeared in fifty feature films. In today's MGM mystery thriller *The 13th Hour*, he played the diabolical Professor Leroy, who is behind a series of thefts and murders always

America's most famous gangster, Al Capone, created a dapper, bon vivant persona that was picked up and promoted by the press. It was also picked up by many authors and filmmakers, and over the years, thinly disguised versions of Capone can be found in dozens of novels, films, and television movies. *Photofest © Photofest*

committed at one o'clock in the morning. Detective Matt Gray searches for the culprit with the help of his German shepherd. When Leroy offers a substantial reward for the capture of the killer, Gray meets him and soon falls in love with his secretary Mary Lyle. By the time he figures out that Leroy is the murderer, Gray is trapped inside the professor's house, which is filled with deadly gadgets and creepy gizmos. But Gray and the dog outwit the professor, rescue Mary, and bring Leroy to justice.

Organized crime in Cleveland was controlled by "Big Joe" Lonardo and Joe Porrello. "Big Joe" and his brother John had control of the bootleg business in the city since 1919 but today both brothers were gunned down after being summoned to a card game at a barber shop owned by Porrello. It was not proved that Porrello was behind the hit, but he soon became the crime boss of Cleveland. Three years later, Porrello himself was gunned down.

AL CAPONE AND ORGANIZED CRIME

Al Capone was at the height of his power in 1927. The New York-born gangster and businessman was only twenty-eight years old but "Scarface" already ran Chicago with little interference, both the mayor and the police being firmly under his thumb. His operations, including bootlegging and gambling, were so effectively run that Capone's businesslike operations gave rise to the expression "organized crime." Capone was something of a hero to the common man, particularly Italian-American immigrants. But his image was damaged after the St. Valentine's Day Massacre in 1929 in which he wiped out seven rival mobsters. Capone's empire started to crumple in 1931, when he was prosecuted for income tax evasion. By the next year, he was in prison, and he died in 1947 from cardiac arrest complicated by his longtime bouts with syphilis.

FRIDAY, OCTOBER 14

As part of their around-the-world flight in their Breguet airplane *Nungesser-Coli*, French pilots Dieudonné Costes and Joseph Le Brix today set off from Saint-Louis, Senegal, and became the first pilots to fly across the South Atlantic Ocean. They arrived the next day in Port Natal, Brazil, the flight taking twenty-one hours and fifteen minutes.

SATURDAY, OCTOBER 15

A little-noticed event today in northern Iraq would eventually alter the world economy: the first discovery of oil in the Middle East. At 3 a.m. a fountain of oil gushed up to the surface from one of the largest oil fields in the world. Located some fifty miles south of Kirkuk in present-day Iraq, the site was named Baba Gurgur, "Father of Eternal Fire" in Arabic. It is estimated that the underground field had been burning for 2,500 years. Oil gushed out for ten days before the Turkish Petroleum Company (today the Iraq Petroleum Company) could control the flow of oil and begin collecting between 35,000 and 95,000 barrels a day. Subsequent discoveries of oil throughout the Middle East would shift the balance of international power as the demand for oil increased over the rest of the century.

There were three tie games today in college football. USC and Stanford University both scored 13, Illinois and Iowa State played to a 12–12 tie, and Minnesota and Indiana ended up with 14 points each. Notre Dame defeated Navy 19–6; Army bested Davis & Elkins College 27–6; and Texas A&M surrendered its first points in a 40–6 win over Arkansas. The rest of the games were shutouts: Yale v. Brown 19–0, Michigan v. Wisconsin 14–0, Georgia v. Furman University 32–0, Pittsburgh v. Drake 32–0, and Nebraska v. Grinnell College 58–0.

Hal Roach's comedy short *Call of the Cuckoo* includes Stan Laurel and Oliver Hardy among its cast members but it is far from a Laurel and Hardy film. Papa Gimblewart hates living next door to the local lunatic asylum, so he foolishly buys a house sight unseen in order to escape his crazy neighbors. The new house is poorly built and has its own loony quality, such as water coming out when you turn on the light switch. There are so many things falling apart or dysfunctional about the house that Gimblewart asks himself what could be worse. Then he sees the lunatics from the old asylum move into the house next door. Laurel, Hardy, Charley Chase, and James Findlayson were among the expert clowns who played the inmates.

Jacob "Little Augie" Orgenstein, a notorious labor racketeer, drug trafficker, and bootlegger, was killed today in a drive-by shooting in Lower Manhattan at the age of thirty-four. The killers were gunmen Louis "Lepke" Buchalter and Gurrah Shapiro. Wounded in the attack was Orgenstein's cohort Jack "Legs" Diamond, who during his life survived so many attempts to kill him that he became known as the "clay pigeon of the underworld."

SUNDAY, OCTOBER 16

Excavations at Chou K'ou Tien (Zhoukoudian) in China had begun in 1921 and remnants of early man had been unearthed there. Canadian anatomist Davidson Black secured funding from the Rockefeller Foundation, which sponsored excavations at the site with both Western and Chinese scientists. Today a tooth was discovered by Swedish paleontologist Anders Birger Bohlin that was estimated to be more than three hundred thousand years old. Black named the find *Sinanthropus pekinensis*, since the site was near the city of Peking (now Beijing). More remains were found over the next ten years and the species was reclassified as *Homo erectus pekinensis*, or Peking Man. Sadly, all the specimens from the site would disappear in 1941 when World War II raged in China.

MONDAY, OCTOBER 17

Baseball executive Ban Johnson, who had founded the American League in 1901, today retired as the league's president. The sixty-three-year-old Johnson cited failing health as the reason he stepped down. He died in 1931 and was inducted into the Baseball Hall of Fame in 1937.

TUESDAY, OCTOBER 18

The French aviator Jacques de Lesseps died today at the age of forty-four when his plane went down off the coast of Quebec. Lesseps was a World War I hero who became a noted aerial photographer after the war. Although the wreckage of his plane was soon found, Lesseps's body did not wash up on the shores of Newfoundland until several weeks later.

The critics may not have been overwhelmed with MGM's comedy *Spring Fever*, but the public was, and the movie turned out to be a big hit. The thin plot concerned the smart-aleck shipping clerk Jack Kelly (William Haines) who bluffs his way into an exclusive country club where he meets and falls head over heels in love with Allie Monte (Joan Crawford). To impress her, Jack poses as a pro golf champ, which wins her heart but also causes complications, such as forcing him to play in the big tournament. By this time Allie has learned the truth and loves Jack for himself, but her family insists she marry a man with money. When Jack wins the $10,000 golf tournament, he is just the man.

Five shows opened on Broadway this night and two of them were moneymakers, both imports from the London theatre. *Interference* was a thriller about a respected British physician, Sir John Marlay, who finds out that his young wife Barbara is being blackmailed by a woman who knows that Barbara's supposedly dead first husband Philip is very much alive. The blackmailer is murdered, Barbara is accused, but it turns out Philip did it. The tight little drama ran twenty-eight weeks. A. A. Milne's fantasy drama *The Ivory Door* ran even longer: thirty-nine weeks. King Perivale (Henry Hull) has been told for years that anyone who enters through a mysterious ivory door never returns the same. His curiosity is so strong that he goes through the door, finds nothing but a dusty hallway, then returns to the palace. But no one recognizes him as the king, and when he insists he is Perivale, the court believes he is bedeviled. Only Perivale's fiancée Princess Lilia believes him and to prove it she goes through the ivory door with him, the two ending up in the future where they are much happier.

A renowned New York City landmark, Sardi's Restaurant, opened in 1921 under the management of Vincent Sardi Sr. In 1927 it moved to its present location on West 44th Street in the Theatre District and has remained a famous eatery ever since.

WEDNESDAY, OCTOBER 19

Pan American Airways was founded in March and today made its first regularly scheduled international flight from Key West, Florida, to Havana, Cuba, in a tri-motor Fokker F-VIII piloted by Hugh Wells. The company, soon changing its name to Pan American World Airways but usually just called Pan Am, grew quickly, expanding its routes and eventually becoming the largest international American air carrier. In the late 1980s, competition, the rise in fuel prices, and other factors caused Pan Am to file for bankruptcy in 1991. By the end of that year, the company ceased operations. Ironically, Pan Am's last flight was, like its first, a Florida-Caribbean one: Captain Mark Pyle flew Pan Am Flight 436 from Bridgetown, Barbados, to Miami on December 4, 1991.

THURSDAY, OCTOBER 20

The first Ford Model A automobiles were manufactured on this day but were not available for sale until December 2. The upscale car came in four standard colors and cost the hefty price of $500 for the Tudor style model and $1,200 for the deluxe Town Car body. Over five million Model A cars were sold over the next five years.

FRIDAY, OCTOBER 21

Construction on the George Washington Bridge, connecting Manhattan and New Jersey, began today on both sides of the Hudson River as a project by the New York Port Authority. Called the Hudson River Bridge when groundbreaking took place, the Port Authority named the structure after the first president in 1931. The $75 million bridge was completed eight months ahead of schedule and was opened to traffic in October of 1931.

SATURDAY, OCTOBER 22

Despite disparaging reviews from the critics when it opened on Broadway in 1922, Anne Nichols's ethnic comedy *Abie's Irish Rose* was an audience favorite and one of the biggest hits of the 1920s. The play about a Jewish boy wedding an Irish girl, much to the consternation of their families, finally closed today after 2,327 performances, a record for a Broadway run. Not until the comedy *Life with Father* opened in 1939 and ran eight years was that record broken.

In college football today, Texas A&M and Texas Christian battled it out but ended up with a tie score of 0–0. Other shutouts included USC v. Caltech (51–0), Minnesota v. Iowa, (38–0), and Michigan v. Ohio State (21–0). Other action saw Georgia trounce Auburn, 33–3; Brown was bested by Lebanon Valley 13–12; Pittsburgh beat its local rival Carnegie Tech 23–7; Illinois snuck by Northwestern 7–6; Notre Dame defeated Indiana 19–6; and Yale beat Army 10–6.

Outfielder Ross "Pep" Youngs died today from a kidney disorder at the age of thirty. Youngs, whose career was cut short in 1926 because of his health, played for the New York Giants from 1917 to 1926, including four National League pennants and World Series championships in 1921 and 1922. He was elected to the Hall of Fame in 1972, a decision that was controversial since the Veteran's Committee consisted of several ex-teammates. All the same, Youngs hit over .300 for nine seasons, eight of them consecutive.

SUNDAY, OCTOBER 23

Disagreements between Leon Trotsky and Joseph Stalin, mainly over political issues and the direction in which the Soviet Union was moving, exploded today, and Trotsky and fellow politico Grigory Zinoviev were expelled from the Central Committee of the Communist Party.

Although newspaper tycoon William Randolph Hearst preferred to see his protege Marion Davies in elegant costume dramas, she always came across best in contempo-

Coming into power in 1922 and removing his rivals in 1927, Joseph Stalin was the undisputed dictator of the Soviet Union for twenty-six more years. It is estimated that during his reign, Stalin ordered the persecution and deaths of more victims than Hitler and Mussolini combined. *Photofest © Photofest*

rary comedies, such as Cosmopolitan Pictures' *The Fair Co-ed*. Davies played Marion Bright, who is not interested in going to college until she meets the school's football star Bob Dixon (Johnny Mack Brown). She enrolls at Bingham College where she finds out he earns his tuition money by coaching the girls' basketball team, so Marion joins the team. Soon she is the best player, but after a tiff with Bob she misses a game and Bingham loses. She and Bob make up and Marion leads the team to victory in the big game. While the plot is featherweight, the cast is charming, Davies in particular showing off her comic (and athletic) skills. Different skills were at work in Universal's *The Chinese Parrot*. Earl Derr Biggers's famous Asian sleuth Charlie Chan first appeared on the screen in 1926. Chan's second film adaptation, *The Chinese Parrot*, opened today with Japanese actor Sojin Kamiyama as the title detective. Everyone who has owned a legendary pearl necklace has either died or been ruined financially or socially. Honolulu detective Chan disguises himself as a servant in the household of the latest victim in order to seek out the murderer. With the help of a parrot who speaks both English and Chinese, he succeeds. Sadly, *The Chinese Parrot* is believed lost.

MONDAY, OCTOBER 24

Alfred Hitchcock's third movie of 1927, the drama *Downhill*, opened in London today and it starred Ivor Novello, his leading man from the popular *The Lodger*. The plot is about the fall from grace of an honest man who is true to a friend. Rugby athlete Roddy Berwick (Novello) and Tim Wakely (Robin Irvine) are best friends at an upper-crust boarding school. When Tim gets the waitress Mabel pregnant, Roddy takes the blame for his friend and is expelled, ostracized by his family, and subjected to a series of misfortunes until years later the truth comes out and he is exonerated. *Downhill*, Hitchcock's fifth movie, has many of the director's distinctive touches, particularly in his use of shadows and during a dream sequence that involves a surreal descent in an elevator. When the film was released in the United States in 1928, it was retitled *When Boys Leave Home*.

Railroad developer and executive S. Davies Warfield died today in Baltimore at the age of sixty-eight. He was responsible for extending the Seaboard Air Line Railway into South Florida and linking the east and west coasts of Florida by railroad. Warfield's rail lines are still in use today. He was also a prominent banker and businessman, serving as the president or director of the Continental Trust Company of Baltimore, the Baltimore Steam Packet Company, the Maryland Casualty Company, and the New York Life Insurance Company.

TUESDAY, OCTOBER 25

The Italian luxury liner SS *Principessa Mafalda* was approaching Porto Seguro, Brazil, today when its propeller shaft fractured and damaged the hull. The ship sank slowly and rescue vessels were soon on the scene, but there was so much panic on board that 314 out of the ship's 1,252 passengers and crew went down with the liner.

A rousingly raucous revival of *The Taming of the Shrew* opened on Broadway and pleased audiences for nearly six months, still a record for that Shakespeare comedy on Broadway. The production by the Garrick Players boasted a fine cast and an intriguing concept: the Renaissance play was set in modern times. Petruchio (Basil Sydney) was a dapper sportsman with a Kodak camera who ran off with his bride Kate (Mary Ellis) in an automobile. While such treatments of Shakespeare's works would become common in the 1930s, this clever production was quite ahead of its time.

The esteemed baseball outfielder Tom Brown died today in Washington, D.C., at the age of sixty-seven. Brown played for nine teams in four different leagues between 1892 and 1898. During the 1,788 games he played, Brown had 1,951 hits. He later managed the Washington Senators and served as an umpire for three seasons.

WEDNESDAY, OCTOBER 26

The trial of the Russian-Jewish poet and Bolshevik Sholom Schwartzbard concluded today with an acquittal on all criminal counts, in particular the assassination of the Ukrainian nationalist leader Symon Petliura in Paris in 1924. Schwartzbard, who had relocated from his native country to Paris in 1920, had seen scores of Jews, including fourteen members of his own family, killed in Petliura's anti-Semitic pogroms in the Ukraine. Schwartzbard's defense was that he assassinated an assassin.

The jazz standard "Black and Tan Fantasy" was recorded today in Camden, New Jersey, by its composers, Duke Ellington and trumpeter Bubber Miley, with Ellington's band, the Washingtonians. At the same session Ellington recorded another jazz favorite, "Creole Love Song," which was based on Joe "King" Oliver's earlier "Camp Meeting Blues."

John Galsworthy's episodic melodrama *Escape* arrived from London and was welcomed on Broadway for twenty-two weeks. The play had been a success in the West End with actor Leslie Howard securing his reputation as one of the finest young actors on the stage. Howard reprised his performance in the New York production and met with another round of raves. He played Matt Denant, a former army captain during the Great War, who comes upon a man beating a prostitute. He interferes and, in the struggle, the aggressive man falls, hits his head, and dies. It turns out the man was a plain-clothes cop, and Denant is tried and convicted of manslaughter. Denant escapes from Dartmoor Prison and encounters a series of people who either help or hinder him as he runs from the police. Galsworthy's plot consists of nine taut episodes and emphasizes character over action, painting a vivid portrait of various Englishmen from different classes. *Escape* was filmed in 1930 with Gerald du Maurier as Denant and in 1948 with Rex Harrison.

Jazz musician, composer, arranger, and bandleader Duke Ellington (at piano) inspired the sound of the Jazz Age perhaps more than anyone else. By 1927 he had been working professionally for a dozen years and he continued to experiment and create jazz innovations for another four decades. *Photofest © Photofest*

THURSDAY, OCTOBER 27

British composer Frank Bridge's *Rhapsody for Orchestra: Enter Spring* premiered today at the Norwich Triennial Festival in England, performed by the Queen's Hall Orchestra. Subtitled a "Symphonic Poem," the composition is a vigorous piece with a pastoral flavor including bird song.

The romantic drama *Dress Parade*, released today by DeMille Pictures, is a routine affair but the performances by stars William Boyd and Bessie Love make it seem special. Boyd plays the small-town athlete Vic Donovan, who visits West Point Academy and is instantly smitten with Janet Cleghorne (Love), the daughter of the Commandant. Vic enrolls at the famous school to pursue Janet but his cocky ways and arrogant attitude earn him neither friends nor Janet's love. Not until Vic performs a selfless act and saves the life of a cadet is he appealing in her eyes.

The most notorious Australian gangster of his day, Squizzy Taylor, died today in Melbourne from wounds suffered during a shoot-out with rival mobster Joseph "Snowy" Cutmore, who also died. Taylor was thirty-nine years old and Cutmore was thirty-two. The details of the shoot-out remain contradictory to this day and many theories about who shot who when and how are disputed. The whole incident was revived in a popular Australian TV miniseries *Underbelly: Squizzy* (2013).

FRIDAY, OCTOBER 28

The Yugoslav revolutionary and political leader Josip Broz, better known simply as Tito, began his seven-month jail sentence in Croatia for his subversive activities. Tito eventually became the first Communist president of Yugoslavia, in office from 1953 to 1980.

Country singer Porter Wagoner, known as "Mr. Grand Ole Opry," was born today in West Plains, Missouri.

FUTURE MUSIC MAKERS

Some notable composers, lyricists, singers, musicians, conductors, and bandleaders who were born in 1927:

Edie Adams (d. 2008)
Mose Allison (d. 2016)
Ed Ames
Liz Anderson (d. 2011)
Hank Ballard (d. 2003)
Billy Barnes (d. 2012)
Harry Belafonte
Mindy Carson
Barbara Cook (d. 2017)
John Dankworth (d. 2010)
Sir Colin Davis (d. 2013)
Val Doonican (d. 2015)
Slim Dusty (d. 2003)
Stan Getz (d. 1991)
Fred Hellerman (d. 2016)
Johnny Horton (d. 1960)
John Kander
Eartha Kitt (d. 2008)
Danny La Rue (d. 2009)

Cleo Laine
Al Martino (d. 2009)
Kurt Masur (d. 2015)
Guy Mitchell (d. 1999)
Gerry Mulligan (d. 1996)
Ram Narayan
Patti Page (d. 2013)
Junior Parker (d. 1971)
Leontyne Price
Boots Randolph (d. 2007)
Johnny Ray (d. 1990)
Red Rodney (d. 1994)
Mstislav Rostropovich (d. 2007)
Ronnie Scott (d. 1996)
Doc Severinson
Ralph Stanley (d. 2016)
Ward Swingle (d. 2015)
Porter Wagoner (d. 2007)
Andy Williams (d. 2012)

SATURDAY, OCTOBER 29

A German luxury ocean liner, SS *Cap Arcona*, began its maiden voyage today, setting sail from Hamburg to Buenos Aires. The ultra-modern ship was 676 feet long, could carry 1,315 passengers, and was powered by eight steam turbines, making her one of the largest and fastest liners on the high seas. The *Cap Arcona* was requisitioned by the German navy in 1940 and was used as a prison ship. It was transporting some five thousand prisoners from Scandinavia to German concentration camps in 1945 when it was sunk by the British Royal Air Force along with sister ships *Deutschland* and *Thielbek*. In all, nearly seven thousand passengers died, making the attack one of the deadliest of World War II.

Polish-born film star Pola Negri was in three movies released in 1927, and they were all splendid. The third was Paramount's *The Woman on Trial*, in which she played the Frenchwoman Julie accused of murder. Based on a Hungarian play by Ernest Vajda, the movie is set in the courtroom where the artist's model Julie tells her story in a series of flashbacks. Her love for the consumptive artist Pierre Bouton, her marriage to wealthy arts patron Moreland to finance Pierre's career and cure, the machinations of the scoundrel Gaston Napier to compromise Julie and lose her child in a divorce case, and her shooting of Napier are all recounted and shown at the trial. In the end, the court acquits Julie and she returns to her now-cured Pierre. Only sections of the movie survive but enough to see that *The Woman on Trial* was Negri at her best. One can see all of the German-British film *Der Geisterzug* (*The Ghost Train*) today and it still has its thrills. Based on Arnold Ridley's 1923 London hit *The Ghost Train*, the plot for the movie is similar. A diverse group of railway passengers are stranded at a remote station where it is said every night a mysterious train quickly passes the station and anyone who looks on it drops dead. There are plenty of chills before it is discovered by a detective in disguise that the station master and some crooks have fabricated the ghost train in order to transport drugs and alcohol. Filmed in Germany by Géza von Bolváry, the movie features mostly a British cast. It opened today in Berlin and then was seen throughout Europe but not officially in the United States until a silent film festival in San Francisco in 2015. Ridley's original play was remade by Gainsborough Pictures (UK) in 1931 and 1941.

In college football today, Illinois shut out Michigan 14–0. There were plenty of other shutouts: USC v. California, (13–0); Army v. Bucknell (34–0); Yale v. Dartmouth (19–0); Nebraska v. Syracuse, (21–0); Georgia v. Tulane, (31–0); and Pittsburgh v. Allegheny (62–0). At least Georgia Tech got 7 points but still lost to Notre Dame 26–7, while Minnesota beat Wisconsin, 13–7.

Influential German architect and author Hermann Muthesius died today in a road accident near Berlin at the age of sixty-six. Muthesius introduced many of the British Arts and Crafts movement ideas to Germany and his ideas formed the basis for the later Bauhaus school of architecture.

SUNDAY, OCTOBER 30

Today an assassination attempt on a Greek naval hero and politician failed. Admiral Paul Kondouriotis, a former president of Greece, was shot in the head by the twenty-five-year-old waiter Zafioios Goussies while Kondouriotis was leaving an Athens conference of Greece's mayors. Miraculously, Kondouriotis survived and was reelected president in 1929.

MONDAY, OCTOBER 31

One of the most popular songs of all time, Hoagy Carmichael's "Stardust," began its journey to fame today when Carmichael recorded a jazz instrumental version of the number in Richmond, Indiana, for Gannett Records. The entrancing melody for "Stardust" had come to Carmichael when he was still a student at Indiana University, but he didn't write it down as a composition until 1927. The recording received moderate attention, mostly by other musicians who noticed the unusual structure of the piece and the innovative chord changes and shifts in the musical line. It was not until 1930 when Mitchell Parish wrote the intoxicating lyric about the "stardust of yesterday" that the piece was published as a song and started to catch on. Soon it was being widely recorded, as with Artie Shaw's 1941 version which sold 2.5 million records. It is estimated that there have been over one thousand different recordings in over forty languages, making "Stardust" one of the most recorded songs of the twentieth century.

The 1927–1928 season at the Metropolitan Opera in New York City opened tonight with Giacomo Puccini's *Turandot* conducted by Tullio Serafin. The Met had presented the American premiere of the opera in 1926 and revived it as the season opener.

If the romance in United Artists' *My Best Girl* seems particularly sincere, it might be because costars Mary Pickford and Charles "Buddy" Rogers fell in love while making the movie and later married. Maggie Johnson (Pickford) works as a stock girl at Merrill's Department Store and supports her oddball family: her elderly postman father, her scatterbrained mother, and her carefree flapper of a sister. Maggie falls in love with the handsome new stock boy Joe (Rogers), who is really the son of the store's owner trying to prove to his father that he is responsible enough to marry the monied Millicent Rogers. There are the usual complications before Joe's affections turn to Maggie, the truth of his identity is revealed, his engagement to Millicent is broken off, and Maggie and Joe end up together. *My Best Girl* was made for less than $500,000 but was an immediate hit with audiences, earning over $1 million on its first release. Such was not the case with the day's other notable opening. Henry Wadsworth Longfellow's narrative poem was the inspiration for the DeMille Pictures Corporation's sea adventure *The Wreck of the Hesperus*. Widower David Slocum, Captain of the *Hesperus*, returns from the sea to his New England village to learn that the woman he loves has been coerced into marrying John Hazzard. The bitter captain returns to sea with his daughter, Gale, and his second mate, Singapore Jack. Coming to the aid of a burning ship, the captain rescues John Hazzard Jr., the son of his rival, and is enraged when his daughter and the young Hazzard fall in love. He tries to separate them, going so far as putting her ashore at one port, but the two are reunited. During a furious storm, the captain ties Gale to the mast for safety, but the ship breaks apart and she is saved from drowning by John. Like producer Cecil B. DeMille's other epic movies, it was expensive to make and did not repay its high costs at the box office.

A true sea adventure with a tragic ending was in the news today. The Japanese fishing vessel *Ryo Yei Maru* was sighted drifting off the coast of Cape Flattery in the state of Washington. The American freighter *Margaret Dollar* went out to investigate and discovered the emaciated bodies of the twelve Japanese crewmen. According to the ship's log, the engine had failed during a gale on December 23, 1926. The log recorded the death of each man on board as he slowly starved to death. The charts on board indicated that the *Ryo Yei Maru* drifted five thousand miles. The next day the ship was towed into Seattle where a Buddhist funeral ceremony was held, the twelve bodies cremated, and the ship burnt.

NOVEMBER

TUESDAY, NOVEMBER 1

The Palestine pound was introduced today. It was the first currency for the British Mandate in Palestine. After the creation of Israel in 1948, the Palestine pound ceased to be legal tender.

Marion Davies was the beguiling leading lady in Cosmopolitan Pictures' *Quality Street*, a screen version of James M. Barrie's very popular play. The improbable, if not downright ridiculous, plot concerns the vivacious Phoebe Throssel (Davies), whose beloved, Dr. Valentine Brown (Conrad Nagel), goes off to fight in the Napoleonic Wars and is gone for ten years. Phoebe patiently waits for him, becoming an old maid in dress and demeanor. When Brown finally returns, he has no interest in the spinster Phoebe, so she changes her dress and attitude and passes herself off as her young niece Livvy. Of course, Brown falls for Livvy, and by the time the truth comes out, he realizes he loves Phoebe. *Quality Street* was remade by RKO in 1937 with Katharine Hepburn and Franchot Tone.

African American singer-dancer Florence Mills, who had recently returned to New York after a triumphal tour of Europe, died today in New York City at the age of thirty-two. The sparkling performer, billed as the "Queen of Happiness," sang and danced in vaudeville, on Broadway, in cabarets, and on tours. The cause of her death is not clear. Mills was suffering from tuberculosis, but it is also believed she died from a ruptured appendix. Her popularity was so great that over ten thousand people came to the funeral home to bid Mills goodbye and thousands attended her funeral. Also dying young today was the German flying ace Karl Plauth, who had shot down seventeen planes for Germany during the Great War. The thirty-one-year-old pilot crashed and was killed during a test flight of a plane he had designed.

WEDNESDAY, NOVEMBER 2

The celebrated American poet T. S. Eliot, born in St. Louis and raised in the Unitarian faith, had lived in England for much of his adult life. On June 29 he was baptized into the Church of England and today he became a naturalized British citizen.

MOST POPULOUS AMERICAN CITIES

The six largest cities in America by population in 1927:

New York City (6.7 million)
Chicago (3 million)
Philadelphia (1.7 million)

Detroit (1.4 million)
Los Angeles (1 million)
Cleveland (800,000)

THURSDAY, NOVEMBER 3

Still considered the worst natural disaster in the history of the state of Vermont, a two-day tropical-like storm began today and broke records for the number of inches of rain that fell. By the time the skies finally cleared, flooding had killed 114 people in Vermont and another 18 in adjoining states.

Thornton Wilder's second novel, *The Bridge of San Luis Rey*, was published today and its first run of four thousand five hundred copies priced at $2.50 sold out within a month. In 1714, the oldest and most famous rope bridge in Peru collapses and sends five people to their deaths. The Franciscan monk Brother Juniper sees the accident and wonders why God chose those five souls. He tries to find out all about each of the five and see if there is a divine intention at work. The novel then tells the story of the five characters and their lives up to the day the bridge collapsed. The wealthy, grasping Marquesa, the widow of a rich but horrid merchant, tries to find a reason for living through her smothering affections for her uncaring daughter Clara, then begins to turn her attentions on the pious servant girl Pepita. The orphaned twins Esteban and Manuel, raised by the holy Abbess of the convent of Santa Maria de la Rosas, have become silent, hardworking adults who live in a private world of two. When Manuel falls in love with the beautiful actress Camila Perichole, the twins' world is turned upside down. Manuel dies from an infected wound, Esteban assumes his brother's identity, and plans to go to sea. The colorful Uncle Pio is Camila's valet and they suffer from a tempestuous love-hate relationship over the years while he changes her from an ignorant peasant to a renowned actress. Pio takes Camila's son to educate him in Lima, but they never make it to the other side of the bridge at San Luis Rey. The novels ends with Brother Juniper completing his research and writing a massive volume about the five people and his conclusions about God's will. But the Church finds the book full of heresy and both Juniper and his life's work are burned in a square in Lima. *The Bridge of San Luis Rey* is at heart a philosophical work trying to determine a pattern in God's actions, yet the characters and the various stories made it an immediate bestseller, a Pulitzer Prize winner, and one of the most acclaimed books of the early twentieth century. There have been screen versions in 1929, 1944, and 2004.

The popular songwriting team of Rodgers and Hart had one of their biggest hits when the musical comedy *A Connecticut Yankee* opened on Broadway today. At a party on the eve of his wedding, Martin (William Gaxton) flirts with Alice Carter (Constance

The songwriting team of Richard Rodgers (music) and Lorenz Hart (lyrics) had musical hits on Broadway before, during, and after the Depression. *A Connecticut Yankee* managed to be a hit twice: in 1927, featuring William Gaxton and Constance Carpenter (pictured here) and again in 1943, starring Dick Foran and Vivienne Segal. *Photofest © Photofest*

Carpenter), which so infuriates his bride-to-be, Fay Morgan (Nana Bryant), that she knocks him unconscious with a blow from a champagne bottle. Martin dreams he is in King Arthur's court, where he falls in love with Alisande La Carteloise (Carpenter), who looks just like Alice. But Martin's attempts to modernize the medieval world are thwarted by Merlin (William Norris) and the sorceress Morgan Le Fay (Bryant), who happens to be the spitting image of Fay Morgan. When he awakes, he decides to marry Alice. Herbert Fields wrote the clever book, loosely based on Mark Twain's *A Connecticut Yankee in King Arthur's Court*, but it was the score by Richard Rodgers (music) and Lorenz Hart (lyrics) that made the musical so entertaining. The engaging "My Heart Stood Still" and the breezy "Thou Swell" were the runaway hits and helped *A Connecticut Yankee* to run fourteen months. The musical was successfully revived on Broadway in 1943, at which time Hart contributed his last Broadway lyric with the hilariously macabre song, "To Keep My Love Alive."

That same day in London, the West End production of the Broadway musical *Hit the Deck* opened, six months after it premiered in New York. There were some name changes, and the story was now set in Plymouth harbor. Ivy Tresmand played the dockside cafe worker Looloo and Stanley Holloway was her sailor sweetheart Bilge. *Hit the Deck* ran a profitable nine months in London then was popular on tour and in Australia.

FRIDAY, NOVEMBER 4

U.S. Army Air Corps officer Captain Hawthorne C. Gray had set new altitude records for balloon ascents earlier this year on March 9 and May 4. Today he broke those records when he reached the height of 42,470 feet in a balloon launch from Scott Field in Illinois. Because his timer failed during his descent, Gray ran out of bottled oxygen at forty thousand feet, lost consciousness, and died. His body and the balloon were found miles away in Tennessee the next day.

Nearly three hundred people died in the town of Nellore, on the Bay of Bengal in India, when a cyclone pounded that community today.

By 1927, there had been at least ten short or feature film versions of Harriet Beecher Stowe's history-making novel *Uncle Tom's Cabin*. Universal's adaptation, which premiered today in New York City, is considered by film historians to be the finest. While previous movies show only scenes or highlights from the book, this film runs 144 minutes, has a literate (though not always accurate) screenplay, and is well directed by Harry A. Pollard (who had played Uncle Tom in a 1913 version). The script combines characters and condenses events and the story is extended to include the Civil War and the Emancipation Proclamation. The movie ends with Simon Legree haunted by the ghost of Uncle Tom and falling to his death trying to battle the specter. One of the most expensive films of its day ($1.8 million), the epic production boasts plenty of spectacle (the chase on the Ohio River is very thrilling) and yet has many intimate character scenes. The production values throughout are superb, from the cinematography to the sets and costumes. Many of the slaves are played by white actors in blackface, a common practice on stage and screen at the time, but several of the performances are not so exaggerated and mannered that the serious scenes don't work. Uncle Tom is played by the African American James B. Lowe and he gives a poignant, sincere performance. Virginia Grey is also very touching as Eva. There are still some grotesque African American stereotypes, and a modern viewer has to keep a lot of things in context to appreciate this movie, but it is a major accomplishment all the same and very much in the spirit of the novel. Unfortunately, the film did only modest box office and lost a lot of money.

In 1925, fifty-seven-year-old Great War veteran Frank Heath and his horse Gypsy Queen set out from Washington, D.C., on a journey that would include all forty-eight states. Today Heath and Gypsy Queen arrived back in Washington, having covered 11,356 miles. When Gypsy Queen died in 1936, she was buried at the Rosa Bonheur Memorial Park in Elkridge, Maryland, and a bronze tablet was erected in her honor in 1938. Heath lived to be seventy-seven years old and was buried in Spokane, Washington.

SATURDAY, NOVEMBER 5

The tenth annual PGA (Professional Golf Association) Championship concluded today at the Cedar Crest Country Club in Dallas, Texas. The PGA was then a six-day match play championship. Walter Hagen defeated Joe Turnesa one up in the finals to win his fourth consecutive PGA title.

Both Notre Dame and Minnesota were undefeated so far during the 1927 college football season, so there was plenty of excitement when they faced each other today. At the end of the game, both teams were still undefeated as the score was a tie 7–7. In a conference game, Stanford bested Washington 13–7. Army shut out Franklin & Marshall, 45–0, as did Michigan to Chicago (14–0), Illinois to Iowa (14–0), and Georgia to Florida (28–0). Yale beat Maryland 30–6, Nebraska bested Kansas 47–13, Texas A&M defeated SMU 39–13, and Pittsburgh tied with Washington and Jefferson 0–0.

An article in today's issue of the *Saturday Evening Post* gave birth to The Seeing Eye in America. American dog breeder Dorothy Harrison Eustis, living in Switzerland, wrote the article about how Germany was using trained guide dogs to assist blind war veterans. Morris Frank, a twenty-year-old blind man living in Nashville, contacted Eustis and with her help established The Seeing Eye, the first school in the States to train canines to be guide dogs for the blind.

The Ikhwan Revolt, a three-year struggle between the Saudi Arabian tribesmen known as the Ikhwan and the established British and Saudi forces in present-day Iraq and Kuwait, began today when a party of Berber tribesmen attacked and killed foreign construction workers and policemen who had been working on a military post in Busaiya.

Warner Brothers' backstage melodrama *Good Time Charley* featured Warner Oland as the title character, a song-and-dance man on the vaudeville circuit at the turn of the century. His modest success is ruined when the corrupt producer John Hartwell sees talent in Charley's daughter Rosita and lures her to Broadway where she marries Hartwell's son John Jr. When Rosita and John upset Hartwell, he has them blacklisted from show business. Charley has been saving his money for an eye operation but instead gives it to the struggling couple, who go to England to start over. In the sentimental conclusion, Rosita finds out about her father's sacrifice and the two are reunited. Opening the same day was the Laurel and Hardy comedy short *Hats Off* presented by MGM. Stan Laurel and Oliver Hardy play salesmen who go door to door trying (not very successfully) to sell washing machines. They lug washing machines up and down flights of stairs without making a sale, continually losing their hats in the process. By the climax of the film, a strong wind blows the hats off several people on the street and a fight breaks out. The police van arrives and hauls everyone to the station except Laurel and Hardy, who are left searching for their hats among the many all over the street. *Hats Off* was a huge success and is thought to have been very influential in the rising popularity of the two comics. Sadly, all that remains of the movie are some photo stills originally used for publicity purposes. *Hats Off* is one of the most sought-after Laurel and Hardy movies by historians and fans.

Great Britain's first automatic traffic light was installed today at the junction of Lichfield Street and Princess Street in the city of Wolverhampton on an experimental basis and was a landmark moment in motor vehicle traffic control.

A scathing review of the Yale professor William Lyon Phelps's book *Happiness* appeared in today's issue of the *New Yorker* magazine, a book "presumably written for God, for Country, and for Yale." The review was signed "Constant Reader," which was Dorothy Parker's moniker for her book reviews.

Bolivian law decrees that only one person be executed for a murder even if it was committed by more than one person. Today the radical Alfredo Jauregui was selected by lottery from four suspected assassins of President José Manuel Pando in 1917 and was executed by firing squad in La Paz. He was twenty-eight years old. The details of the ten-year-old assassination of Pando were never satisfactorily uncovered, and it is likely that none of the four suspects was involved in the murder.

One of the most beloved and popular European stage clowns of the past, Marceline Orbes, committed suicide by gunshot today in a New York City hotel at the age of fifty-three. Internationally known simply as "Marceline the Clown," the Spanish-born physical comedian had filled theatres from the 1890s to the late 1910s with his farcical antics but then fell out of favor and went bankrupt from bad business decisions.

The pioneering neurologist Augusta Déjerine-Klumpke died today in Paris at the age of sixty-eight. Although she was born in San Francisco, Déjerine-Klumpke's parents recognized her medical knowledge at a young age and the family moved to Paris where she was among the first women to study and practice medicine. Most known for her pioneering work and books on the nervous system, Déjerine-Klumpke was the first woman to become a member of the Société de Neurologie de Paris. Today the condition of a nerve injury affecting the use of the arm is called Klumpke paralysis.

SUNDAY, NOVEMBER 6

Hal Roach's latest Our Gang comedy short *Chicken Feed* is one that has dated poorly because of its racial stereotypes. The teenage magician Presto Misterio performs his act in the neighborhood, seemingly turning Jean into a rabbit. The gang is so impressed that they steal some of the magic powder and use it to try and turn Mango, the little sister of Farina, into a rabbit as well. Instead out of the box comes a monkey escaped from a zoo, and Farina spends the rest of the short trying to turn Mango back into a human.

MONDAY, NOVEMBER 7

An antigovernment protest took place today in Moscow during the tenth anniversary of the Communist takeover in Russia. The annual parade was disrupted by a group of marchers demonstrating against First Secretary Joseph Stalin. The police attacked the protesters and the parade continued. The next day the Soviet government blamed Leon Trotsky, Grigory Zinoviev, and Lev Kamenev for organizing the protest. Not until 1991 would such a show of opposition to the Communist Party again be seen in Russia.

Few Broadway playhouses have such a diverse history as the theatre that opened today as the Gallo Opera House. Impresario Fortuna Gallo hoped to rival the Metropolitan Opera with his playhouse decorated with marble and mirrors. The premiere production was Puccini's *La Boheme* performed by the San Carlo Opera Company. Gallo struggled to find an audience and, when the opera folded inside of three weeks, he renamed it the Gallo Theatre and offered plays. But they all failed, and he sold the playhouse in 1930, when it was renamed the New Yorker Theatre. During its checkered history, the playhouse was turned into New York's first theatre restaurant (Billy Rose's Casino de Paree), was remodeled into a radio studio for CBS, then in 1977 it became the popular disco Studio 54, which was famous for the difficulty that anyone but stars had in getting in. When the two owners ended up in prison for suspicious accounting and selling of drugs, the venue closed and had other uses until 1998, when it was bought by the Roundabout Theatre and returned as a legitimate Broadway house called Studio 54 Theatre, the name it retains today.

In 1927 New York City surpassed London in population, making it the largest city in the world.

TUESDAY, NOVEMBER 8

Actress Helen Hayes scored a triumph on Broadway with *Coquette*, a play by George Abbott and Ann Preston Bridgers, which opened to rave notices. In the melodrama, Norma Besant (Hayes) is the quintessential flirtatious flapper who loves Michael Jeffrey, a handsome, insolent, and shiftless young man. Norma's father, Dr. Besant, refuses to consider Michael's request to marry Norma until Michael tells him that he and Norma have slept together. The doctor shoots Michael, and, rather than face the physical examination that would almost certainly be demanded at her father's trial, Norma commits suicide. The critics praised the play but their highest accolades were for Hayes's touching performance. *Coquette* ran ten months on Broadway and Hayes was contracted to then do a tour of the hit melodrama, but she got pregnant and would not do it. Producer Jed Harris took Hayes to court and sued her for breach of contract, but the court decided that having a baby was "an act of God" and sided with Hayes. The court decision was a landmark case, and Hayes's offspring was called the "Act of God Baby."

WEDNESDAY, NOVEMBER 9

The Norwegian composer Ole Olsen died today in Oslo at the age of seventy-seven. Olson wrote operas, choral works, cantatas, orchestral pieces, and other genres of music. He was also a highly-esteemed conductor and musician (pipe organ, piano, and violin).

THURSDAY, NOVEMBER 10

General Motors today proudly declared the largest dividend in history up to that time. GM investors received $3.75 per share, totaling $65,250,000 on their 17,400,000 shares of stock.

Two American warships were launched today; both would suffer the same fate because of Japanese aggression. The river gunboat USS *Panay* was built in Shanghai and spent its history in Chinese waters, usually patrolling the Yangtze River and protecting American property and personnel. The *Panay* was destroyed by Japanese naval aircraft in 1937, long before America was involved in World War II. The submarine USS *Argonaut* was also launched today, but in Portsmouth, Maine, where it was built. One of the many V-boats manufactured by the United States in the 1920s, it was the largest (381 feet long) submarine until the first nuclear sub in 1953. Luckily, the *Argonaut* left Pearl Harbor a few days before the Japanese attack in 1941 and saw action during World War II until it was sunk by a Japanese destroyer off the coast of New Guinea in 1943.

FRIDAY, NOVEMBER 11

Today Britain, France, the United States, and other allies of the Great War celebrated Armistice Day, the annual holiday commemorating the armistice signed in 1918 that ended the war. After World War II, the holiday was changed to Veterans Day.

One of Irving Berlin's most beguiling ballads, "The Song Is Ended (but the Melody Lingers On)," was published today by Berlin's music company. The quietly captivating piece about how a song (and romantic feelings) resound after the music (and lover) depart was recorded by Annette Hanshaw and Ruth Etting in 1927, followed by dozens of other discs over the decades.

In a special Armistice Day college football game, the Texas A&M Aggies shut out the Rice University Owls in Houston, 14–0.

The noted American historian and author Frances Gardiner Davenport died today at the age of fifty-seven. She was an expert on treaties, both American and European, and wrote about them in many books and pamphlets.

SATURDAY, NOVEMBER 12

Leon Trotsky and fellow politico Grigory Zinoviev were expelled today from the Soviet Communist Party. Eighty-one members who supported or sympathized with Trotsky were also expelled within the next month. Such a drastic move left the field open for Joseph Stalin to take total control of the party and, consequently, the Soviet Union.

The Holland Tunnel, the world's longest continuous underwater vehicular tunnel as well as the world's first tunnel designed specifically for automobile traffic, opened today in New York City. Although there were existing underwater tunnels for railroad traffic in New York, the Holland was the first constructed for cars, running underneath the Hudson River between Jersey City, New Jersey, and Canal Street in Manhattan. President Coolidge presided over the opening ceremony, then the tunnel was open to pedestrians only that first day. About twenty thousand people walked through it before the tunnel was opened to auto traffic at midnight. The Holland Tunnel, which took eight years to build and cost $48.4 million, is still in busy use today.

Notre Dame's Fighting Irish changed their blue jerseys for green ones beginning with today's college football game at Yankee Stadium against Army, but it brought them no luck; Notre Dame had its first loss of the season with Army's 18–0 victory. Georgia shut out Clemson (32–0) while Pittsburgh beat Nebraska (21–13); USC trounced Colorado 46–7; Yale beat Princeton 14–6; Minnesota defeated Drake 27–6; Michigan bested Navy 27–12; and Illinois won over Chicago 15–6.

Paramount's satiric *She's a Sheik* made fun of the desert sheik movies of the 1920s, in particular Rudolph Valentino and *Son of the Sheik* (1926). This time around, it is a woman who does the seducing. She is the half-Spanish and half-Arab Zaida, played with panache by comic actress Bebe Daniels. Zaida decides she wants a white man as her mate, so she kidnaps the French captain Colton (Richard Arlen) and brings him to her desert camp. It doesn't take long for the captive Colton to fall in love with Zaida, but the French troops come to rescue him and delay the happy ending for a while. Even the climactic battle between the French and the Arabs is satirical, with the French projecting a movie clip of an attacking army on a big screen and frightening away the Arabs. Daniels was praised by the critics for her comedics and her swashbuckling as well. It is unclear whether *She's a Sheik* is lost or not.

The Mexican priest Father Margarito Flores García was executed today in Tulimán at the age of only twenty-eight. His death was part of the anticlerical persecution throughout Mexico by secularist president Plutarco Calles. Flores García was canonized as a Roman Catholic saint in 2000.

SUNDAY, NOVEMBER 13

Warwick Deeping's 1925 British novel *Sorrell and Son* was as popular as it was controversial, so it has been adapted for the screen and television three times. The last reel of United Artists' 1927 version, which premiered in New York today, is believed missing, but what remains reveals an outstanding performance by H. B. Warner. He plays Stephen Sorrell, a hero of the Great War who returns home to find that his wife has abandoned him and their young son, Kit. Sorrell works as a porter in a hotel to make ends meet and raises his son, even finding the money for Kit to go to medical school. Mrs. Sorrell tries to come back into her son's life but the adult Kit will have nothing to do with her. Kit becomes a successful doctor and realizes that his terminally ill father has only months of suffering ahead of him, so he reluctantly euthanizes Sorrell. It was this mercy killing in the plot that made the book and film so controversial. Warner's performance as Sorrell in the silent version is superior and, because he reprised the role in the 1933 British remake of *Sorrell and Son*, it is somewhat documented. The novel was also turned into a British television miniseries in 1984.

MONDAY, NOVEMBER 14

The world's largest natural gas storage tank exploded today in Pittsburgh, killing twenty-eight people and injuring nearly five hundred others. The five-million-cubic-foot gasometer, operated by the Equitable Gas Company, erupted at 8:45 in the morning. The blast was so strong it destroyed the nearby Pittsburgh Clay Pot Company, which had 140 employees inside at the time. The cause of the explosion is not certain, though some witnesses reported seeing repairmen using blow torches to seal a leak in the tank the morning of the blast.

British playwright-actor Noel Coward, whose work was very popular on stages on both sides of the Atlantic in the 1920s, brought his newest play, *The Marquise*, to Broadway on this day. The French aristocrat, the Marquise Eloise de Kestournel (Billie Burke), in eighteenth-century Paris, learns that her daughter has fallen in love with the son from her former marriage to a Marquis. To keep the half-siblings from marrying, Eloise finds new mates for them as well as a new one for herself. The charming costume play was well received in London the previous February and ran 129 performances on the strength of the fine cast, particularly the star turn by Marie Tempest as Eloise. *The Marquise*, now with an American cast, did not repeat its earlier success in New York. The critics disapproved of the comedy, but there was high praise for Billie Burke's flighty, funny performance as the Marquise, so the play ran ten weeks.

In a study conducted for insurance companies, it was determined that only 64 percent of American children under eighteen were in school, 54 percent of those in elementary school.

TUESDAY, NOVEMBER 15

The comet 29P/Schwassmann-Wachmann was discovered today by astronomers Arno Wachmann and Arnold Schwassmann at the Hamburg Observatory in Bergedorf, Germany. It is an unusual comet in that about seven times each year it has an outburst that raises its magnitude ten-thousand times its usual brightness. Wachmann and Schwassmann were able to discover it photographically when the comet was in one of these outbursts.

Since 1923, the producing Shubert Brothers usually offered a musical revue titled *Artists and Models* that was better known for its practically-nude chorus girls in artistic poses than for its songs and comics. Today's edition was even leaner on music and comedics, but there were one hundred females on view as well as twenty-five chorus boys. The critics were not impressed, but audiences were satisfied enough to let *Artists and Models* run nineteen weeks in the large Winter Garden Theatre.

WEDNESDAY, NOVEMBER 16

The United States Navy's second aircraft carrier, the USS *Saratoga*, was commissioned today. Originally planned as a battleship in 1920, the *Saratoga* was redesigned as an aircraft carrier to comply with the Washington Naval Treaty of 1922. The carrier participated in several crucial battles in the Pacific during World War II. In 1946 the *Saratoga* was among the ships sunk in an atomic test.

The Communist politician Adolph Joffe committed suicide today in Moscow at the age of forty-four. A strong ally of Leon Trotsky, Joffe was ordered by the Soviets to leave the country when Trotsky was expelled from the Communist Party. Sickly and bed-ridden, he decided to take his own life instead.

Four days after he knocked out Leo Gates in four rounds in a bout in New York City, former middleweight boxing champion Theodore "Tiger" Flowers died today during a routine operation to remove some scar tissue from around his eyes. Flowers was the first African American to become a middleweight boxing champ. He won the title in 1926 when he defeated Harry Greb. Ironically, Greb had died later in 1926 while undergoing minor surgery to repair his nose and respiratory tract. Both Flowers and Greb were thirty-two years old when they died.

THURSDAY, NOVEMBER 17

The Washington, D.C., area was hit badly today when a tornado touched down near Alexandria, Virginia, and cut a fifteen-mile path through Anacostia, the District of Columbia, and Maryland. Winds measured at 125 mph demolished several homes and buildings, injured about fifty people, and killed one person who was struck by lightning during the storm.

Bus manufacturer Leyland Titan today introduced a new style of double-deck bus with a low chassis that made it easier for passengers to board and exit. Called the TD1, the new bus was also longer (twenty-five feet) and carried more people (forty-eight seated) than previous models. The Leyland Titan double bus was soon the most used bus, not only in Great Britain but also in Ireland, Australia, India, Spain, and South Africa for the next forty years.

Moulay Youssef, Sultan of Morocco, died today in Rabat of uremia at the age of forty-five. He had sat on the throne since 1912. There was much infighting within the royal family after Youssef's sudden death, but the youngest son, Sidi Mohammed, prevailed and was crowned Mohammed V.

> The average cost of a newly constructed home in the United States in 1927 was $5,000.

FRIDAY, NOVEMBER 18

After eighteen months of marriage, actress Helen Menken divorced future film star Humphrey Bogart today, charging cruelty and even battery. Ironically, the two actors remained friends for the rest of their lives.

The song standard "Washboard Blues" was given a significant recording today by Paul Whiteman's Orchestra on the Victor label. Hoagy Carmichael composed the piece as an instrumental in 1926, but it found more fame once Fred B. Callahan and Irving Mills added a lyric about a woman so weary of washing clothes that she just wants to throw herself into the river. For the Whiteman recording, Carmichael did the vocals.

The vaudeville and Broadway singer Emma Carus died today in Venice, California, at the age of forty-eight after a long illness. The German-born contralto had first found fame on the Broadway stage in 1897 and was the featured star in the first *Ziegfeld Follies* in 1907. Carus introduced or popularized many popular songs in the years surrounding the turn of the twentieth century, none more famous than Irving Berlin's "Alexander's Ragtime Band," which was first noticed when she sang it in Chicago in 1911.

SATURDAY, NOVEMBER 19

The Phillips Petroleum Company opened its first Phillips 66 service station today in Wichita, Kansas. When the company's gasoline was being tested on U.S. Highway 66 in Oklahoma, the test car reached the breathless speed of 66 mph, so the new fuel was named Phillips 66 and consequently so was the station. Today the original Phillips 66 station is maintained by the historical society of Wichita.

Myrna Loy had appeared in bit parts or supporting roles in thirty-two movies before Warner Brothers gave her the leading role in *The Girl from Chicago*, an early gangster film that opened today. The movie is considered lost, but we do know Loy played the southerner Mary Carlton, who goes to New York pretending to be a gangster's moll from Chicago in order to save her brother Bob from the electric chair. Mary knows Bob is innocent and so she befriends two big time hoods, Handsome Joe and Big Steve Drummond, to find out who framed her brother. It turns out Joe is an undercover detective, and he and Mary get to the truth and save her brother.

James Thurber was getting the attention of readers of the *New Yorker* magazine with today's issue in which he wrote a gentle and knowing article titled "The Old Lady" about the aged owner of the Murray Hill Hotel.

It was a very busy day for college football with Stanford beating California 13–6 to close their season at 8–2–1. Yale closed its season by shutting out Harvard (14–0). Other shutouts included USC v. Washington State (27–0); Illinois v. Ohio State

(13–0); Notre Dame v. Drake University (32–0); Army v. Ursinus College (13–0); and Nebraska v. Kansas State (33–0). Georgia bested Mercer 26–7 and Minnesota finished out its season by defeating Michigan 13–7.

SUNDAY, NOVEMBER 20

Prominent music publisher John Stillwell Stark died today in St. Louis at the age of eighty-six. Stark is most known for discovering Scott Joplin, publishing his rags, and making ragtime music so popular.

MONDAY, NOVEMBER 21

Thirty miles northwest of Denver, in Lafayette, Colorado, the coal mine operated by the Columbine Mine Rocky Mountain Fuel Company was the scene of one of the most infamous labor disputes of the decade. About five hundred striking miners were attacked by the Colorado State Police with a machine gun, killing five and wounding dozens of others, including two women. For years the incident was referred to as the Columbine Massacre. Ironically, a high school shooting in nearby Littleton in 1999 was also called the Columbine Massacre.

United Artists' adventure romance *The Gaucho* not only afforded Douglas Fairbanks one of his most dangerously sexy roles but it introduced the Mexican actress Lupe Velez, who had enough sex appeal of her own to be later labeled the Mexican Spitfire. High up in the Andes Mountains, a girl survives a great fall and is blessed with special powers from the Blessed Virgin. Soon pilgrims come from all over Argentina to Miracle City to be blessed and cured by her, many from leprosy. The corrupt General Ruiz steals the money the pilgrims leave behind, so the outlaw known as the Gaucho (Fairbanks) and his men overthrow Ruiz. The Gaucho plans to keep the money himself until he undergoes a conversion when the Blessed Virgin (Mary Pickford) appears to him. The romantic side of the tale is supplied by a fiery "mountain girl" (Velez) who is so feisty that she spends as much time fighting the Gaucho as she does making love to him. Fairbanks's performance is darker and less playful than in his usual adventure movies. He is still dashing and romantic but there is a sinister subtext to the character that he conveys with skill. *The Gaucho* was a giant hit for Fairbanks and for United Artists.

The Theatre Guild offered a sterling cast in today's revival of George Bernard Shaw's *The Doctor's Dilemma*, one of the playwright's most thought-provoking works. The 1906 drama was first seen on Broadway in 1915 for a short run so the play was new to most New York critics and playgoers. Baliol Holloway played the esteemed physician Sir Colenso Ridgeon who has developed a serum to cure tuberculosis but can test it only on a limited number of patients. Jennifer Dudebat (Lynn Fontanne) pleads with the doctor to select her husband Louis (Alfred Lunt), a very promising artist, to use the serum on. But Dudebat is an egotistical brute and Dr. Ridgeon despises Louis even as he is falling in love with the wife. When the physician chooses not to include Louis and he dies, Jennifer vents her contempt for Ridgeon, thereby ending any possible romance between them. The popular revival of *The Doctor's Dilemma* ran fourteen weeks and helped to keep the nonprofit Theatre Guild solvent. A film version was not made until 1958 with Dirk Bogarde as Louis, Leslie Caron as Mrs. Dudebat, and John Robinson as Ridgeon.

The Danish artist Laurits Tuxen died today in Copenhagen at the age of seventy-three. He was a painter and sculptor known for his portraits ranging from European royalty to Danish fishermen. Tuxen founded the art academy Kunstnernes Frie Studieskoler in Stockholm in 1882 as an alternative to the Royal Danish Academy of Fine Arts.

TUESDAY, NOVEMBER 22

The sentimental ballad "Among My Souvenirs" had been recorded earlier in 1927 but the song by Horatio Nicholls (music) and Edgar Leslie (lyric) did not become a hit until a version by Paul Whiteman's Orchestra, which was recorded today on the Victor label.

A new Broadway theatre offered a new Broadway hit musical today. The Alvin Theatre was named by its owners Alex A. Aarons and Vinton Freedley by combining parts of their first names. (Today the playhouse is known as the Neil Simon Theatre.) The musical was *Funny Face* with a score by the Gershwin brothers and starring the brother-sister team of Fred and Adele Astaire. The strict guardian Jimmie Reeves (Fred Astaire) refuses to allow young Frankie (Adele Astaire) to take possession of the jewels that she will eventually inherit. Frankie is furious and arranges for her friend Peter Thurston (Allen Kearns) to steal the jewels. Two comic burglars, Herbert (Victor Moore) and Dugsie (William Kent), are also after the jewels, but they get in an argument and Herbert is about to shoot Dugsie until he realizes he has forgotten to get a shooting license. Jimmie relents and Frankie gets her jewels and her sweetheart Peter. The book was funny if slight but the music by George Gershwin and lyrics by Ira Gershwin were top-drawer, most memorably the wry duet "The Babbitt and the Bromide," the flowing love song "He Loves and She Loves," the sprightly "'S Wonderful," and the adoring title song. The Astaires were in top form as was the entire Aarons and Freedley production, which ran over two years. *Funny Face* is also notable for Fred Astaire wearing top hat and tails for the first time, a classic look he would repeat in later shows and in the movies. In 1957, Fred Astaire starred in the movie *Funny Face*, which was not based on the stage musical but used some of the Gershwin tunes. Decades later, a very loose adaptation of the stage *Funny Face*, retitled *My One and Only* (1983), opened on Broadway with Tommy Tune and Twiggy in the leading roles. It also was a hit and it also ran two years.

For sixteen years before Fred Astaire made his first movie, he thrilled Broadway audiences with that distinctive Astaire singing and dancing charm. He was an original then, and he remained so throughout his extraordinary Hollywood career. Here he poses with some of the chorus girls in the hit Gershwin Broadway musical *Funny Face*. *Photofest © Photofest*

That same night an American play, the exciting melodrama *The Racket*, opened to appreciative reviews and ran fifteen weeks. Bartlett Cormack's play offered a colorful set of characters, including the racketeer Nick Scarsi (Edward G. Robinson), who is protected by some powerful politicians; the cop Captain McQuigg (John Cromwell), who is after Scarsi; and Scarsi's kid brother Joe (Edward Eliscu), who is used as a pawn between Nick Scarsi and McQuigg. There are some twists in the plot and a few bodies on the stage before McQuigg gets a confession out of Nick Scarsi and the political boss is named. The drama was realistic in dialogue and setting and the critics deemed *The Racket* to seem quite authentic. The melodrama was filmed in 1928 with Thomas Meighan as McQuigg and Louis Wolheim as Scarsi.

The Mexican priest Pedro Esqueda Ramirez was executed by firing squad today in Teocaltitán by the Mexican government secularists. He was forty years old. Ramirez was named a saint in 1992 by Pope John Paul II.

WEDNESDAY, NOVEMBER 23

U.S. Army pilot Rusty Rowell, on a reconnaissance aircraft mission in Nicaragua, today located the hidden mountain base El Chipote which was used by Sandinista rebels for raids against American troops occupying Nicaragua and for attacks on the Nicaraguan National Guard. Rowell reported his discovery to the military staff and plans to take El Chipote commenced.

The controversial Polish literary figure Stanisław Przybyszewski died today in Jaronty at the age of fifty-nine. Przybyszewski wrote poetry and novels in both German and Polish but was best known for his symbolist dramas.

The widely beloved Mexican Jesuit priest Miguel Agustín Pro was executed by firing squad today in Mexico City at the age of thirty-six. Pro was accused of participating in the bombing and assassination attempt on former Mexican president Álvaro Obregón. Pro was arrested and declared guilty without a trial. For his execution he was tied in a cross-like posture. Some four hundred thousand people lined the streets of Mexico City for Pro's funeral procession and another twenty thousand attended his burial. Pro remained a much-revered martyr for many years and he was beatified by Pope John Paul II in 1988.

THURSDAY, NOVEMBER 24

The annual Macy's Thanksgiving Day Parade, in its fourth year, usually included live animals from the Central Park Zoo. This year they were replaced by some giant balloon animals designed by Tony Sarg and built by the Goodyear Tire and Rubber Company in Akron, Ohio.

A Thanksgiving Day celebration at California's maximum-security Folsom Prison turned into a riot and a hostage situation that left two guards and seven prisoners dead. While most of the prison's twelve hundred inmates were watching a movie, a group of prisoners overwhelmed the eight guards and attempted an escape. None of the guards had keys, so the escapees were still locked inside the prison. About four hundred inmates took control of the interior of the prison and held five guards as hostages. Some three hundred members of the California National Guard arrived to assist two hundred civil officers, bringing with them tanks and machine guns. The standoff lasted all night, but by daybreak the inmates released their hostages unharmed then returned to their cells.

The Thanksgiving Day college football game that garnered the most interest was that between Pittsburgh and Penn State. With a record of 8–0–1, Pitt had outscored its opponents 283 to 20 this season with seven shutouts. They shut out Penn State today, 30–0, which meant Pitt would meet Stanford in the Rose Bowl game on January 1, 1928. Other holiday games included Nebraska over New York University 27–18 and Texas A&M closing its season with a 28–7 win over Texas.

Thanksgiving Day also marked another episode in the bizarre history of J. Frank Davis's reincarnation drama *The Ladder* on Broadway. Free performances of the play began today and curious patrons took advantage of the odd opportunity and filled the house. *The Ladder* was a clumsy melodrama about a woman who dreams about her previous lives. The oil mogul Edgar B. Davis, an avid believer in reincarnation, funded the production, which opened on October 22, 1926, to scathing reviews. Davis felt so strongly about spreading the word about reincarnation that he continued to pour money into the production even as attendance dwindled. Legend has it that some evenings the cast played to an audience of two or three people. Davis cut ticket prices until the show was as cheap as a movie, which boosted attendance for a while, but word of mouth repeated the critics' opinions. Refusing to close *The Ladder*, Davis announced that as of Thanksgiving Day, the play would be free and open to all. For a time, people came, but after the holidays the cast was again playing to practically empty houses. Davis finally gave up in May of 1928 and closed *The Ladder* after 640 performances. It is estimated he spent close to a $1 million on his pet project.

Indiana had more paved or "surfaced" roads in 1927 than any of the other forty-eight states. Ohio had the second most paved roads.

FRIDAY, NOVEMBER 25

Eleven-year-old violinist Yehudi Menuhin made his New York concert debut today at Carnegie Hall performing the Beethoven concerto with the New York Symphony Orchestra under the conductor Fritz Busch. The American-born Menuhin, who died in 1999, is considered one of the finest concert violinists of the twentieth century.

The influential Hungarian artist József Rippl-Rónai died today in Kaposvár at the age of sixty-six. He is credited with introducing modernist art to Hungary and is known for his paintings as well as for his stained-glass windows and interior designs.

SATURDAY, NOVEMBER 26

The fifteenth annual Grey Cup, the championship prize of the Canadian Football League (CFL), was won today by the Toronto Balmy Beach Beachers who defeated the Hamilton Tigers 9–6. The championship game was played at Varsity Stadium in Toronto.

A crowd of one hundred twenty-three thousand turned out at Soldier Field in Chicago to watch Notre Dame's Fighting Irish (6–1–1) play USC's Trojans (7–0–1) in what was arguably the biggest game of the college football season. On the strength of a blocked extra point attempt, Notre Dame triumphed 7–6, giving USC its first loss of the season. Almost as highly anticipated was the Army-Navy game which was played at the Polo Grounds in New York with some seventy thousand spectators on hand. They saw Army come back from 9–0 down at halftime to win 14–9. Also played today was Georgia beating Alabama 20–6 in Birmingham.

The twenty-two-year-old Austrian religious novice Maria Kutschera, the tutor to the seven children of widower Captain Georg Von Trapp of the Austrian navy, today married her employer, who was twenty-five years her senior. Facing financial difficulties after the Crash of 1929, they formed the Trapp Family Singers, and their story became the inspiration for the 1959 Broadway musical and the 1965 film *The Sound of Music*.

SUNDAY, NOVEMBER 27

Danish composer Carl Nielsen's orchestral rhapsody *An Imaginary Trip to the Faroe Islands* premiered today at the Royal Danish Theatre in Copenhagen with Nielsen conducting. The piece is divided into five sections celebrating the different musical moods suggested by a recent visit to the Faroe Islands off the coast of Norway in the North Atlantic.

Columbia's by-the-numbers campus comedy *The College Hero* had a plot that was already old hat in 1927, but moviegoers loved movies about college sports and romance. The expected triangle in this film involves friends and football teammates Jim Halloran and Bob Canfield who both pine for Vivian Saunders. Jim goes so far as to physically injure Bob on the field, but the old school spirit kicks in and Bob still manages to win the crucial game. For comic interest, cross-eyed comedian Ben Turpin plays the dorm valet. *The College Hero* was an early effort by distinguished Hollywood director Walter Lang. Opening in London on that same day was Gaumont's *The Arcadians,* a loose adaptation of the very popular 1909 British musical fantasy. London nightclub owner Smith (Ben Blue) escapes from his creditors and parachutes down into the Land of Arcady where truth and beauty rule. Smith is cured of his crooked ways by the Pool of Truth then returns to London as the shepherd Simplicitas. There he leads a crusade to convert everyone to the simple life of the Arcadians and, after several curious exploits, he does. This cockeyed tale was more plausible on the stage with one of the greatest musical scores of the Edwardian era. Yet even without the songs the screen version was very popular in Great Britain. *The Arcadians* also marked the directorial debut of prolific director-producer Victor Saville. The movie is believed lost and is much sought after by British film historians and silent movie enthusiasts.

MONDAY, NOVEMBER 28

The Pittsburgh Pirates today traded right fielder Hazen "Kiki" Cuyler to the Chicago Cubs for infielder Sparky Adams and outfielder Pete Scott. The reason behind the trade was not because of Cuyler's performance on the ballfield but his many disagreements with management. Looking back, baseball historians view the trade as one of the worst ones in the Pirates' history. Adams and Scott were gone from the team within two years while Cuyler had six more seasons in which he hit over .300 on his way to induction into the Baseball Hall of Fame.

Forty-three-year-old Billy Evans quit as an American League umpire today to become business manager of the Cleveland Indians. Known as the "Boy Umpire," Evans began umpiring in Major League Baseball in 1906 when he was only twenty-two years old. He was later inducted into the Baseball Hall of Fame.

One of the classics of Irish drama, Sean O'Casey's *The Plough and the Stars*, had its Broadway premiere today to complimentary notices, but the grim play had little audience appeal and closed after four weeks. Set in Dublin during the Irish Rebellion of 1915–1916, the residents of a tenement house have different opinions about the cause of Irish Independence as fighting, looting, and dying surrounds them. The pregnant Nora pleads with her husband Jack not to continue in the Irish Citizen Army but he is faithful to the cause and is killed in one of the encounters. Nora loses her baby and nearly her life when her neighbor Bessie Burgess dies shielding Nora from a stray bullet. The drama is filled with rich and lively characters and stinging dialogue and would eventually be recognized as a masterwork. But in 1927 many playgoers were more interested in lighter entertainment, such as the musical revue *Delmar's Revels*, which opened that same night. Producer-director Harry Delmar assembled a top-notch cast for this satirical look at New York life, in particular the contemporary theatre. The musical numbers, written by various songwriters, were also sarcastic, such as an undersea ballet with dancing jellyfish and octopuses. Comic Frank Fay, singer Winnie Lightner, and comedienne Patsy Kelly were featured but it was newcomer Bert Lahr who stole every sketch and song he was in. *Delmar's Revels* played a profitable fourteen weeks.

TUESDAY, NOVEMBER 29

Legend has it that MGM's screen version of Leo Tolstoy's novel *Anna Karenina* was retitled *Love* because the studio could not resist advertising the movie as "Greta Garbo and John Gilbert in *Love*." The title was not the only change made in Tolstoy's classic tale, but the spirit of the Russian masterpiece was there and it remains a very powerful film. Garbo is a low-key but luminous Anna, Gilbert is a magnetic if sometimes cruel Count Vronsky, and the supporting cast is first rate. The studio shot two endings to the film: a tragic one that adhered to the novel, and a contrived happy one in which Anna's husband dies and she and Vronsky are reunited. Theatre owners in the United States had their choice of which to show, but only the Tolstoy ending was seen internationally. Regardless of the ending, *Love* was a tremendous hit and both Garbo and Gilbert enjoyed their last hit together before sound came in.

WEDNESDAY, NOVEMBER 30

Jimmie Rodgers, who would become the first country-western singing star, went into a major recording studio today in Camden, New Jersey, and recorded on the Victor label four of his earliest discs: "Ben Dewberry's Final Run," "Mother Was a Lady," "Blue Yodel No. 1 (T for Texas)," and "Away Out on the Mountain."

Amy Lowell's anthology *Selected Poems* (edited by Melissa Bradshaw and Adrienne Munich) was published and released today, bringing renewed attention to the modernist writer who had died in 1925 and won the Pulitzer Prize in 1926. Although Lowell was much read and discussed before World War I for her modernist and even feminist ideas, she fell out of favor in the 1920s. She was rediscovered by a new generation in the 1960s and 1970s.

One of the most famous of all novelty songs, "Ice Cream" by Howard Johnson, Billy Moll, and Robert King, was first recorded today by Fred Waring's Pennsylvanians (vocal by Waring and Poley McClintock) for the Victor label. The silly ditty is better known by its shouting subtitle "I Scream, You Scream, We All Scream for Ice Cream!"

Perhaps no other Broadway playhouse was known across the nation as well as the one that opened today as Hammerstein's Theatre. Most Americans knew it decades later as the Ed Sullivan Theater, home of the popular television show from 1948 to 1971, then even later as the studio theatre for *Late Night with David Letterman*. The premiere production at Hammerstein's Theatre was the operetta *Golden Dawn*, a ridiculous tale about the white beauty Dawn (Louise Hunter) who is raised in Africa as a tribal princess. She falls in love with Steve Allen (Paul Gregory), an American prisoner of war held by the Germans, but their romance is thwarted by the cruel overseer Shep Keyes (Robert Chisholm). The happy ending came about when the tribal chief announced that Dawn is white. Such nonsense was made bearable by the romantic music by Emmerich Kalman and a thrilling number called "The Whip." The theatre was well named. It was built by producer Arthur Hammerstein in honor of his late father, impresario Oscar Hammerstein I; the musical was codirected by Reginald Hammerstein; and the book and lyrics were by Oscar Hammerstein II with Otto Harbach. *Golden Dawn* managed to run twenty-three weeks and turn a profit.

Retired baseball second baseman and manager Jimmy Wood died today in San Francisco at the age of eighty-four. He spent his fifteen-year Major League career in the National Association as either a player or a manager for the Chicago White Stockings, the Troy Haymakers, the Brooklyn Eckfords, and Philadelphia White Stockings. Wood moved from second baseman to manager in 1874 when an infection necessitated the amputation of one of his legs.

DECEMBER

THURSDAY, DECEMBER 1

The world was introduced to one of the most famous and beloved fictional characters, Miss Jane Marple, when she appeared in the Agatha Christie short story "The Tuesday Night Club" today in *Royal Magazine*. In the village of St. Mary Mead, spinster Miss Marple has a gathering at her house where the talk turns to solving mysteries. The former Scotland Yard officer Sir Henry Clithering tells the group about a case in which three people fell ill after a dinner party and then one of them died. Clithering gives the others all the facts available, including the coroner's report that the victim died of arsenic poisoning. The members of the group argue and offer different theories, but it is the quiet, reclusive Miss Marple who figures out who the murderer was and how he did it. "The Tuesday Night Club" was reprinted in the Christie short story collection *The Thirteen Problems* in 1932. Miss Marple appeared in twelve Christie novels and twenty short stories before making her farewell in *Sleeping Murder* in 2001.

The American-educated Chinese activist Soong Mei-ling today married General Chiang Kai-shek, and became known as Madame Chiang Kai-shek. She was a Christian, so an Episcopal marriage ceremony took place in English at Miss Soong's home, then a traditional Chinese civil ceremony was held at the Majestic Hotel in Shanghai. When General Chiang was made China's leader the following year, she became the first lady and remained so for forty-eight years.

Today Annette Hanshaw was the first artist to record a vocal version of the peppy song "Plenty of Sunshine" by Ray Henderson (music), B. G. De Sylva, and Lew Brown (lyric). Her recording with Lou Gold's Orchestra was the first of many versions of the song about being happy because the sun is shining.

Fallen Angels, Noel Coward's second play on Broadway in 1927, fared no better than *The Marquise*. If fact, it folded inside of five weeks. Two married women, Julia Sterroll (Fay Bainter) and Jane Banbury (Estelle Winwood), both loved the Frenchman Maurice Duclos years ago and now arrange to meet with him while he is visiting London. While the two women wait, they reminisce, argue, and drink too much and are at each other's throats by the time the no-longer-young Maurice arrives. The nearly plotless comedy was dismissed by the critics and then little heard of until a revival thirty years later that was a hit.

Retired baseball shortstop Germany Smith died today after being hit by an automobile in Altoona, Pennsylvania, at the age of sixty-four. Between 1884 and 1898 he played for seven different teams, most notably for the Brooklyn Grays/Bridegrooms during seven seasons.

FRIDAY, DECEMBER 2

The Model A Ford automobile went on sale today for the first time. One million would be sold in the first two months. By the time production stopped in 1931 to make way for the Model B, nearly five million Model A's had been sold.

The fifteenth Congress of the All-Union Communist Party began its seventeen-day conference today. The Congress was attended by 898 delegates who had voting rights and 771 members of the Party with a consultative vote. Many subjects were debated during the conference and several issues were voted upon, but it was clear that there was plenty of disharmony and rival factions among the Bolsheviks.

Debate over abolishing the death penalty in France went back to 1791 and continued today when the Chamber of Deputies rejected a proposal to end the death penalty by a vote of 376 to 145. Not until 1981 would France finally abolish the death penalty.

NEW CARS

These automobiles were among those introduced in 1927 and were made until the designated year:

Adler Standard 6 (1934)	Opel 7/34 PS (1930)
Austin 16 (1937)	Peugeot Type 183 (1931)
Bugatti Royale Type 41 (1933)	Renault Monasix (1932)
Chevrolet Series AA Capitol (1927)	Rover 10 (1947)
Dodge Fast Four (1928)	Rover 10/25 (1933)
Fiat 520 (1930)	Rover Two-Litre (1932)
Ford Model A (1931)	Studebaker Commander (1964)
MG 14/40 Mark IV (1929)	Studebaker Dictator (1937)
Mercedes-Benz S-Series (1933)	Triumph Super 7 (1934)
Nash Ambassador (1974)	Vauxhall 20-60 (1930)

The African American activist Marcus Garvey, the leader of a mass movement called Pan-Africanism and the founder the Universal Negro Improvement Association and African Communities League (UNIA-ACL), had been charged with mail fraud and was sentenced to prison but the sentence was commuted by President Coolidge. Garvey was released but deported today from the United States on the SS *Saramacca* from New Orleans and returned to his native Jamaica where he was greeted by a crowd of followers in Kingston.

SATURDAY, DECEMBER 3

Crooner Gene Austin's recording of the ballad "My Blue Heaven" by Walter Donaldson and George Whiting today hit the best-seller charts. The record would go on to sell over twelve million copies, the biggest seller until Bing Crosby's "White Christmas" came along two decades later.

MGM's horror film *London after Midnight* starring Lon Chaney was released today and both critics and audiences at the time declared it a classic in the genre. Since the film is lost today, we only have movie stills to suggest how effective this thriller was. When Sir Roger Balfour is found shot dead in his London home, it is ruled to be suicide but Roger's friend, Inspector Edward Burke (Chaney), is not satisfied. Five years later, living next door to the abandoned Balfour house, Burke starts to notice figures coming and going into the house. Neighbors notice a man in a beaver-skin hat with dark sunken eyes and fangs and rumors circulate that it is Balfour come back from the dead. It turns out the creature is Burke in disguise, using the ploy to discover who murdered Balfour. Tod Browning coproduced, cowrote, and directed *London after Midnight*, which was released in Great Britain as *The Hypnotist*. Under either title, the movie is one of the most sought after of all lost silent films.

Hal Roach's early Stan Laurel–Oliver Hardy comedy short *Putting Pants on Philip* gets a lot of mileage out of its thin premise. Young Scotsman Philip (Laurel) arrives in America wearing full Scottish regalia, including a kilt, which greatly annoys his uncle, J. Piedmont Mumblethunder (Hardy). The gags as the uncle tries to get trousers on his nephew are clever and keep coming right up to the hilarious climax.

The college football season officially concluded today as USC defeated Washington State 33–13. More notable was the contest between the Georgia Bulldogs (9–0–0) and the Georgia Yellow Jackets (7–1–1) in Atlanta. Georgia Tech won 12–0, spoiling the Bulldogs' chance for an undefeated season.

E. B. White, writing in today's edition of the *New Yorker* magazine, reported on his attendance at the first free showing of the Broadway melodrama *The Ladder* on Thanksgiving, wryly commenting on the dazed reaction of the audience to the dreadful play. He also noted that the cast, used to playing to a handful of people each night, seemed to be just as dazed by the packed house. In the same issue, Robert Benchley, another constant contributor to the *New Yorker*, offered a comic piece in "The Press in Review" section titled "Football Lingo," having fun with gridiron phrases and acronyms.

SUNDAY, DECEMBER 4

Pittsburgh Pirates right fielder Paul Waner was today named the Most Valuable Player (MVP) in the National League for the 1927 Major League Baseball season.

Duke Ellington and his orchestra became the house band at Harlem's famed Cotton Club starting tonight. Ellington and his eleven-piece ensemble were so popular that their gig at the club lasted five years. In 1929, the CBS Radio Network began broadcasting the live show from the Club, bringing national fame to the twenty-eight-year-old jazz musician.

MONDAY, DECEMBER 5

Dmitri Shostakovich's Symphony no. 2 in B Major, op. 14 premiered today in Leningrad to honor the tenth anniversary of the Russian Revolution. It was performed by the Leningrad Philharmonic Orchestra and the Academy Capella Choir under the direction of Nikolai Malko. The short symphony, written in one movement with four sections, is sometimes abstract, other times neoclassical. The political statement about the revolution was made in the verses sung by the mixed chorus. An extended version of the symphony premiered in Moscow a few months later. On the same night as Shostakovich's premiere, the Czech composer Leoš Janáček's *Glagolitic Mass* was performed for the first time in Brno, Czechoslovakia, by the Brno Arts Society conducted by the composer. The piece calls for orchestra, organ, a double chorus, and soloists and is sung using the Glagolitic alphabet which was an early Slavic alphabet, the predecessor of the modern Cyrillic alphabet. The *Mass* is pro-Slavic in its music and its content.

The University of Illinois football team, the Illini, was awarded the Rissler Cup today after finishing first in the Dickinson System ratings for college football teams. The award was determined under a formula devised by University of Illinois economics professor Frank G. Dickinson. The Illini had a 7–0–1 record; second place was held by the University of Pittsburgh Panthers (8–0–1).

A raccoon fur coat, an iconic garment of the Roaring Twenties, cost about $40 in 1927. A man's suit, consisting of a coat, vest, and two pairs of trousers, cost approximately $16.

TUESDAY, DECEMBER 6

The fictional, unflappable butler Jeeves, first introduced to readers by author P. G. Wodehouse in 1915, was featured in the short story "Jeeves and the Yule-tide Spirit," which appeared in the December issue of the *Strand* in London and later in the month in *Liberty* magazine in the States. Jeeves is disappointed when his employer, the frivolous Bertie Wooster, tells him that instead of going to Monte Carlo for the holidays they are going to Skeldings Hall because Bertie is smitten with the hostess Lady Wickham's daughter Bobbie. Jeeves does not approve of the destination nor of Bobbie and manages to thwart Bertie's revenge plan on Tuppy Glossop and show Bobbie in her true colors. Jeeves and Bertie end up abandoning Skeldings Hall and head to Monte Carlo.

WEDNESDAY, DECEMBER 7

The Canadian freighter S.S. *Kamloops*, making its last run through the Great Lakes before the winter season halted all nautical travel, encountered an ice storm in Lake Superior and sank today along with all twenty-two crew members. Some of the bodies were recovered in the spring on the shores near Isle Royale, Michigan, but the 250-foot-long *Kamloops* was not found until August of 1977, when it was discovered by two scuba divers.

THURSDAY, DECEMBER 8

One of America's earliest "think tanks" was created today. Robert S. Brookings had founded the Institute for Government Research in 1916 with the mission of becoming "the first private organization devoted to analyzing public policy issues at the national level." Today that organization merged with the Institute of Economics and the Robert Brookings Graduate School of Washington University in St. Louis to become the renowned Brookings Institution, which is still in operation in Washington, D.C.

Although the last reel of MGM's pacifist drama *The Enemy* is lost, the movie is still a powerful indictment of war and boasts a superb performance by Lillian Gish. She plays Pauli Arndt, the daughter of a professor who is dismissed for teaching that war is evil while America is engaged in the Great War. Pauli's husband, Carl, is drafted and serves overseas while his wife and child are destitute. Pauli turns to prostitution, Carl is reported missing in action, but the movie ends happily without weakening its antiwar message. Loosely based on a successful 1925 play, *The Enemy* raised some controversy but most agreed that Gish's performance was what mattered.

FRIDAY, DECEMBER 9

The hot jazz favorite "Struttin' with Some Barbecue" was recorded today by trumpeter Louis Armstrong and His Hot Five. Most assume Armstrong also composed the swinging instrumental piece, but in fact it was written by his then wife Lillian Hardin Armstrong. The lyric by Don Raye was not added until 1941.

Mythology was given a comic treatment in First National's *The Private Life of Helen of Troy*. Only sections of the beginning and the end of the movie survive, but there is enough footage to see that this merry telling of the unfaithful Helen (Maria Corda); her Trojan lover, Paris (Ricardo Cortez); and her frustrated husband, Menelaus (Lewis Stone) was not to be taken seriously. After the Trojan War and when Helen is returned to Menelaus, he has a customary right to kill her, but she is still too enticing, so there is a happy ending. The comedy is very anachronistic, Helen coming across more like a flirtatious 1920s flapper than a Grecian queen, and some of the title cards are very slangy and modern. Alexander Korda was the sly director.

SATURDAY, DECEMBER 10

WSM-Radio in Nashville had been broadcasting a show called *Barn Dance* since 1925 with WSM director George D. Day presenting country music acts. Today's broadcast followed the NBC Radio Network show *Music Appreciation Hour*, and when *Barn Dance* came on the air, the host, George Hay, remarked, "For the past hour, we have been listening to music taken largely from Grand Opera. From now on, we will present the 'Grand Ole Opry.'" From that night on, the program was called *Grand Ole Opry*, and it went on to become the longest continuous show in the history of radio.

MGM's western *Spoilers of the West* was better than many movies of that genre thanks to a solid story, a fine cast, and tight direction by W. S. Van Dyke. When white trappers and squatters trespass on Native American territory, the tribesmen go on the warpath. It is the job of Army lieutenant Lang to clear out the intruders before violence erupts. Lang manages to drive off all the trespassers except for the Benton gang. It turns out that young Miss Benton runs a trading post on the land and refuses to budge; that is, until she meets and falls in love with the handsome lieutenant.

SUNDAY, DECEMBER 11

The Chinese civil war reached new levels of carnage this week. Today the city of Guangzhou (then known as Canton) was attacked in the middle of the night by twenty thousand Communists, who took the city by surprise. Gaining control of police stations and the prison, they murdered police and guards, seized the arsenal, and released political prisoners from jail. The Communists then announced the formation of a new government called the Canton Soviet. Their victory and control of Guangzhou lasted only two days.

MONDAY, DECEMBER 12

Tommy Loughran defended his title as the world light heavyweight boxing champion today at New York's Madison Garden when he defeated Jimmy Slattery in a fifteen-round decision.

An ice storm in London paralyzed motor and foot traffic today, sending over fifteen hundred Londoners to the hospital for injuries incurred on the icy streets.

The Disney cartoon short *Empty Socks* featuring Oswald the Lucky Rabbit was released today in time for the holiday season. The socks of the title referred to Christmas stockings belonging to a group of orphans that are indeed empty until Oswald plays Santa and brings treats to the orphans. It was Walt Disney's first cartoon with a Christmas theme. He retold the same story in the 1931 sound short *Mickey's Orphans*. *Empty Socks* was considered a lost film for many years until a copy showed up in a library in Norway in 2014.

REDISCOVERED SILENT FILMS

Some films from 1927 that were believed to have been lost but were later rediscovered:

The Beloved Rogue (USA) John Barrymore adventure. Rediscovered by Mary Pickford in the late 1960s.
The Cave of the Silken Web (China) Directed by Dan Duyu. Found in a library in Norway in 2013.
A Diary of Chuji's Travels (Japan) Directed by Daisuke Ito. A trilogy, portions of which were found in Japan in 1991.
Duck Soup (USA) A short featuring Laurel and Hardy. A copy found in 1974.
Empty Socks (USA) A Disney Oswald the Lucky Rabbit cartoon. A copy found in Norway in 2014.
Eyes of the Totem (USA) Melodrama directed by W. S. Van Dyke. Found in a New York City vault in 2014.
Garras de oro [*Claws of Gold*] (Colombia) Anti-American political drama. Portions found and screened in 2008.
Her Wild Oat (USA) Comedy starring Colleen Moore. Copy found in Prague in 2001.
It (USA) Comedy-drama starring Clara Bow. Copy found in Prague in the 1960s.
Metropolis (Germany) Severely edited in 1927, the lost portions were found in Argentina and in New Zealand in 2008.
Mickey's Circus (USA) Comedy short with Mickey Rooney featured for the first time. Found in Amsterdam in 2014.
Mockery (USA) Drama about the Russian Revolution starring Lon Chaney. Rediscovered in the mid-1970s.
Sorrell and Son (USA) Drama featuring H. B. Warner. Found and a partially restored version shown in 2005.

Stark Love (USA) Smokey Mountain melodrama. Found in Prague in 1967.

Tarzan and the Golden Lion (USA) Adventure film featuring James Pierce. Copy found in a French asylum in the 1990s.

Upstream (USA) Backstage comedy-drama directed by John Ford. Rediscovered in New Zealand in 2010.

Why Girls Love Sailors (USA) Comedy short starring Laurel and Hardy. Copy found in 1985.

See February 19 for lost 1927 silent films.

TUESDAY, DECEMBER 13

Charles Lindbergh set off today on a "Good Will Tour" of sixteen Latin American countries that would last until February 8, 1928. While making the nonstop flight from Washington, D.C., to Mexico City, Lindbergh got caught in bad weather and lost his bearings somewhere in Mexico. When the weather cleared today, he flew low enough to try and find some landmarks that he could locate on his map. Legend has it that Lindbergh spotted the word "Caballeros" at a railroad depot but could not find it on his map. He eventually landed in Mexico City and only later learned that "Caballeros" was the Spanish word for "Gentlemen" and that the sign indicated the men's toilet.

Today the Chinese Nationalist Army retook the city of Guangzhou from the Communist rebels and their retaliation was fierce. Over two thousand Communists were arrested and executed, and another four thousand civilians were killed during the five-day-long massacre, which was called the "White Terror."

WEDNESDAY, DECEMBER 14

The Book of Common Prayer, in use in Great Britain since the Reformation when it was first published in 1549, was the subject of debate in Parliament. The Archbishop of Canterbury's request for approval of a revision to the book of prayer today passed in the House of Lords with a vote of 241 to 88. The next day the revision was voted down by the House of Commons by a vote of 247 to 205, the members arguing that the new version was too "papist." Subsequent attempts to revise the book also failed but much later versions that departed from the original became widely used, such as the *Alternative Service Book* (1980) and *Common Worship* (2000).

The House of Representatives in Washington today voted unanimously to confer the Medal of Honor on Charles Lindbergh, who now held the rank of colonel. Sometimes called the Congressional Medal of Honor, it had been established in 1861 and only rarely has been given for valor that was not part of military activity. The medal was presented personally to Lindbergh by President Coolidge on March 21, 1928.

THURSDAY, DECEMBER 15

Twelve-year-old Marion Parker, the daughter of an important Los Angeles banker, was kidnapped as she left Mount Vernon Junior High School today. A ransom note from "The Fox" demanded $1,500, which was paid by her father, but the girl was not returned alive. After the ransom money was picked up on December 17, Marion's body was thrown out of the kidnapper's car. Her arms and legs had been cut off and her throat had been slit. A manhunt involving over twenty thousand police officers and American Legion volunteers began and a reward of $50,000 (soon doubled to $100,000) was offered for the identification and capture of the kidnapper, dead or alive.

FRIDAY, DECEMBER 16

Ten years after Russia had turned to godless Communism, the Vatican finally cut off relations with the Soviet Union. Today Cardinal secretary of state, Pietro Gasparri, was instructed by Pope Pius XI to stop discussions and other communications with the Soviet Union. This directive would not change until 1961 when Premiere Nikita Khrushchev reopened relations with the Vatican.

The Stamps All-Star Quartet (Otis Echols, Roy Wheeler, Palmer Wheeler, and Dwight Brock) recording of "Give the World a Smile" was distributed to music stores today for the first time. The disc not only became the first recorded gospel music bestseller but the optimistic song of joy is said to have created the genre of gospel music in the music business.

The nineteen-year-old Australian batsman Don Bradman made his first-class cricket debut today playing for New South Wales against South Australia. Over the next twenty years, Bradman would be recognized as one of the greatest cricket players in the history of the game with nicknames such as the Don, the Boy from Bowral, Braddles, and the White Headley.

SATURDAY, DECEMBER 17

A peacetime naval tragedy that occurred today brought heavy criticism on the U.S. Navy. The submarine *S-4* was surfacing off the coast of Provincetown, Massachusetts, when it accidentally hit the Coast Guard destroyer USS *Paulding*. The sub and its crew of forty-six men sank immediately. Six men trapped in the torpedo room survived the collision and sent word that they were alive by tapping in Morse code on the sub's hull. Some rescue divers heard them and efforts were made to get to the trapped men over the next three days but torrential weather foiled all rescue attempts and the six sailors died.

The African American activist Hubert Harrison, considered the Father of Harlem Radicalism, died today in New York City from complications from an appendectomy at the age of forty-four. Harrison was an outspoken author, orator, poet, and critic who founded the International Colored Unity League (ICUL) in 1924. Although he was largely forgotten by the 1930s, there has been a resurgence of interest in the new century in Harrison's writings, and he is now considered one of the most influential African American spokespersons in American history. On the other side of the globe, another radical, India's revolutionary Rajendra Nath Lahiri, was hanged today in the Gorkakhpur District jail by the British for his participation in a bombing and a train robbery. He was only twenty-six. Lahiri was an active member of the Hindustan Republican Association whose aim was the removal of the British from India. Two days later, three other members of the anti-British Hindustan Republican Association—Pandit Ram Prasad Bismil, Thakur Roshan Singh, and Ashfaqulla Khan—were also hanged in the same jail.

SUNDAY, DECEMBER 18

Joseph Stalin celebrated his forty-ninth birthday by seeing Leon Trotsky and ninety-eight of his other enemies officially expelled by a vote by the Fifteenth Congress of

Many historians consider Communist theorist, writer, and politician Leon Trotsky a true interpreter of the Marxist philosophy. But he opposed Stalin's form of Communism and was seen as a threat to Stalin's total power, so he had to be eliminated. Stripped of all his Party positions, Trotsky fled to Mexico, where he continued to write about his ideas until Stalin ordered him assassinated in 1940. *Photofest © Photofest*

the Soviet Communist Party. Trotsky was eventually sent into exile in Turkey, then Mexico, where he was assassinated in 1940.

Although considered a lost film, the First National melodrama *The Love Mart* is of interest to film historians because of its superior cast, including a young Boris Karloff in a supporting role. The movie's star was Billie Dove, who played Antoinette Frobelle in nineteenth-century New Orleans. When she refuses the amorous advances of the corrupt Captain Remy (Noah Beery), he forges papers saying she is a quadroon, having Negro blood in her, and can be sold as a slave. Remy plans to buy Antoinette and make her his mistress, but the wily adventurer Victor Jallot (Gilbert Roland), who loves Antoinette, figures out how to discredit Remy and save her. George Fitzmaurice directed *The Love Mart*, which was well received when it premiered on this day.

MONDAY, DECEMBER 19

For the first time in its history, the Dow Jones Industrial Average broke 200 points. This stock market index, which measured the health and wealth of the American market, would continue to climb, getting as high as 386.10 on September 3, 1929. The stock market crashed a month later and the Dow and the economy collapsed. It reached its lowest point on July 8, 1932, when the Dow closed at 41.22.

> In 1927, the amount of money in the United States equaled that of Great Britain, France, Italy, Germany, the Soviet Union, and the rest of Europe combined.

In a Nicaraguan jungle near the Honduras border, a joint force of the U.S. Marines and Nicaraguan National Guard numbering one hundred eighty marched on the Sandinista secret base at El Chipote, which had recently been discovered by air. Before an attack on the base could begin, two hundred rebels counterattacked and, after an eighty-minute battle, pushed the marines and guardsmen back into the jungle. The Americans and Nicaraguans retreated and returned to their base. They would return with greater numbers on January 1, 1928, and rout the Sandinistas during the Battle of Las Cruces.

In the Vatican in Rome, Pope Pius XI today appointed five non-Italian cardinals—from Spain, Hungary, Canada, and two from France—to fill vacancies in the sixty-six-member College of Cardinals. It was the first time in the history of the Roman Catholic Church that there were as many non-Italians as there were Italians in the College of Cardinals.

The Irish Players, who had presented *The Plough and the Stars* so well but with little success in November, revived Sean O'Casey's earlier play *Juno and the Paycock* (1924) for forty performances. Arthur Shields played the boisterous Captain Jack Boyle and

Sara Allgood was his crafty wife, Juno, who sees her family torn apart over drink, their daughter's pregnancy, and their son's death.

TUESDAY, DECEMBER 20

The much-publicized trial of Cincinnati lawyer and bootlegger George Remus, who had shot his wife to death in a public park on October 6, concluded today with Remus acting as his own lawyer and pleading temporary insanity. The jury deliberated for only nineteen minutes before acquitting him.

An explosion in the Franco Mine No. 1, a coal mine at Stiritz, Illinois, that employed four hundred miners, instantly killed seven. Luckily the blast occurred during the night shift when only twenty men were working or the number of fatalities would have been much greater.

WEDNESDAY, DECEMBER 21

Lucille King, who worked for the John Schroeder Lumber Company in Milwaukee, Wisconsin, had for a few years been making toys to be used as teaching aids for young children. Today she registered the trademark name Playskool, and by 1928 the new division of the lumber company was manufacturing toys that soon became very popular. As a subsidiary of Hasbro, Playskool is still in operation today.

Australian cricketer Jack Saunders died today in Melbourne at the age of fifty-one. He is most remembered as the left-hand bat on the Australian team of 1902 which toured England and South Africa.

THURSDAY, DECEMBER 22

William Edward Hickman, who had kidnapped and dismembered the twelve-year-old Los Angeles girl Marion Parker a week earlier, was arrested today in the town of Echo, Oregon. He had a criminal record and was identified by his fingerprints on the girl's clothing. Hickman confessed to the crime which, he told police, was motivated by money and fame. He entered a plea, recently established in California law, of not guilty by reason of insanity, but he was tried, found guilty, and hanged in October of 1928.

Playwright Robert E. Sherwood was starting to get recognition because of his play *The Road to Rome*, which had opened the previous January. But his new entry, the comedy *The Love Nest*, was rejected by the press and public and closed in three weeks. Based on a story by Ring Lardner, the comedy was a satire on Hollywood. Cecilia Gregg has lost her patience with her egotistical movie-director husband Lou Gregg and gets drunk before doing a movie magazine interview in which she lambasts her husband, Hollywood people, and the whole movie business. Lou is so caught up in his career that he doesn't even notice when Cecilia takes her children back to New York City to live.

FRIDAY, DECEMBER 23

Few stories have been reincarnated in so many forms as the satirical *Chicago*, the silent screen version of which premiered today. In 1924 two women, Beulah Annan and Belva Gaertner, were separately arrested and tried for murdering their lovers but were acquitted by the court. Reporter Maurine Dallas Watkins covered the trials for the *Chicago Tribune* and then fictionalized the stories into the play *Chicago* in 1926. In the stage version, Roxie Hart shoots her lover and gets her husband, Amos, to say he did it thinking it was a robbery. But the police see through the false confession and Roxie is arrested. Newspaper reporter Jake smells a good story and takes Roxie under his wing, getting the hotshot lawyer Billy Flynn to defend her and convincing columnist Mary Sunshine to write sob stuff about Roxie in the paper. Coached by Flynn, Roxie performs the role of the innocent, convent-educated girl at the trial and is acquitted. When she is free, she dumps Amos and goes into vaudeville. The scathing satire of celebrity in the Roaring Twenties was applauded by the press and enjoyed by the public for five months on Broadway. DeMille Pictures Corporation filmed the play in 1927 and made a few changes to the script. Roxie (Phyllis Haver) is as publicity hungry as in the stage version, but husband Amos is more likable and even ends up with the housemaid Katie, who has loved him all along. *Chicago* on screen is a fast-paced, raucous, and contemporary spoof of America's fascination with crime and celebrity. The nominal director was Frank Urson, but it is rumored that producer Cecil B. DeMille directed most of the movie and kept his name off the credits because he didn't want to be associated with such an amoral tale when his biblical epic *King of Kings* was in theatres. *Chicago* was remade as a talkie by 20th Century-Fox in 1942 as *Roxie Hart* with Ginger Rogers as the title heroine. The 1975 Broadway musical version of *Chicago* made many changes to the original, most of which were retained for the successful and popular 2002 film adaptation.

The annual Caddy Championship, in which young golfers compete at the Glen Garden Country Club in Fort Worth, Texas, concluded today, and the final round was played by two future golf legends: Byron Nelson and Ben Hogan. Both were fifteen years old at the time. Nelson defeated Hogan by one stroke.

Frances Wilson Grayson, the niece of Woodrow Wilson, and three crew members disappeared today off the coast of Nova Scotia as she attempted to become the first woman to fly across the Atlantic Ocean. Grayson became interested in aviation after she divorced her husband John Brady Grayson, but she had no flying experience. She got financing to build a new Sikorsky S-36 amphibian plane, which she named *Dawn*, then recruited Royal Norwegian Navy lieutenant Oskar Omdal as pilot, Brice Goldsborough as navigator, and Frank Koehler as radio engineer. (Grayson intended to do some of the piloting herself.) The plan was to begin the transatlantic flight from Newfoundland, but the *Dawn* and its four crew members took off from Long Island today and were never seen again.

In what became known as the Santa Claus Bank Robbery, the First National Bank of Cisco, Texas, was robbed of $12,400 by a man dressed in a Santa outfit and three accomplices. Ex-con Marshall Ratliff entered the bank as Santa, then three other armed ex-cons joined him to collect the money. Over one hundred shots were fired both inside and outside the bank, leaving the town's police chief and a deputy dead and six civilians wounded. After one of the biggest manhunts in Texas history, the four culprits were found, brought to trial, and eventually executed, Ratliff by a lynch party.

SATURDAY, DECEMBER 24

During a skirmish of the civil war in China, the Standard Oil refinery in the city of Tientsin caught fire and the blaze threatened to burn down the entire city. American marines stationed there put out the fire and saved Tientsin.

A difficult film for modern audiences to watch is Warner Brothers' World War I comedy *Ham and Eggs at the Front*. Privates Ham (Tom Wilson) and Eggs (Heinie Conklin) are friends in an African American regiment stationed in France. The village innkeeper Friml (William Irving) is a spy for the Germans and has his Negro waitress Fifi (Myrna Loy) flirt with the soldiers to obtain information. She gets friendly with Ham and Eggs, but the officers find out that Friml is a spy and that Fifi is his accomplice. Friml flees and Ham and Eggs are ordered to learn his whereabout from Fifi or shoot her. Fifi escapes, Ham and Eggs follow in a merry chase that sets them adrift in a balloon, and when they parachute out, they land on Friml and become heroes. The fact that Wilson, Conklin, and Loy are white actors who play their characters in blackface is not only distracting but very uncomfortable to watch.

SUNDAY, DECEMBER 25

It was a white Christmas for most of southern England and Wales today when the Christmas Blizzard of 1927 started mid-day and continued for two more days. All transportation was halted as winds created snowdrifts up to twenty feet high in some areas. When the snow started to melt in January, the river Thames flooded.

Indian activist Dr. B. R. Ambedkar, leader of the Dalit caste known as the "untouchables," led thousands of followers to the city of Mahad to burn in public copies of *Manusmriti*, the Hindu holy book that established the rules for the caste system in India. The act of protest marked an important date in the Dalit struggle against traditional

Brahminism. Every year on December 25 the Dalits still celebrate the day as Manusmriti Dahan Din (Manusmriti Burning Day).

An ongoing labor dispute at a stove plant in South Pittsburg, Tennessee, came to a bloody climax on Christmas Day with a shootout between laborers and the law on the streets of the town. Two sheriffs, two city marshals, and a policeman died in the ten-minute gun battle; a number of workers were wounded but survived. To this day, bullet holes can still be seen in the brick building that housed the stove company.

Colleen Moore was the star of First National's comedy *Her Wild Oat* which opened today. She played Mary Brown who saves the money she has earned from her lunch wagon to vacation at a ritzy summer resort where she can hobnob with high society. But the other guests snub Mary, so the reporter Tommy Warren, desperate for a story, convinces Mary to pass herself off as the Duchesse de Granville. He trains her on how to behave and she is successful until Philip Latour, the son of the Duke of Granville, arrives at the resort and things get sticky. Happily, Philip falls for Mary, and he solves her dilemma by proposing marriage. Moore was one of the best light comediennes of the time and *Her Wild Oat* is one of her best films.

Diplomat and statesman Sergey Sazonov, the former foreign minister of the Russian Empire, died today in Nice, France, at the age of sixty-seven. He was minister during the turbulent years of 1910–1916, and his role in promoting or discouraging Russia's entry into World War I has been much debated. Opposed to the Communists, Sazonov immigrated in 1917 to Britain and then France.

THE FIRST ACADEMY AWARDS

The Academy of Motion Picture Arts and Sciences Awards were presented for the first time at a banquet in the Blossom Room of the Hollywood Roosevelt Hotel on May 16, 1929. Movies from 1927 and 1928 were considered eligible. Douglas Fairbanks (Senior) announced and presented all the awards. The categories, nominees, and winners (in **bold** print) were:

Production

The Last Command (Paramount)
The Racket (United Artists)
7th Heaven (Fox)
The Way of All Flesh (Paramount)
Wings (Paramount)

Artistic Quality of Production

Chang (Paramount)
The Crowd (MGM)
Sunrise (Fox)

Actress

Louise Dresser in *A Ship Comes In* (Pathé-RKO)

Janet Gaynor in *7th Heaven* (Fox), *Street Angel* (Fox), and *Sunrise* (Fox)

Actor

Richard Barthelmess in *The Noose* (First National) and *The Patent Leather Kid* (First National)
Charles Chaplin in *The Circus* (Chaplin-United Artists)
Emil Jannings in *The Last Command* (Paramount) and *The Way of All Flesh* (Paramount)

Director

Frank Borzage for *7th Heaven* (Fox)

Herbert Brenon for *Sorrell and Son* (United Artists)

King Vidor for *The Crowd* (MGM)

Comedy Direction

Charles Chaplin for *The Circus* (Chaplin-United Artists)

Lewis Milestone for *Two Arabian Knights* (United Artists)

Ted Wilde for *Speedy* (Paramount)

Writing (adaptation)

Glorious Betsy—Anthony Coleway (Warner Brothers)

The Jazz Singer—Alfred Cohn (Warner Brothers)

7th Heaven—**Benjamin Glazer** (Fox)

Writing (original story)

The Last Command—Lajos Biro (Paramount)

The Patent Leather Kid—Rupert Hughes (First National)

Underworld—**Ben Hecht** (Paramount)

Title Writing

The Private Life of Helen of Troy—Gerald Duffy (First National)

The Fair Co-ed—Joseph Farnham (MGM)

Laugh, Clown, Laugh—Joseph Farnham (MGM)

Telling the World—**Joseph Farnham** (MGM)

Oh Kay!—George Marion Jr. (First National)

Cinematography

The Devil Dancer—George Barnes (United Artists)

Drums of Love—Karl Struss (United Artists)

The Magic Flame—George Barnes (United Artists)

My Best Gal—Charles Rosher (Pickford-United Artists)

Sadie Thompson—George Barnes (United Artists)

Sunrise—**Charles Rosher** and **Karl Struss** (Fox)

The Tempest—Charles Rosher (United Artists)

Interior Decoration

The Dove—William Cameron Menzies (United Artists)

7th Heaven—Harry Oliver (Fox)

Sunrise—Rochus Gliese (Fox)

The Tempest—**William Cameron Menzies** (United Artists)

Engineering Effects

The Jazz Singer—Nugent Slaughter (Warner Brothers)

The Private Life of Helen of Troy—Ralph Hammeras (First National)

Wings—**Roy Pomeroy** (Paramount)

Special Awards

Warner Brothers for producing *The Jazz Singer*, the outstanding pioneer talking picture, which has revolutionized the industry.

Charles Chaplin for versatility and genius in writing, acting, directing, and producing *The Circus*.

MONDAY, DECEMBER 26

The word "astronaut" was invented today when the Belgian science fiction author J. H. Rosny used it at a meeting of the Société Astronomique de France (French Astronomical Society) in Paris. The Society requested a word to describe a person who travels through space and Rosny proposed *l'astronautique*, taken from the Greek root words for navigation and stars.

A simple innovation in sports was made today during the East-West Shriner football game. For the first time, each player's number was on both the front and the back of each jersey. The Shriners started the fund-raising games in 1925, the nation's first college all-star football game. Also in football news, the Hominy Indians, a team comprised entirely of Native Americans, bested the New York Giants 13–6 in an exhibition game.

British prime minister Stanley Baldwin made the cover of *Time* magazine in today's issue on the occasion of his being made a fellow of the Royal Society. Although the Society was a group of learned scientists, Baldwin was welcomed because of his efforts to bring government-sponsored electricity into private and public buildings in Britain.

In the midst of its busiest season, Broadway had its busiest night ever: eleven shows opened. Nine of the offerings were original plays, one was a revival of a French drama, and one was a new musical. That many openings on the Great White Way had never happened before or since. Alas, only two of the productions were hits. The melodrama *Excess Baggage* was about a couple in vaudeville whose marriage breaks up when Elsa (Miriam Hopkins) temporarily leaves her juggling husband Eddie (Eric Dressler) to go to Hollywood. The play was well reviewed and ran a profitable twenty-seven weeks. *Excess Baggage* was made into a partial talkie by MGM in 1928. The night's other success (though a modest one) was *Behold the Bridegroom*, a play by George Kelly that was more serious than the playwright's usual fare. The spoiled Antoinette (Judith Anderson) rejects several wealthy suitors but falls for a business man (John Marston) only to be turned down for the first time in her life. Reviews were mixed but there was plenty of praise for Anderson, who helped the play run eleven weeks. Also giving a lauded performance was Alice Brady in *Bless You, Sister*. She played an Aimee MacPherson-like revivalist preacher who works with a con man in mesmerizing crowds of people across the country. But she eventually sees the error of her fake miracles and settles down with her hometown boyfriend. The melodrama ran three weeks, the same length of time as *Restless Woman*. A bored housewife (Mary Young) leaves her husband and moves into a love nest in Greenwich Village with a young artist. He gets tired of the older woman and ends up with her daughter. Author Fannie Hurst was an expert at weepy books, plays, and movies, but she didn't succeed with her *It Is to Laugh*, a melodrama about a Jewish family who gets rich and moves uptown, only to find heartbreak and despair. The play held on for four weeks, which was three more than *Celebrity* lasted. This boxing drama had thinly disguised versions of Gene Tunney and Arnold Rothstein as characters. Neither boxing fans nor theatergoers were interested. Also running one week but much more interesting was Rachel Crothers's futuristic drama *Venus* set in a time when there are regularly scheduled airplane flights to the planet Venus. Crothers was known for her thought-provoking plays about the sexes and *Venus* was no exception. A doctor has created a pill that makes women behave more masculinely and reduces men to emotional weaklings. The night's third play to only survive a week was *Paradise*, a romance about spinster Winnie Elder in New York City who has written to her sisters back in Paradise, Ohio, that she has married a handsome man. When one of the sisters decides to visit, Winnie panics, reveals that her husband has died, and finds a body to prove it. Happily, she ends up in the arms of a doctor. The night's only adventure play was *Mongolia*, about a Russian general who in 1919 uses an American couple to get his nephew, one of the surviving Romanovs, out of Russia. The play lasted six weeks but the production was so expensive that the producers couldn't make a profit. The evening's revival was the old French warhorse of a melodrama *L'Aiglon* which had served both Sarah Bernhardt and Maude Adams very well in the past. The star this time was Michael Strange, whose only claim to fame was the fact that she was married to John Barrymore at the time. Audiences were curious for one week only. The day's only musical sounded promising. *The White Eagle* was an operetta by Rudolf Friml (music), Brian Hooker, and W. H. Post (book and lyrics), based on the famous play and film *The Squaw Man*. Allen Prior played the British gentleman James who takes the blame for his brother's thievery and escapes to the Wild West where he weds the Native girl Silverwing. When James inherits the family fortune and considers bringing Silverwing back with him to England, she commits suicide. Critics enjoyed the familiar story and some of Friml's music but little else, so *The While Eagle* closed after six unprofitable weeks. Although no major works came from the evening of December 26, 1927, it still remains Broadway's busiest night.

TUESDAY, DECEMBER 27

One of the most important works of the American musical theatre, *Show Boat*, premiered on Broadway today and opened up new possibilities for the art form. *Show Boat* was the first musical play, as opposed to musical comedy. The musical dealt with racism, alcoholism, divorce, gambling addiction, and miscegenation, yet was still highly entertaining even as it was moving in a way not experienced in a musical before. Oscar Hammerstein adapted Edna Ferber's best-selling novel and wrote the lyrics to Jerome Kern's masterful music that included operetta, blues, musical comedy, and folk. When Cap'n Andy (Charles Winninger) and his wife, Parthy Ann (Edna May Oliver), bring their show boat *Cotton Blossom* into a Southern river town for a performance, their daughter, Magnolia (Norma Terris), meets and falls for a handsome professional gambler, Gaylord Ravenal (Howard Marsh). Magnolia seeks advice from the African American work hand Joe (Jules Bledsoe), who tells her only the Mississippi River knows what's to be, and it "don't say nothin'." The boat's leading lady, Julie (Helen Morgan), is accused of having Negro blood and she is forced to leave, taking her husband (and the troupe's leading man) with her. Magnolia and Gaylord are pressed into assuming the lead roles on the show boat, eventually getting married (much against Parthy's wishes) and going off together. Years later, living in Chicago, Gaylord's gambling luck has run out, so he deserts Magnolia and their young daughter, Kim. Magnolia applies for a job singing at a

The landmark Broadway musical *Show Boat* went places and explored topics rarely attempted before on the musical stage. In this scene in which Cap'n Andy (Charles Winninger) addresses the audience on the *Cotton Blossom*, notice the "colored section" in the balcony. *Photofest © Photofest*

nightclub where Julie, now a drunkard, works. Julie recognizes Magnolia and sacrifices what is left of her own career to help Magnolia begin hers. On New Year's Eve, Magnolia is a hit and goes on to become a famous entertainer. More years pass and Magnolia and the grown-up Kim visit the *Cotton Blossom* where they meet up with the aging Gaylord. To his relief he is welcomed by Magnolia and the two are reunited as they joyfully watch their daughter launch her own career. The famous score included the folk-like anthem "Ol' Man River," the playful duet "Make Believe," the bluesy "Can't Help Lovin' Dat Man," the rhapsodic "You Are Love," the torch song classic "Bill," the lullaby-like "Why Do I Love You?," and the wry frolic "Life upon the Wicked Stage." *Show Boat* was presented by Florenz Ziegfeld in a memorable staging that received raves from the press and the public, allowing the large and expensive production to run 572 performances in the Ziegfeld Theatre. It would return to Broadway several times during the next ninety years and would inspire three film versions.

Somewhat overshadowed by *Show Boat* was a first-rate comedy of manners titled *Paris Bound* by Philip Barry, which opened on Broadway that same night. For six years, Mary (Madge Kennedy) and Jim Hutton (Donn Cook) seem the ideal young couple; then, Mary discovers that Jim has not been totally faithful to her. Back on their wedding day, Jim's divorced father, James Sr. (Gilbert Emery), had warned them to overlook occasional straying, lest it ruin their marriage as it had destroyed his. At first, Mary is bitter and determined on divorce. But when she realizes that Jim has ignored her own flirtation with a handsome young composer, Richard Parrish (Donald MacDonald), she decides to live and let live. The critics applauded the witty script and the fine cast, helping the Arthur Hopkins production to run a profitable thirty weeks. *Paris Bound* was filmed by Pathé in 1929 with Ann Harding and Fredric March as the troubled couple.

WEDNESDAY, DECEMBER 28

The bohemian journalist and social activist Dorothy Day today was baptized in the Roman Catholic Church at the age of thirty. In 1933 Day founded the Catholic Worker Movement and for the next five decades was arguably the most political radical in the Catholic Church in America.

The last notable Broadway offering of the year was the comedy *The Royal Family* by George S. Kaufman and Edna Ferber, which opened today and ran nearly a year. The Cavendishes are the greatest acting family in America, presided over by the aging Fanny Cavendish (Haidee Wright). Her daughter, Julie (Ann Andrews), is the leading contemporary actress, while Julie's daughter Gwen (Sylvia Field) is a promising ingenue. Fanny's dashingly handsome son Tony (Otto Kruger) could have been the greatest performer of all, but he prefers the celebrity that comes with being a film star. His wild affairs with women and other escapades keep him perpetually on the run. Hovering over the family is the great producer Oscar Wolfe (Jefferson De Angelis). Both Julie and

Gwen are toying with marriage and abandoning the frenzied world of the theatre. For all their complaints about their lives, the call of the stage is irresistible, so Julie and Gwen look forward to the next theatre engagement and Fanny quietly dies while planning yet another tour. Jed Harris produced the satiric spoof of the famous Barrymore and Drew families; the play so infuriated Ethel Barrymore that she refused to talk to or associate herself with the two authors for the rest of her life. *The Royal Family* has enjoyed numerous revivals, most memorably a very successful 1975 Broadway production that made the old comedy popular all over again.

THURSDAY, DECEMBER 29

The eruption of an undersea volcano today between Perboewatan and Danan near Krakatoa in the Pacific Ocean created a lava dome that pushed its way to the surface within a few days. Two burning islands formed but were soon cooled and eroded away by the sea. Yet they created the foundation for the Anak Krakatau Island, which was formed in 1930 and still exists.

Broadway's last new offering of 1927 was the musical *Lovely Lady*, which was a modest success at twenty weeks. Based on a French farce, the slim plot had Folly Watteau convince Paul deMorlaix to pose as her husband when she stays at the Hotel Royale. To no one's surprise they fall in love and end up as man and wife. The songs were as forgettable as the characters and story, but audiences found it an entertaining enough way to spend an evening or a matinee.

The Indian doctor and activist Hakim Ajmal Khan died of heart failure today in Delhi at the age of sixty-four. An activist for Muslim rights in British India, he also cofounded Jamia Millia Islamia University and Tibbia College, where he was chancellor when he died.

FRIDAY, DECEMBER 30

The first subway system in Asia opened today when the Tokyo Metro dedicated its first route, the Giza Line, a two-mile run between Asakusa and Ueno. Today the capital city has two separate subway systems carrying ten million passengers a day.

The last issue of Henry Ford's weekly newspaper, the *Dearborn Independent*, was published today. Started by Ford in 1919, the paper reached a peak circulation of nine hundred thousand in 1925, but the high numbers were due to a sales quota imposed on Ford dealers. The paper often expressed Ford's anti-Semitic views and was castigated by many. By 1927 there were so many lawsuits against the *Independent* that Ford decided to stop publishing it.

The Bellanca Aircraft Company was founded today by Italian-American airplane designer Giuseppe Mario Bellanca in Richmond Hill, New York. Bellanca had worked with various companies before setting off on his own and Bellanca Aircraft was soon one of the major manufacturers of planes in America. The name of the company was changed to AviaBellanca Aircraft in 1983, and it is headquartered in Alexandria, Minnesota.

SATURDAY, DECEMBER 31

United Artists' melodrama *The Dove* was based on a popular 1925 play about corruption in Mexico, but the studio feared alienating the Latin American audience, so the story was reset in some unnamed Mediterranean country. The political thug Don José (Noah Beery Sr.) is passionately in love with the cabaret dancer Dolores (Norma Talmadge), and he is not happy when she prefers the gambler Johnny Powell (Gilbert Roland). Using his powerful connections, Don José frames Johnny for murder and he is sentenced to die by firing squad. Dolores pleads on Johnny's behalf, telling Don José that if he were a truly macho man, he would release Johnny. The ploy works and the lovers are reunited. The superior art direction for the movie was by the young William Cameron Menzies, one of Hollywood's greatest designers. He won an Oscar for *The Dove*. The movie was remade in 1932 as *Girl of the Rio*, then again in 1939 as *The Girl and the Gambler*.

The last notable film of 1927 was a dandy: the Laurel and Hardy short *The Battle of the Century*, which contains one of the cinema's most memorable cream pie fights. A

The brilliant screen comics Stan Laurel (left) and Oliver Hardy (pointing) are barely recognizable in the famous pie fight in the comedy short *The Battle of the Century*. Unlike many comics, Laurel and Hardy were fortunate to make a successful transition from silent movies to the talkies. *MGM / Photofest © MGM*

boxing manager (Oliver Hardy) has a problem with his client Canvasback Clump (Stan Laurel) who loses every bout. So the manager takes out an insurance policy on Clump and tries to arrange for the boxer to have an accident. When he places a banana peel on the sidewalk where Clump is sure to walk, a pastry chef slips and falls on it instead. In anger, the chef throws a pie in the manager's face, the manager responds with another pie, and soon everyone on the block is throwing pies at each other. Legend has it that between three and four thousand pies were used in the famous sequence.

Retired baseball player Jack Sharrott died today in Los Angeles at the age of fifty-eight. A pitcher and outfielder, he played in the Major Leagues from 1890 to 1893 with the New York Giants and Philadelphia Phillies, then in the minors from 1894 to 1903. In his later years Sharrott coached at Worcester Polytechnic Institute.

MAN OF THE YEAR

On January 2, 1928, *Time* magazine initiated a new feature: the annual "Man of the Year" issue. The journal named Charles Lindbergh the Man of the Year for 1927. The first woman to be named "Man" of the Year was Mrs. Wallis Simpson, whose romance led to the abdication of King Edward VIII in 1936. *Time* changed the name of the honor to "Person of the Year" in 2000.

EPILOGUE

New Year's Day, 1928

Hangovers and optimism ruled the day as the new year began. For many Americans, not much had changed since last year's January 1st. If anything, things were better. The Stock Market and the Dow Jones continued to climb. Technology, particularly aviation and the radio, would blossom. More Americans were buying houses and cars as well as luxury items unheard of a decade earlier. It looked like 1928 would be an even better version of 1927. Internationally, that was not the case. Communism was faltering in Russia and struggling in China. Before 1928 was over, the Marxist idea would predominate in both countries. Similarly, in Germany and Italy, Fascism would strengthen and prevail. Japan would recover from its financial crash of 1927 and end up a major industrial and military power. Americans did not notice, but the nightmares of the 1930s had already started overseas.

The party that was 1927 would continue in the United States for twenty-two more months then come crashing down in October 1929. The country had never been taken by such a surprise. There had been financial crashes, depressions, recessions, runs on banks, and other money setbacks in the past, but the Great Depression outdid them all. There were a few sputters and glitches during those twenty-two months that, looking back, foreshadowed the disaster to come. When the crisis came, many felt Herbert Hoover, the nation's very popular president, would fix it. Some of that optimism of 1927 still held on. It didn't take long for Americans to realize that the 1920s were a luxury that was bought on borrowed time and with money that had quickly dried up. By the time Franklin Roosevelt was elected president in 1932 in hopes of saving a sinking ship, 1927 was already distant history. Many Americans felt it was a time that seemed long gone and never likely to happen again. Perhaps they were right.

BIBLIOGRAPHY

Affron, Charles. *Lillian Gish: Her Legend, Her Life*. Oakland: University of California Press, 2002.

Allen, Frederick Lewis. *Only Yesterday: An Informal History of the 1920s*. New York: Harper Perennial, 2010.

Allvine, Glendon. *The Greatest Fox of Them All*. New York: Lyle Stuart, 1969.

Appel, Marty. *Pinstripe Empire: The New York Yankees from before the Babe to after the Boss*. New York: Bloomsbury USA, 2012.

Astaire, Fred. *Steps in Time: An Autobiography*. New York: Dey Street Books, 2008.

Aylesworth, Thomas G. *Broadway to Hollywood*. New York: Gallery Books, W. H. Smith Publishers, 1985.

Bair, Deirdre. *Al Capone: His Life, Legacy, and Legend*. New York: Anchor, 2017.

Balio, Tino. *United Artists*. Madison: University of Wisconsin Press, 1976.

Barrios, Richard. *A Song in the Dark: The Birth of the Musical Film* (2nd ed.). New York: Oxford University Press, 2009.

Barry, John M. *Rising Tide: The Great Mississippi Flood of 1927 and How It Changed America*. New York: Touchstone Books, 1997.

Bawden, Liz-Anne. *The Oxford Companion to Film*. New York: Oxford University Press, 1976.

Behr, Edward. *Prohibition: Thirteen Years That Changed America*. New York: Arcade Publishing, 2011.

Berg, A. Scott. *Lindbergh*. New York: Berkley, 1999.

Bergreen, Laurence. *As Thousands Cheer: The Life of Irving Berlin*. Boston: Da Capo Press, 1996.

———. *Capone: The Man and the Era*. New York: Simon & Schuster, 1996.

Bilby, Kenneth. *The General: David Sarnoff and the Rise of the Communications Industry*. New York: HarperCollins, 1986.

Bingen, Steven. *Warner Bros.: Hollywood's Ultimate Backlot*. Lanham, MD: Taylor Trade Publishing, 2014.

Bloom, Ken. *Broadway: An Encyclopedic Guide to the History, People and Places of Times Square*. New York: Facts on File, 1991.

Bloom, Ken, and Frank Vlastinik. *Broadway Musicals: The 100 Greatest Shows of All Time*. Norwalk, CT: Easton Press, 2004.

Boardman, Barrington. *From Harding to Hiroshima: An Anecdotal History of the U.S. from 1923–1945*. New York: Dembner Books, 1988.

Bolton, Kerry. *Stalin: The Enduring Legacy*. London: Black House Publishing, 2012.

Bordman, Gerald. *American Theatre: A Chronicle of Comedy & Drama, 1914–1930*. New York: Oxford University Press, 1995.

———. *Jerome Kern: His Life and Music*. New York: Oxford University Press, 1980.

Bordman, Gerald, and Thomas S. Hischak. *The Oxford Companion to American Theatre* (3rd ed.). New York: Oxford University Press, 2004.

Bordman, Gerald, and Richard Norton. *American Musical Theatre: A Chronicle* (4th ed.). New York: Oxford University Press, 2011.

Botto, Louis, and Robert Viagas. *At This Theatre*. New York: Hal Leonard Corporation/Applause Theatre & Cinema Books, 2010.

Brantley, Ben (ed.). *The New York Times Book of Broadway*. New York: St. Martin's Press, 2001.

Brennan, Thomas. *The Million Dollar Man: Jack Dempsey*. Berkeley, CA: Regent Press, 2017.

Bret, David. *Greta Garbo: Divine Star*. London: Robson Press, 2013.

Brower, Steven, and Mercedes Ellington. *Duke Ellington: An American Composer and Icon*. New York: Rizzoli, 2016.

Bryson, Bill. *One Summer: America, 1927*. New York: Anchor, 2014.

Carmichael, Hoagy, with Stephen Longstreet. *The Stardust Road & Sometimes I Wonder: The Autobiography of Hoagy Carmichael*. Boston: Da Capo Press, 1946/1999.

Carradice, Phil. *The Shanghai Massacre: China's White Terror, 1927*. Barnsley, UK: Pen and Sword Military Press, 2018.

Carter, Randolph. *Ziegfeld: The Time of His Life*. London: Bernard Press, 1988.

Cavanaugh, Jack. *Tunney: Boxing's Brainiest Champ and His Upset of the Great Jack Dempsey*. New York: Ballantine Books, 2007.

Coolidge, Calvin. *The Autobiography of Calvin Coolidge*. Honolulu: University Press of the Pacific, 2004.

Creamer, Robert. *Babe: The Legend Comes to Life*. New York: Simon & Schuster, 1992.

Crowther, Bosley. *The Lion's Share: The Story of an Entertainment Empire*. New York: E. P. Dutton, 1957.

Curcio, Vincent. *Henry Ford*. New York: Oxford University Press, 2013.

Davis, Martin. *The Greatest of Them All: The Legend of Bobby Jones*. Greenwich, CT: American Golfer, 1996.

Decker, Todd. *Show Boat: Performing Race in an American Musical*. New York: Oxford University Press, 2015.

Deford, Frank. *Big Bill Tilden: The Triumphs and the Tragedy*. New York: Simon & Schuster, 1976.

Deutscher, Isaac. *The Prophet Unarmed: Trotsky 1921–1929*. London/New York: Verso, 2004.

Dick, Bernard F. (ed.). *Columbia Pictures: Portrait of a Studio*. Lexington: University of Kentucky Press, 1991.

DuRose, Richard A. *1927: A Brilliant Year in Aviation*. CreateSpace Independent Publishing, 2013.

Eames, John Douglas. *The MGM Story*. New York: Crown Publishers, 1975.

———. *The Paramount Story*. New York: Crown Publishers, 1985.

Eig, Jonathan. *Luckiest Man: The Life and Death of Lou Gehrig*. New York: Simon & Schuster, 2006.

Elleman, Bruce. *Moscow and the Emergence of Communist Power in China, 1925–30: The Nanchang Uprising and the Birth of the Red Army*. Abingdon-on-Thames, UK: Routledge, 2009.

Everson, William K. *American Silent Film*. Boston: Da Capo Press, 1998.

Eyman, Scott. *Lion of Hollywood: The Life and Legend of Louis B. Mayer*. New York: Simon & Schuster, 2008.

———. *The Speed of Sound: Hollywood and the Talkie Revolution, 1926–1930*. New York: Simon & Schuster, 2015.

Fitzgerald, Michael G. *Universal Pictures: A Panoramic History*. Westport, CT: Arlington House, 1977.

Freedland, Michael. *Jerome Kern: A Biography*. New York: Stein and Day, 1981.

———. *Jolson: The Story of Al Jolson*. London: Virgin Books, 1995.

Frommer, Harvey. *Five O'Clock Lightning: Babe Ruth, Lou Gehrig and the Greatest Baseball Team, the 1927 New York Yankees*. Lanham, MD: Taylor Trade Publishing, 2015.

Fury, David. *Johnny Weissmuller: Twice the Hero*. Waterville, ME: Thorndike Press, 2001.

Geduld, Harry M. *The Birth of the Talkies*. Bloomington: Indiana University Press, 1975.

Giddins, Gary. *Satchmo: The Genius of Louis Armstrong*. Boston: Da Capo Press, 2009.

Gish, Lillian. *Lillian Gish: The Movies, Mr. Griffith, and Me*. Upper Saddle River, NJ: Prentice-Hall, 1969.

Godfrey, Donald. *Philo T. Farnsworth: The Father of Television*. Salt Lake City: University of Utah Press, 2001.

Golden, Eve. *John Gilbert: The Last of the Silent Film Stars*. Lexington: University Press of Kentucky, 2013.

Green, Stanley. *Encyclopedia of Musical Film*. New York: Oxford University Press, 1981.

Greenberg, David. *Calvin Coolidge*. New York: Times Books, 2006.

Grode, Eric. *The Book of Broadway*. Minneapolis: Voyageur Press, 2015.

Halliwell, Leslie. *Halliwell's Film Guide* (7th ed.). New York: Harper & Row, 1989.

Hampton, Dan. *The Flight: Charles Lindbergh's Daring and Immortal 1927 Transatlantic Crossing*. New York: William Morrow, 2017.

Hirschhorn, Clive. *The Columbia Story* (2nd ed.). London: Hamlyn Press, 2001.

———. *The Universal Story*. New York: Crown Publishers, 1981.

———. *The Warner Bros. Story*. New York: Crown Publishers, 1979.

Hischak, Thomas. *The Oxford Companion to the American Musical: Theatre, Film, and Television*. New York: Oxford University Press, 2008.

Jarret, John. *Gene Tunney: The Golden Guy Who Licked Jack Dempsey Twice*. London: Robson Books, 2003.

Jeansonne, Glen. *Herbert Hoover: A Life*. New York: Berkley, 2016.

Jewell, Richard B., and Vernon Harbin. *The RKO Story*. New York: Arlington House, 1982.

Karney, Robin (ed.). *Cinema Year by Year, 1894–2002*. London: Dorling Kindersley Books, 2002.

Katz, Ephraim. *The Film Encyclopedia* (3rd ed.). New York: Harper Perennial, 1998.

Kellen, Stuart. *The Roaring Twenties*. San Diego: Greenhaven Press, 2002.

Khlevniuk, Oleg V. *Stalin: New Biography of a Dictator*. Translated by Nora Seligman Favorov. New Haven, CT: Yale University Press, 2017.

Kobel, Peter. *Silent Movies: The Birth of Film and the Triumph of Movie Culture*. New York: Little, Brown, 2007.

Kobler, John. *Capone: The Life and World of Al Capone*. Boston: Da Capo Press, 2003.

Konigsberg, Ira. *The Complete Film Dictionary* (2nd ed.). New York: Penguin, 1997.

Kotkin, Stephen. *Stalin: Paradoxes of Power, 1878–1938*. New York: Penguin, 2014.

Kreuger, Miles. *Show Boat: The Story of a Classic American Musical*. New York: Oxford University Press, 1978.

Lasky, Betty. *RKO: The Biggest Little Major of Them All*. Englewood Cliffs, NJ: Prentice-Hall, 1984.

Leerhsen, Charles. *Ty Cobb: A Terrible Beauty*. New York: Simon & Schuster, 2016.

Leinwand, Gerald. *1927: High Tide of the 1920s*. New York: Four Walls Eight Windows, 2002.

Lennig, Arthur. *The Immortal Count: The Life and Films of Bela Lugosi*. Lexington: University Press of Kentucky, 2010.

Lewis, David Levering. *When Harlem Was in Vogue*. New York: Penguin, 1997.

Lindbergh, Charles A. *The Spirit of St. Louis*. New York: Scribner, 1953/2003.

Louvish, Simon. *Stan and Ollie—the Roots of Comedy: The Double Life of Laurel and Hardy*. New York: Thomas Dunne Books, 2002.

Mantle, Burns (ed.). *The Best Plays of 1926–1927*. New York: Dodd, Mead, 1928.

——. *The Best Plays of 1927–1928*. New York: Dodd, Mead, 1929.

McCoy, Donald R. *Calvin Coolidge: The Quiet President*. Newtown, CT: American Political Biography Press, 2000.

Meyer, Jean. *La Cristiada: The Mexican People's War for Religious Liberty*. Garden City Park, NY: Square One, 2013.

Monsen, Marie. *The Awakening: Revival in China, 1927–1937*. Shoals, IN: Kingsley Press, 2011.

Montville, Leigh. *The Big Bam: The Life and Times of Babe Ruth*. New York: Anchor, 2007.

Moore, Lucy. *Anything Goes: A Biography of the Roaring Twenties*. London: Atlantic Books, 2009.

Mordden, Ethan. *The Hollywood Studios*. New York: Alfred A. Knopf, 1988.

——. *Make Believe: The Broadway Musical in the 1920s*. New York: Oxford University Press, 1997.

——. *Ziegfeld: The Man Who Invented Show Business*. New York: St. Martin's Press, 2008.

Newton-Matza, Mitchell (ed.). *Jazz Age: People and Perspectives*. Santa Barbara, CA: ABC-CLIO, 2009.

Okrent, Daniel. *Last Call: The Rise and Fall of Prohibition*. New York: Scribner, 2011.

Olney, Martha L. *Buy Now, Pay Later: Advertising, Credit, and Consumer Durables in the 1920s*. Chapel Hill: University of North Carolina Press, 1991.

Ortega, Daniel, and Tomas Borge. *Nicaragua: The Sandinista People's Revolution*. New York: Pathfinder Press, 1985.

Parrish, Susan Scott. *The Flood Year 1927: A Cultural History*. Princeton, NJ: Princeton University Press, 2017.

Perrett, Geoffrey. *America in the Twenties*. New York: Simon and Schuster, 1982.

Peters, Margot. *House of Barrymore*. Seattle: Touchstone Press, 1991.

Pollock, Howard. *George Gershwin: His Life and Work*. Oakland: University of California Press, 2007.

Razlogova, Elena. *The Listener's Voice: Early Radio and the American Public*. Philadelphia: University of Pennsylvania Press, 2012.

Rose, Lisle A. *Explorer: The Life of Richard E. Byrd*. Columbia: University of Missouri Press, 2008.

Rosenberg, Deena. *The Brothers Gershwin: Their Lives and Work Together*. New York: Atheneum, 1990.

Rubenstein, Joshua. *Leon Trotsky: A Revolutionary's Life*. New Haven, CT: Yale University Press, 2013.

Ryan, Jason. *Race to Hawaii: The 1927 Dole Air Derby and the Thrilling First Flights That Opened the Pacific*. Chicago: Chicago Review Press, 2018.

Schickel, Richard, and George Perry. *You Must Remember This: The Warner Bros. Story*. Philadelphia: Running Press, 2008.

Sennett, Ted. *Warner Brothers Presents*. Secaucus, NJ: Castle Books, 1971.

Sheward, David. *It's a Hit! The Back Stage Book of Longest-Running Broadway Shows*. New York: Back Stage Books, 1994.

Shindo, Charles. *1927 and the Rise of Modern America*. Lawrence: University Press of Kansas, 2015.

Shipman, David. *The Story of Cinema*. New York: St. Martin's Press, 1982.

Shlaes, Amity. *Coolidge*. New York: Harper Perennial, 2014.

Sinyard, Neil. *Silent Movies*. New York: Gallery Books, 1995.

Skretvedt, Randy. *Laurel & Hardy: The Magic behind the Movies*. Aliso Viejo, CA: Bonaventure Press, 2016.

Smith, Sally Bedell. *In All His Glory: The Life and Times of William S. Paley and the Birth of Modern Broadcasting*. New York: Random House, 1990.

Snow, Richard. *I Invented the Modern Age: The Rise of Henry Ford*. New York: Scribner, 2014.

Stillman, Edmund O. *The Roaring Twenties*. CreateSpace, 2017.

Sudhalter, Richard M. *Stardust Melody: The Life and Music of Hoagy Carmichael*. New York: Oxford University Press, 2003.

Swenson, Karen. *Greta Garbo: A Life Apart*. New York: Scribner, 1997.

Symonds, Dominic. *We'll Have Manhattan: The Early Works of Rodgers and Hart*. New York: Oxford University Press, 2015.

Taylor, Jay. *The Generalissimo: Chaing Kai-Shek and the Struggle for Modern China*. Cambridge, MA: Belknap Press, 2011.

Teachout, Terry. *Duke: A Life of Duke Ellington*. New York: Avery, 2013.

Tejada, Susan. *In Search of Sacco and Vanzetti*. Lebanon, NH: Northeastern University Press, 2012.

Temkin, Moshik. *The Sacco and Vanzetti Affair: America on Trial*. New Haven, CT: Yale University Press, 2009.

Thomas, Henry W., and Shirley Povich. *Walter Johnson: Baseball's Big Train*. Lincoln, NE: Bison Books, 1998.

Thomas, Lawrence B. *The MGM Years*. New York: Arlington House, 1971.

Thomas, Tony, and Aubrey Solomon. *The Films of 20th Century-Fox*. Secaucus, NJ: Citadel Press, 1979.

Ullrich, Volker. *Hitler: Ascent, 1889–1939*. New York: Vintage Press, 2017.

Weissmuller, Johnny Jr., with William Reed and W. Craig Reed. *Tarzan, My Father*. Toronto: ECW Press, 2008.

Wellman, William, Jr. *Wild Bill Wellman: Hollywood's Rebel*. New York: Pantheon, 2015.

Whyte, Kenneth. *Hoover: An Extraordinary Life in Extraordinary Times*. New York: Alfred A. Knopf, 2017.

Wilber, C. Martin. *The Nationalist Revolution in China, 1923–1928*. Cambridge, UK: Cambridge University Press, 1985.

Wiley, Mason, and Damien Bona. *Inside Oscar: The Unofficial History of the Academy Awards*. New York: Ballantine Books, 1996.

Wintz, Cary D. *Black Culture and the Harlem Renaissance*. Houston: Rice University Press, 1996.

INDEX

Note: Page numbers with photographs appear in bold.

ABOUT THE AUTHOR

Thomas S. Hischak is an internationally recognized author and teacher in the performing arts. He is the author of thirty non-fiction books about film, theatre, and popular music, including *The Oxford Companion to the American Musical, 1939: Hollywood's Greatest Year, The Woody Allen Encyclopedia, The 100 Greatest Animated Feature Films, The Encyclopedia of Film Composers, The Rodgers and Hammerstein Encyclopedia, Broadway Plays and Musicals, Through the Screen Door, The Tin Pan Alley Encyclopedia, Disney Voice Actors, The Disney Song Encyclopedia* (with Mark A. Robinson), *Word Crazy: Broadway Lyricists, American Literature on Stage and Screen, Theatre as Human Action,* and *The Oxford Companion to American Theatre* (with Gerald Bordman).

He is also the author of fifty published plays, which are performed in the United States, Canada, Great Britain, and Australia. Hischak is a Fulbright scholar who has taught and directed theatre in Greece, Lithuania, and Turkey.

Hischak is emeritus professor of theatre at the State University of New York at Cortland, where he has received such honors as the 2004 SUNY Chancellor's Award for Excellence in Scholarship and Creative Activity and the 2010 SUNY Outstanding Achievement in Research Award. He currently teaches film at Flagler College in St. Augustine, Florida.

Website: ThomasHischak.com